TERMINAL IDENTITY

TERMINAL IDENTITY

THE VIRTUAL SUBJECT IN

POSTMODERN SCIENCE FICTION

SCOTT BUKATMAN

DUKE UNIVERSITY PRESS   Durham and London 1993

2nd printing, 1994

Batman, and all related characters, the distinctive likenesses

thereof and all related indicia are trademarks of DC Comics Inc.

Printed in the United States of America on acid-free paper ∞

Typeset in Cheltenham by Keystone Typesetting, Inc.

Library of Congress Cataloging-in-Publication Data

appear on the last printed page of this book.

This is for my mother, and for Dave.

CONTENTS

ACKNOWLEDGMENTS

If I have never tired of this work over the many years of its development, it is because of my regard and fondness for those I worked with. A quick perusal of *Terminal Identity* will reveal my debt to two scholars in particular. Annette Michelson's support has been unyielding, but even more rewarding has been our decade-long friendship. Annette always had a faith in my abilities and a respect for my loopy little interests while making certain that my thinking was as rigorous and grounded as it could be. She has introduced me to so much, and no one has ever pushed me harder or encouraged me more. Vivian Sobchack has exemplified the notion of a "colleague" in all respects, and this book would simply not be what it is without her input at all points. Her work has moved from excellent to inspired; I'm glad that I could be along for the ride.

Paul Arthur worked overtime on this project. The care, the interest, and the humor he showed are reflected on every page of this work. Paul combines passion, imagination, and rigor to a degree rare in academia, and I value his friendship. Richard Allen's insights into the philosophical conundrums underlying these fictions were helpful indeed. Ken Wissoker of Duke University Press has shown a real appreciation and respect for my approach; I hope his faith is rewarded. Tassie Cameron put extraordinary effort into the preparation of the index and I am indebted to her care and good humor.

One of the rewards of my project has been my exposure to an assemblage of scholars from different fields, united through their interest in cyberspaces and cybercultures. I warmly recall hours of telephone calls with Brooks Landon and my voluminous e-mail correspondence with Istvan Csicsery-Ronay, Jr.—brilliant and exuberant thinkers, both. More recently, Mark Dery and Larry McCaffery have fired ideas across my neural net. These are my trusted cyborg comrades.

Karen Sacks has almost singlehandedly defined *family* for me: she is a sustaining and wonderful part of my life. Steve Barnes and Joe McElhaney have taught me more about film aesthetics than I can say. And I am still not altogether accustomed to all I have received from Alex Juhasz. Alex helped me finish this work and read it with interest. When things were especially good, she even deigned to watch *Mystery Science Theater 3000* with me. Her intelligence, strength, warmth, and humor are slowly redefining my relationship to the world, as she tries to teach me the value of a *non*-terminal identity.

On the nonhuman side, my cats (Corwyn, and now Pook and Bama) and my Macs made life much happier. Thanks to Bootsy, Miles, and Pere Ubu for the cyberfunk.

Finally, I must thank David Samuels, my best friend for over two decades (!). Aside from general life-support, Dave has helped this project in many ways: whether testing a new computer game (he *always* wins), listening to me read chapters over the phone, stirring up trouble on Compuserve, or sitting in on my science fiction course (much the stronger for his presence), whenever I have needed him he has been *right there*. It's impossible to imagine life without him. Dave is a careful scholar with unique (and sometimes wacky) insight.

While showing my affection and appreciation has never been terribly easy, I hope that these people and others not mentioned understand all that they have meant to me.

When I began this project, Max Headroom did not yet exist, while now he has become a quaintly nostalgic figure. Naturally, I accept full responsibility for all errors in the text. But I accept no responsibility for a terminal reality that is simply changing too rapidly to chronicle.

"The entire planet is being developed into *terminal identity* and complete

surrender . . ."—William S. Burroughs

TERMINAL IDENTITY

INTRODUCTION

Across the communications landscape move the spectres of sinister technol-

ogies.—J. G. Ballard ¶ No longer has information any tangible, kinetic

analogue in the world of the senses, or in the imaginations of writers of

fiction. Gone are the great arrays of vacuum tubes, the thousands of toggles

that heroes of space fiction would flick *almost* faster than the eye could

see as they dodged space "torpedoes," outflanked alien "battle lines,"

steered through asteroid "storms"; gone, more importantly, is any sus-

tained sense of the autonomy, in space and time, of gross visible individual

human actions. And if "actions" are now invisible, then our fates are like-

wise beyond our grasp. We no longer feel that we penetrate the future; fu-

tures penetrate us.—John Clute ¶ Our machines are disturbingly lively,

and we ourselves frighteningly inert.—Donna Haraway ¶ Mankind's a

dead issue now, cousin.—Bruce Sterling, *Schismatrix*

The visible symbols of technological aspiration that characterized the Space Age reached an apotheosis with the massive Saturn V rockets lifting off from Cape Kennedy, but they have disappeared from our vision and our consciousness. The newly proliferating electronic technologies of the Information Age are invisible, circulating outside of the human experiences of space and time. That invisibility makes them less susceptible to representation and thus comprehension at the same time as the technological contours of existence become more difficult to ignore—and all of this is occurring during a lengthy period of diminished economic expectation. In this time of advanced industrialism coupled with economic exhaustion, a deep cultural ambivalence has made itself evident across a range of phenomena. Fredric Jameson has labeled the resultant ambivalent, and sometimes contradictory, formations of postmodernism "the cultural logic of late capitalism." There has arisen a cultural crisis of visibility and control over a new electronically defined reality. It has become increasingly difficult to separate the human from the technological, and this is true rhetorically and phenomenologically. Within the metaphors and fictions of postmodern discourse, much is at stake, as electronic technology seems to rise, unbidden, to pose a set of crucial ontological questions regarding the status *and power* of the human. It has fallen to science fiction to repeatedly narrate a new subject that can somehow directly interface with—and master—the cybernetic technologies of the Information Age, an era in which, as Jean Baudrillard observed, the subject has become a "terminal of multiple networks."[1] This new subjectivity is at the center of *Terminal Identity.*

The crises of the Information Age are rooted in the Space Age: the profound reorganization of society and culture that accompanied its onset and the dissolution of energy that succeeded it. It is common knowledge that the complacency of the postwar United States was shattered with the Soviet launch of the Sputnik satellite in October 1957. Historian Walter McDougall argues that the premises of American technological superiority and the "evident superiority of American liberal institutions" were challenged by the beeping orbiter that circled above.[2] The American mainland was under a direct threat for the first time in well over a century, and anxiety was epidemic. The result was an enormous influx of capital and labor power as the technocratic state became firmly established as a peacetime phenomenon. The state took direct responsibility for technological development, in America and other industrially advanced countries, leading to a centralized belief in the "utopian notion that man could truly invent his own future."[3]

MacDougall's history of the Space Age emphasizes the establishment of a comprehensive technocracy in the United States: "What began as an extraordinary governmental initiative to reassure the world that individualism, free enterprise, and limited government were still superior came in [NASA administrator James E.] Webb's mind to be a vehicle for 'revolution from above.' NASA's destiny was to serve as prototype for reallocation of national power for social and political goals."[4] The citizen is defined within an encompassing techno-political system, reinforcing a view of the human that arose with the advent of *cybernetics* (post-WWII) and its "functional analogy" between human and computer.[5]

The era between Sputnik and Apollo was marked by simultaneous experiences of "euphoria and fear."[6] McDougall refers to Daniel Bell, who "argued that technology governs change in human affairs while culture guards continuity. *Hence technology is always disruptive and creates a crisis for culture*."[7] While the grandly utopian pronouncements of the New Frontier have ebbed to nothing, the scope of technological development that had been initiated in an era of Cold War expansionism continues unabated, as does the cultural crisis that exists around that accelerated development. In the absence of any mitigating utopian discourse, in fact, that crisis is even more emphatically displayed.

In his oft-cited, oft-contested, but indispensable essay on postmodernism, Fredric Jameson has constructed a periodization of culture that corresponds to Ernest Mandel's periodization of economic development. Mandel had proposed three economic revolutions governed by revolutions in *power technology:* the steam engine of 1848, the rise of electricity and the combustion engine in the late nineteenth century, and most recently (since the 1940s), the development of nuclear and electronic technologies. In these three "long waves" of capitalist development, an initial moment of increased profits (due to the new

technologies in place) yields to a phase of gradually decelerating ac-
cumulation.[8] According to Mandel, we are in the second, later, phase of
the third long wave. According to Jameson, this is the period of postmodernism.

Much of the upheaval surrounding accelerated technological development is not unique to the Information Age: contemporary culture
overlaps and restates many of the fears that inhered during the Machine and Nuclear Ages. Technological spaces and objects prevail in the
public imagination and serve as loci for the anxieties that arise in
response to rapid change: diabolical factories and locomotives are
superseded by melt-downable reactors; such machineries of destruction as thunderous tanks and machine guns are nothing against the
power of a neutron bomb; the Little Tramp among the grinding gears of
Chaplin's *Modern Times* (1936) is replaced by the mushroom cloud
montage of Kubrick's *Dr. Strangelove* (1963). Technology, after all, always creates a crisis for culture, and the technologies of the twentieth
century have been at once the most liberating and the most repressive
in history, evoking sublime terror and sublime euphoria in equal mea-
sures.

The representation of electronic technology thus connects to the
enormous discourse on technology that cuts through American history
(see, for examples, Leo Marx on "the rhetoric of the technological
sublime" in the nineteenth century or the rise of the industrial designer
as a heroic figure in the 1920s).[9] Technology, whether figured in the
exaggerated modalities of the sublime or the cooler pragmatism of an
elite technocracy, defines the American relation to manifest destiny and
the commitment to an ideology of progress and modernity ("A utopian
faith in technology reinforced a longstanding American ideal of creating
a new world").[10] Destiny, however, is undercut by anxiety. Writing in
1924 about the New God of the machine, Paul Strand envisioned a task
for America and American artists: "the New God . . . must be humanized
lest it in turn dehumanize us."[11] This theme recurs, of course, in the
Amazing Stories SF from the same era, with their quaintly anthropomorphized robots and rationalist technological triumphs, but it continues
through the Space Age and beyond. McDougall finds the same underlying aspiration in *Star Trek* (1964–66) and *Star Wars* (1977) and notes that
"We want to believe that we can subsume our individualism into the
rationality of systems yet retain our humanity still." Phenomenologist
Don Ihde characterizes this pervasive desire—"I want the transformation that technology allows, but . . . I want it in a way that it becomes
me," but he further argues that: "Such a desire both secretly *rejects*

what technologies are and overlooks the transformational effects which are necessarily tied to human-technological relations. This illusory desire belongs equally to pro- and antitechnology interpretations of technology."[12] In short, a desire for the extension of power that technologies permit is accompanied by the concomitant fear of a *loss* of power and the weakening of human control in the Machine, Nuclear, *and* Information Ages.

There is a chronology of *emergence* here: electronic follows nuclear which followed mechanical. Their supersession is another matter. Nuclear anxieties continue to proliferate, while worries about the Machine are hardly obsolete for large parts of the population. Under postmodernity, these techno-anxieties commingle. There is little doubt though, that electronic technologies most contour first world existence, and for many critics this technological shift inaugurates the postmodern era. Jameson follows Mandel's periodization, which is rooted in technologies that affect economic production. Jean Baudrillard and Donna Haraway, for all their differences, are united in their recognition of the enveloping and determining parameters of a fully technologized existence that has forced a crisis around untenable definitions of the human. While Paul Strand's proclamation demonstrates the substantial overlap of anxieties between Machine and Information Ages, it also hints at some differences. After all, what relevance can "humanized technology" retain in an era of blurred ontologies? Technology and the human are no longer so dichotomous.

Larry McCaffery has summarized the differences between machine and electronic paradigms and notes that "While railroads, steel mills, and assembly lines were fundamentally altering America's landscapes and mind-sets during the nineteenth century, it was still possible for the average American to grasp the mechanisms and principles responsible for such changes."[13] The kinetic icon of the machine challenged traditional fields of representation, but an array of new strategies developed to explore it. This hyperbolically visible technology moved with endless power, before its conceptual bankruptcy became clear: "Cape Kennedy is gone now, its gantries rising from the deserted dunes. Sand has come in across the Banana River, filling the creeks and turning the old space complex into a wilderness of swamps and broken concrete" (Ballard, "The Dead Astronaut").[14]

The Space Age thus overlaps postmodernism, but postmodernism really gets going around the *exhaustion* of the Space Age; the end of that period of aspiration, centralization, technologization, and expansion. Now the inertial shell of the personal computer replaces the thrusting power of the Saturn V as the emblem of technological culture. Invisible spaces now dominate, as the *city* of the modernist era is replaced by the *non-place urban realm*[15] and *outer space* is superseded by *cyberspace*. According to Jameson, the postmodern era is marked by, among other things, a fundamental sense of disorientation within "the bewildering world space of late multinational capital."[16] The works of postmodernism either emphasize that sense of dislocation or produce some form of *cognitive mapping* so that the subject can comprehend the new terms of existence.

There is simply no overstating the importance of science fiction to the present cultural moment, a moment that sees itself *as* science fiction: "The cyberpunks [science fiction writers] are perhaps the first SF generation to grow up not only within the literary tradition of science fiction but in a truly science-fictional world"; "We live science fiction"; "We have annexed the future into our own present"; "We are already living out the existences predicted by earlier generations of SF authors"; "The future was now."[17] The Situationist provocateur Ivan Chtcheglov once lamented that "The various attempts to integrate modern science into new myths remain inadequate," and while most science fiction is unflaggingly conservative in its language and iconography, it remains the genre that has represented, since the onset of the Space Age, the most sustained attempt to identify and narrate the ambiguities that mark the technological contours of contemporary culture.[18]

Jameson himself has stated that cyberpunk is "henceforth, for many of us, the supreme *literary* expression if not of postmodernism, then of late capitalism itself."[19] His comment reveals a salient truth: science fiction has, in many ways, prefigured the dominant issues of postmodern culture. Jameson's own essay, for example, is strikingly anticipated by J. G. Ballard's introduction to his high-tech porn novel, *Crash*. It was Ballard who, in advance of Jameson, isolated "the death of affect," the "moratorium on the past," and the irrelevance of "the subjective nature of existence" as hallmarks of contemporary life.[20] Without *postmodernism* as a label, Ballard wrote in unmistakable terms of the end of literary modernism, characterized by "its sense of individual isolation, its mood of introspection and alienation." This mind-set was more characteristic of the nineteenth century than our own: "Among those areas neglected by the traditional novel, are, above all, the dynamics of human societies (the traditional novel tends to depict society as static), and man's place in the universe" (96–97).

Perhaps most importantly, Ballard, like Jameson, sees the movement away from the forms of modernism as something other than a moment in the history of aesthetics, but as the signifier for a broader cultural transition. Ballard, too, sees a new "cultural dominant" at work, one defined by accelerated technological change (especially electronic technology): "Across the communications landscape move the spectres of sinister technologies and the dreams that money can buy. Thermonuclear weapons systems and soft drink commercials co-exist in an overlit realm ruled by advertising and pseudoevents, science and pornography" (96). Ballard's 1974 description echoes Guy Debord's 1964 analysis of *The Society of the Spectacle* on one side while it anticipates the writing of Jameson, Jean Baudrillard, and Paul Virilio on the other. Here, however, there is none of the ambivalence that characterizes Baudrillard's later cyberpunk philosophy—the new state of things is seen as literally nightmarish. "Will modern technology provide us with hitherto undreamed-of means for tapping our own psychopathologies?" he asks. Ballard's ambiguously autobiographical fictions, published more recently, emphasize the emotional trauma that underlay his explorations of inner space and a technological unconscious and refigure Ballard's affectless fictions as a psychopathological symptom. Still, this latest revision is intentionally vague in its relation to reality and is only another possible interpretative layer.[21] In the introduction to *Crash* the new landscape is "an ambiguous world," and the reader of Ballard's fiction would have to acknowledge uncertain pleasures in these appropriations of a postmodern media culture.

For Ballard, science fiction replaced the focus on individual psychology with a broader vision of cultural operations, and it participated in the "moratorium on the past" by insisting upon *the future* as its structuring principle. Science fiction was thus an apt discourse for describing and exploring the myths of the Space Age. "I wanted to write a fiction about the present day," Ballard wrote. "To do this in the context of the late 1950s, in a world where the call sign of Sputnik I could be heard on one's radio like the advance beacon of a new universe, required completely different techniques from those available to the 19th century novelist" (97). Science fiction offered (and continues to offer) an alternative mode of representation, one more adequate to its era: "However crudely or naively, science fiction at least attempts to place a philosophical and metaphysical frame around the most important events within our lives and consciousness." Ballard's predecessor and ally, William S. Burroughs, summarized his task as an experimental writer by claiming that his "purpose in writing has always been to express human potentials and purposes relevant to the Space Age."[22]

In an interesting essay, Bruce Mazlish recalls Freud's suggestion that there were three "ego-smashing" historical moments for humanity: the Copernican revolution, which displaced the earth from its central position in the universe; Darwin's theories, which "robbed man of his peculiar privilege of having been specially created, and relegated him to a descent from the animal world"; and Freud's own contribution, which demonstrated that the subject "is not even master in his own house," but is subject to the unknowable operations of the unconscious. Jerome Bruner noted that these revolutions all eliminate the discontinuity between human and nature.[23] Mazlish argues that a *fourth* discontinuity "still exists in our time. It is the discontinuity between man and machine. In fact, my thesis is that this fourth discontinuity must now be eliminated—indeed, we have started on the task—and that in the process man's ego will have to undergo another rude shock."[24]

Mazlish himself seems to be caught in the "functional analogy" that Donna Haraway describes (he writes that "the same conceptual schemes, for example, that help explain the workings of his brain also explain the workings of a 'thinking machine,'" somehow forgetting where those conceptual schemes came from in the first place), but this fourth discontinuity is nevertheless important, if for no other reason than that it might represent the *master-narrative* that underlies postmodern culture itself. Although Walter McDougall is an historian, and not a literary theorist, he has effectively tied the fourth discontinuity to traditional science fiction: "What do we fear most, that technocracy will be perfected, or that it won't be? Americans delight in such futuristic epics as *Star Trek* and *Star Wars* precisely because the human qualities of a Captain Kirk or Han Solo are always victorious over the very technological mega-systems that make their adventures possible. We want to believe that we can subsume our individualism into the rationality of systems yet retain our humanity still."[25] The ambivalence that McDougall describes so well also permeates a more stylistically adventurous science fiction. Larry McCaffery proposes that through its deployment of new "terminologies and metaphors," contemporary American science fiction has "produced a body of work that addresses and analyzes . . . new technological modes of 'being in the world.'"[26] His language strikes me as exactly right—it is not technology per se that characterizes the operations of science fiction, but the interface of technology with the human subject. The narration of new *technological modes of being in the world* represents a significant attempt to grapple with, and perhaps overcome, the fourth discontinuity that Mazlish described.

I would argue that it is the purpose of much recent science fiction to construct a new subject-position to interface with the global realms of data circulation, a subject that can occupy or intersect the cyberscapes of contemporary existence. Bruce Sterling, an important cyberpunk author and editor, has expressed the need for a new term to describe the subject in the electronic era. Referring to "the remorseless drive of technology," he adds that, "there should be a better term, the 'techno-state of mind,' perhaps."[27] A "better term" might be found in the work of William Burroughs, who has coined so many contemporary neologisms. The Nova Mob are moving in on Earth: "The entire planet is being developed into terminal identity and complete surrender."[28] *Terminal identity:* an unmistakably doubled articulation in which we find both the end of the subject and a new subjectivity constructed at the computer station or television screen.

The category, or subgenre, of writing that concerns us here might thus be termed *terminal identity fictions:* a grouping intended to encompass not only the cyberpunk narratives, but also the techno-prophecies of Marshall McLuhan and the cultural analyses of Baudrillard and Haraway. It is a term that describes a coupling of both stylistic *and* thematic approaches to the problem of the subject in the electronic era. Nearly all the works analyzed in this study have appeared since 1960; many date from the early 1980s. Not all of the texts are literary: *terminal identity* pervades a range of media: visual representations (illustrations, comics, and cinema) and electronic representations (video, computer graphics, and computer games) are essential components of the discourse. In true postmodern fashion, the boundaries between genres, between media, between "high" and "low," and between mainstream and experimental forms have dissolved into irrelevance: if terminal identity is as endemic as I propose, then we could expect nothing less than its full penetration into the cultural continuum (*your entire planet is being developed into terminal identity*). Also, cyberpunk is heavily prefigured in both cinema and comics (*Blade Runner* [1982] and the *Heavy Metal* comics of the 1970s inform every page of William Gibson's *Neuromancer*), and many creators have crossed between media.[29] The best cyberpunk, techno-surrealism, and postmodern textual praxis challenge conventional systems of meaning in disturbing ways, often from a position *within* (or aligned with) the commercial structures of mass culture.[30] The characteristic textual strategies of William Burroughs, J. G. Ballard, Philip K. Dick, Joanna Russ, David Cronenberg, James Tiptree, Jr., Howard Chaykin, Donna Haraway, William Gibson, Pamela Zoline, and Bruce Sterling all confront the boundaries of human meaning and value.[31]

Science fiction narrates the dissolution of the very ontological structures that we usually take for granted. Theorists of poststructuralism and postmodernism are fond of cataloging the crumbling of such foundational oppositions as "organic/inorganic, male/female, originality/duplication (image/reality, artifice/nature), human/nonhuman" (this typical list is McCaffery's). Russ has spoken about her attraction to science fiction (note the anticipation of Haraway's cyborg manifesto):

> One of the best things (for me) about science fiction is that—at least theoretically—it is a place where the ancient dualities disappear. Day and night, up and down, 'masculine' and 'feminine' are purely specific, limited phenomena which have been mythologised by people. They are man-made (not woman-made) . . . Out in space there is no up or down, no day and night, and in the point of view space can give us, I think there is no "opposite" sex—what a word! Opposite what? The Eternal Feminine and the Eternal Masculine become the poetic fancies of a weakly diamorphic species trying to imitate every other species in a vain search for what is 'natural.'[32]

Russ was one of the major figures of the New Wave that exploded in the 1960s with an onslaught of radical stylistic and thematic experimentation that allegorized the characteristic dissolutions of postmodernity. Postmodernism, itself a provisional term of uneasy periodicity, augured a massive upheaval in the understanding of human *being,* and McCaffery is correct when he writes that "SF writers share with their postmodernist cousins a sense of urgency about the need to re-examine central narrative assumptions and metaphorical frameworks."[33] Science fiction informed the language strategies of such novelists as William Burroughs, Italo Calvino, Donald Barthelme, Thomas Pynchon, Kathy Acker, Don Delillo, Umberto Eco, and Jay Cantor, as well as the sociological writings of Marshall McLuhan and Alvin Toffler and the philosophical discourses of Jean Baudrillard, Donna Haraway, and Gilles Deleuze. The 1980s saw the advent of the aforementioned cyberpunk science fiction that affected not only the representations of technological culture, but the very uses to which those technologies are put.

Science fiction constructs a *space of accommodation* to an intensely technological existence. Through language, iconography, and narration, the shock of the new is aestheticized and examined. Jameson writes about the intersection of science fiction and postmodernism, and his book-length theorization of postmodern culture begins by proposing that "It is safest to grasp the postmodern as an attempt to think

the present historically in an age that has forgotten how to think historically in the first place."[34] Here are the contradictions and conundrums
that are endemic to the postmodern, but here as well is the postmodern
offering at least the *possibility* of a critical discourse on "the present."
Later, he discusses SF in relation to a discourse of history: "[I]f the
historical novel 'corresponded' to the emergence of historicity, of a
sense of history in its strong modern post-eighteenth-century sense,
science fiction equally corresponds to the waning or the blockage of
that historicity, and, particularly in our own time (in the postmodern
era), to its crisis and paralysis, its enfeeblement and repression."[35]
What science fiction offers, in Jameson's words, is "the estrangement
and renewal of our own reading present."[36] The "multiple mock futures"
of science fiction work by "transforming our own present into the
determinate past of something yet to come."[37] McCaffery, who has
edited several volumes of writing on what he and I both call "postmodern science fiction," similarly writes that SF possesses the capacity to
"*defamiliarize* our science fictional lives," reflecting them back to us in
more hyperbolic terms.

This hyperbolic language, which characterizes the philosophy of
Baudrillard as well as the cyberpunk of William Gibson, constitutes a
new mimesis—it is a language of spectacle and simulation, a language
designed to be appropriate to its era.[38] But the language is more than
mimetic: McCaffery writes that the reader of science fiction is forced to
"temporarily inhabit worlds" comprised of "cognitive distortions and
poetic figurations of our own social relations—as these are constructed
and altered by new technologies."[39] The thematic and stylistic estrangement offered by the most challenging science fiction permits that renewal (and cognitive mapping) of the reader's present to which Jameson referred.

Samuel Delany and Teresa deLauretis each contend that the distinctiveness of science fiction results from the unique strategies of
reading required of its audience. Even in its most banal forms, SF can be
characterized by a continual linguistic play that resists any totalization
of meaning: "The science fiction text appears as a discontinuous set of
sign-functions which produces an indefinite set of semantic constructs
by dislocating the subject in the reading process."[40] DeLauretis draws
directly from the fictional and metafictional work of Delany, who has
demonstrated the subversion of tradition-bound concepts of language
and narrative that he sees as the semantic function of the genre. A
sentence such as, "The red sun is high, the blue low," involves the
reader in a constant activity of revision and reorientation; it is not until

the final word has been assimilated that the reader is emplaced: diegetically far from earth, generically within a science fiction text.[41] The neologistic excess and literalization of language foreground the reading process in a manner perhaps more characteristic of poetry than of narrative prose ("Her world exploded," becomes a potentially dual statement in SF, possessed of *both* figurative and literal possible readings). Thus, deLauretis and Delany would argue, science fiction is inherently "writerly" in the Barthesian sense of positing an active reader who must wittingly construct the text in the process of reading it.

In more recent criticism Delany has become even more occupied by the differing reading protocols demanded by science fiction and "mundane" literature (from the Latin, *mundus:* world).[42] Science fiction, when practiced by writers as diverse as Heinlein, Disch, Gibson, or Russ, encourages—demands—a tremendous inferential activity from the reader. Sentences such as, "The door dilated," or "Daddy married, a man this time, and much more happily," constantly allude to the complexity of a world which must be constructed through inference. (Delany further notes that it is the failure to comprehend this which results in the bafflement of readers new to the genre.)[43] The distance between the world of the reader and the diegetic construct is always an issue; the text therefore enacts a continual defamiliarization. At its best the language of science fiction, and the distance between its signifiers and the reader's referents, becomes its ultimate subject (cinematic analogues might be found in Godard's *Alphaville* [1965] and Kubrick's *2001* [1968]). The language structures of science fiction bear an inherent reflexivity, although not always exploited, that can denaturalize language by foregrounding the processes by which meaning is made.

The science fiction film reveals a similar reflexivity in its "language" but is also something of a special case because of its mainstream positioning, big-budget status, and technological sophistication. While many SF novels or comics need sell only a few thousand copies to recoup their costs, and while video or performance are largely funded through grants, mainstream film is committed to finding a mass audience that will generate major returns. The mode of production of the science fiction film has committed it to certain kinds of narratives, conflicts, and closures that must find a profitable commercial niche. As with many works of popular culture, however, the narratives of such massive successes as *Star Wars* and *Terminator 2* (1991) are riven with internal complexities and contradictions regarding the status of technology and the definition of the human. But the significance of science fiction surely transcends its narrative content. While science fiction cinema is neither a writer's nor a director's genre (with few exceptions), style, and even auteurist consistency, can be located in the fields of art- and effects-direction. The meaning of SF films is found in their visual organization, and in their inevitable attention to the act of seeing, the significance of special effects begins to emerge.

It is a commonplace of critical approaches to the cinema that special effects constitute an unfortunate sideshow. Neither participating in the satisfying *telos* of cinematic narrative nor fully inscribed by the terms of an alternative avant-garde, special effects are doubly compromised. Because of the tremendous capital investment involved, special effects are primarily associated with mainstream American cinema, and thus inevitably function as a sign of the *commodity* rather than the author or artwork. Compromise or commodification: I would join those critics who hold that special effects in fact constitute a privileged locus of meaning.[44] The reflexive spectacularity of special effects challenge many paradigms of film theory, derived as they are from theories of narrative.

Special effects in the cinema, of course, hearken back to the films of Méliès, although this too-easy historicism must be augmented with reference to precinematic presentations of spectacle, from fairground attractions to panoramas and magic lantern performances. And in the field of cinema, it should be clear that even the supposedly naturalistic Lumiére brothers were purveyors of spectacle and novelty. Writings on early cinema by Tom Gunning and Miriam Hansen describe a "cinema of attractions"; an "unabashed eclecticism" that was figured in a direct address to the viewer. "[T]his is an exhibitionistic cinema," Gunning argues, while Hansen writes that "The frontality and uniformity of view-point is clearly the mark of a *presentational*—as opposed to *represen-tational*—conception of space and address."[45] The dominance of the presentational would ultimately yield to the emergence of a univocal narrational system that not only stabilized space, but that also intro-duced "the segregation of the fictional space-time on the screen from the actual one of the theater or, rather, the subordination of the latter under the spell of the former." The events onscreen would no longer be presented directly to the audience, but would be subordinated to the *represented* experiences of the spectator's onscreen surrogate, as "pat-terns of linear causality around individual characters and their psychol-ogy" emerged.[46]

Nevertheless, Gunning has argued that the fascination of the attrac-tion "does not disappear with the dominance of narrative, but rather goes underground, both into certain avant-garde practices and as a component of narrative films, more evident in some genres (e.g., the musical) than in others."[47] The genre of science fiction often exhibits its spectatorial excess in the form of the *special effect,* which is especially effective at bringing the narrative to a temporary and spectacular halt. Effects are exhibitionistic rather than voyeuristic—in other words, they are designed *to be seen.* Science fiction participates in the presentational mode through the prevalence of optical effects that *re*-integrate the spatiality of the spectacle with the "actual" spatiality of the theater to create a phenomenologically significant experience.

Further, the special effect is often a product of the very technologies that the narrative attempts to explain and ground. The interiorized cyberspaces of *TRON* (1982) are produced through computer-enhanced and computer-generated images, while the visual presentation of a liquid metal Terminator in *Terminator 2* is a "state-of-the-art" technical marvel, much like the android itself. Here, and elsewhere, the special effect presents the previously inconceivable in detailed, phenomenologically convincing forms. In the Information Age this has additional ramifications. The invisible workings of electronic technology are made manifest, in varying ways and to varying degrees, but more importantly, the ontological anxieties of the present are endowed with a concreteness and literalness of form. McCaffery's comments regarding contemporary science fiction in general are particularly applicable to SF cinema: "in many cases, terms that were previously purely speculative abstractions ('immortality,' 'illusion') whose 'existence' was tied to matters of semiotics and definition have now suddenly become literalized."[48] The special effects of *TRON* and *T2* construct new objects and spaces that visualize abstract cultural concerns and permit a provisional re-embodying of the human subject in relation to those concerns.

Reviewing the cinematic and literary functions of science fiction language is obviously important, but the paradigmatic representational forms in the age of postmodernity have been the media of electronic communications, especially video. Video possesses different temporal properties than film and carries a real-time, global simultaneity—or *instantaneity*—that video artists and broadcast television both exploit.[49] More recently the movement has been away from an illusion of live-ness and toward a heavily processed whirlwind of images that results in a reduction of temporality. Stanley Cavell notes of video installations, "The multiplicity of monitors . . . encodes the denial of succession as integral to the basis of the medium. . . . Succession is replaced by switching, which means that the move from one image to another is motivated not, as on film, by requirements of meaning, but by requirements of opportunity and anticipation."[50] In the implosion of everything within this electronic monitor/computer/object, the object is on display, indisputably *there,* as much an object to look at as a channel of transmission. By contrast, cinema's durational effect is quite pronounced—the darkened room, the invisibility of the screen and the hiding of the apparatus all emphasize the temporality of watching. Video is more synchronic: it is continuous with its environment and its succession is less determinate: as in the Zone of Pynchon's *Gravity's Rainbow,* there is "no serial time over there, events are all there in the same eternal moment."[51]

The electronic "presence" of video, to use Vivian Sobchack's term, overlaps with that dissolution of ontological structures found in science fiction and postmodern philosophy. The blurring of boundaries between human and machine results in a superimposition that defines contemporary aesthetics. The density of information is often manifested as an overlap or juxtaposition of forms. Whether the technique is graphic or narrative, the cyberblitz effect is the same. Elements commingle within the same space, creating a metaphorical connection. Rather than privileging discontinuity, postmodernism often tends to reduce experience to an ersatz continuity; a simultaneity or coexistence without history. More effective works emphasize the displacement within (and through) that continual interface of forms, images, and technologies.

I am not suggesting that superimposition is strictly a postmodern attribute—Ernst, Eisenstein, Joyce, and Man Ray are obviously implicated in strategies of juxtaposition and spatiotemporal distortion. These manifestations are, however, connected to the very different historical phenomenon of modernism; they respond to different representational forms and different master-narratives. The superimpositions of the present integrate responses to electronic technologies that are more immediate, less diachronic, more ambiguous and less reliable. The mutational works of postmodernity are neither representations of the character's nor the artist's unconscious, but they might be the inscription of a *technological* unconscious. Baudrillard writes that, "We are in a system where there is no more soul, no more metaphor of the body— the fable of the unconscious itself has lost most of its resonance."[52] The prevailing attitude is that technology imposes itself upon human experience to such a degree that the very concept becomes irredeemable. Samuel Delany's *paraspace,* which allegorizes technology as it stages the death of the Subject (see chapter 2), is quite evidently a displacement of the unconscious itself—the rhetoric of science fiction supplants psychology with technology. This is far from the utopian playfulness of Dziga Vertov or René Clair.[53]

Cyberpunk, *TRON,* and *T2* offer examples of the pervasive concern regarding the dissolution of boundaries and the electronic challenge to subject definition. That concern is no less endemic to the field of cultural theory, as such writers as Baudrillard, Haraway, and Arthur and Marilouise Kroker indicate, and all of these writers have recourse to rhetorics of superimposition and the language of science fiction to express the postmodern crisis of a body that remains central to the operations of advanced capitalism as *sign,* while it has become entirely superfluous as *object.* The body exists only as a rhetorical figure: "its reality is that of refuse expelled as surplus-matter no longer necessary for the autonomous functioning of the technoscape."[54] Simply put, the body is not a requisite for the survival of the technocratic system. In cyberpunk science fiction the body finds and occupies a new space; a realm in which a control over the dataspheres of capitalism is restored. Within the intersecting planes of cyberspace, the body is re-placed and the subject's autonomy is resurrected. But only to a degree: in *Neuromancer* and Joan Vinge's *Catspaw,* the data systems merge into a fantastically complex organism in which humans operate as cells or mere units of data. The artificial mind becomes a body on its own (albeit a noncorporeal one), rendering the human superfluous once more.

While Baudrillard maintains that "No narrative can come to metaphorize our presence," this would seem to be precisely the function of science fiction. As a genre, SF has long engaged in preserving definitions of the human against the merely *bodily,* but those days are over, at least for now. Science fiction, from at least the 1960s, has expanded the parameters that once contained the definition of the human. The American science fiction film, for example, has staged a passage from ontological certainty to *un*certainty, centering upon the relation between Utopia and human definition. While utopian fiction is a foundation of SF literature, it is largely absent from the action-packed xenophobia of most films. Yet there *is* a utopia to be found in the science fiction film, a utopia that lies in *being human,* and if utopia is always defined in relation to an *other,* a nonutopia, then the numberless aliens, androids, and evil computers of the SF film are the barbarians storming the gates of humanity.

Jameson regards utopias as privileged discursive objects because they permit the emergence of cultural anxieties. A structuring tension between rationality and biology, power and infantilism, civilization and its discontents exists in SF film, but it was once recontained by God's will, manifest destiny, human "nature," etc. Observe the *deus ex biologia* at the end of *War of the Worlds,* which has very different implications in the 1953 film than it did for H. G. Wells in 1898. While the novel emphasized mankind's complacency, shattered by the Martian invasion, the film presents a perfect Earth as the only desirable spot in the solar system (who *wouldn't* want to invade us?). America, the inevitable new site of the invasion, becomes the paradigm for the world, while despite their scientific superiority the Martians remain puny and infantile—little more than high-tech third-worlders. The bacteria that devastates the invaders permits the humans of the novel an opportunity to reconsider human purpose, while in the film it serves only to affirm humanity's triumphal destiny.

By the 1980s the ontological certainties of an earlier science fiction cinema yielded to increasingly tortured attempts to contend with challenges to human definitions that remained rooted in Western, masculine, heterosexist—"natural"—paradigms. The mutability of the Alien, the Thing, the liquid metal Terminator, and any Cronenberg protagonist signify a slippage in human definition. The loss of power over the form of the human, the visible sign of our being, combines with the absence of the moral certainties that once guided that power. Hence, in *The Thing* (1982) the thing is bad because it takes over our bodies, but the film never tells the viewer just what that might *mean.* The human retains no fixed or certain meaning, even against the terms of an *anti-*human invader. Following Klaus Theweleit's analysis of male fantasy, Claudia Springer, Mark Dery, and Hal Foster argue that the powerful cyborgs of contemporary mainstream cinema represent a last bastion of overdetermined human, masculinist, definition, bodies armored against the malleability and invisibility of the present (see chapter 5). Like the Terminator himself, the utopian promise of the science fiction film—the superiority of the human—may be battered and beleaguered, but it is still in there, fighting for validation.

Terminal Identity constructs a trajectory that propels the subject into the machine. In "Terminal Image" the centrality of television culture is explored in intriguingly hyperbolic terms. The chapter begins with the phenomenon of *image addiction*—a culture built around its devotion to the televisual image—that appears in science fiction by Philip K. Dick and J. G. Ballard, in the comic book *American Flagg!* by Howard Chaykin, and in the British television film that introduced Max Headroom to the world. Following Guy Debord's elaboration of a *society of the spectacle,* these pervasively reflexive and auto-critical works might be called *the science fiction of the spectacle.* The latter part of the chapter moves to the image *virus,* an invasive formation in which the danger is no longer from the *content* of TV programming but issues from the technology itself. The subject is so overtaken by the forces of the spectacle that simulation becomes a new reality. Baudrillard's philosophies of the simulacrum are exemplary of such "image virus" writings, which are anticipated and echoed by William Burroughs, by Philip K. Dick's extraordinary *UBIK,* and by *Videodrome,* the 1982 film by David Cronenberg. "Terminal Image" is an extended introduction to the crisis of the subject in terminal culture that tracks the assault on the mind and body of the spectating citizen/subject.

The next chapter moves beyond the barrier of the screen. "Terminal Space" concentrates on the numerous representations of electronic space that provide both conceptual and perceptual metaphors for this crucial, invisible arena of cultural activity. These representations *dramatize* the cybernetic, electronic, cosmos and thus re-place the human subject at its center. Following the theories of Henri Lefebvre, Jameson has proposed that postmodernism depends on a "supplement of spatiality" that results from its evacuation of history and consequent exaggeration of the present. "Space has become for us an existential and cultural dominant," Jameson continues, and although this slights the astonishing spatialities of such modernists as Baudelaire, Joyce, and Eisenstein, there is something to his claim.[55] Cyberspace represents the most convincing defense of his argument: a completely malleable realm of transitory data structures in which historical time is measured in nanoseconds and spatiality somehow exists both globally *and* invisibly. Through the operations of their narratives as well as their operant spatialities, *Blade Runner, Neuromancer,* and *TRON* construct a phenomenological interface between human subject and terminal space.

The second chapter concludes by examining the allegorical languages of postmodern fiction and science fiction, both of which narrate "parallel" spaces, or *zones,* of transformation and instability. Within the zones of postmodern fiction the reader finds a polymorphous stage for the dissolution of ontological boundaries; for the collision of competing and transmutating worlds. The parallel spaces of SF stage the breakdown of language, rationality, and subjectivity. A dislocation of the subject (character and reader) is represented by a movement (physical and textual) through an excruciatingly technological, radically decentered, and rhetorically exaggerated space. Cyberspace exemplifies the paraspaces of science fiction: spaces that deconstruct the transparency of language to refuse the subject a fixed site of identification.

The visual and rhetorical apperception of cyberspace prepares the subject for a more direct, bodily engagement, and this engagement is the topic of the third chapter. "Terminal Penetration" concentrates on the *cybernaut*—the subject *in* cyberspace. Terminal culture could be defined as the era in which the digital has replaced the tactile, to use Baudrillard's terms, but he further argues that physical engagement "returns as the strategy of a universe of communication—but as the field of a *tactile* and *tactical* simulation."[56] In Baudrillard's worldview, virtual reality constitutes a simulation of an embodied presence, and thus a deception that further separates the subject from the fields of control. While a welcome corrective to the utopian prognostications that dominate writing on VR (virtual reality), Baudrillard's text is equally unilateral in its understanding of technology. *Contra* Baudrillard, Timothy Leary reminds us that, "The word cybernetic-person or cybernaut returns us to the original meaning of 'pilot' and puts the self-reliant person back in the loop."[57] The human gains the ability to move within the worlds of information. The construction of a new cyberspatial subject thus depends upon a narration of *perception* followed by *kinesis.* This is a striking recapitulation of the development of the subject described in Merleau-Ponty's phenomenology, in which just such a process of *physiognomic perception* "arranges around the subject a world which speaks to him of himself, and gives his own thoughts their place in the world."[58] Actions become visible once more as the cybernaut penetrates the terminal future. As might be expected, *Neuromancer* and *TRON* are again prominent examples, but other modes of physiological/narrative interface are considered in this chapter, from computer games to the hypertechnologized spaces of Walt Disney World. The physical interface with a world constructed of data is also the impetus behind the computer-generated sensory environments of virtual reality.[59] "Terminal Penetration" concentrates on all these insertions of the body into the hitherto bodiless realms of terminal space.

"Terminal Flesh," the fourth chapter, continues the emphasis on the body by presenting a bestiary of cyborg formations. *The body* has long been the repressed content of science fiction, as the genre obsessively substitutes the rational for the corporeal, and the technological for the organic. Libidinal energies are redirected toward a new invention, a virgin planet or an alien Other. It is horror, rather than SF, that has continued to stage the return of the repressed in the form of a hyperbolic body, but terminal identity fictions frequently blend elements of horror and science fiction to construct their own emphatic, techno-organic reconstructions of the flesh.

While previous chapters described the penetration of the human into technology, "Terminal Flesh" narrates technology's penetration into the human (what cyberpunk Walter Jon Williams calls the "bodily incarnation of the i-face").[60] The body is often a site of deformation or disappearance—the subject is dissolved, simulated, retooled, genetically engineered, evolved, and de-evolved. Istvan Csicsery-Ronay, Jr. has proposed *the cyborg* as the central thematic of contemporary SF, and the figure of the cyborg dominates the science fiction sociologies of Haraway and Baudrillard as well.[61] "We cannot think any longer of man without a machine," Bruce Mazlish observes,[62] and the cyborg literalizes this inseparability. The cyborg is a cut-up with multiple meanings: in the form of the "computer-generated" television personality Max Headroom, the cyborg represents the very *embodiment* of media culture, while the hybrid superhero bodies of Robocop and the Terminator embrace technology at the same time as they armor the human against the technological threat. There is, underlying these works, an uneasy but consistent sense of human obsolescence, and at stake is the very definition of the human. The narratives of terminal flesh offer a series of provisional conclusions wherein the subject is defined, at different times, as its *body,* its *mind,* or sometimes its *memory.* This proliferation of definitions reveals the absence of definition: our ontology is adrift.

"Terminal Flesh" includes some radical work that owes much to Georges Bataille. William Burroughs may have been the first to wed Bataille's psychoanalytically and anthropologically inflected discourse with the rhetoric and concerns of the Space Age, but Ballard, Bernard Wolfe, and David Skal have all produced SF that touches upon Bataille's paradigmatic tropes of sacrificial excess and bodily affirmation, and Baudrillard, Gilles Deleuze, and Félix Guattari have also mapped Bataille onto the terrain of a technological reality. The libidinal energies of the unconscious move to occupy reality itself—Ballard writes: "Freud's classic distinction between the latent and manifest content of the dream, between the apparent and the real, now needs to be applied to the external world of so-called reality."[63] In terms that are similar, but more explicitly technological, Baudrillard proclaims that "The cool universe of digitality absorbs the world of metaphor and of metonymy, and the principle of simulation thus triumphs over both the reality principle and the pleasure principle."[64] This movement of the libido beyond the bounds of the individual psyche marks the emergence of a techno-surrealism, what Jameson must mean by "surrealism without the unconscious."[65]

The *subject* narrated by terminal identity fiction has both positive and negative attributes, as demonstrated in my final chapter, "Terminal

Resistance/Cyborg Acceptance." In the fantasies of technological symbiosis that cyberpunk presents, the subject's control is actually enhanced by its disappearance into the imploded spaces of electronic technology. The dissolution of the body, and its replacement by its own imploded simulacrum, is repeatedly posited as *empowering*. Technology is thus introjected and bound to a subject position strengthened but otherwise unchanged. Using Klaus Theweleit's psychoanalytic study of the proto-Nazi *Freikorps*, Mark Dery and Claudia Springer have analyzed the Robocops and Terminators in our midst to discover the misogyny that informs their existence (and the spectre of feminized technologies, as Springer claims). The romance of the subject's penetration into, and assimilation of, the telematic matrices of terminal culture becomes untenable, while in the most radical works emerging from feminist positions, it becomes unimaginable.

Reading SF through the matrices of feminist science fiction and theory, one encounters another set of human-technology relations in which the techno-organic fusion produces something other than cyberpunk's ambivalent euphoria. Given a thematics profoundly engaged with social

structures and sexual difference and potentially heterotopic discursive practices, the relevance of SF to a feminist politics should not be mysterious. The affinity between the generic structures of science fiction and the concerns of postmodernism clarifies the feminist attention to the production and consumption of science fiction, as the body has been figured in postmodern art and cultural theory as a site of cultural crisis. Within these discourses, the politics of the body is already vastly more complex than in cyberpunk's fantasies of an inevitably masculine empowerment. "The Girl Who Was Plugged In," a brilliant novella by James Tiptree, Jr. (Alice Sheldon), provides a counterpoint to the exultant kinesis of *Neuromancer* and *TRON*.

Feminist science fiction acknowledges the pervasive interface of human and technology, but it also confronts the ambivalent and profound dilemmas created by that interface. "Cyborg Acceptance" begins with a review of Donna Haraway's cyborg manifesto. Haraway has offered a utopian redefinition of the cyborg as a figure that might elude the (racial, gendered, or class-based) dichotomies of western culture. Her call for a "cyborg politics" poses the possibility of technological symbiosis as a progressive alternative, rather than a simple masculine fantasy of "natural" mastery and domination. The section concludes with a very different perspective: Deleuze and Guattari's celebration of the Body without Organs, a deconstruction of organic wholeness and organicism, and a refusal of technocratic controls over the subject.

The world has been refigured as a simulation within the mega-computer banks of the Information Society. Terminal identity exists as the metaphorical mode of engagement with this model of an imploded culture. Terminal identity is a form of speech, as an essential cyborg formation, and a potentially subversive reconception of the subject that situates the human and the technological as coextensive, codependent, and mutually defining. A new subject has emerged: one constituted by electronic technologies, but also by the machineries of the text. Terminal identity is a transitional state produced at the intersection of technology and narration, and it serves as an important space of accommodation to the new and bewildering array of existential possibilities that defines our terminal reality.

1 TERMINAL IMAGE

INTRODUCTION

In the real world of television, technology is perfectly interiorized: it comes *within* the self.—Kroker and Cook ¶ Television is the sincerest form of imitation.—Fred Allen

Several sections of Chris Marker's 1982 film, *Sans Soleil,* present contemporary Tokyo as a science fiction metropolis. Marker does not understand the Japanese language, and the resultant disorientation, when coupled with the high-technology compactness of this urban environment, creates the effect of a futuristic alienation. Like the protagonist/narrator of Edward Bellamy's 1888 novel *Looking Backward* (the significantly surnamed Julian West), Marker has awakened to find himself dislocated, both spatially and temporally. Unlike West, Marker has few guides to his brave new world, and those that do exist serve to distort more than to clarify. Cinematically, his alienation is conveyed through montage, sound/image disunion, and an evocation of the surfeit of signifiers, signs for which Marker can only guess at possible referents.[1] Passengers doze on a commuter train as the electronic soundtrack drones, punctuated by a series of beeps and bleeps reminiscent of old Astroboy cartoons.[2] The commuter train is intercut with shots of the space-borne locomotive from the popular animated film *Galaxy Express,* further implicating the film in a web of intertextual and inter-

galactic reference. These associations also have the effect of infantilizing the narrator, as alienation engenders a retreat to the images of
childhood—or children's media.

Marker does not simply map Tokyo onto the field of science fiction,
but onto the field of the media-spectacle as well. What characterizes Tokyo is the domination of the image: not simply the static, over-
sized posters with their staring eyes ("voyeurizing the voyeurs," as the
narrator says), but the endless flow of images across the television
screen and the endless televisions which multiply across Marker's solitary cinematic frame. Tokyo constitutes the "world of appearances" for
Marker—how could it be otherwise, given his selective and seemingly
deliberate cultural illiteracy—but it is also a realm devoted to the surface, to the external. Tokyo exists as pure spectacle; that is, as a proliferation of semiotic systems and simulations which increasingly serve to
replace physical human experience and interaction. Television brings
the signs of a peculiar sexuality into Marker's hotel room, videogames
serve as furniture in numberless arcades, sumo-wrestling fans gather to
watch their favorites do combat along walls of TV monitors; a serial
multiplication of the same image-flow extended onto a grid formation
like Warhol's Marilyn or Elvis panels. Video monitors are so prevalent
that the narrator finally concludes that in Tokyo, "Television is watching *you.*"

Ultimately, the narrator finds a kind of solace with a companion
who has designed a video-synthesizer as a means of resisting the onslaught of images, the bombardment of signals. Their electronically re-
processed world is dubbed the Zone (in homage to Tarkovsky's *Stalker*
[1979]). In the Zone the image is regrounded *as* image rather than
functioning as a surrogate reality. The passivity engendered by the
spectacle has ostensibly been shattered; the filmmaker has reappropriated control of the image.

Sans Soleil presents, in compact form, a remarkable number of the
tropes which recur in both contemporary science fiction and the critical discourse regarding the media. The pervasive domination by, and
addiction to, the image might be regarded as a primary symptom of
terminal identity. The "image addict" is a metaphor which exists in and
through the media, subject to forces which might at first seem to be
controlled by the instrumental forces of government and/or big business, but that ultimately seems to signify the passage into a new reality.
The spectacular world of television dominates and defines existence,
becoming more "real" (more familiar, more authoritative, more satisfying) than physical reality itself. Much science fiction recognizes that we

now inhabit what techno-prophet Alvin Toffler has called "blip culture," a rhetorical (and perhaps "real") construct within which citizens are becoming blips: electronic pulses which exist only as transitory bits or bytes of information in a culture inundated with information.[3] The science fiction of the 1950s resisted the advent of the spectacular society (in works by Ray Bradbury, Frederik Pohl and C. M. Kornbluth, and Robert Sheckley, for example), while more recent texts acknowledge, analyze, and sometimes apparently embrace this new state of things.[4] A spectacular ambivalence pervades science fiction cinema, television, and comics. Television and computer cultures have repeatedly been posited as formations of spectacular control, but it is important to note that the new modes of challenge and resistance have themselves become spectacular in form.

In its discursive play, including its images, music, and narration, this section of *Sans Soleil* aspires to the condition of science fiction. The narrator's Tokyo journey takes him from an initial state of radical alienation in the face of the constant flow of images, through periods of an almost palpable terror of assault and invasion by the forces of blip culture. Finally, the journey into the Zone represents an adaptation to, and appropriation of, the society of the spectacle. Marker utilizes the rhetorical strategies of the genre of science fiction to evoke the experience of disorientation before the media eruption of Tokyo. Similarly, the film *The Man Who Fell to Earth* (1976), in its depiction of an alien abroad in a distant world, bombarded by the images and sounds of the media culture which is America, might be regarded as the fictional analogue to Marker's avant-garde documentary.[5]

This conflation of science fiction and media criticism is neither unique nor even unusual in recent years. It is already evident in the writings of Marshall McLuhan, replete with their metaphors of neurology and bodily transformation. It is evident in Alvin Toffler's paeans to technological development and cybernetic adaptation. But it is equally apparent in the more negative postures of the Situationists, in their concern with urban redefinition and individual existence; and it exists, perhaps most clearly, in the profound ambivalence of Jean Baudrillard's cyborg rants, which loudly declaim the new state of things while maintaining an ironic distance.

In all these cases, and others less notorious, the cyberneticized orientation of the respected critic aligns him or her with society's debased prophet of the technological: the science fiction writer. But the conflation of SF and critical discourse doesn't only exist on the referential level, it extends to the deployment of signifiers. If it is true, as Samuel R.

Delany and Teresa deLauretis contend, that the use of language in science fiction is sufficiently idiosyncratic as to demand new strategies of reading,[6] then it is in the similitude of the *signifiers* of science fiction and media criticism that the real consequences of this conflation might be discovered. The language of science fiction provides a self-critical discursive level from which theories of language and media benefit.

That which requires continual demonstration by theorists of natural language is already something of a truism in media criticism: the medium is the message; language and its structures transform cultural activities into signs of a "natural" order; dominant language usage is complicit with dominant ideological formations. The clear and demonstrable imbrication of TV, radio, and the press with the political, economic, and technical bases of the social system makes perceptible a relationship which still remains elusive when dealing with the apparently "un*media*ted" circulation of language in everyday life.[7] The media belong to the mainstream, and any tolerance of divergent views or lifestyles is only a token nod to pluralistic diversity. Such clichés of spectacular society are, of course, equally applicable to, although not as evident in, less spectacular forms of communication such as writing or speech.

Frequently, however, the discourse of media criticism posits a separation, as though the difference was one of *kind* rather than *degree*. The mass media are, correctly, perceived as a *hyper-language* possessed of unimaginable powers of reification; the unfortunate correlate is that other discourses are thereby inscribed as the "voice" of truth. The shortcomings of this argument ought to be obvious enough, yet it remains implicit in much of the critical work produced on, and by, media culture.[8]

Writings on the mass media, and television in particular, concentrate on the passivity of the audience in the face of the spectacle. The seductiveness of the media have apparently resulted in the decline of moral values, the trivializing of politics, the increase of illiteracy, shorter attention spans, and a heightened capacity for violent behavior—all from the surrender of the consumer.[9] The invasion of "the real" by the proliferating forms of "the spectacle" in much science fiction and critical theory might in fact serve as a metaphorical projection of the threatened subversion of *language* and its claims to veracity. In Bradbury's *Fahrenheit 451* (1967), to take an obvious example, books are burned and written language has been forcibly superseded by television—an explicit turning against the *word*. Book burning is no idle choice on Bradbury's part, summoning up as it does overwhelming images of the Inquisition, the Holocaust, and the successive waves of fundamental hysteria in contemporary America. The overthrow of the Word is presented as tantamount to the overthrow of Reason itself, leaving an infantilized—if not barbaric—citizenry poised passively before the pseudo-satisfactions of the spectacle, bereft of the ability to think, judge, and know. The 1966 film adaptation by Truffaut emphasizes this by limiting reading matter to wordless comic books, an evocation of the preliterate status of the young child.[10] In fact, and as a large number of contemporary artists (Barbara Kruger and Jenny Holzer, for example) have acknowledged, the Word has become a complicit part of the image culture, especially within the constructs of consumer society.[11]

It seems that many works about *the spectacle* are, in fact, concerned with preserving and protecting the power of the word against the barbarizing forces of image culture (which is frequently linked to commodity culture and mass forms, most unlike the rarefied discourses of criticism or literature).[12] I would further suggest that the anxiety surrounding the spectacle is not privileging any specific discursive form such as written or spoken language, but that it is directed at the feared manipulation of representational *truth* at a time when the complex interplay of data and representations have usurped earlier forms of cultural and physical engagement and validation. Television, computers, and the hybrid forms of virtual reality having arisen to comprise Toffler's blip culture, the loss of the often unexamined, empirically accepted category of "the real" has instantiated a crisis throughout our hardwired cultural circuits.

To take one example, the advent of digitally "retouched" photographs, which can seemingly (and seamlessly) reconstruct the representation of events and spaces, has raised questions about the relation of the photograph to truth. What is most fascinating, in the face of this electronic onslaught, is the retrospective instantiation of the photograph as the very sign of truth. The *New York Times* (which might admittedly have some stake in its position) reports, "Ever since its invention a shade more than 150 years ago, photography has been seen as a medium of truth and unassailable accuracy."[13] While this may have been true in the years immediately following the invention of photography, the establishment of photography as an "art form" (encouraging creative manipulation) and a tradition of doctored photographs quickly called this attitude into question.[14] The complex mediation of reality that marks the photographic process has also produced a range of complex artistic and philosophical meditations, and not the uncritical acceptance the writer implies.[15]

Fred Ritchin (whose book on computer imaging prompted the article) notes that with digital technology, "there is no equivalent to an original archivally permanent negative." There is thus a loss of representation, a loss of the object, and finally, a lost relationship to the real.[16] What we regard as "reality" stands revealed as a construction—a provisional and malleable alignment of data. "If photographs can no longer be perceived as unalloyed facts peeled from the surface of the real world, what will replace them?" the *Times* asks, but there is no answer. Video, a startlingly ubiquitous documentary medium, is also the archetypal electronic—and hence manipulable—form. It is increasingly evident that society, ever more defined by a system of electronic representations, is based on an accepted fiction, or a "consensual hallucination," to use William Gibson's definition of cyberspace.

The perception of a spectacular assault on the dominance of written language stands revealed as a defense of pre-electronic representational forms (writing, photography, and even cinema) which actually reifies a pre-electronic, empirically verifiable definition of "the real." Although much science fiction participates in precisely such a reification, a significant set of reflexive works, across a range of media, acknowledge a more complex relation with a world increasingly defined by electronic data circulation and management. A more reflexive critical discourse is required to combat a writing in which the critic or scholar is inscribed as the bearer of truths produced through "natural" language structures.

It is in this context that the appropriation of the *forms* of science fiction, and what Delany has called its "reading protocols," can be considered. If, as Delany and deLauretis argue, science fiction de-naturalizes language through an inherent reflexivity of form, then something is added in what we may term the science fiction of the spectacle. Textuality now becomes an explicit *theme* in the science fiction work; language will comprise the *content* of the discourse as well as determine its form. Reflexivity is extended as the text turns in upon its own production. The constant meditation upon the mediation of the real, the usurpation of traditional experience, and the reduction of reality to a representation is emphasized by a text that foregrounds its own textual status, a text that emphasizes the estrangement of the sign. The science fiction of the spectacle, even in its more diluted instances, acknowledges its own complicity with the spectacularizing of reality.

Paul de Man has written that "the allegorical representation of Reading [is] the irreducible component of any text,"[17] and it is indeed easy to situate spectacular science fiction within such a paradigm of textuality. He further notes, "The allegory of reading narrates the impossibility of reading," by which we can understand that de Man refers to the impossibility of reading *through* to an unproblematic, nonfigural, totalizing meaning. The range of approaches which exists within the genre of science fiction toward comprehending the society of the spectacle might be provocatively reexamined within such an allegorical model. In his scholarly work, *The Soft Machine,* David Porush has productively demonstrated the relevance of the "science" of cybernetics to a range of postmodern narratives (by Beckett, Pynchon, and Burroughs, among others), all of which emphasize communication, control, and information management (and, in these fictions, a pervasive and strategic information disruption and willful *mis*-management).[18] While Porush unfortunately neglects science fiction in his study, an oversight he has corrected in his subsequent writings, his postulations concerning the existence of an emergent "cybernetic fiction" are especially relevant. The cyborg formations of *terminal culture,* the melding of human and machine, would then further represent the dialectic of reality and representation, the dialectic which exists between the "natural" semiosis of the referent and the cybernetic "machinery" of the text: terminal identity fictions are a cyborg discourse.

Within the matrices of consumer culture, science fiction offers a new complexity of form to replace the absolutism and transparency of most writing. The polemic is rendered spectacular in an avoidance of any assumption of an uncontaminated discourse and in a diegetic and textual acknowledgment of an already existent complicity. The simultaneous technologism and reflexivity of the text permits a deeper engagement with the issues raised by the spectacle while maintaining the distance of the writerly, the ambivalent, the self-aware. Whether used by Toffler to evoke an era of technological promise and prophecy or by Baudrillard to construct a labyrinthine discourse of technocratic control, science fiction functions as a dominant language within the society of the spectacle. As J. G. Ballard wrote, "Science and technology multiply around us. To an increasing extent they dictate the languages in which we speak and think. Either we use those languages, or we remain mute."[19] *Sans Soleil* incorporates science fiction as a metadiscourse on spectacle, in a movement which fully participates in what it might at first appear to simply condemn.

The analysis performed in this chapter concentrates on the axiomatic form of electronic spectacle: television. In the first section television becomes an important social control by substituting its own pseudo-realities for the "real thing," while in the next TV operates in a more explicitly malevolent manner, penetrating and invading the physical body of the viewer like a virus. In both cases the viewer becomes little more than an adjunct or extension of the media.

Many of the SF texts reviewed here induce a deliberate state of informational overload, pushing language beyond its transparent narrational function to a largely visual spectacularity, leaving the reader to grapple with the (more or less) random patterns of noise and criss-crossing informational systems. The more recent texts, in a movement which again parallels the tactics of many contemporaneous artworks and theories of media culture, advocate a resistance to control which is itself a part of the spectacle: the collagist cut-ups of William S. Burroughs and the passage into the "video word made flesh" in David Cronenberg's *Videodrome* (1982); the new tangibility of the word in the comic book *American Flagg!* and the surfeit of mediated media imagery in the television production of the adventures of Max Headroom. A prevalent concern with the representation of the electronic, information "noise" which pervades (post)modern culture is evident in recent science fiction, a generic transformation which acknowledges the text's complicity in the maintenance and construction of the society of the spectacle. In these works the image no longer exists as a sign, but rather as an object: a commodity, a virus, a weapon, an identity. This chapter, then, traces the first phase of terminal identity: the recognition and ambivalent acceptance of the spectacularization of human culture and human beings.

THE IMAGE ADDICT   I think it's terribly important to watch

TV.—J. G. Ballard   ¶ Watching TV will patch them back into the world's mixing board.—Bianca O'Blivion, *Videodrome*

According to numerous cultural theorists, we are living in the era of the blip. Alvin Toffler has written of the bombardment of the individual by these "short, modular blips of information," which can take the form of ads, news items, music videos, and so forth.[20] For Arthur Kroker and

David Cook the blip is more pervasive and more crucial in its implications for identity, and their writing constructs a subject who has, in the 1980s and 1990s, *become* a blip: ephemeral, electronically processed, unreal.[21] In the evocative, hyperbolic prose of several postmodern critics, subjectivity has itself receded within an electronically constituted system, exemplified by the ubiquity of television. The blip subject exists only within this system, becoming a sign of an increasingly imploded culture. Many have noted a passage into such a state of *implosion,* the passage of experiential reality into the grids, matrices, and pulses of the information age. The rhetoric of expansion and outward exploration has been superseded by one dominated by the inward spirals of orbital circulation—in cybernetic terms, the feedback loop.

The 1930s saw a minor craze for thin, horizontal "speed lines." Designers including Raymond Loewy, Norman Bel Geddes, Otto Kuhler, and Henry Dreyfuss incorporated the motif on everything from railway cars to Thermos bottles, leading the editor of *Architectural Forum* to remark on the "curious cult of the 'three little lines' . . . few objects have escaped the plague of this unholy trinity."[22] In *Populuxe,* Thomas Hine's account of consumer design in the 1950s and 1960s, there is an account of the pervasiveness of the boomerang or parabola motif among the works of the designers of that time.[23] Everything became aerodynamic: automobiles, alarm clocks, and jukeboxes. Objects were now potential vessels, ready to "lift off" in the next moment. An explosion of new forms celebrated the Jet Age and the Rocket Age and the Space Age. In the imploded society of the 1980s, technological change has had a similar effect.[24] Graphic design in the present celebrates the centrality of terminal culture—a new ontology transmitted through the parallel electronic terminals of television and computer. Beginning with Paul Rand's logo for IBM (c. 1960), stark geometric forms have become increasingly synonymous with a powerful corporate identity. The graphic equivalent of the International Style in architecture, these forms are monolithic and unrevealing: ornamentation consists only of the simplest geometric flourish—a shaved corner, a rakish tilt. Like the IBM logo, many are intersected by horizontal lines, like the scan-lines on a television screen or computer monitor. In Rand's own words the signs become suggestive of "technology and computers by association."[25] The explosion of the Space Age has yielded to the implosion of the Information Age; everything exists as data, and the real worlds of production and commerce exist largely as an afterthought. As Karrie Jacobs writes: "In the information age figurative logos carry too much baggage. They're reminders of historic and geographic ties, of the dark ages when American corporations wanted to be known for making particular things, for doing particular things instead of selling services and sending binary impulses careening around the globe."[26] As with our politicians, corporations now attempt to construct a new identity which bears little relation to real space, real time, real activity.

Television is the model for the new technological era "as it implodes the space and time of lived human experience to the electronic poles of the 'screen and the network.'"[27] Baudrillard, in his most science fictional mode, uses gravitational metaphors to describe the implosion of human experience within fields of information transmission. Orbital circulation becomes the matrix of the implosive process, replacing the dialectical passage between poles.[28] An orbit implies a constant turning-in, and Baudrillard adds the image of the black hole: that massive anomaly which draws all into it and from which no information can reliably emerge. Below the event horizon lies only abstraction and hypothesis; direct experience is, by definition, impossible.

Social reality undergoes a "gravitational collapse" beneath the weight of the accumulated data that defines the Information Society. Baudrillard describes a society at critical mass, a society collapsing into itself. "Information devours its own contents," he has written, and in the Information Society, the same entropic process occurs.[29] Acknowledging the strength of McLuhan's axiom, "the medium is the message" ("the key formula of the age of simulation"), Baudrillard further states that it is not only this implosion of the message in the medium which is at stake, but also the concurrent "*implosion of the medium and the real* in a sort of nebulous hyperreality."[30] The world has undergone a significant restructuring, as direct experience is replaced by the recursivity of countless data-based simulations. This restructuring is fundamental to Baudrillard's middle writings, and it is just as central to the science fiction of the spectacle.

Television, still the axiomatic form of electronic simulation due to its mass penetration and continually functioning national and global networks, can therefore not be regarded as presenting an image or mirror of reality (neutral or otherwise), but rather as a constituent portion of a *new* reality. Society, the arena of supposed "real" existence, increasingly becomes "the mirror of television."[31] Jameson argues that "the most likely candidate for cultural hegemony today . . . is clearly video," because of its ubiquity and because it is "so closely related to the dominant computer and information technology of the late, or third, stage of capitalism."[32] "The result of this image bombardment," Toffler wrote in *Future Shock*, "is the accelerated decay of old images, a faster

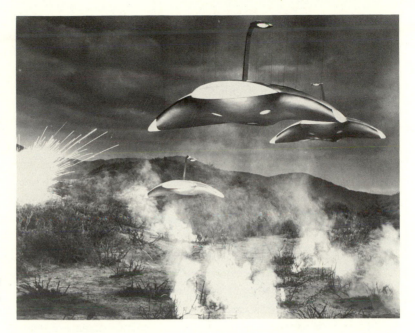

TERMINAL   *War of the Worlds* (Paramount Pictures, 1953). Populuxe industrial design over middle America.

IMAGE   intellectual through-put, and a new, profound sense of the impermanence of knowledge itself."[33] In John Sladek's science fiction novel, *The Müller-Fokker Effect,* a character realizes, "The truth was that reality was televised"; and this "truth" allows him a comforting lack of engagement with the political realities around him.[34]

Reality has moved inside an electronic "nonspace": everything has become data. In *Videodrome,* media prophet Brian O'Blivion (not his real name, but his "television name") declares that soon "everyone will have special names . . . names designed to cause the cathode-ray tube to resonate." In the fictions of cultural theory and SF, a new subject emerges, one that begins its process of being through the act of viewership: "The TV self is the electronic individual *par excellence* who gets everything there is to get from the simulacrum of the media."[35]

The Society of the Spectacle

Guy Debord's 1967 manifesto, *Society of the Spectacle,* begins by acknowledging the passage into a new mode of phenomenological and commercial existence: "In societies where modern conditions of production prevail, all of life presents itself as an immense accumulation of *spectacles.* Everything that was directly lived has moved away into a representation" (Thesis 1).[36] An onslaught of news, advertisements, paid political announcements, fashion, living room wars, celebrity and urban sprawl constituted a new experiential terrain, one contemporaneously explored in the Pop Art of Warhol and the cinema of Godard.

The fundament of the spectacle is its unilateralism. Greil Marcus later observed: "One could not respond, or talk back, or intervene, but one did not want to. In the spectacle, passivity was simultaneously the means and the end of a great hidden project, a project of social control."[37] The citizen/viewer, no longer participating in the production of reality, exists now in a state of pervasive *separation,* cut off from the producers of the surrounding media culture by a unilateral communication and detached from the mass of fellow citizen/viewers as a new "virtual" community of television families and workplaces arises to invisibly take their place.

The spectacle controls by atomizing the population and reducing their capacity to function as an aggregate force, but also by displaying a surfeit of spectacular goods and lifestyles among which the viewer may electronically wander and experience a simulation of satisfaction. The conditions of late capitalism lead Debord to write, "When economic necessity is replaced by the necessity for boundless economic development, the satisfaction of primary human needs is replaced by *an uninterrupted fabrication of pseudo-needs* which are reduced to the single pseudo-need of maintaining the reign of the autonomous economy" (Thesis 51, my emphasis). As for the citizen/consumer, "The real consumer becomes a consumer of illusions" (Thesis 47). (Kroker and Cook describe the 1980s self as "a blip with a lifestyle.")[38] Marcus writes that the "earthly base" for the society of the spectacle was "modern capitalism:"

> an economic mode of being that by the 1950s had expanded far beyond the mere production of obvious necessities and luxuries; having satisfied the needs of the body, capitalism as spectacle turned to the desires of the soul. It turned upon individual men and women, seized their subjective emotions and experiences, changed those once evanescent phenomena into objective, replicable commodities, placed them on the market, set their prices, and sold them back to those who had, once, brought emotions and experiences out of themselves—to people who, as prisoners of the spectacle, could now find such things only on the market.[39]

The spectacle had come to exist on more than a public level (via televised politics, say), it had colonized and co-opted all levels of private existence as well.[40] The spectacle *became* the world.

Debord's post-Frankfurt School polemic is paralleled by a number of science fiction texts which pre- and postdate it. Science fiction (from the 1950s onward), like the critical writing on the media (beginning much earlier), has frequently portrayed the mass media as a pacifying force, an opiate. In *Fahrenheit 451,* for example, the wife of the book-burning fireman is addicted to both tranquilizers and television.[41] The juncture of technology, control, and addiction produced in Debord's writing further points to the work of the author of *Naked Lunch* and the Nova Trilogy.

The incantatory prose of William S. Burroughs evokes a world—a galaxy—completely given over to the pervasiveness and vulnerability of addiction. Addiction is pervasive in that the phenomenon transcends the use of narcotics: in Burroughs's fiction one can be addicted to money or to dope; there are orgasm addicts, control addicts, and image addicts. Vulnerability exists because when the desperation of the addictive need is brought into being, the potential for manipulation escalates. "The pusher always gets it all back. The addict needs more and more junk to maintain a human form . . . buy off the Monkey. Junk is the mold of monopoly and possession." Burroughs then discusses the relation between addiction and capitalist control: "Junk is the ideal product . . . the ultimate merchandise. No sales talk necessary. The client will crawl through a sewer and beg to buy . . . the junk merchant does not sell his product to the consumer, he sells the consumer to his product."[42]

The nexus commodity/addiction/control, powerfully delineated by Burroughs, is replicated in Debord's analysis of the role of the spectacle in the contemporary era. The spectacle is the ultimate commodity in that it makes all others possible: in its role as advertisement, the spectacle generates the conditions for consumption, and therefore for production as well. The spectacle is infinitely self-generating; it stimulates the desire to consume (the only permissible participation in the social process), a desire continually displaced onto the next product and the next.

In the society of the spectacle, all images are advertisements for the status quo.[43] The commodity is replaced by its own representation, and the fulfillment of need is replaced by a pseudo-satisfaction of desire. A citizenry alienated by the industrial-capitalist mode of production is granted an illusion of belonging and participation; the fragmentation of the productive and social realms is replaced by *the appearance* of coherence and wholeness. Debord: "The spectacle presents itself simultaneously as all of society, as part of society, and as *instrument of unification.* As a part of society it is specifically the sector which concentrates all gazing and all consciousness. Due to the very fact that this sector is *separate,* it is the common ground of the deceived gaze and of false consciousness, and the unification it achieves is nothing but an official language of generalized separation" (Thesis 3).

Ultimately, the spectacle takes on the totalizing function of any addictive substance; it differs from dope only in that its addictive properties remain hidden within the rational economic structures of the capitalist society. Contrast Burroughs's statements on junk to these by Debord: "The spectacle is the moment when the commodity has attained the *total occupation* of social life." "The spectacle is a permanent opium war which aims to make people identify goods with commodities and satisfaction with survival." "[T]he spectacle is the *main production* of present-day society." "The spectacle subjugates living men to the extent that the economy has totally subjugated them. It is no more than the economy developing for itself" (Theses 42, 44, 15, and 16).

The positioning of the subject as a *consumer of illusions* recurs in science fiction, and the more revealing critiques of spectacular culture are based in voluntarism. There is, after all, no need to force the citizenry to do what they are already doing quite willingly ("One could not respond, or talk back, or intervene, but one did not want to"). The addiction to the video narcotic means that the control apparatus is emplaced and operating invisibly to secure a false consciousness of cohesion, democratic order, and freedom. Conversely, works such as *Fahrenheit 451* or Orwell's *1984* ignore the crucial postulate of Marcuse's "democratic domination": that an effectively functioning ideological state apparatus replaces the need for overt exercises of power by the repressive apparatus. "The perfection of power," Michel Foucault wrote, referring to the panoptic structures of the disciplinary society, "should tend to render its actual exercise unnecessary." Or, as William Burroughs observed, "A functioning police state needs no police."[44]

Cut-ups and White Noise
The technologies of the mass media have been crucial to the maintenance of instrumental reason as a form of rational (and hence natural, invisible, and neutral) domination. "Domination has its own aesthetics," wrote Marcuse, "and democratic domination has its democratic aesthetics."[45] The plurality of channel selections serves as a kind of guarantee of the freedom of the subject to choose, to position *oneself* within the culture, while the constant flow of images, sounds, and narratives seemingly demonstrate a cultural abundance and promise.

In the era of implosion, the citizen has become a supplicant before the altar of the spectacle, a TV self, without any need for overt coercion.

Yet, as so many have argued, the range of choice is illusory. The viewer is always passive before the spectacle; the act of viewing amounts to an act of surrender.[46] Television functions to maintain order; it provides the state with the unprecedented ability to interpellate many of its citizens into the proper sociopolitical positions with unprecedented simultaneity and constancy. Those who believe that the media serve simply to barbarize culture frequently miss the continual level of social recuperation which occurs.[47] Such recuperation can occur through the functioning of the media itself, quite apart from issues of content. In an early article Jean Baudrillard wrote: "It is useless to fantasize about state projection of police control through TV. . . . TV, by virtue of its mere presence, is a social control in itself. There is no need to imagine it as a state periscope spying on everybody's life—the situation as it stands is more efficient than that: it is the *certainty that people are no longer speaking to each other.*"[48] "TV . . . is a social control in itself," regardless of the specific images or messages the medium transmits or promulgates.

There are ways to challenge or even to resist the controlling power of the spectacle from within spectacular culture itself. The means of resistance have themselves become spectacular in form. One example of such a "spectacular anti-spectacularity," and one which serves as a touchstone for much science fiction of the spectacle, is found in Burroughs's appropriation of science fiction for his own "mythology of the space age." It is in the field of language that his interest in the genre primarily resides. There is no writer's work in which the dislocating power of the language of science fiction is brought more fully into play.

In Burroughs's mythos, language and communication serve as the controlling forces of instrumental reason. Burroughs and his collaborator Brion Gysin evolved the *cut-up* as a simultaneous form of appropriation and resistance: "Cut the words and see how they fall."[49] The cut-up clearly inherits from the modernist history of collage, in which nontraditional and aesthetically undervalued materials were combined with the fine arts tradition of painting. Collage repudiated the purity of the art, the definition of artistic beauty, and the very hand of the artist. Further, as in the work of Schwitters, the collage also acknowledged the aesthetic dimension found in the products of a culture that was becoming increasingly industrialized and consumerist. The cut-up continues this tradition of textual heterogeneity. The text (original or co-opted) is folded, cut, and reshaped into a new, but randomized, continuity. It is to be deployed as a new form of poetic creation, one which is antirational through the inadvertent collisions of the rearranged pieces of a cut-up page of prose. "You cannot *will* spontaneity," Burroughs wrote, "But you can introduce the unpredictable spontaneous factor with a pair of scissors."[50] In the Nova Trilogy the cut-up becomes an hallucinatory science fiction language: an alien—or insect—discourse that constantly devours itself.

The cut-up becomes a critical weapon against the spectacular society. Like the randomly assembled "poems" of a Dadaist performance, in "The Electronic Revolution" (1971), Burroughs advocates extending the cut-up to both audio and video tape. This passage functions almost as an aleatory score for a cut-up (de)composition: "To discredit opponents: Take a recorded Wallace speech, cut in stammering coughs sneezes hiccoughs snarls pain screams fear whimperings apoplectic sputterings slobbering drooling idiot noises sex and animal sound effects and play it back in the streets subways stations parks political rallies."[51] He adds, "The control of the mass media depends on laying down lines of association. When the lines are cut the associational connections are broken. President Johnson burst into a swank apartment, held three maids at gunpoint, 26 miles north of Saigon yesterday."[52] The spectacular forms of mass media are cut-up, randomized, and returned to circulation. The scrambling of language defamiliarizes it, revealing its pervasiveness and operant illusions. Burroughs performs an incisive violence on the body of the text (this textual machine is a medical apparatus), and the incoherence of the results are obvious. The "images" produced by this textual body are freed from any illusory totality to instead serve as the partial and fragmented representations that they are. Relations among signifiers having been lost, each must then exist in glittering isolation, outside temporality, outside history. The cut-up techniques reject the position of control or mastery over the image/text, replacing the rational *telos* of the narrator with the random bombardments of the spectacular society.

The cut-up enhances the displacement of Burroughs's time-tripping narratives, generates a surfeit of science-fictional neologisms, and dislocates the reader searching for the rationality of linear structure. Cut-ups of audio tapes and filmstrips permit us to turn the mechanisms of the spectacle against their creators (the Nova Mobs or the Subliminal Kids). Finally, cut-ups reveal the very strategies of spectacle itself. J. G. Ballard, stressing the importance of collision and opposition in Burroughs's writing, notes, "Far from being an arbitrary stunt, Burroughs' cut-in method is thus seen as the most appropriate technique for the marriage of opposites, as well as underlining the role of recurrent images in all communication."[53]

More recently, the transitory sense of the Information Age is eloquently demonstrated in Don Delillo's novel *White Noise,* another work that shares much with media criticism and science fiction.[54] "White noise" is, after all, the soundtrack that accompanies this era of postmodern implosion. Delillo mixes diegetic dialogue and TV chatter in a collage reminiscent of cut-ups, but here the collage is not the result of a subversive authorial intervention, but is instead diegetically anchored to demonstrate the blip culture bombardment which *already prohibits* the reception of information. Delillo's characters search for a level of phenomenal, emotional reality against the white noise of a culture where the only monument is "The Most Photographed Barn in America" and where Hitler is an academic department. *White Noise* takes place entirely within the cut-up continuum of Burroughs and the imploded America of Baudrillard's hyperbolic prophecies.

J. G. Ballard and the Mediascape

The terrain is changing within the postmodern condition, and under the pressures of a continuous movement of perceived implosion the landscape is increasingly figured as a *mediascape.*[55] The science fiction writer who has been the longest inhabitant of this new territory is J. G. Ballard. Ballard's science fiction has rejected the explosive trajectories associated with the macrocosmic realms of faster-than-light travel and galactic empire, in favor of the imploded realms of what he has termed "inner space."[56] Such a term might imply that Ballard is constructing a psychological science fiction, a science fiction centered upon individual subjectivity, but this is not quite the inner space to which he refers. His work is marked instead by its sustained refusal of individual psychology and his construction of a world which itself bears the marks of the writer's own interior, but socially derived, landscape. The cities, jungles, highways, and suburbs of Ballard's fiction are relentlessly claustrophobic, yet empty; spectacular, but not seductive; relentlessly meaningful, yet resistant to logic. The repetition and obsessiveness of these works suspends temporality while it shrinks space. His characters are without ego, and they become only a part of the landscape, and the landscape becomes a schizophrenic projection of a de-psychologized, but fully colonized, consciousness. As in melodrama or surrealism, everything becomes at once objective and subjective.

The iconography of Ballard's landscape bears strong affinities to Pop Art, and especially the darker Pop of the British wing of the movement, as represented by the work of the Independent Group in the late 1950s and early 1960s ("Artists were revealing a sense of the city . . . as a symbol-thick scene").[57] To the Independent Group "science fiction was one of the few areas in which modern technology was being discussed."[58] The future as presented in *Crash* (1973), *High-Rise* (1975), and *The Atrocity Exhibition* (1970) might well be called, after the famed Independent Group exhibition of contemporary art, "This is Tomorrow." That 1956 event, celebrating the arrival of the present into the future, also turned to science fiction as the metaphorical discourse most appropriate to contemporary life, but rejected much of the utopian flavor of the genre. Commercial and technological cultures were accepted as fact in Pop, just as the SF in the British journal *New Worlds* (a frequent publisher of Ballard) advocated: "Before we begin to investigate [the effects of a new industrial revolution], we must accept the existence of the situation. This . . . is what authors are now beginning to do."[59]

There is thus a link between science fiction and Pop. "In essence," Ballard has written, "science fiction is a response to science and technology *as perceived by the inhabitants of the consumer goods society.*"[60] *New Worlds*'s fiction, dominated by the influence of J. G. Ballard and its editor Michael Moorcock, was littered with the signs of consumer culture: advertisements, news broadcasts and billboards; commodities, chrome, and cars; reentering space capsules;[61] Jackie Kennedy, Andy Warhol, and Lee Harvey Oswald; cleaning products, satellites, and supermarkets; Elizabeth Taylor.[62]

This panoply of pop images and forms comprises the *mediascape* (in Situationism and SF): an external reality ontologically transformed by the multiplicity of electronic signals in the air. Reality becomes an extension of the mass media—television especially, but also color magazines, billboards, rock and roll radio, and even cinema and newspapers (*TRAK news agency—"We don't report the news—We write it"*).[63] First the public's response to reality and finally reality itself are affected. David Pringle notes that in stories such as Ballard's "The Subliminal Man," where huge "billboards" flash a constant barrage of subliminal advertising messages, "even the unconscious is annexed by the media landscape."[64] Television especially exerts a fascination for Ballard: "I think it's terribly important to watch TV. I think there's a sort of minimum number of hours of TV you ought to watch every day, and unless you're watching 3 or 4 hours of TV a day you're just closing your eyes to . . . the *creation* of reality that TV achieves."[65]

Ballard's story, "The Intensive Care Unit" (1977), is an Information

Age update of E. M. Forster's "The Machine Stops" (1909); it also recalls the social science fiction of the 1950s, but with an unprecedented savagery. Ballard stages a future in which all social interaction occurs through the medium of television—schooling, marriage, child-rearing—there is no unmediated personal contact. The surrogate experience provided by the media has fully usurped, and even surpassed, the potentials of actual existence. A doctor by training, the protagonist observes as his "more neurotic patients . . . presented themselves with the disjointed cutting, aggressive zooms and split-screen techniques that went far beyond the worst excesses of experimental cinema."[66] By contrast, his own family life is modeled on very different cinemas: "I relished the elegantly stylized way in which we now presented ourselves to each other—fortunately we had moved from the earnestness of Bergman and the more facile mannerisms of Fellini and Hitchcock to the classical serenity and wit of Rene Clair and Max Ophuls, though the children, with their love of the hand-held camera, still resembled so many budding Godards" (201–2). Cinematic style becomes a part of social and gestural rhetoric, an integral part of the presentation of self in the era of terminal identity. Mysteriously driven to meet his wife and children in the flesh, the protagonist triggers off a kind of nuclear family war. "True closeness is television closeness," he belatedly concludes. "Only at a distance could one find that true closeness to another human being which, with grace, might transform itself into love" (204).

Ballard's mission is to sift through the array of signals in order to locate the latent meanings in the mediascape—to tease out the "deviant logic" found in the random geometries of pop-historical artifacts: "In the past we have always assumed that the external world around us has represented reality, however confusing or uncertain, and that the inner world of our minds, its dreams, hopes, ambitions, represented the realm of fantasy and the imagination. These roles, too, it seems to me, have been reversed."[67] The distinction between "latent and manifest content . . . now needs to be applied to the external world of so-called reality." Objects in juxtaposition allude to an infinity of significance which reason alone cannot possible contain: "Captain Webster studied the documents laid out on Dr. Nathan's demonstration table. These were: (1) a spectroheliogram of the sun; (2) tarmac and take-off checks for the B29 Superfortress Enola Gay; (3) electroencephalogram of Albert Einstein; (4) transverse section through a Pre-Cambrian Trilobite; (5) photograph taken at noon, 7th August, 1945, of the sand-sea, Quattara Depression; (6) Max Ernst's 'Garden Airplane Traps.' He turned to Dr. Nathan. 'You say these constitute an assassination weapon?' "[68]

Ballard's reference to Ernst inevitably recalls that artist's dadaist recourse to collage as the means of exploring the relation between the private psyche and the public world. Drawing his materials from medical and mechanical catalogs, as well as engravings and illustrations from the history of the fine arts, Ernst permitted a new logic to emerge, one at odds with traditional reason. In Ballard's text, which so clearly derive from Ernst's strategies, it is only the fact of coincidence that is meaningful, the randomness of collision, the cut-ups of a postmodern experience that's *already* cut up.

Ballard discusses the field of science fiction by providing another collage: "The subject matter of SF is the subject matter of everyday life: the gleam on refrigerator cabinets, the contours of a wife's or husband's thighs passing the newsreel images on a color TV set, the conjunction of musculature and chromium artifact within an automobile interior, the unique postures of passengers on an airport escalator."[69] Ballard's language is reminiscent of Situationist rhetoric in its attention to the meaningful structures of "everyday life" and its random wanderings—its *dérive*—through the territories of consumer existence.

A necessary ambivalence pervades these texts that makes them easier to quote than to paraphrase. The increasing compression of Ballard's prose through the 1960s renders it even more resistant to summary, as it moved closer to the condition of the advertisement ("What can Saul Bellow and John Updike do that J. Walter Thompson, the world's largest advertising agency and its greatest producer of fiction, can't do better?").[70] To this end Ballard developed the form of the "condensed novel."[71] As Pringle and James Goddard describe them, "the narratives are stripped of surplus verbiage and compounded until they are only skeletal representations of what they might otherwise have been."[72] The linear progress of the minimal narrative that remains is further broken by a division into separately headed paragraphs; the temporal and spatial relations between fragments are variant. As did the cut-ups, Ballard's narrational style derives from the collage techniques of the surrealists: "The techniques of surrealism have a particular relevance at this moment, when the fictional elements in the world around us are multiplying to the point where it is almost impossible to distinguish between the 'real' and the 'false'—the terms no longer have any meaning."[73]

The terrain of the mediascape and the form of the condensed novel were not Ballard's alone. One of the most celebrated works in the SF canon is Pamela Zoline's 1967 *New Worlds* short story, "The Heat Death of the Universe."[74] Zoline narrates a day in the life of Sarah Boyle, witty and dangerously intelligent, who is preparing her child's birthday party. The story is divided into discrete numbered and labeled sections (a familiar *New Worlds* trope). Sections on entropy, light, ontology, and dada are interspersed with a catalog of Sarah's activities ("AT LUNCH ONLY ONE GLASS OF MILK IS SPILLED"). Zoline evokes both entropic dispersal and cosmic connectedness, as the quotidian experience of a housewife is described in language usually reserved for astronomical phenomena: a fine example of the estranging rhetorics of science fiction.[75] The narrative builds to her inevitable breakdown on the kitchen floor, smashing glassware, scrawling graffiti, and throwing eggs. But this is not only about psychological breakdown: through Zoline's complex structures, Sarah Boyle signifies the prevalent, contradictory, and mediated inscriptions on women in consumer culture: "(24) Sarah Boyle's blue eyes, how blue? Bluer far and of a different quality than the Nature metaphors which were both engine and fuel to so much of precedent literature. A fine, modern, acid, synthetic blue . . . the deepest, most unbelievable azure of the tiled and mossless interiors of California swimming pools. The chemists in their kitchens cooked, cooled and distilled this blue from thousands of colorless and wonderfully constructed crystals, each one unique and nonpareil; and now that color, hisses, bubbles, burns in Sarah's eyes." In Zoline's story the authority of scientific discourse is ironically undermined by the commodification of both everyday life and the known universe.

The implosion of meaning in the mediascape, in blip culture, dictates the rise of new literary forms. The "novels" operate as a condensation of the iconography of consumer culture and the compactness of consumerist forms. The traditions of "literature" prevent readers from engaging with the realism of such supposedly "experimental" writing. In the absence of such preconceptions, Ballard argues that people "would realize that Burroughs' narrative techniques, or my own in their way, would be an immediately recognizable reflection of the way life is actually experienced." He continues by defining the state of terminal culture and image addiction: "We live in quantified non-linear terms— we switch on television sets, switch them off half an hour later, speak on the telephone, read magazines, dream and so forth. We don't live our lives in linear terms in the sense that the Victorians did."[76]

Both the cut-ups of William Burroughs and Ballard's condensed novels continue the collagist traditions of their modernist forebears in the surrealist, dadaist, and cubist projects. Given the fullness of that appropriation, it would be false to immediately confer a "postmodern" status upon these writers, and yet the history of postmodern science fiction (and indeed, postmodernism itself) is inconceivable without them. Clearly the writers of cyberpunk, a thoroughly postmodern phenomenon, derive much from Burroughs and Ballard. The shift from modernism to postmodernism is evident in Ballard's recognition that his and Burroughs's techniques are largely mimetic of a profoundly transformed reality. The prejudice against "experimental" writing, which prevents readers from perceiving the mimetic aspects of their prose, has been elided in the more narratively grounded work of the cyberpunks. There, cut-ups and condensations moved from being antinarrative experimental practices (even within science fiction's own avantgarde) to a phenomenon grounded in lived reality. The notorious first sentence of William Gibson's *Neuromancer,* for example ("The sky above the port was the color of television turned to a dead channel"), describes the reality of "Chiba City," but it also recalls Ernst's collages, filtered through the white-noise sensibilities of electronic culture. Ballard and Burroughs, then, are crucial transitional figures positioned between the psychoanalytic modernism of the Surrealists and the electronic postmodernism of the cyberpunks.

Thus the development of new spectacular forms is a project that dominates the production of recent science fiction, and the compression of Ballard's work will find echoes, not only in cyberpunk, but also in the music video aesthetic of *Max Headroom* and the dense layering of panels in Howard Chaykin's comics. Note that Ballard does not necessarily embrace the emergent order of things, and the series of technological disaster novels he has produced reveal a profound suspicion of the new cultural formations. Yet the act of acceptance is paramount: Ballard's protagonists are marked by their acceptance of the altered circumstances of reality: "In *The Drowned World,* the hero, Kerans, is the only one to do anything meaningful. His decision to stay, to come to terms with the changes taking place within himself, to understand the logic of his relationship with the shifting biological kingdom . . . is a totally meaningful course of action. The behavior of the other people, which superficially appears to be meaningful—getting the hell out, or draining the lagoons—is totally meaningless."[77] This acceptance, as noted, extends to the new forms of the mediascape: the shifting *electronic* kingdom. There is an acknowledgment, rare in fiction, that this is where we all live.

The Man Who Fell to Earth—Loving the Alien

Before moving to the science fiction works concerned with the control *of* the media, it is worth taking a brief look at a film that effectively portrays the control *by* the media and that demonstrates the addictive need for the substitute reality of the spectacle. Nicolas Roeg's *The Man Who Fell to Earth* presents an alien (David Bowie) whose knowledge and experience of our world is entirely mediated by television. Here the science fiction narrative serves as a metaphor for a less cosmic alienation: the British alien adrift in America—another "world of appearances" (Marker).[78] Roeg's cinematography and mise-en-scène continually stress angularity, reflectivity, and prismaticity; the geometry of intersecting light and images; a substantial insubstantiality. Thomas Newton, the alien, watches television (or *televisions:* six, twelve, or more).[79] "Strange thing about television is that it doesn't tell you everything," he muses. "It *shows* you everything about life on Earth, but the mysteries remain. Perhaps it's the nature of television." Debord provides an analysis of Newton's observation: "The spectacle originates in the loss of the unity of the world, and the gigantic expansion of the modern spectacle expresses the totality of this loss: the abstraction of all specific labor and the general abstraction of the entirety of production are perfectly rendered in the spectacle, whose *mode of being concrete* is precisely abstraction" (Thesis 29). The expression of the loss of unity could only take the form of a massive displacement from sign to sign. There could be no totalizing system of reference to ground it in order to engender cohesion and produce concrete meaning.

In *The Man Who Fell to Earth,* real life is trivialized and made banal. Newton's quest to rescue his family is parodied by a camera commercial: togetherness through picture taking. The photograph becomes an instant substitute and a surrogate memory.[80] As in advertising, TV at once reveals and hides the lack, providing him with parodic distortions of the family he does not have, the community he does not share, the experiences from which he remains separate. Television serves simply as noise for Newton; the white noise of American culture. The wealthy Newton purchases no extraneous commodities other than the multiple television monitors; as Debord noted, the spectacle is the ultimate commodity, for it contains all the others (Thesis 15).

Like the alien figure of *Sans Soleil,* Newton feels a force which emanates from television, a control which pulls him in. "Get out of my mind, all of you!" he moans to his wall of screens. "Stay where you belong." Television is both pervasive and invasive, evidently serving as a drug, an electronic analogue for the pollution of Newton's body with alcohol. The more Newton engages the world of appearances, the less real his own body, his own appearance, becomes. The spectacle holds the "monopoly of appearance" (Debord, Thesis 12), representing the cohe-

The Man Who Fell to Earth (British Lion, 1976). David Bowie as a prisoner of the spectacle.

sion that is no longer locatable in the real. "The externality of the spectacle in relation to the active man appears in the fact that his own gestures are no longer his but those of another who represents them to him" (Debord, Thesis 30). The struggle to resist the spectacle marks the *return* to alienation from the affectless one-dimensional state so accurately described by Marcuse: the return to a recognition of spectacle as spectacle. The status of the alien thus allows the *privilege* of alienation, a state that exists beyond (or more accurately *before*) the acceptance of spectacle.

The Schizoculture of Philip K. Dick

The paranoid sensibility of Philip K. Dick, in dozens of science fiction novels and stories, explores the alienation that results from seeing *through* the spectacle. The spectacle pervades Dick's universe as a benign and effective mode of control; the spectacle constitutes the parameters of reality for the citizen. The central characteristic of Dick's protagonists involves their crises of subjectivity; crises which begin when the categories of the real and the rational begin to dissolve their boundaries. In Dick's best work, such a metaphysical dilemma does not simply represent a failure of the individual to map him or herself onto the social realm, but is interwoven with the changes in the physical world, primarily with the rise of spectacle and the expansion of the technologies of reproduction. Jameson has written that, "in the weaker productions of postmodernism the aesthetic embodiment of such [re-productive processes] often tends to slip back more comfortably into a mere thematic representation of content—into narratives which are about the processes of reproduction, and include movie cameras, video, tape recorders, the whole technology of the production and reproduction of the simulacrum."[81] Despite Jameson's caution, it is nevertheless important to understand and accept the iconographic force with which these objects have become endowed. It is undeniable that, more than any other science fiction writer (including the more recent cyberpunks), Dick's novels and stories are "about" the pro-cesses of reproduction and yet, through repetition and variation, the plethora of apparatuses of reproduction and simulation are bestowed with a force and obsessiveness that often transcend the concerns of any particular work.[82] In *The Simulacra* (1964), a relatively minor novel dating from the period of Dick's highest productivity, the panoply of spectacular simulations informs the novel's tightest structure.

The novel presents a future one-party state that maintains power by dominating the airwaves with light entertainment: while TV watching is entirely voluntary, it is the means by which an increasingly atomized society engages in a form of collective activity, hosted by Nicole, the First Lady: "[Nicole's] face faded, and a sequence showing unnatural, grotesque fish took its place. This is part of the deliberate propaganda line, Duncan realized. An effort to take our minds off Mars and the idea of getting away from the Party—and from her. On the screen, a bulbous-eyed fish gaped at him, and his attention, despite himself, was captured. Jeez, he thought, it *is* a weird world down there. Nicole, he thought, you've got me trapped" (22).[83] It is the noncompulsory and hopelessly banal nature of this viewing situation (the opposite of those horrific situations presented in, say, *1984* or *A Clockwork Orange*) which links it so readily to the society of the spectacle as delineated by Debord. The *addiction* to the image places the responsibility for viewership on the citizen rather than the state and masks the centralized manipulation that constructs the citizen's social definition and very existence.

In *The Simulacra,* the spectacle of the commodity, the advertisement, is no longer restricted to the usual media: "The commercial, fly-sized, began to buzz out its message as soon as it managed to force entry. 'Say! Haven't you sometimes said to yourself, I'll bet other people can see me!

And you're puzzled as to what to do about this serious, baffling problem of being conspicuous, especially—' Chic crushed it with his foot" (44). This annoying advertisement is a robot—a simulation of a life form—and these simulations comprise a second category of images which circulate within this future. It is worth noting the spiel of the advertisement, which invokes an anxiety over public appearance, thus contributing to the atomized, and therefore controlled and centralized, conditions of existence. Dick's satire prefigures not only Debord's work, but also the analysis performed by Richard Sennett in *The Fall of Public Man,* in which he argues that "Electronic communication is one means by which the very idea of public life has been put to an end." Just as Nicole provides a guided tour of the world without requiring the active participation of the viewer, Sennett states: "The media have vastly increased the store of knowledge social groups have about each other, but have rendered actual contact unnecessary."[84]

Entrepreneurs in *The Simulacra* market "famnexdo" (family-next-door) units to interplanetary colonists so that they will have neighbors. Another novel by Dick postulates a barren, future Mars where a handful of disillusioned and isolated colonists ingest a drug to enter the 1950s suburban dreamworld of Perky Pat and her friends (imagine Barbie and Ken as a role-playing game or virtual reality experience).[85] In another, a corporate mogul of the far future employs a staff to supply him with authentic items from Washington, D.C., circa 1935, the props of a huge simulacrum which he uses as a retreat: "There, he blossomed. He restored his flagging biochemical energy and then returned to the present, to the shared, current world which he eminently understood and manipulated but of which he did not psychologically feel himself a native."[86] The imploded environment of television serves as an ersatz collectivism, advertisements detail the horror of public existence, and simulations and docile simulacra are everywhere present to mimic the vanished public sphere (Debord proclaimed the moving away of reality into the forms of spectacle, adding that "the spectacle originates in the loss of unity of the world" [Thesis 29]).

One of Dick's most effective and developed novels, *Martian Time-Slip,* presents a terrifying portrait of schizophrenic breakdown in an alien and alienating environment.[87] The future Earth of *Martian Time-Slip* is marked, like the future according to *The Simulacra,* by massive and monadic cooperative housing structures that reflect the utopian aspirations of urban planning boards and modernist architects. These are the very aspirations which led to the construction of such projects as the Pruitt-Igoe buildings in St. Louis in the mid 1950s. Then, the ideal of

urban social cooperation crumbled before the reality of social ano-
nymity and nonexistence, as crime and vandalism assumed massive
proportions. The result of pragmatic planning from above was the
emergence of a resistant anarchism from below. The profoundly unin-
habitable buildings were finally dynamited by the city government in
1972, and it is in this moment of explosion, writes Charles Jencks, that
the utopianism of modern architecture died.[88]

One of the novel's central characters is Jack Bohlen, whose occupation as repairman links him to the fragile technocracy which has consol-
idated some limited power among the trickle of off-world colonists.
Bohlen has a history of mental illness, with one serious schizophrenic
period in his precolony existence. After his relocation to the frontier-
like Martian colony, Bohlen is dismayed to learn that Earth's cooperative housing plan is to be expanded to Mars. Looking at architectural
drawings, he says, "It looks like the co-op apartment house I lived in
years ago when I had my breakdown." Manfred, an autistic child, draws
his own version of these new housing projects, but his gift for perceiving future events leads him to draw the buildings as ruins or slums. "At a
broken window of the building, Manfred drew a round face with eyes,
nose, a turned-down, despairing mouth. Someone within the building,
gazing out silently and hopelessly, as if trapped within" (123). In the
1990s this image is horribly familiar, and it is easy to imagine such a face
at a window in Pruitt-Igoe or Southcentral L.A.

Bohlen's original breakdown, perhaps connected to this architectural
monadism and isolation, led to hallucinations:

> He saw, through the man's skin, his skeleton. It had been wired
> together, the bones connected with fine copper wire. The organs
> which had withered away, were replaced by artificial components,
> kidney, heart, lungs—everything was made of plastic and stainless
> steel, all working in unison but entirely without authentic life. The
> man's voice issued from a tape, through an amplifier and speaker
> system. . . . He was not sure what to do; he tried not to stare too
> hard at the manlike structure before him. . . .
> "Bohlen," the structure said, "are you sick?" (69)

The psychosis is defined by a slippage of reality, a perception of the
world which strips it of its status as real, and constructs it instead as a
mechanical simulacrum of reality: a spectacular mimicry of the natural
world. A diagnosis of schizophrenia is inevitable, but Dick has begun to
suggest the social and material roots of Bohlen's psychotic reaction.

In fact Dick uses the discourse of science fiction to complicate and even negate the naturalistic discourse of psychologized characterization. In Bohlen's capacity as Martian repairman, he is summoned to a school to recondition a faulty teaching machine. These machines are standardized models of human simulacra: characters such as Kindly Dad, Angry Janitor, and Mr. Whitlock ("a combination of Socrates and Dwight D. Eisenhower") instruct all children in the important and apparently universal social values. The apprehension evidenced by Bohlen while in the presence of these simulacra is couched in the language of spectacle and even a prefiguration of Althusserian interpellation: "[H]e felt repelled by the teaching machines. For the entire Public School was geared to a task which went contrary to his grain: the school was there not to inform or educate, but to mold, and along severely limited lines. It was the link to their inherited culture, and it peddled that culture, in its entirety, to the young. It bent its pupils to it; perpetuation of the culture was the goal, and any special quirks in the children which might lead them in another direction had to be ironed out" (63). In his encounter with the teaching machines, Bohlen is reminded of his schizophrenic perception of an inauthentic humanity—but now only this "psychosis" can adequately provide an understanding of the *actual* state of things. The mental instability of psychosis has been superseded by the ontological upheavals of a new reality. Here, Bohlen addresses Kindly Dad in the same folksy tone used by this affable simulacrum: "'I know your purpose, Kindly Dad. We're a long way from Home. Millions of miles away. Our connection with our civilization back Home is tenuous. And a lot of folks are mighty scared, Kindly Dad, because with each passing year that link gets weaker. So this Public School was set up to present a fixed milieu to the children born here, an Earthlike environment. For instance, this fireplace. We don't have fireplaces here on Mars; we heat by small atomic furnaces'" (73). Bohlen's sickness permits him to perceive the spectacle *as spectacle* rather than as surrogate reality. In the postmodern, post-alienated future posed by Philip Dick, the movement into a state of alienation is simultaneously both regression and progression; a crucial ambivalence which avoids any reification of the "natural," but which also rejects the unequivocal embracing of the instrumental reason of a new technocratic order. "[T]he spectator feels at home nowhere, because the spectacle is everywhere" (Debord, Thesis 30).

Like Debord, Dick finds little to celebrate in a social and technological formation in which the real is so ably and readily simulated, yet his work recognizes a fundamental contradiction of late capitalism. In the words of economist Ernest Mandel: "Capitalist automation as the mighty development of both the *productive forces of labor and the alienating and destructive forces of commodity and capital* thus becomes the quintessence of the antimonies inherent in the capitalist mode of production."[89] While Dick may evidence a profound suspicion of technology, it must be remembered that the technological societies of his fiction are overwhelmingly capitalistic and largely fascistic. It is less technology per se than the mythifying uses to which it is directed by the forces of an instrumental reason that serve as the targets of Dick's satire. Debord has noted, and Dick would surely assent, that "the spectacle is not a collection of images, but a social relation among people, mediated by images" (Thesis 4). Once again, the individual's pseudo-need to participate in the spectacle permits the real political structure to exist autonomously, behind the "screen" of a rational order which, in fact, only exists in spectacular form.

Dick constructs a decentered narrative structure wherein multiple characters interact in a futile quest to fix reality, and therefore themselves, in place. In *The Simulacra* the psychoses and aspirations of the more than one dozen integral characters form a network within which the central action of state takeover is subsumed. Science fiction author Kim Stanley Robinson, in his thesis on the writings of Philip Dick, has referred to this "polyphonic narrative structure that employs five to ten privileged point-of-view characters": "Almost from the beginning Dick's works contained the reality breakdowns I have defined, and so in that sense Dick's subject was always ontological. . . . But when six or eight characters at different levels of the class system of the fictional worlds are portrayed, employing and working for each other, in control or in rebellion, then the narrative is necessarily political, no matter what miraculous reality breakdown is impinging on them all."[90] Whether or not one accepts that this "necessarily" defines fiction as political, Robinson is firmly correct with regard to Dick's novels.

This narrational tactic first reflects the domination of the linear and rational order which governs the characters' lives, but it finally challenges that very rationality. Dick focalizes the action through characters who occupy both the inside and the outside of the government power structure, such as Duncan, who watches the image of Nicole, and Nicole, who is actually an actress hired to play this "ageless" First Lady (and whose status is thus that of an image of an image). The *Geheimnistrager* (bearers of the secret) are ostensibly opposed to the *Befelhaltrager* (mere carry-outers of instructions), but the narrative finally deconstructs this opposition: the focalization through characters at all sociopolitical strata finally demonstrates that information is partial at all levels. A totalizing perspective is impossible; control eludes even the controllers.

The reader of *The Simulacra* is exposed to the neologistic excess which characterizes the science fiction text. The first pages, frequently the most defamiliarizing in any SF novel, introduce a pattern of acronyms (EME), abbreviations (Art-Co), and new products (Ampek F-a2) which, in their abundance, render the text less readable. Each condensed form or typographical anomaly opens a hermeneutic gap while emphasizing the signifier's sign-function. These terms cannot be read *through,* for the unfamiliarity they engender is precisely their purpose. They are never fully clarified or translated for the reader, who must either infer their meanings or accept the terms as signs of *difference*— that is, signs of a future that differs from the reader's own present. In *The Simulacra* the "reading protocols" of science fiction are not deployed with the gleeful abandon of such contemporaries as William Burroughs or Alfred Bester; nevertheless, the technologies of simulation and reality-production in Dick's diegesis have a real analogue in the written and spoken languages which comprise the reader's reality, a position which his language and narrative structures are constantly in the process of demonstrating. "Jeez," the reader might remark while staring at the page, "it *is* a weird world down there." Unlike Nicole, however, Dick will not allow the possibility of the spectacle as pseudo-escape; it is postulated instead as a problematic and omnipresent mediation.

Having elaborated the radical aspects of Dick's project, his limitations must also be acknowledged. Some of these are simply a function of the business for which he labored. Dick wrote prolifically in an industry which paid a flat rate for each delivered novel—quantity, and not quality, determined the shape of his output. Many works, even from his most successful periods, bear the marks of their commodity status: some novels are carelessly cobbled-together rewrites of earlier novellas, others are clearly first-draft efforts, and, most notoriously, one novel was written to accompany *a title* being pushed by Dick's publisher. Additionally, despite recoveries in individual works, Dick's later writing (from about 1966 onward) is increasingly grounded in an elaborate theological framework (which Dick referred to as his Exegesis) and features a much-reduced cast of characters. Robinson makes a distinction between Dick's early and later works and argues that the shift occurs "not in *what* Dick wrote about, but in *how* he structured what he wrote about:" "In these later stripped-down narrative schemes there are not enough private individual concerns clashing to form larger political narratives, and very often the private concerns of the single protagonist have to do with the basic nature of reality."[91] With a reduced emphasis on the broader social formations through which "reality" gains meaning, works such as *VALIS* (1981) are, to my mind, less compelling and surely less relevant.

In works such as those analyzed here, though, the value of Philip Dick's writing becomes evident. *The Simulacra* is not simply a "mere thematic representation" of new reproductive technologies. By producing a narrative labyrinth around the problem of a politically constructed reality, Dick challenges the spectacle by foregrounding the quest for elusive meaning. Without any significant departure from the rhetoric or form of the science fiction novel, *The Simulacra* displays an abundance of reproductive technologies within a decentered and dispersed narrative structure. *Ubik,* discussed later in this chapter, pushes the instabilities further, producing an hallucinatory tour de force that approaches the technological paranoia of Pynchon, Burroughs, or Vonnegut. The disorientation of the reader in Dick's diegesis must confront that of the characters, but without the aid of Nicole (or a shot of Ubik) to provide reassuring guidance through the resonating unrealities of a society comprised almost solely of the spectacle.

Superheroes for a New Era

1. American Flagg! *and Nam June Paik*

An effective and original engagement with spectacular culture is represented by *American Flagg!,* a comic book written and illustrated by Howard Chaykin.[92] In Chaykin's future, the government has been replaced by the Plex (a government cum communications network cum corporate power) which has provided elaborate shopping malls (Plexmalls) and vid-programming to the beleaguered urban areas. From Mars to Chicago comes Reuben Flagg, ex-Plex vid-star, new Plexus Ranger, eager to see the America where his parents were raised. His experience is quickly disillusioning, as he witnesses the sellout of American values to the corruptive commercialism of the Plex. Flagg gains control of a private vid-station, an alternative to Plex programming, which he intends to use toward nothing less than the moral and political overhaul of his adopted world and country.

The coalescence of government and media is handled with particular wit in *American Flagg!* The ultimate function of the Plex on Earth is simply to acquire capital, partly through selling the assets of the country (including the country itself) to the highest bidders. Because the populace must be kept docile and cooperative, the Plex provides a government, or at least its simulacrum. The malls and entertainment that it provides are spectacular formations which foster the illusion of the re-institution of a governing power—their very existence promises control, stability, and *containment*. As Debord wrote, "The spectacle is the material construction of the religious illusion" (Thesis 20). The world of the Plex exists as undiluted spectacle with no backing reality: the Plex is a floating signifier. Chaykin deliberately grants the Plex only the vaguest status; the reader can be no more certain of its meaning than the citizens of its future (who suspect it to be anything from the Mafia to the telephone company). The literal *displacement* of the government from Earth to Mars further demonstrates that "everything that was lived directly" will continue to "move away" into a state of representation and simulation. The state is replaced by its own simulacrum and the population barely notices.

The media are used by the Plex as a direct locus of social control. Urban riots are encouraged by the Plex for their entertainment value: "The Plex supplies 'em with conventional weapons, vidunits and American Plexpress cards. They know the rules—no aircraft, no nukes, no combat in commercial zones and, of course, *no suburban adventurism.*" In return the Plex gets "the highest rated vidshow on three planets. The Plex makes a fortune in ad revenues and these guys get to be on TV. Fair exchange." Even the antisocial actions of the rioters are appropriated in the calculating interests of a commercial rationality, as the population is served the bread and circuses of spectacular reality: the most popular program is "Bob Violence"™ ("When you're threatened by mob violence, *Bob Violence,*" the ads proclaim). Patrick Brantlinger has written that: "From its cultural beginnings in the late 1940s, television has been accused more often—and from more ideological perspectives—of causing cultural and political decadence than has any other communications medium. Whatever it broadcasts is apt to be interpreted as antithetical to high culture. It appears to be a sort of anti-classical apparatus for automatic barbarization."[93] The description of a process of "automatic barbarization" seems particularly apt in describing the world of *American Flagg!*, although Chaykin never exempts his own discourse from the lowbrow pleasures of spectacular textuality.

Flagg's discovery that the Plex might function as something other than a purely benign force is accidental: he alone is capable of consciously perceiving the subliminal commands encoded onto the images of Bob Violence. The effect of the subliminals is to provoke gogang riots and thereby force a state of permanent crisis. The Plex strategy recalls *Nova Express,* where the Intolerable Kid is up to his tricks: "And he breaks out all the ugliest pictures in the image bank and puts it out on the subliminal so one crisis piles up after the other right on schedule."[94] Chaykin's satirical technique is to exaggerate the effects of the media. Bob Violence, like the underground broadcast of Videodrome (from the film of the same name), represents a nadir in public entertainment—as someone remarks of Videodrome, it's "a scum show." While it commands a massive viewership, the decision to watch remains voluntary. The subliminal commands embedded in both programs only augment the *already existing* powers of suggestion which pertain to the mass media. Bob Violence is hyperbolically violent entertainment; the explicit sadism of Videodrome (discussed at length below) encourages pornographic fantasies: in each case, the content of the television program *already* engenders a response that is merely augmented, translated into physical activity, by the addition of a subliminal transmission.

Flagg himself, as the former star of "Mark Thrust: Sexus Ranger,"[95] is no stranger to the phenomenon of the spectacle, and it is in fact the technological advancement of the forms of spectacle that accounts for this presence as a Ranger: he has been replaced by a "tromplographic" simulation (as in trompe l'oeil). "*I* get cancelled," he complains, "but the show goes on." Flagg functions as a hero in several ways. Like many a comic book hero before him, Flagg possesses a secret "super-power," yet his is neither a function of strength nor speed, but of perception: he perceives the subliminal messages; his is the power to decode signs. Like other heroes, Flagg also possesses a secret fortress: but his is a pirate video station rather than a crime lab (Batman) or private fortress (Superman). Reuben Flagg is thus positioned within the society of the spectacle in three distinct ways: as victim (the "Mark Thrust" simulation), as decoder/mythologist (his ability to see the spectacle as spectacle), and as controller/producer (owner-operator of station Q-USA). Chaykin's achievement here is to have preserved the genre of the superhero comic book while constructing a hero for these postmodern times.[96]

The language of the spectacle infects everyday discourse in the world of *American Flagg!* Products are referred to by their brand names, such as Mañanacillin™, the day-after contraceptive and antibiotic, or Nachtmacher™, a blackout-producing riot control device. Chaykin even includes the "™" superscript to indicate the trademarks, signs of the corporate ownership of language. The subscript also represents an important inclusion of nonphonetic writing, which leads to a deliberate confusion in the text between spoken and written discourses. Video screens are ubiquitous, located even in public spaces, and Chaykin frequently includes this transmitted speech in dialogue sequences. As in

The original opening page of Howard Chaykin's first *American Flagg!*
(© Howard Chaykin, Inc.)

White Noise, the effect is of constant chatter and an ongoing process of randomization and dislocation, the cut-up as lived postmodern experience.

In a number of 1980s comic books, the syntagmatic progression of panels, inflected by cinematic storytelling techniques, was partially supplanted by a synchronic display of shapes and forms heavily influenced by the graphic arts. As Howard Chaykin has continually demonstrated, the comic book is a medium uniquely suited to the depiction of spectacular society. The conjunction of image, color, text, and typography is exploited with continual variation in his work. In another series, the more openly experimental *Time²*, Chaykin incorporates commercial trademarks, photographs, hand-lettering, typeset lettering, Hebraic calligraphy, varying panel sizes and page layouts, as well as overlapping and overlaid illustrations (to catalog only some of his materials). In *Flagg!* and especially *Time²*, the characters are literally surrounded by a plethora of signs. The setting of the latter work is no accident: Times Square has long been famed for its obtruding and massive signs. Chaykin's unorthodox pictorials establish a distance from the standard syntagmatic organization of panels on the page, while the deployment of texts as *visual objects* replaces the traditional emphasis on phonetic language (what Robert Smithson has called "language to be looked at").[97] Synchrony replaces diachrony as the sign (image and text) is stripped of its transparency and becomes a material form: a commodity.[98]

The opening of *Flagg!* exemplifies Chaykin's approach. The saga begins as the Mars-Luna shuttle bringing Flagg to his new station in Chicago requests landing instructions. As the shuttle makes its approach, the electronic "air" is shown to be filled with violent or sexually explicit vid-material, as well as political broadcasts, game shows, advertisements, computer readouts, and graphic displays. Space is hardly empty, it is instead filled with all the signs and signals of the social system. Chaykin makes this even more evident in a more recently added prologue, as the shuttle accidentally plows into a communications satellite. The prologue continues with a channel by channel overview of vid-programming which restores a diachronic progression, but one which makes no sense (recalling Burroughs's adage that "TV is a *real* cut-up").[99] The reader is introduced to the culture via the media, much as the viewer encountered Tokyo in *Sans Soleil*.

The layout of the title page, as the shuttle makes its final approach to Chicago, further emphasizes this future America's full incorporation into its own spectacular constructions. The page demolishes the clear demarcation of space into separate panels in favor of an overlapping and largely synchronic display, in an inspired foregrounding of the white noise which prevails in contemporary culture. The ability of the comic book format to present both words and images in iconic form allows Chaykin to render this noise physically and tangibly, filling the

Chaykin's *Time²: The Epiphany.* (© Howard Chaykin, Inc.)

air in a spatial, as well as an electronic, sense. The reader of *American Flagg!* must find an orientation within this newly opened space of the page. Such a conception of space corresponds to the dominant characteristics of postmodern architecture, as elaborated by Charles Jencks, in its celebration of hybrid (rather than univocal) expression, complexity (rather than linearity), eclecticism (rather than an historicized homogeneity), and "variable space with surprises."[100]

The architectural model retains its relevance when considering the existence of the Plexmall, a building which deaccentuates its entrances in favor of its monadic interior. The Plexmall is not a building to enter or exit so much as it is one to be already in. The mall, even in our own time, represents the implosion of the public space of the village green or town center; this new unit "aspires to being a total space, a complete world, a kind of miniature city," as Jameson writes in his famed analysis of the Bonaventura Hotel. Therefore, it "ought not to have entrances at all, since the entryway is always the seam that links the building to the rest of the city that surrounds it: for it does not wish to be a part of the city, but rather its equivalent and replacement or substitute."[101] The mall can serve as metaphor to the implosive concentration of images and text in *American Flagg!* For Jameson the elaborate postmodern "hyperspace" represents the transcendence of the individual's capacity to comprehend the surrounding territory: the inability to get one's bearings thus becomes a further indicator of the crises of subjectivity and rationality which obtain within postmodern culture.[102] What Venturi and Portman have achieved in architecture is analogous to Chaykin's accomplishment in *American Flagg!* and *Time²:* the images presented to the reader initiate the same cartographic failure that Jameson observed.

The postmodern paradigm originally developed by Jencks for categorizing architectural styles has clearly had a broader impact. There are real affinities between Jencks's schema and the medium of video, with its imploded space, hybridization, and the absolute proliferation of signs and symbols. Venturi has discussed the effectiveness of the designs along the Las Vegas Strip, where the clarity of signs ensures "comprehension at high speeds."[103] So it is with television and its images that must hold the viewer who may, at any moment, zoom off to other channels. There is no beginning and no end; just the flow of signs. As J. Hoberman wrote, "Movies are events: TV is a continuum that, like the Blob, oozes out in all directions."[104] (The Blob . . . the very incarnation of implosion.)

Chaykin's suggestion of an almost entirely televisual reality can recall the work, both early and late, of artist Nam June Paik. The gardens, aquariums, and articles of clothing which Paik constructed around the simulacrum/object of the television are easily linked to the plethora of simulations in science fiction: in John Shirley's *Eclipse,* garments are woven of cathode-ray filaments, and video images flash across bodies in a random, ever-changing array.[105] "As collage technic replaced oil paint," Paik wrote in a now-famous proclamation, "the cathode ray tube will replace the canvas."[106] In its inherent capacity to generate

unpredictable, random sets of images, television becomes the medium
for a new era, an era of information bombardment or *cyberblitz*.[107] Fields
of multiple screen installations enhanced randomization through the
collision of images in space as well as time. As a character in *The
Watchmen,* a comic book by Alan Moore and Dave Gibbons, observes,
multiscreen viewing is the equivalent of William Burroughs's cut-ups as
a randomizing technique which foregrounds and estranges the white
noise of the imploded society.[108] Art must privilege the random to reveal
its existence and thereby defamiliarize the alienating effects of blip
culture.

In Paik's movement into videotape production was inevitable. To operate within the object is to acknowledge the implosive force which
television represents. His tapes are simulacra of television, as is Chaykin's work, blending synthesized effects, talking heads, overlapping
images, textual overlays, and a staggering sensation of total flow, combined to represent TV as a random but all-inclusive process of program
switching and channel-hopping. The works operate "in such an incredi-
bly dense manner that one is subliminally bombarded by information in
rhythmically shifting time perspectives, leaving one with a feeling of
video exhaustion: information overload as the battle fatigue of the
future."[109]

In *American Flagg!* and *Time²*, Howard Chaykin has replaced the
model of cinema in comic book narrative style with the more "terminal"
model of video. Like comics, video incorporates a flow of images of
varying shapes and sizes (within the frame of the picture tube, just as
comics are bounded by the page), the images are often overlapping,
text frequently shares space with the image, and text (in the form of
logos, for example) functions as a physical and iconic element, as well
as a symbolic one. Television is the aesthetic model for the postmodern
era, and Chaykin's inclusion of that aesthetic reveals new possibilities
and signals a new importance for the medium of comics.

In *American Flagg!* an involvement with spectacle thus operates narratively and narrationally. A society in which images become a primary
mode of devaluing the human and the social is depicted through the
deployment of images which emphasize their own spectacular nature.
The evacuation of the real is represented by a spatial construction
which fails to provide the reader with a clearly delineated and rational
sequence to follow. The relation between image and control, a relation
so clearly posited within the diegesis, is emphasized through strategies
of deliberate incoherence and materiality. The analysis of mass culture,
coupled with Chaykin's gift for nomenclature and the modern idiom,

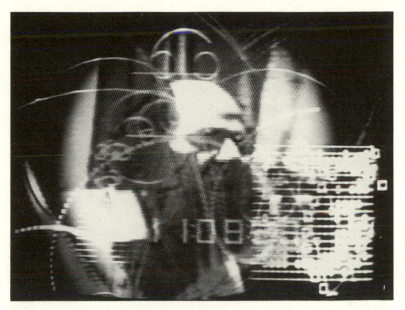

Nam June Paik, *Allan 'n Allen's Complaint* (1982). Informational density constitutes *cyberblitz* . . . (Courtesy Electronic Arts Intermix)

results in a work of remarkable sophistication. *Flagg!* effects a deconstruction of a culture profoundly engaged with images; a culture which allows images to construct a whole and reassuring—but entirely false—image of itself.

2. Max Headroom—20 Minutes into the Future

The concept of a society of the spectacle has passed from the realms of critical theory and avant-garde practice, through the generic structures of science fiction, to the mainstream spectacular empire of television itself. The British television film, *20 Minutes into the Future* (1985, aka *The Max Headroom Story*)[110] posits a near-future society in which "television is the only growth industry." Most discussions of this significant work have justifiably concentrated on the figure of Max Headroom "himself"—the first "computer-generated" television personality—but the carefully developed satirical setting for Max's emergence is also worthy of attention.[111] While derivative of much science fiction, especially recent science fiction film,[112] *20 Minutes* incorporates sufficient stylistic innovation, even in its more mainstream position, to serve as a valuable and ultracontemporary reflection on blip culture.

The only major corporations visible in *20 Minutes* are the massive television networks, frantically battling to increase their market shares.

The cutthroat boardroom meetings, the unabashed drive to maximize profits at any cost, and the knowing deployment of an addictive force all recall the popular science fiction work, *The Space Merchants* (1953) by Frederik Pohl and C. M. Kornbluth. In that novel, advertising agencies dominated economics and politics: "He explained how the Government—it's odd how we still think and talk of that clearinghouse for pressures as though it were an entity with a will of its own."[113] *20 Minutes* makes no such explicit statement regarding the state, but the analogous position of the corporation might permit, or dictate, the assumption of a similar analogue regarding government power. An episode of the American *Max Headroom* television series depicted a government election as a pure media event; the results of interactive television voting are falsified by the network.

Most journalistic media criticism chides political candidates for relying too heavily on media consultants to create an "image" for themselves. The widespread belief is that the issues should dictate the image and not the reverse. Other critics, though, note that in the present circumstances, the spectacle is all that exists.[114] By displacing government in favor of spectacle, *20 Minutes* is aligned with this latter group. The spectacle no longer makes any pretense of representing reality: it has replaced reality. Debord: "It is not a supplement to the real world, an additional decoration. It is the heart of the unrealism of the real society. In all its specific forms, the spectacle is the present model of socially dominant life" (Thesis 6). For Debord, spectacle and reality are indistinguishable concepts, and the progression of works considered in this chapter demonstrates a deepening imbrication of lived and spectacular realities. He continues: "One cannot abstractly contrast the spectacle to actual social activity: such a division is itself divided. . . . Lived reality is materially invaded by the contemplation of the spectacle while simultaneously absorbing the spectacular order, giving it positive cohesiveness" (Thesis 8). This is a subtle side of Debord's analysis: the recognition that the spectacle is a supplement only in the Derridean sense of an addition which demonstrates the incompleteness of the whole.[115] "Objective reality is present on both sides," he concludes one section, "reality rises up within the spectacle, and the spectacle is real. This *reciprocal alienation* is the essence and the support of the existing society" (Thesis 8, my emphasis).

The hero of *20 Minutes* is, appropriately, a mediator or interface between these two realities. Edison Carter is the video-journalist responsible for the "What I Want to Know Show," serving as an audience/citizen surrogate. Like Reuben Flagg, he appropriates spectacle in the name of truth: a potentially reactionary recuperation partially belied by the complexity of the discursive formations of the two works (Carter and Max, his telematic alter-ego, will be discussed more fully in chapter 4).

"Blipverts" are the new advertising strategy deployed by the preeminent Network 23. By compressing thirty seconds of programming into three, Blipverts prevent viewers from changing stations during advertising breaks. Their problem is that they overstimulate the electrical currents of human nerve cells. As their creator explains: "In some subjects, this causes a short circuit. Some particularly slothful viewers literally explode. Simple as that." A network executive sees no problem: "The only people who are that inactive are pensioners, the indigent and the unemployed. And they have no spending power." Image addiction becomes more than a form of social control, now it yields a means of weeding out less desirable members of the population.

In appropriately condensed form, Blipverts ingeniously parody a number of issues pending for media culture. First, they recall the arguments that too much TV is bad for your health: arguments institu-

tionalized by Jerry Mander's *Four Arguments for the Elimination of Television* (1978). Mander maintains that exposure to the cathode ray tube is harmful, as Blipverts abundantly demonstrate. Additionally, the Blip-

vert problem reveals that the executives' concern only involves demographics ("I am talking about *ratings!*" "And I am talking *people.*" "Same thing."). The citizen only exists as part of the machinery of the spectacle (although the more liberal executives resist such reductions).

Blipverts satirize the very real fear in the television industry over the loss of viewers. The dominance of the remote-controlled channel selector has brought about the activity of "zapping" along an expanded range of programming choices, pausing briefly, then zapping off again.[116] The advent of the videocassette recorder has given rise to the complementary activity of "zipping"—fast-forwarding past the advertisements (or programs). Blipverts thus acknowledge the changing status of the audience from spectator to participant. For Alvin Toffler, interactive telecommunications are the key to breaking with existing centralized power structures. In the field of video, for example, video games, cable television, video recording, and interactive television systems allow the viewer a new power: "they are changing from passive receivers to message senders as well. They are manipulating the set rather than merely letting the set manipulate them."[117] Blipverts are an attempt to subvert this new power about which Toffler expresses such optimism; they are the means by which the potential for a real freedom (to provisionally grant the validity of Toffler's analysis) is replaced by its mere simulacrum.

The negation of a bilateral communication has further consequences. *American Flagg!* began by explicitly centralizing the communications media. The Mars-Luna shuttle requests landing instructions, only to be "answered" by this message: "-clik-'Bob?—Mandy. Could you, uh, land it yourself? You know where the runway is . . .' (This recording will not repeat)." Similarly, the first image of *20 Minutes* is of static, as the voice-over of star video-reporter Edison Carter requests a clear communications link. It could be stated that the difficulty in establishing clear comm-links is the basic problem faced by a postmodern culture.[118] In this instance it certainly foreshadows the conflict with a faceless authority that tries to deny Carter access to the informational network that defines his mode of being. Carter's problem and the problem faced by *Flagg!'s* hapless shuttle pilot are hardly unique: it is a tenet of media criticism that the predominant "communication" systems are, in fact, overwhelmingly one-directional: "this 'communication' is essentially unilateral" (Debord, Thesis 24). Baudrillard adds that the mass media "fabricate non-communication."[119]

The opening moments of both *20 Minutes* and *Flagg!* promise an interaction which is not to be. The apparently simple trope of a missed, blocked, or broken communication which initiates both works represents more than an aberration: it reveals the sham nature of interactive communications; control figures are solicited, but do not respond. The failures present, in a synecdochical form, the pervasive difficulties with communications which plague not only the protagonists, but the world they inhabit. Far from "de-massifying" society, as Toffler would have it, the proliferation of communicative technologies serves only to disguise the existence of a fully centalized base of power. "Response" is only the *appearance* of response and the *illusion* of communication: a palliative for the spectacular society.

20 Minutes into the Future is marked by the self-conscious excess common to much SF cinema of the 1980s, here distinguished by its devotion to the forms of the televisual spectacle. In the first place the entire film is only one hour long, applying the compression, condensation, and hyperactivity of the music video format to a narrative structure and also recalling the condensed novels of J. G. Ballard.[120] This is a work which seems to be as much *of* its future society as it is *about* it. As with much science fiction, the film begins in medias res, as Carter descends by helicopter to report a story. In keeping with the emphasis on the media-spectacle, every image in this first section is mediated by other image generators. The images all derive from diegetic sources, and there are four of them:

—Carter's video-camera is recognizable by the uneven, handheld quality of its images, which are recorded in color and live-on-site.

—The securicam (security camera) system presents largely static images, punctuated by minimal lateral panning. These are poor quality, wide-angle, black & white images, and reveal the Network 23 controllers' area.

—View-phone images are in color and are entirely static, with extensive distortion caused by an extremely wide-angle lens.

—Computer graphics simulate environments and produce data. Images on screen are magnified or scanned in a manner which does not replicate the capabilities of the human eye. Graphics are colored on a black background.

All images are overlaid to varying degrees with lines of videotex, informing the attentive viewer of time, place, image source, and other pertinent data. Rapid editing amongst these sources produces a nearly incoherent jumble of activities and image types. No images are recorded directly onto film until Carter returns to base (accompanied by the first nondiegetic music, further emphasizing a more legibly *cinematic* discourse). This panoply of mediated forms, largely eschewed in the version produced for American television, goes far in describing a world in which the spectacle is so predominant. Like *The Atrocity Exhibition* or *American Flagg!*, *20 Minutes* succeeds in representing the noise of the imploded society, creating a nearly synchronic overflowing of informational systems to replace the diachronic progression of cinematic or literary narrative forms.

Episodes of the American *Max Headroom* television series retreated, both stylistically and thematically, from the excesses of the original. All the episodes explored aspects of spectacular culture (including violent spectator sports [a favored bread and circuses motif], information control and the invasion of privacy, television evangelism, and terrorism and the media), but in distressingly recuperative terms. Network 23, under more liberal leadership (iconically represented by tweed jackets rather than business suits), polices its own behavior, voluntarily drawing an ethical line beyond which it will not venture in pursuit of profit. The corporation is therefore presented, entirely without irony, as the caretaker, rather than the exploiter, of society. Carter is usually the first to discover unethical programming practices, but these are presented as aberrational rather than systemic. The original head of Network 23 even returns to head another, glaringly unscrupulous, network, "proving" that it is the individual who causes the system to break down. Spectacle and reality, once intertwined in a state of "reciprocal aliena-tion," are separated and hierarchically positioned. The spectacle, in the forms of Edison Carter, Network 23, and Max Headroom, now operates in unambiguous service to the real.

The series also reduced the stylistic range of the original production, so that the spectacle of computer-generated Max or of Network 23 programming are now opposed to the "real" Edison Carter and his "real" life: the two realms no longer exist as immixture. Baudrillard has wittily claimed that the hyperreality of Disneyland's simulated America ultimately makes the spectacular reality of contemporary Los Angeles seem more truly real,[121] and the same is true of the *Max Headroom* series: by first exaggerating and then containing the spectacular excess of Network 23, the rest of television is itself redeemed and its ideological foundations solidified. This is the program that *Newsweek* called a "thoroughly subversive video parody."[122]

The schismed nature of the series is exemplified by one episode in which "The Blanks"—citizens who have opted out of blip culture by erasing all electronic data pertaining to their existence—threaten to disrupt all television programming. The premise has promise: as terror-ists are always portrayed as playing *to* the media, their assault *on* the media is logical. Yet when Carter locates them, he can only give the traditional TV speech regarding amateur terrorist actions ("I sympa-thize with the principle, but your methods stink"). The idea of no TV (!) thus loses all the ironic force originally implied; television is actually *not* to be toyed with, not even by "thoroughly subversive" Max Headroom. Debord has called the spectacle a "pseudo-sacred entity" (Thesis 25) representing the nexus of social wholeness, and the more reaction-ary *Max Headroom* became, the more this pseudo-sacred nature was revealed.

A paranoid conception dominates in the writings of Burroughs and Dick in which the state is monolithic, faceless, and fully in command of the spectacle. Their attitude toward the power of the capitalist state aligns them with Debord (although neither is a Marxist), who pro-nounced the spectacle to be "the image of the ruling economy" (Thesis 14). He adds, "The concentration of 'communication' is thus an ac-cumulation, in the hands of the existing system's administration, of the means which allow it to carry on this particular administration" (Thesis 24). The passage from Debord's "spectacle" to Baudrillard's "simula-tion" is precisely a shift from a state which constructs the spectacle, to a spectacle which now constructs the state. Later science fiction of the spectacle, including *American Flagg!, 20 Minutes into the Future,* and even *Videodrome,* displace paranoia onto the omnipresent corporation. As in *The Space Merchants,* capitalist power is still ascendent but without the niceties of government to mask its operations. This is only a provisional accommodation—while the self-sustaining power of the market might stand more clearly revealed, its condensation into a single Machiavellian corporate entity disguises the influx of the spectacle into all sectors of public *and private* existence.[123] This paranoia about state or corporate control of spectacle and simulation can ultimately be read as a metaphor for any totalizing system of control or even any totalizing system of meaning. As such, these works produce a valuable rejection of any prespectacular, empirically verifiable system of "truth" and point toward the larger cultural shift in electronic culture which has produced profound transformations of space, time, and being.

The image addict is a helpless prisoner of the spectacular society. The spectacle is a force of pacification, exploitation, control, and containment which functions as either a supplement or simulacrum of the state. The citizen becomes a blip circulating within the feedback loop of the imploded society: terminal identity begins. In this set of science fiction texts, a trajectory has been described, largely tied to the chronological production of the works themselves, which expresses a changing understanding of the spectacle. Over the last twenty years the science fiction of the spectacle has moved from a resentment regarding the infantilizing function of the media to a deeper recognition of the powerfully controlling force of the spectacle; from the depiction of the passive consumer of images to the image-controlling hero; from a rationalist rejection of the "false consciousness" engendered by the spectacle to the ambivalent postmodern strategies (barely introduced as yet) involving simultaneous acceptance and resistance through the proliferation of a spectacular noncoherence. In the end, image addiction is no longer posited as a disease: it has instead become the very condition of existence in postmodern culture.

THE IMAGE VIRUS   "Your reality is already half-video hallu-

cination."—Dr. Brian O'Blivion, *Videodrome* ¶ "I suffer a little from video

burn."—Bruce Sterling, *Schismatrix*

The Electronic Nervous System

According to Marshall McLuhan in his essential 1964 analysis *Understanding Media,* our (post)modern technological capabilities function as "the extensions of man."[124] Furthermore, the proliferation of the technologies dedicated to information and communication comprise an extension, outside the body, of the central nervous system: that elaborate, electrical, message-processing system. The metaphor is intended to reassure by fostering an acceptance of media culture as a natural and evolutionary state. Everything is now different, but there is no need to worry: it is also the same. The nervous system is constructed for bilateral communication. The brain receives neural messages caused by alterations in external stimuli and transmits messages to control bodily position and action. The myriad pathways and branches of the neural structure are dominated by the processing centers of the brain, to which all roads lead. To extend the nervous system outside the body, then, is to further empower the brain and to further centralize the individual. In McLuhan's view the procession of new technologies gives us more to control.

"During the mechanical ages we had extended our bodies in space," McLuhan wrote, while today, "we have extended our central nervous system in a global embrace, abolishing both time and space as far as our planet is concerned" (19). This bit of postmodern science fiction is summed up by contrasting the explosion of mechanical technologies to the *implosion* of the media age: the reduction of all the things in the world to blips, to data, to the message units contained within the brain and its adjunct, the computer.

McLuhan envisions technological advance as a simultaneous process of projection and denial. A medically derived physiological metaphor dominates his writing on this topic. The nervous system "shuts down" under the impact of an overloading of stimuli; the brain performs a kind of "autoamputation" to escape the sensations of irritation or of threat. "The function of the body, as a group of sustaining and protecting organs for the central nervous system, is to act as a buffer against sudden variations of stimulus in the physical and social environment" (53). Mechanical technologies such as the wheel were developed to ease the stress on the body, while the "electric technologies" allowed new protection for the central nervous system: "To the degree that this is so, it is a development that suggests a desperate and suicidal autoamputation, as if the central nervous system could no longer depend on the physical organs to be protective buffers against the slings and arrows of outrageous mechanism" (53). Stress stimulates development, but there occurs a consequent "numbing" of the system, a denial of the adaptation. We therefore, "naturally," come to regard our technologies as separate from ourselves instead of more properly understanding them as extrusions of our organs and neural passages.

McLuhan is a great believer in the unity that underlies disjunction. Discontinuity, as Foucault wrote regarding traditional historiography, is the stigma which must be erased.[125] The mass media will create a mass man living within the intimacy of the global village, or—more accurately—new technologies will reveal the unity that is everywhere already present: "With the extension of the central nervous system by electric technology, even weaponry makes more vivid the fact of the unity of the human family" (300). New technologies necessitate a recasting of global political structures. "The very inclusiveness of information as a weapon becomes a daily reminder that politics and history must be recast in the form of 'the concretization of human fraternity'" (300). That this will in fact occur strikes McLuhan as inevitable.

Other theorists are less sanguine. Guy Debord clearly posits the media as unilateral forms of communication which exist as an *intrusive* force: "Lived reality is materially invaded by the contemplation of the spectacle" (Thesis 8). J. G. Ballard has written, "Despite McLuhan's delight in high-speed information mosaics we are still reminded of Freud's profound pessimism in *Civilization and its Discontents*. Voyeurism, self-disgust, the infantile basis of our dreams and longings—these diseases of the psyche have now culminated in the most terrifying casualty of the century: the death of affect."[126] By electing to ignore the psychosexual and sociopolitical realities which govern the use of technologies, McLuhan's prognostications become science fiction (and not very good science fiction at that, recalling the liberal-Utopian voyages in the contemporaneous *Star Trek*). The printing press might hold the technological possibility of revolutionizing society but, since "freedom of the press is guaranteed only to those who own one," the possibility also exists that it will serve to *consolidate* rather than *disseminate* power.[127] Power is the operative lack in McLuhan's discourse, rendering his vision compelling but inadequate.

Debord plays down the technology of spectacular society in favor of its politics. The paradigm of spectacle is indeed separable from the technological power of the mass media (T. J. Clark has demonstrated how the great Impressionist paintings reveal a Paris already constructed along the lines of a bourgeois spectacle).[128] Debord's model is thus more evolutionary, more gradual, than McLuhan's (although McLuhan seems to waver between evolution and revolution). The mass media reify existing power structures with unprecedented effectiveness, but the act of reification is not itself a new development.[129]

The Electronic Virus

Frequently linked to McLuhan, Jean Baudrillard's writings on the media share his fascination with technological change, but this is always accompanied by a massive sense of the reification of power. Baudrillard describes, as does Debord, a mediated and imploded society in which all power to act has been transformed into the power to appear. The world has passed into a pure simulation of itself. The media are an intrusive force which not only prevent response, but render the very concept irrelevant.[130] Baudrillard differs from Debord in several significant ways which distance him from a more traditional Marxist position. First, technology is as central to Baudrillard's writing as it is to McLuhan's, and it replaces Debord's economics as the structuring principle of the discourse on power. Second, there is Baudrillard's rejection of the Marxist doctrine of "use-value" and its consequent privileging of human labor as a fixed point of reference, in favor of a position which guarantees no rigid site of meaning, no transcendental signified.[131] Finally, Baudrillard argues that power has been subsumed by technological forces to such a degree that it is no longer the province of the state, much less the citizen.[132]

In Baudrillard's imploded universe, power—as wielded by humans—has itself become a simulation: "if it is possible at last to talk with such definitive understanding about power, sexuality, the body and discipline, even down to their most delicate metamorphoses, it is because at some point *all this is here and now over with.*"[133] The real power now resides in a technology that holds humanity in its thrall (SF again serves as metaphor, but if McLuhan's utopianism is akin to *Star Trek's,* then Baudrillard's dark visions suggest something closer to *Alien*). Resistance or response are irrelevant because there is no one to respond *to.* The media are invading; there will be no survivors.

This extraordinary cynicism accounts for the tactics of Baudrillard's prose, which shifted from a rationally argued Debordian resentment at the deployment of spectacular power to a hypertechnologized, jargon-ridden language that refused the possibility of a critical position. Baudrillard became a science fiction writer, using language to enact the process his earlier writings merely described: "Private 'telematics': each person sees himself at the controls of a hypothetical machine, isolated in a position of perfect and remote sovereignty, at an infinite distance from the center of his universe of origin. Which is to say, in the exact position of an astronaut in his capsule, in a state of weightlessness that necessitates a perpetual orbital flight and a speed sufficient to keep him from crashing back to his planet of origin."[134] This passage clearly ties in to the protocols of science fiction discourse in its evocation of space travel and the center of the universe, as well as its pervasive sense of decentering through weightlessness and timelessness. Its conflation of the centrifugal force of outer space exploration with the centripetal implosion of the terminal image of the computer anticipates the precise strategies employed by William Gibson in *Neuromancer,* but the language here is even more hyperbolic and vertiginous.

The usurpation of power by the new technologies of information management and control leads to Baudrillard's rejection of McLuhan's neural metaphors in favor of another biological trope. He begins by proclaiming that, "There is no longer any medium in the literal sense; it is now intangible, diffuse and diffracted in the real, and it can no longer even be said that the latter is distorted by it." The new "*immixture*" represents "a *viral,* endemic, chronic, alarming presence of the medium . . . the dissolution of TV into life, the dissolution of life into TV."[135] Invasion gives way to an image of *viral infiltration.*

This is interesting with regard to the historical reception of television itself. Lynn Spigel has elaborated an early popular ambivalence surrounding the new object:

> Television would seem to hold an ideal place here because it was a "window on the world" which could never look back. Yet, the magazines treated the television set as if it were a problem window through which residents in the home could be seen. . . . Even the design of the early television consoles, with their cabinet doors which covered the TV screen, suggested the fear of being seen by television. Perhaps, this fear was best expressed in 1949 when the *Saturday Evening Post* told its readers, "Be Good! Television's Watching!"[136]

Spigel, in fact, goes on to mention a reflexive episode of a science fiction anthology show, *Tales of Tomorrow,* in which the week's episode is "interrupted" by a reflected image of its own viewers (engaged in a tale of conspiracy and murder).[137] And clearly, Orwell's *1984* effectively encapsulates the anxiety about television as an electronic Panopticon. Fictions such as these foreshadow Baudrillard's polemic, if not his tone. Addiction has begun to give way to infection. The media are no longer the extensions of man; man has instead become an extension of them: a "terminal of multiple networks."[138]

Science fiction and video art repeatedly hypostatize a Baudrillardian immixture of reality and simulation. The videotapes of California-based artist Max Almy, for example, address the overload of an imploded tele-visual culture in a manner which fully participates in the production of spectacle. Her works are technically sophisticated, even slick, with the concision of an advertisement, and *Perfect Leader* (1983) also evokes the music video in its length, soundtrack, special effects, and graphic force. Almy's 1985 tape, *Lost in the Pictures,* is most explicitly concerned with image addiction and the invasive image virus. After a day in front of his computer terminal, a man lies in bed watching televised images of war, fire, and sexuality. A UFO emerges from the TV screen as the images suddenly overflow their medium, surrounding him and drawing him into the televisual reality. What at first appears to be an explosion of images becomes, with this envelopment, an act of implosion. The simulation has invaded, infected, and taken over the host reality.

Almy's work relies on the malleability of the digital, electronic image. Real space and time are compressed and concentrated, while the human figure(head) of *Perfect Leader* is morphed to become the very embodiment of authoritative reassurance. For all its embracing of spectacular forms, there is still no deep ambivalence to Almy's productions. Her didacticism presents television only as pervasive, manipulative, and false: how, then, can her own productions, fully imbricated as they are in the rhetoric of the medium, be progressively received or regarded? Science fiction authors such as Chaykin or Cronenberg, while grounded more firmly within commodity production, achieve a more complex postmodern perspective on the pervasiveness of spectacular culture. The telematic-didact, Max Headroom—anchorman of postmodernism—was the *really* perfect leader for a cultural moment that seems to be twenty minutes into its own future. In comparison Almy's work appears nostalgic and unwittingly paradoxical.

William Burroughs, the Nova Mob, and the Silence Virus

The figure of the media-virus greatly predates Max Almy and Jean Baudrillard. William Burroughs had deployed virus extensively as a metaphor for all the infiltrating forces of control to which people are subjected. *Junky, Naked Lunch,* and *Cities of the Red Night* all incorporate viral figures, but it is in the Nova Trilogy, and especially in *Nova Express,* that the control virus appears in the form of an image: a media-form controlled by an invading alien force.[139] The Nova Mob is on Earth to enslave or exterminate humanity; their strategies are technological, with biological warfare and mind control techniques most prominent.

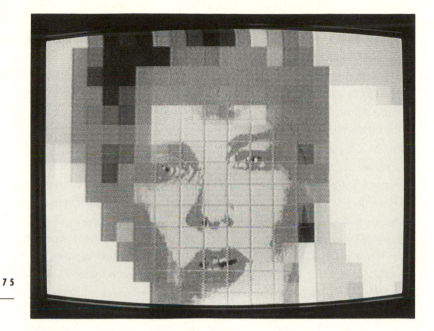

TERMINAL   *Leaving the 20th Century* (1982), a videotape by Max Almy. (Photo: Marita Sturken, Courtesy Electronic Arts Intermix)

IMAGE
Biology, psychology, and the media are linked through the node of the image. Images are tangible and material forces, neither ephemeral nor temporary. A death-dwarf is a literal image-addict:

> "Images—millions of images—That's what I eat—Cyclotron shit—Ever try kicking that habit with apomorphine?—Now I got all the images of sex acts and torture ever took place anywhere and I can just blast it out and control you gooks right down to the molecule—I got orgasms—I got screams—I got all the images any hick poet ever shit out—My power's coming—My power's coming—My power's coming. . . . And I got millions of images of Me, Me, Me, meee." (*Nova Express* [*NE*], 45)

Image is a form of junk, an addictive substance that controls its user. Burroughs has constructed a mythology around the nexus of junk, virus, addiction, control, and surrender: "Heaven and hell exist in my mythology. Hell consists of falling into enemy hands, into the hands of the virus power, and heaven consists of freeing oneself from the power, of achieving inner freedom, freedom from conditioning."[140] In the Nova trilogy, "image is virus," and "junk is concentrated image." A report from the Nova Police states: "it was found that the image material was not dead matter, but exhibited the same life cycle as the virus. This virus released upon the world would infect the entire population and turn them into our replicas" (*NE*, 48).

The virus is a powerful metaphor for the power of the media, and Burroughs's hyperbolic, and perhaps parodic, Manichaeism does not completely disguise the accuracy of his analysis. There is some disagreement over the precise biological status of the virus. Whether the viral form is an actual living proto-cell or simply a carrier of genetic *information,* it clearly possesses an exponentially increasing power to take over and control its host organism. The virus injects its genetic material into the host cell, seizing control of the reproductive mechanism. The cell now becomes a producer of new viral units, and so forth. The injection of information thus leads to control and passive replication: the host cell "believes" that it is following its own biologically determined imperative; it mistakes the new genetic material for its own: "What does virus do wherever it can dissolve a hole and find traction?— It starts eating—And what does it do with what it eats?—It makes exact copies of itself that start eating to make more copies that start eating to make more copies that start eating and so forth" (*NE*, 68). The image/virus is posited as invasive and irresistible, a parasite with only self-replication as its function. It is a soft machine.

Compare this to Debord's economic analysis, where the pervasiveness of the spectacle serves the similar function of creating a deception for the purpose of regeneration. The commodity has become an "actually real illusion, and the spectacle is its general manifestation" (Thesis 47). Images and their promise of the satisfaction of desire are manipulated and controlled. The consumer of images becomes a consumer of commodities as the subject becomes further colonized by the forces of capital. The coherence of the subject is revealed as illusory, indeed, imagistic. Control over these images is elusive; in fact, impossible.

The recurrent image of the virus (the virus of the image) biologizes the waning autonomy of the individual in the face of the consumerist spectacle. The subject becomes a "carrier" of spectacle, of image, of pseudo-reality, without ever recognizing the substitution. "Reality," constructed as it is through our images and our perceptions, is itself subject to control: "The scanning program we accept as 'reality' has been imposed by the controlling power on this planet, a power primarily oriented towards total control—In order to retain control they have moved to monopolize and deactivate the hallucinogen drugs by effecting noxious alterations on a molecular level—(*NE*, 51–52). The experience of reality, as it emerges through the labyrinthine structures of *Nova Express,* is the experience of images which can be controlled to reconstruct reality as well as the subject. This is what Eric Mottram has called "the virus transformation into undifferentiated man, the terminal image of man as patient-victim."[141]

McLuhan, while retaining his vision of an externalized, global nervous system, writes of *Nova Express* that it takes place "in a universe which seems to be someone else's insides," and he clearly recognizes that Burroughs's work represents an inversion of his own.[142] Power is the absent center of McLuhan's theories, while it is Burroughs's only topic. In restating his electronic neurological model, McLuhan notes, ominously, "The human nervous system can be reprogrammed biologically as readily as any radio station can alter its fare." In this statement, which foreshadows the appearance of *Videodrome,* there is an acknowledgment of political and social control that is rare in McLuhan and that allows a perception of the unasked question which lurks behind a reading of his works: whose nervous system is this, anyway? Within the new mythology of William Burroughs, it is the nervous system of the forces of control that are extended, consequently co-opting and eroding the power of the individual. The media are the extensions of the state at the expense of the power of the citizen. For most of the population, then, the new information technologies represent *in*trusions rather than *ex*trusions.

Burroughs's attempt to construct a new mythology of the virus power and the struggle for freedom has been noted: "I may add that none of the characters in my mythology are free. If they were free they would not still be in the mythological system, that is, in the cycle of conditioned action."[143] Myth therefore implies an intrinsic lack of freedom for Burroughs.[144] The generic structures of science fiction provide him with an already existing set of crudely aestheticized materials involving technology, science, and rationality. Otherness, dystopianism, alternate worlds, and time travel all function as cosmic tropological systems in science fiction, but such radically decentering reconceptions of the universe are usually—almost inevitably—masked by their aesthetic banality. Science fiction nevertheless succeeds in constructing a new cosmology based upon cultural and technological development. By engaging with the received, and authorless, structures of science fiction, Burroughs is able to excavate a new mythology, in which the avant-garde potentials of the genre are finally realized.

Burroughs also utilizes the structures of received language, in particular the discourses of popular culture, to reject the notion of an original or pure self. Like Warhol, Burroughs replaces *self* with *culture* as the source for the expressive and communicative forms of language. From the Nova Trilogy, with its emphasis on the discourse of science fiction, to *Cities of the Red Night,* with its evocation of boys' adventure stories, Burroughs has spoken, as we all do, through other voices.[145] The names and neologisms that pepper the Nova Trilogy (the Silence Virus, Nova Police, Interzone, Carbonic Caper, and, of course, the Heavy Metal Kid) suggest the incorporation of the languages of science and technology, of advertising and comic books, of drugs and disease, into the construction of a (post)modern idiom, at once satirical and expressive. "Whatever his reservations about some aspects of the mid-20th century," Ballard wrote, "Burroughs accepts that it can be fully described only in terms of its own language, its own idioms and verbal lore."[146] Needless to say, the rationality of technical discourse is undercut by the collisions generated by Burroughs's textual operations. The language of *Nova Express* possesses no directly referential function and serves instead to foreground the proliferation of mediating discourses that produce our reality. As Roland Barthes wrote of avant-garde writing practices in 1968, "In the multiplicity of writing, everything is to be *disentangled,* nothing *deciphered.*"[147] The textual practices of Burroughs, the neologisms, discursive appropriations, and especially the cut-ups, literalize Barthes's statement through a particularly pronounced act of *en*tanglement. The cut-up represents an immunization against the media-virus: a strengthening of the host organism against the infectious agent. "Communication must become total and conscious," Burroughs wrote, "before we can stop it."[148]

Burroughs and Cronenberg—Word and Body

The similarities between the writings of William Burroughs and David Cronenberg are certainly extensive. The invasion of the body, the loss of control, the transformation of self into Other are as obsessively deployed in the works of the latter as in those of the former. As Christopher Sharrett has written, the pervasive concern in the works of Burroughs and Cronenberg is "the rise of the addictive personality cultivated by dominant culture and the changing structures of power." He adds that, "Neither Burroughs nor Cronenberg finds a solution in organized revolt since the new technological environment absorbs and dilutes ideological principles and abstract values."[149] Both can be read through this observation by Baudrillard: "All the movements which only bet on liberation, emancipation, the resurrection of the subject of history, of the group, of speech as a raising of consciousness, indeed of a 'seizure of the unconscious' of subjects and of the masses, do not see that they are acting in accordance with the system, whose imperative today is the overproduction and regeneration of meaning and speech."[150]

Baudrillard's pessimism regarding the co-optation of the spectacle by more progressive forces is entirely complicit with Burroughs's textual destructions. Language, and more specifically *textuality,* is the space of conflict, as demonstrated most extensively in the Nova Trilogy. Language is, in multiple senses, the definition and controller of the self, the site of identity—an attitude entirely commensurate with Burroughs's self-awareness as a writer. Burroughs pushes beyond the limits of traditional identity by breaking the boundaries of traditional language usage. His incorporation of other texts from the genres of poetry, fiction, and medical and scientific discourses undermines the hegemony of the novel. The technique of the cut-up is explicit in its evocation of a surgical procedure, metaphorically linking the textual and corporeal bodies, but it also suggests a form of torture or dismemberment. Whatever the metaphor, the cut-up demolishes the linear coherence that produces the identity of the text.

As a final escape from the controllers of the language/self, Burroughs advocates the use of the Silence Virus, which can be partially regarded as a retreat into the unwritable. (David Porush observes that the "noise" generated by the cut-up is itself a form of silence,[151] and the black hole of Baudrillard's sci-fi philosophy is also pertinent.) Transcendence might involve an escape from the text or medium over which the subject has no control. Baudrillard's position is here significantly different from that of Burroughs: for the former, the mass media function as a hyper-language which accelerates the process of information entropy. Through overload, the proliferation of informational systems produce their own resistance: "Instead of informing as it claims, instead of giving form and structure, information neutralises even further the 'social field'; more and more it creates an inert mass impermeable to the classical institutions of the social, and to the very contents of information."[152] The new resistance takes the form of a hyper-conformity: the citizens are so overly addressed, that the address ceases to function. In the same text, however, Baudrillard also writes of terrorist activity as the production of a meaningless, that is to say a *silent,* speech.[153] For both Burroughs and Baudrillard, then, a spectacular silence constitutes one possible—but ultimately inadequate—form of resistance to the spectacular order.

Cronenberg replaces this emphasis on the structures of language with an attention to the image of the body. The body serves as both an iconic and symbolic sign for this filmmaker, and it is a sign of tremendous complexity. Cronenberg constructs an elaborate semiotics of the body in his work (but it is only in *Videodrome,* to date, that he fully addresses the construction of the body of the text: the cinematic signifier). The body represents the self in this set of films, and the transformations that the body undergoes rival Burroughs's cut-ups for their violence, randomness, and capacity to produce confusion. The penile organ emerging from Marilyn Chambers's armpit in *Rabid* (1976), the extruded "children" of *The Brood* (1979), and the biological cut-up represented by the human/fly genetic mélange in *The Fly* (1986) all enact the breakdown of human coherence through the deployment of new technologies. Burroughs wrote: "The realization that something as familiar to you as the movement of your intestines the sound of your breathing the beating of your heart is also alien and hostile does make one feel a bit insecure at first."[154] Through his linking of the alien with the technological, David Cronenberg is *the* filmmaker of terminal identity.

Annette Michelson and, more recently, Fredric Jameson have characterized science fiction as primarily a spatial genre. For Jameson, writing about science fiction literature, space serves so many metaphorical functions, and pervades the genre in such a thorough and distinct manner, that it can be seen as a defining characteristic of the field. In contrast to the psychologized space in "realist" fiction, science fiction space becomes totalizing, formalized, and reflexive, and a reader's experience of a literary science fiction text becomes an experience of that uniquely overdetermined spatiality.[155] Science fiction film, as Michelson has demonstrated in her reading of Kubrick's *2001,* can extend the spatial experience of the viewer into the realm of the theatre itself: the spatial experience becomes physical and bodily in the cinema through the kinesthetic effects and appeal engendered by the cinematic apparatus (despite the fact that few films have matched *2001*).[156]

The films of David Cronenberg are also involved in a particular spatial play, one which at first glance owes more to the horror genre than to science fiction. Further analysis reveals a new spatialization that marks the texts as science fictional, although in a way more closely aligned with Jameson's literary conception than to Michelson's cinematic phenomenology. Space serves a complex metaphorical function in the Cronenberg film, as the inner workings of the body and mind are spatialized and co-opted by the forces of spectacle.

Cronenberg's insistent figuration of the body as the site of psychosexual, social, or political conflict represents a first level of movement from the invisible to the visible, a step toward a more fully realized spatialization. This aspect of the Cronenberg text is surely the most striking and startling, and as his most insistent trope it has not escaped the notice of other writers. The compellingly repugnant bodily transformations are frequently seen to indicate a playing through of a new Cartesian split—the rational mind lost before the onslaught of the unleashed and irrational desires of the body. This is most clearly on display in *The Brood,* in which a new psychotherapeutic technique transforms mental anguish into physical symptoms (the doctor responsible has published a treatise called *The Shape of Rage*).[157] As one patient with lymphatic cancer notes, "Dr. Raglan encouraged my body to revolt; now I've got a small revolution on my hands, and I'm not putting it down very well."

The mind-body dualism, according to William Beard's lengthy review of Cronenberg's work, leads to the necessity for "a precarious balance between rationality and instinct. . . . [The] dichotomy is, so to speak, a two-way street: when the confident head tries to manipulate the gut, it not only fails but also provokes the gut to rise up and have its way with the head—often literally."[158] Thus the rabid physicality of the Cronenberg text belongs firmly to the traditions of the horror film: "monsters from the id" are rendered physical, and figures of desire roam the landscape. One significant difference is that the "landscape" is now the *body* of the protagonist, and the contusions, tumors, lesions, and new organelles are the "monsters" roaming free.

Beard is correct to point out that a Cronenberg film does not, for all its graphic detail, revel in the return of the repressed, as so many horror films do, from the films of James Whale through those of Terence Fisher and George Romero. There is a sobriety to Cronenberg's work, evident in *The Brood, Videodrome,* and *The Fly* in particular, which marks them as different from most horror films and, in fact, as probably being more repressed themselves (in Cronenberg's world, smoking, drinking, or sexual activity produce disastrous consequences).

There is no need to review the appearance of the mind/body dichotomy in every film by this filmmaker, but it should be noted that the bodily transformations which recur are not, I think, able to be completely subsumed within such a Cartesian system. The humanistic balance stressed by Beard simply does not fully account for the evident and pervasive antihumanism of Cronenberg's production, as demonstrated by the recurrent fears of human contact, sexuality, or physicality in any form. David Cronenberg is the filmmaker of *panic sex,* to use Arthur Kroker's pungent phrase, with the body as the overdetermined metaphorical site for the expression of profound social anxiety.[159] Human emotion is not the subject of the Cronenberg film, *contra* Beard, it is instead, as Sharrett has correctly argued, the structures of external power and control to which the individual (in body *and* soul) is subjected. The dissolution of identity into new forms is increasingly posited as a consequence of contemporary existence, connected to the rise of new technologies. This has become greatly evident in three films: *Scanners* (1981), *Videodrome,* and *The Fly,* in which the apparent mind/body dichotomy is superseded by the *tri*-chotomy of mind/body/machine. While all of his films involved scientific developments (e.g., in parasitology, psychology, pharmacology, immunology, and—in *Dead Ringers* [1989]—gynecology), in these films science takes the explicitly technologized forms of media, computers, transporters, and genetics. Carrie Rickey is closer to the mark when she writes that Cronenberg is: "a visionary architect of a chaotic biological tract where mind and body, ever fighting a Cartesian battle for integration, are so vulnerable *as to be easily annexed by technology.*"[160] The mind/body struggle is a blind, in Rickey's view (and I concur), for the larger Burroughsian issues of addiction, technological control, and the malleability of reality and identity.

This movement beyond the boundaries of the individual, to which the mind/body model is largely limited, is troped through Cronenberg's treatment of space, a treatment which distances him from the realm of the horror film and which places him squarely within the traditions of the science fiction text as characterized by Jameson and Michelson. If mental processes are rendered physical, played out on the body, then we should also recognize that both mental *and* biological processes are granted spatial dimension. The space of the film becomes a specifically *bodily* space. In *They Came from Within* (1975), a modern high-rise apartment building is the site of a parasitic infestation. First one resident, then more, succumb to a bizarre new organism which inhabits the body and releases libidinal forces. At last, the invasion complete, the residents calmly drive into the city, presumably to further spread this new plague. The high-rise serves as a mega-organism; the space itself becomes biologized. An extension of this spatial figuration is present in *The Brood.* Dr. Raglan's most successful patient at his "psychoplasmic" institute, Nola, grows bizarre offspring from her body that strike back at all those for whom she feels anger (giving new meaning to the notion of "acting out" one's feelings). As Raglan wanders through the attic where her eerie brood is housed, Nola argues with her husband on the floor below. Her increasing tension is intercut with her brood's growing restiveness. Here the topography of the mind is given a literal spatiality, as Dr. Raglan searches through a psychic realm of pain, rage, and anguish.

Scanners, Cronenberg's first high-tech production, is extensively involved with the physical representation of invisible psychic processes. An elaborate soundtrack, replete with overlapping voice-overs, the beeping of an EKG machine, and electronic music and effects fill the visible space with evidence of the hidden mental struggles of the telepathic protagonist. One sequence is staged within a massive work of modernist art—a giant head—precisely enacting that formalized, reflexive, and overdetermined space within which Jameson locates science fiction. Later, as a telepath "scans" a computer, melding their "minds," Cronenberg's camera tracks across the vast landscape of—a microchip. The mind of the computer is granted spatiality, as the movement of the camera begins to dynamize and dramatize the invisible electronic processes at work.

Each of these instances reveals a space which becomes a body: a contained and closed circulatory system prone to infection and disruption. In *Videodrome* it is not simply an architectural space, but the space of reality itself that becomes so infected. The viral forces of invasion, imagistic or otherwise, assume their full metaphorical value within Cronenberg's construction of a bodily space. While Cronenberg can be linked to McLuhan's vision of a new stage in the development of man, there is an evident concern with the parasitism of other forces which are introduced from without. Cronenberg's spatialization of both bodily and viral forces presents a collision between McLuhan's extension of the body beyond its biological boundaries and Baudrillard's vision of the usurpation and dissolution of individual power.

The repeated spatializing of the body results in a treatment of space very different from more traditional horror filmmakers. Cronenberg's films contain very little sense of the space off-screen, that realm of the unknown and taboo which has served as the central spatial metaphor for the genre. Cronenberg's films are about *presence* rather than *absence,* experience and transformation rather than threat and investigation. The spaces are relentlessly *interior*—apartments, offices, laboratories—and never more so than in *Videodrome, Dead Ringers,* and, obviously, *They Came from Within.* Enclosure, separation, and isolation define the on-screen realm of Cronenberg's filmmaking, and the profu-

sion of slow-tracking shots across these spaces emphasizes the emptiness of what is present, rather than the completion demanded by what
is not. In other words, the forces of the repressed are always already
present and are never displaced to some "other," absent region to await
reemergence.

Space figured as body also illuminates the use of architecture in
Cronenberg's films from *Stereo* (1969) through *Dead Ringers.* Akin to the
design of *2001's* space station and moon base, the architecture in these
films is bland, geometrically precise, and, above all, sterile.[161] This
orderly space, which serves as a security corporation headquarters in
Scanners, a high-rise in *They Came from Within,* and a research facility in
both *Stereo* and *Crimes of the Future* (1970), represents the forces of
control that are in combat with the chaotic processes of the body. By
analogy, then, the humans who inhabit this space of order, this space
which is also the space of a mega-body, must themselves be regarded as
microorganisms and, in addition, as parasites and agents of chaos. The
externalization or spatialization of the biological thus simultaneously
constructs the body as something that inhabits space and as a space to
be inhabited. The human is doubly defined as both host and virus.

The sterility of the architecture in its debased, high-modern blandness points to Cronenberg's rejection of the "purity" of mind, or even of
body. The explicit upheavals of bodily transformation are by contrast,
firmly sensual, yet still discomfiting (if not actually terrifying). The most
significant failing of the Cronenberg film is not, as some suggest, the
failure to resolve this dichotomy—this pervasive ambivalence indeed
recommends his work—but rather the apparent inability to present
either side of the dichotomy as possessed of positive attributes. If
sterility is inadequate then so, clearly, is physical contact. There is an
absence of dialectic in Cronenberg's universe, but this is somewhat
offset by the refusal to finally privilege either term in this physical/non-
physical schism. Cronenberg avoids the Manichaeism of Burroughs,
but so far has rarely achieved the truly transgressive ambivalence of
other scripters of the physical, such as Bataille.

The spatialization of the body does make problematic any rigid division of the world into the dichotomous categories of inside and outside.
Outside forces invade the body and destroy it from *inside.* The interior
bodily space is displayed within an exterior architectural space, although one which retains an emphasis on interiors. Baudrillard had
claimed that the infusion of informational and communicational technologies has brought about an abrupt dissolution of the traditional

boundaries of cultural existence and, moreover, a disruption of those borders which had previously served to guarantee the hegemony of the individual in body as well as soul. The dissolution of the human, which Baudrillard describes in his highly technologized language derived from the discourses of cybernetics and electronics, is performed by the Cronenberg film in a disturbingly visceral manner. For all their stylistic separation, Baudrillard and Cronenberg are both notable for their deliberate ambivalence; for regarding this dissolution with simultaneous fascination, acceptance, and revulsion.

Videodrome

In *Videodrome,* which might stand as the ultimate statement on the place of the image in terminal culture, Cronenberg's overt fascination with McLuhanism is supplemented by what seems to be a prescient figuration of Baudrillard. The mediation of the image as a hyperlanguage and hyperreality allows Cronenberg to situate his bodily figurations and demands a reading through the tropes of postmodernism, in which the negation of a mind/body dichotomy takes its place within a set of such negated oppositions and boundary dissolutions, including self/other, private/public, and spectacle/reality.

Videodrome presents a destabilized reality in which image, reality, hallucination, and psychosis become indissolubly melded, in what is certainly the most estranging portrayal of image addiction and viral invasion since Burroughs. "Videodrome" itself, apparently a clandestine television broadcast, is referred to as a "scum show" by its own programmers and depicts brutal torture and sadism in a grotesque display which exerts a strong influence upon its viewers. Cable-station operator Max Renn desires "Videodrome": as a businessman he needs it to rescue his foundering station; as an individual he finds himself irresistibly drawn to its horrors. Renn must track down the source of this mysterious program (which emanates from either South America or Pittsburgh). Larger themes are connected to Renn's quest, such as the pervasiveness of the media-dominated spectacle in a postmodern world and, further, the passage beyond mere spectacle to the ultimate dissolution of all the boundaries which might serve to separate and guarantee definitions of "spectacle," "subject," and "reality" itself.

At times *Videodrome* seems to be a film which hypostatizes Baudrillard's most outrageous propositions. Here, for example, with remarkable syntactic similarity, Baudrillard and a character from Cronenberg's

film are both intent upon the usurpation of the real by its own representation; upon the imbrication of the real, the technologized, and
the simulated. The language is hypertechnologized but antirational;
Moebius-like in its evocation of a dissolute, spectacular reality:

> *Jean Baudrillard:* "The era of hyperreality now begins . . . it signifies
> as a whole the passage into orbit, as orbital and environmental
> model, of our private sphere itself. It is no longer a scene where the
> dramatic interiority of the subject, engaged as with its image, is
> played out. We are here at the controls of a micro-satellite, in orbit,
> living no longer as an actor or dramaturge but as a terminal of
> multiple networks. Television is still the most direct prefiguration
> of this. But today it is the very space of habitation that is conceived
> as both receiver and distributor, as the space of both reception and
> operations, the control screen and terminal which as such may be
> endowed with telematic power."[162]
>
> *Professor Brian O'Blivion:* "The battle for the mind of North America
> will be fought in the video arena—the Videodrome. The television
> screen is the retina of the mind's eye. Therefore the television
> screen is part of the physical structure of the brain. Therefore
> whatever appears on the television screen emerges as raw experi-
> ence for those who watch it. Therefore television is reality and
> reality is less than television."

Cronenberg and Baudrillard both, in fact, seem to be following Debord's program that "When *analyzing* the spectacle one speaks, to some
extent, the language of the spectacular itself in the sense that one moves
through the methodological terrain of the very society which expresses
itself in spectacle" (Thesis 11: the dictum strongly informs all the science fiction analyzed in this chapter). Baudrillard embraces a high-tech,
alienating, and alienated science fictional rhetoric to explore high-tech
alienation, while Cronenberg's horror films about the failure of interpersonal communications are an integral part of an industry which privileges the spectacular over the intimate, and pseudo-satisfaction over
genuine comprehension. Both construct discourses of antirationalism
in an attempt to expose and ridicule any process or history of enlightenment which might occur through the exercise of a "pure" reason. The
complexity and evasiveness of Baudrillard's prose complements the
visceral and hallucinatory image-systems of Cronenberg's cinema.

Videodrome presents a most literal depiction of image addiction. The
title of the film is presented as a video image; following a flash of
distortion, the title is replaced by another, this one on a diegetic televi-

sion screen, while an accompanying voice-over announces, "CIVIC TV . . . the one you take to bed with you." Dr. Brian O'Blivion is the founder of the Cathode Ray Mission, a kind of TV soup kitchen for a derelict population. Scanning the rows of cubicles, each containing a vagrant and a television, Max Renn asks, "You really think a few doses of TV are gonna help them?" O'Blivion's daughter replies, "Watching TV will patch them back into the world's mixing board." On the street a derelict stands with his television set and a dish for change in what is presumably a watch-and-pay arrangement.

Within the diegesis, television frequently serves as a medium of direct address. Renn awakens to a videotaped message recorded by his assistant. O'Blivion refuses to appear on television "except *on* television": his image appears on a monitor placed beside the program's host (in a gesture reminiscent of Debord's own prerecorded lectures).[163] As Renn awaits his own talk-show appearance, he chats with Nicki Brand, the woman next to him, but an interposed monitor blocks any view of her. The image on the monitor is coextensive with its own background, however—Magritte-like—and consequently, the conversation is between a live Renn and a video Brand. Further examples of direct address proliferate, offering a preliminary blurring of any distinction between real and televisual experience.

This parody of McLuhanism serves as backdrop to the enigma of Videodrome, which is finally revealed to be a government project. The explanation for Videodrome is at least as coherent as any from Burroughs: Spectacular Optical, a firm which specializes in defense contracts ("We make inexpensive eyeglasses for the Third World, and missile guidance systems for NATO"), has developed a signal which induces a tumor in the viewer. This tumor causes hallucinations which can be recorded, then revised, then fed back to the viewer: in effect, the individual is reprogrammed to serve the controller's ends. Burroughs, at his most paranoid, offered a similar vision of the subject:

> you are a programmed tape recorder set to record and play back
> who programs you
> who decides what tapes play back in present time[164]

While the images which accompany the transmission of the Videodrome signal are not directly significant, it is the violence and sadism of Videodrome (the program) which "open receptors in the brain which allows the signal to sink in."

But as Barry Convex of Spectacular Optical asks Renn, "Why would anyone watch a scum show like 'Videodrome?' " "Business reasons," is

Renn's fast response, to which Convex retorts with a simple, "Sure. What about the other reasons?" Convex is correct: Renn's interest in the Videodrome broadcast transcends the commercial. "You can't take your eyes off it," is only his initial response in what becomes an escalating obsession. Asking what sort of program he might himself produce, a client asks, "Would you do 'Videodrome?'" Coincident with his exposure to the Videodrome signal is his introduction to Nicki Brand, an outspoken, alluring radio personality for C-RAM radio.[165] Transgression thus functions in Renn's life in at least three modes: the social transgression represented by his soft-porn, hard-violence cable TV station; the sexual transgression of his forays into sadomasochistic sexuality with Brand; and the political and sexual transgressions of Videodrome's sadistic presentations of torture and punishment. The three levels are linked in a spiraling escalation which culminates in Renn's own appearance on Videodrome, whipping, first Brand, then her image on a television monitor. Brand is the guide who leads Renn toward his final destiny; after her death, her image remains to spur him on. Her masochism might indicate a quest for real sensation: this media figure admits that, "We live in overstimulated times. We crave stimulation for its own sake." Brand wants to "audition" for Videodrome: "I was made for that show," she brags, but it might be more accurate to say that she was made *by* that show. Bianca O'Blivion tells Renn, "They used her image to seduce you."

The Videodrome program is explicitly linked by both Renn and Convex to male sexual response (something "tough" rather than "soft") and penetration (something that will "break through"). Renn takes on the "tough" sadistic role with Brand, and yet there is no doubt that it is she who controls the relationship, she who dominates. Similarly, the power granted by the Videodrome program to observe and relish the experience of torture and vicious brutality disguises the actual function of the program to increase social control: to establish a new means of dominance over the population. Renn is superficially the master of Brand and Videodrome, but ultimately the master becomes the slave. In a Baudrillardian revision of the Frankenstein myth, even Brian O'Blivion is condemned: Videodrome's creator is its first victim.

There is a distinctly Third World flavor to the mise-en-scène of the Videodrome program in its low-technology setting, electrified clay walls, and the neo-stormtrooper guise of the torturers. All this exists in contrast to the Videodrome technology: electronic and invisible, disseminated "painlessly" through the mass media. "In Central America," Renn tells Brand, "making underground videos is a subversive act." In

North America it is too, it would seem, as the Videodrome signal subverts experience, reality, and the very existence of the subject.

Once again, it is the voluntarism of the television experience, the "free choice" of the viewer, which permits the incursion of controlling forces. A strictly political-economic reading of *Videodrome* could easily situate the work within Debord's *Society of the Spectacle*. Images stand in for a lost social whole, the spectator's alienation is masked via the reified whole of the spectacle, the capitalist forces are thereby able to reproduce themselves at the expense of the worker/consumer/spectator. Cronenberg has replaced the structures of power absent from McLuhan's schema: Brian O'Blivion envisioned Videodrome as the next step in the evolution of man, but his utopian technologism is usurped by the technocratic order of state control.

But *Videodrome* moves beyond this classically political reading through its relentless physicality. The film's politics have less to do with economic control than with the uncontrolled immixture of simulation and reality. In *Videodrome* the body literally opens up—the stomach develops a massive, vaginal slit—to accommodate the new videocassette "program." Image addiction reduces the subject to the status of a videotape player/recorder; the human body becomes a part of the massive system of reproductive technology (*you are a programmed tape recorder*). The sexual implications of the imagery are thus significant and not at all gratuitous: video becomes visceral.[166]

Following his own exposure to the Videodrome signal, Renn begins his series of hallucinations with a spectacular immersion in the world of the spectacle. When his visiting assistant, Bridey, reaches for the Videodrome cassette, Renn assaults her. In a series of shot/reverse shot pairings, Bridey becomes Brand, then Bridey again. Disoriented, Max apologizes for hitting her. "Hit me?" she answers, "Max . . . you didn't hit me." The videotape she has delivered from Brian O'Blivion breathes and undulates in his hand; he drops it and kicks it lightly, but it only lies there, inert. As O'Blivion tells him: "Your reality is already half-video hallucination."

The videotaped message from O'Blivion suddenly becomes more *interactive*. "Max," he says, all trace of electronic filtering abruptly gone from his voice. "I'm so happy you came to me." O'Blivion explains the history of the Videodrome phenomenon while being readied for execution: the executioner is Nicki Brand. "I want you, Max," she breathes. "Come to me. Come to Nicki." Her lips fill the screen, and the set begins to pulsate, to breathe. Veins ripple the hardwood cabinet; a videogame joystick waggles obscenely. All boundaries are removed as the diegetic

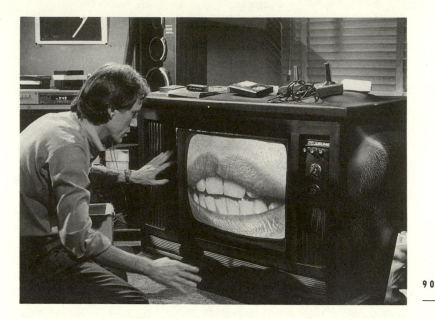

Video becomes visceral in Cronenberg's *Videodrome,* 1982. (Courtesy Photofest)

frame of the TV screen vanishes from view: the lips now fill the movie screen in a vast close-up. Renn approaches the set as the screen bulges outward to meet his touch, in a movement which literalizes the notion of the screen as breast. His face sinks in, his hands fondle the panels and knobs of the set as the lips continue their panting invitation.

Cronenberg moves the viewer in and out of Renn's hallucination by creating a deep ambiguity regarding the status of the image. It is easy to accept the attack on the assistant as real, although the transmigration of identities clearly demarcates Renn's demented subjectivity. Yet, it turns out, the attack was entirely hallucinated: the "real" cinematic image is unreliable. In the extended hallucination of the eroticized, visceral television, the filmmaker gracefully dissolves the bounds that contain the spectacle. O'Blivion's voice is no longer marked as a mediated communication once the electronic tone of his speech ceases. The TV screen is contained by its own frame, but Cronenberg's close-up permits the image to burst its boundaries and expand to the nondiegetic limits of the cinema screen. In a later hallucination, a video-Brand circles Renn with whip in hand, proferring it for him to wield. The image moves from video hallucination to cinematic reality within a single shot: Renn accepts the whip, but Brand is now no longer present in corporeal form; she only exists, shackled, on a TV screen. Renn attacks the bound(ed) image with fervor: another moment which recalls the visual punning of René Magritte. These shifts in visual register mark the passage from spectacle as visual phenomenon to spectacle as new reality.

Cronenberg, then, does not mythologize the cinematic signifier as "real," but continually confuses the real with the image and the image with the hallucination. When Renn pops a videotape into his machine, Cronenberg inserts a blip of video distortion over the entire visual field before cutting to O'Blivion's image on-screen. This does not mark the hallucination, but it "infects" the viewer with an analogous experience of dissolution and decayed boundaries. These confusions, between reality, image, and hallucination, pervade the film. There is no difference in the cinematic techniques employed, no "rational" textual system, which might serve to distinguish reality from hallucination for the film viewer. Each moment is presented as "real," that is, as corresponding to the conventions of realist filmmaking. Discourse itself is placed in question in *Videodrome* through the estrangement of cinematic language. Where the hallucination might have begun or ended remains ambiguous, uncertain. These unbounded hallucinations jeopardize the very status of the image: we must believe everything and nothing, equally. In the words of the Master Assassin Hassan-i-Sabbah, (used as the epigraph to Cronenberg's adaptation of *Naked Lunch* [1991]) "*Nothing is true. Everything is permitted.*"[167]

Renn hallucinates his appearance on Videodrome, but is Videodrome a program comprised entirely of recorded hallucinations? If so, then there is a progression from hallucination, through image, to reality: the scene is real because it is televised, it is televised because it is recorded, it is recorded because it is hallucinated. The illusory rationality which guides the society of the spectacle emanates from the irrational recesses of the libidinal mind. On the medium of television, Baudrillard writes: "The medium itself is no longer identifiable as such, and the merging of the medium and the message (McLuhan) is the first great formula of this new age. There is no longer any medium in the literal sense: it is now intangible, diffuse and diffracted in the real, and it can no longer be said that the latter is distorted by it."[168] Society becomes the mirror of television (Kroker) as television becomes the new reality. A slit opens in Max Renn's stomach, and Barry Convex holds up a videocassette, which breathes. "I've got something I want to play for you," he says and inserts the cassette. The human body thus becomes a part of the technologies of reproduction observed by Jameson: the ultimate colonization under late capitalism and the ultimate penetration of technology into subjectivity. The reprogrammed Renn later retrieves a gun from this new organ, a gun which extends cables and spikes into his arm in an inversion of McLuhan's sense of technology as human extension. Here the man becomes the extension of the weapon: a servo-mechanism or perhaps a terminal. There is none of McLuhan's hypothetical "numbing" in this most painful of cinematic displays. We are instead still trapped within a universe which seems to be someone else's insides.

In its themes and structure the film serves as a graphic example of what Baudrillard termed "the dissolution of TV into life, the dissolution of life into TV." Baudrillard terms this immixture "*viral,*" echoing Burroughs's injunction that "image *is* virus." The viral metaphor is strikingly apt when applied to *Videodrome:* the literalized invasion of the body by the image and the production of tumors which produce images. Image is virus; virus virulently replicates itself; the subject is finished.

Body and image become one: a dissolution of real and representation, certainly, but also of the boundaries between internal and external, as the interiorized hallucination becomes the public spectacle of the Videodrome program. Here *Videodrome* echoes *The Simulacra,* in which a character's psychosis results in a physical transformation (his organs telekinetically appear outside, as objects in the room are reciprocally introjected). In the postspectacle society delineated by Baudrillard, all such boundaries will dissolve, will become irrelevant through the imperatives of the model of communication (simultaneous transmission and reception):

> In any case, we will have to suffer this new state of things, this forced extroversion of all interiority, this forced injection of all exteriority that the categorical imperative of communication literally signifies; . . . we are now in a new form of schizophrenia. No more hysteria, no more projective paranoia, properly speaking, but this state of terror proper to the schizophrenic: too great a proximity of everything, the unclean promiscuity of everything which touches, invests and penetrates without resistance.[169]

The subject has "no halo of private protection, *not even his own body,* to protect him anymore" (emphasis mine). The works of David Cronenberg, as well as those of Philip Dick, repeat several of these tropes. The subject is in crisis, its hegemony threatened by centralized structures of control, by a technology which simultaneously alienates and masks alienation, by a perception of its own helplessness. Even the last retreat, the physical body, has lost its privileged status: hence the schizophrenic terror undergone by the protagonists. Even the libido, site of the irrational, seat of desire, is invaded, enlisted in the furtherance of an obsolescent technological rationalism.

Again, these texts are not simply reactionary moments of nostalgia, but bring a profound and progressive ambivalence to the imbrication of simulation and reality, subject and other. The slippage of reality that marks the textual operations of *Videodrome* can certainly be associated with the commensurate process in the writings of the saboteur Burroughs, who repeatedly declared that we must "Storm the Reality Studio and retake the universe."[170] This cinematic metaphor reaches a kind of apotheosis in *Videodrome,* as the images flicker and fall, their authority ultimately denied, but there is no glimpse of a Reality Studio behind the myriad levels of reality production.

Ubik and the Reality Fix

This territory of reality-slippage, with its echoes of Plato's cave, is not only the province of William Burroughs: Philip K. Dick lives there, too. *Ubik* (1969) constructs a diegesis peopled by telepaths, who (logically enough) function as corporate spies and counter-spies; and half-lifers, dead people who still retain some residual brain function and who exist in a cryogenic partial existence.[171] Boundaries between self and other, and living and dead therefore hold little significance. Following an elaborate assassination attempt, Joe Chip (a blip culture name if there ever was one) and his team of telepaths are subjected to an accelerating process of reality erosion, as temporality itself seems to reverse its valence around them. New cigarettes are stale, food is spoiled, currencies are obsolete (*real* money features the faces of Disney or Castro). The space of this temporal shift expands and soon the objects, then the rooms, buildings, and city blocks around them are figured in earlier and earlier manifestations: the 1950s, the 1930s, the 1900s. Only Ubik, a product packaged in historically appropriate forms (aerosol, ointment, elixir), can briefly restore the familiar temporal surroundings of the present day, and so the narrative propels its characters on a quest for answers and for Ubik.

Chip first suspects that they have been projected into the shadow-world of half-life, implying that they "died" in the explosion. Runciter, Chip's boss, is not with them, and the shifting realities may be the result of his attempts to reach out, to transmit a message to them. Evidence then points to Pat, an enemy telepath with the power to change the past without anyone becoming aware of the alteration. Finally an underlying truth is discovered: Chip and company are in cold-pack, where a battle of shadow-minds is ensuing between the psychotic mind of a peripheral character named Jory, another half-lifer, controlling Chip's reality, and Runcicter (via his half-lifer wife), who provides Ubik. But even this reality may be yet another shadow.

Reduced to its narrative skeleton, and bereft of the work's compression and wit, *Ubik* stands as a Platonic meditation on the rift between appearance and reality. Objects in the world are only shadows of an ideal form, which is why Joe Chip's refrigerator devolves from computerized servant to freon-based cooling system to primitive icebox: this is a reversed succession of manifestations of the Idea of a Refrigerator.

Appearance, image, and spectacle are obviously homologous terms when placed in dichotomous opposition to the notion of "the real": if *Ubik* were to remain at this Platonic level, it would be notable only for its ultimate dependence upon a reality that underlies the shifting levels of appearance or spectacle, but *Ubik* penetrates to further levels that undermine any Platonic idealism. Pat's ability to manipulate the past implies the existence of myriad presents, none finally more real than any other. After Jory's confession Chip is overwhelmed by the notion that this "world" has been constructed solely for himself, but Jory responds, "It's not very large. One hotel in Des Moines. And a street outside the window with a few people and cars. And maybe a couple of other buildings thrown in: stores across the street for you to look at when you happen to see out" (160). Chip has been privileged to look upon the final level, what might actually comprise real reality, the Reality Studio where reality is staged; but in a satisfyingly paranoid moment, the ultimate reality is revealed to be nothing more than the fantasies of a dysfunctional madman.

An important final shift in perspective moves the reader out from Chip's half-life experience to Runciter's position in the moratorium. In his pocket Runciter finds currency adorned with the image of Joe Chip, just as Chip had earlier found Runciter-money in his own pockets: a reversal and continuation of the first moment of reality-slippage in the novel. "This was just the beginning," the book ends. If the final reality presented in the book is itself only a shadow, then the work replaces the reification of the real with infinite regression and oscillation. *Ubik* does not present a dichotomy of appearance and reality, but an unresolved dialectic.

However, a statement denying the existence of the real is, if not meaningless, then at least useless. *Ubik* gains its force and originality by examining the central importance of the *idea* of reality, while resisting the fact of "reality" as an absolute concept. Ubik, the product, is in demand because it *fixes* reality (in both senses of the word: it *repairs* the real and *locks it in place*), and this allows the group to function. The idea of reality thus exerts a tangible influence on appearance and existence. Appearance, then, is not negated as a deception; it is instead postulated as a necessary condition of existence. *Ubik* suggests, still largely within a Platonic model (although without the emphasis on the importance of Ideal Forms), that although appearance may not be synonymous with reality, it remains our sole epistemological realm. Reality is finally not even to be taken on faith, but simply replaced by an acceptance of a conditional and malleable appearance.

Dick lures the reader into a series of false understandings that are accepted because of the premise, inherent in the structures of "escapist literature," of a final and binding revelation which enacts the process of closure: the ending as Ubik.[172] The false ending, which is also explicitly a beginning (a resonant variation on the science fiction/monster movie cliché, "The End?"), reveals the plot as only another appearance, again producing an infinite regression with which the reader must be satisfied. The narrative pretends to a linearity ultimately denied by the false clues, shifting protagonists, and denial of closure.

Similar tendencies mark the fascinating screenplay Dick fashioned from his novel five years later, commissioned by Jean-Pierre Gorin.[173] Although largely faithful to his own plot and dialogue, Dick succeeds remarkably well at conceiving cinema as a spectacular form with particular relevance for *Ubik*. In a maneuver which recalls the strategies of Burroughs's screenplay-novel, *The Last Words of Dutch Schultz* (from 1975, nearly contemporaneous with the *Ubik* screenplay),[174] film becomes a physical object for Dick. The author of this novel on regression wanted his film to end by regressing to black and white stock, silent footage, flickering effects, and by finally bubbling and burning to a halt. The screenplay retains some of this: Chip's unsteady driving in the 1930s recalls "a Laurel and Hardy film"; a drive through the simulated landscape concocted by Jory features repeating backgrounds such as those found in the cheap cartoons produced for television; a character oscillating in and out of existence speaks with defective sound synchronization; a late scene is described thus: "Visual flickering; like with hand-cranked projector. Again the lobby of the Meremont Hotel, but very dim, as if 'bulb' is weak in 'projector.' Colors washed out, low hues only; yellow filter over everything."[175] Film becomes an object to be regarded, a physical substance that might bear the traces of reality, but which is nevertheless pure appearance. Dick's manipulations of the cinematic apparatus reveal cinema as a signifying mechanism and deny its status as transparent conduit of truth.

The novel, and especially the screenplay, perform an effective deconstruction through their very structures, but it is in that commodity of commodities, Ubik, that the work rejoins the analysis of the spectacle performed by Debord, Baudrillard, Burroughs, and Cronenberg. Ubik is the product which permits the maintenance of appearance. In the novel each chapter begins with an advertisement for this mysterious and ubiquitous balm: "Could it be that I have bad breath, Tom? Well, Ed, if you're worried about that, try today's new Ubik, with powerful germicidal foaming action, guaranteed safe when taken as directed" (157). "It takes more than a bag to seal in food flavor; it takes Ubik plastic wrap—actually four layers in one. Keeps freshness in, air and moisture out. Watch this simulated test" (148). These commercials further interrupt the already staccato progress of the diegesis and place the reader in a position analogous to Chip, scanning the advertisements for clues and hidden messages. In Burroughs's *The Soft Machine,* a character reports: "So I am a public agent and don't know who I work for, get my instructions from street signs, newspapers and pieces of conversation." Chip gets his instructions from package labels and Alpha-bits: in the screenplay for *Ubik,* the floating letters in Chip's cereal spell out a message from Runciter.

The screenplay uses these commercials to literally interrupt the action, anticipating such later works as *American Flagg!* and *Robocop* (1987), but they also serve as a superimposition, a layering of images which blocks appearance. The first instance presents only a blank "Andy Warhol colored-dot type austere graphic representation of a spray can," without a label. "Since it is drawn and without writing, we understand that despite its fidelity to graphic representationalism, it is incomplete" (31). Dick's description is dense with meaning. The viewer is promised future revelations regarding this can, but more importantly the spectacle is displayed in spectacular fashion, faithful to reality but, through its apparent incompletion, not interchangeable with it. "Something has come between us and what we have been watching," he continues, "something in a sense more real or anyhow real in a visibly different sense." Over the hallucinatory deformations which prefigure *Videodrome,* in *Ubik* diegetic reality is shattered in a gesture which reflects on the experience of the real through the experience of the cinematic.

Ubik appears again and again throughout book and screenplay, usually through the medium of advertising. Advertising generates anxieties and makes the subject aware of lacks (perhaps in self-*image* or personal *appearance*). In becoming a consumer and acquiring a commodity, the subject fixes the lack, repairs appearance, becomes an image. The commodity, of course, is also a primary example of reification for Marx, in that the abstraction of the labor process is therein contained, bounded, and fixed.[176] In both of these conceptions of the commodity, Ubik stands as the ultimate example: the *ur-commodity*. The modern commodity functions as both reassurance and threat in that it confirms one's relation to and position in the world, but only by constructing a temporary state of pseudo-satisfaction which lasts only until the can is empty or the next commercial is viewed. For Burroughs, commodity and advertisement unsurprisingly function within the realm of addiction and control:

> SMOKE TRAK CIGARETTES. THEY LIKE YOU. TRAK LIKE ANY YOU. ANY TRAK LIKE YOU. SMOKE TRAKS. THEY SATISFY. THEY SERVICE. TRAK TRAK TRAK[177]

In *Ubik,* the final state (but one) presents Chip in half-life, seeking Ubik to maintain the state of world/self/identity. *Ubik* becomes *the* work of commodity fetishism, featuring a product whose function is *only* to sustain the illusion of coherence. "I came to Ubik after trying weak, out-of-date reality supports," beams a happy and secure(d) housewife (104).

Videodrome—The Death of Representation

In *Videodrome* appearance is also put into radical question, both diegetically and discursively. Reprogrammed by Bianca O'Blivion, Max Renn prepares to take the next step. "You've become the video word made flesh," she tells him. "Death to Videodrome—long live the new flesh." The terror must be overcome, the attachment to the body surrendered. Renn makes his way to a rusted hulk—a "condemned vessel"—in the harbor. The reddish-brown of the decaying walls matches the color of his suede jacket. Renn is another "condemned vessel" as long as he remains trapped within the confines of the old flesh, an outmoded conception of the body and the self. Aboard the vessel, Max fires at his own temple and there the film concludes; ambiguously, unsatisfyingly. What is the new flesh?

One postulation might hold that Max has attained the paradoxical status of pure image—an image which no longer retains any connection with the "real" and which is therefore a perfect Baudrillardian simulation. "The real is no longer what it used to be" he writes. "Henceforth, the map precedes the territory."[178] *Videodrome* comes strikingly close to moving through the four successive phases of the image characteristic of the era of simulation that Baudrillard described.[179] First, the image functions as "the reflection as a basic reality." Clearly, until the hallucinations begin, the viewer trusts the cinematic image as the sign of truth. Doubts may be raised earlier concerning the enigmatic video image of the Videodrome program—its ostensible Third World aesthetic belied by its Pittsburgh transmission point: here the image "masks and perverts a basic reality." In the third phase the image "masks the absence of a basic reality," which has, in fact, been the argument behind most of the works explored in this chapter. The film propels its audience along this trajectory, possibly achieving the status of Baudrillard's fourth phase, in which image "bears no relation to any reality whatever: it is its own pure simulacrum." Being beyond representation itself, such an image could not be represented, and thus the screen goes black and the film ends. *Videodrome,* then, enacts the death of the subject and the death of representation simultaneously, each the consequence of the other.

Videodrome presents a destabilized reality in which image, reality, hallucination, and psychosis become indissolubly melded, and it is on this level that the film becomes a work *of* postmodernism, rather than simply a work *about* it. The film is more than a "mere thematic representation of content" (Jameson): from the moment the videocassette begins to respire, Cronenberg moves his film to another, profoundly ambivalent, level of meaning. The subversion of conventional structures of filmic discourse here corresponds to the "progressive" use of language in science fiction, producing that "discontinuous set of sign-functions" and yielding "an indefinite set of semantic constructs by dislocating the subject in the reading process" (deLauretis). The viewer of *Videodrome* (the film) is in a position analogous to the viewer of "Videodrome" (the TV show): trapped in a web of representations which infect and transform reality.

The science fictions of Cronenberg and Dick are profound and disturbing, and the diegeses of *Videodrome* and *Ubik* are situated at the point where spectacle and reality are no longer at all separable. Society has become the mirror of television. In *Videodrome* the immixture of images of sexuality, disorder, technology, and biology demolishes traditional visions of subjectivity, reality, and rationality and marks Cronenberg as heir to the discourses of both Burroughs and Baudrillard. While Dr. Brian O'Blivion seems to parody the oblique discursive strategies of Baudrillard, *Videodrome* and other Cronenberg films serve as an equally intensive, equally ambivalent confrontation with the dissolution and simulation of the real. This "infection" of reality marks the first sign of the extensive and astonishing restructuring of time, space, and being that will be explored in the following chapters.

The final stage of Baudrillard's four phases of the image, wherein the image no longer bears a relation to an unmediated reality, is the hallmark of the age of postmodernism and simulation, but the potential trauma that might be expected to accompany the realization that representation is no longer tied to referent is frequently elided by a regression to simple nostalgia, as both Baudrillard and Jameson have noted.[180] Arthur Kroker has further written that, "The postmodern scene is a panic site, just for the fun of it," an era of crises for their own sake, where the injunction of crisis now ironically covers over the abyss of nonmeaning.[181] The disturbing visions of *Videodrome,* on the other hand, communicate a more sustained air of crisis by obsessively biologizing spectacle and simulation. The insistent figurations of Baudrillard, Cronenberg, and Dick represent a stunning hypostatization of the concerns of postmodern culture and comprise a discourse which retains the power to unsettle, disorient, and initiate the crucial action of questioning the status of the sign in sign culture: a spectacular immunization against the invasive powers of the image virus.

2 TERMINAL SPACE

INTRODUCTION—ELECTRONIC SPACE We used

to live in the imaginary world of the mirror, of the divided self and the stage,

of otherness and alienation. Today we live in the imaginary world of the

screen, of the interface and the reduplication of contiguity and networks. All

our machines are screens. We too have become screens, and the interac-

tivity of men has become the interactivity of screens.—Jean Baudrillard ¶

. . . imaginary waves are actually breaking on an imaginary beach . . .

—Richard Mark Friedhoff and William Benzon

At MIT's Media Lab, one ongoing experiment involves the development
of a Vivarium ("an enclosed environment for life"). The environment is a
computer and the task is to create artificial life: to create the environ-
mental and behavioral parameters for a set of digitized "creatures."

"[I]nvent and then unleash realistic [?] organisms in whole 'living' computerized ecologies—learn about the universe's creation by doing some of their own. The animals they create would behave, learn, even evolve independently."[1] An ecology of such cellular automata occurs within that ambiguous region which falls between reality and simulation. Enthusiasts of "artificial life" argue that real life forms have been created via electronic, rather than genetic, coding. The creatures of the Vivarium, or Polyworld, could never occupy the space of their biological counterparts, it is true, but neither could a biological form inhabit the electronic realms of the computer: this *terminal space*.[2]

In Theodore Sturgeon's story, "Microcosmic God" (1941), a biochemist abruptly produces a flood of revolutionary inventions from his island retreat. Those problems which confront a beleaguered humanity drop away: food, energy, production, and war all cease to distress the global population. The source of such miracles, it turns out, is not the biochemist but his creations, the Neoterics, a miniature race of beings with accelerated metabolisms and evolutionary patterns. The scientist functions as a deity in his microcosmic empire, altering the physical conditions of the Neoterics' existence to observe the resultant adaptations. Their solutions are then passed on to the world in the form of new technologies.

Sturgeon's pre-electronic story can thus be retrospectively recognized as a tale of modeling and simulation, of a programmer working with biological blips. Given the ability to alter the conditions of the Vivarium, by compressing time, for example ("In real time these changes take aeons, and experiment is impossible. The only way to see evolution in action is to make computer models"),[3] the programmer could become a powerful force akin to Sturgeon's "microcosmic god." If the technology has changed, the story nevertheless stands as one of the most prophetic in science fiction—witness physicist Heinz Pagel's assessment of the Vivarium project and others like it: "Understanding artificial life may someday enable us to design it appropriately and put these new life forms to work for us solving complex problems. They will, in effect, become our computational slaves"[4]—*Neoteric* is, at least, the nicer name.

The Vivarium typifies, in its conceits and possibilities, the absolutism of the powers which are imagined to inhere within an electronic reality. The computer has, along with television, altered the social and psychological experiences of space and time in an unprecedented and unexpected manner. The rise of a global communications network involving an avalanche of data in the form of image or voice, statistics or directives, pixels or hard copy has already defined concepts of commerce, government, work, and leisure; "the network nation," one company advertises:[5] "the great new way to meet people without ever leaving your home or office!" boasts another. The result is an intensification of the dissolution of the boundaries between public and private realms, physical and electronic spaces, which were discussed in the previous chapter: we must, in the words of a Media Lab researcher, "say something about transborder data flows."[6] "This is an Information Era," proclaims a world leader in an SF novel, "and our lack of territory—mere topsoil—no longer restrains us."[7]

Since most of us are not programmers, after all, we are denied that godlike status within this "armchair universe" of simulation and control[8] and are, rather, excluded from this new space which remains foreign, decentering, and relentlessly other, its physical parameters reduced to the space of the terminal monitor while its electronic parameters seem literally boundless. One of John Shirley's cyberpunk novels features a video-graffiti artist (who "writes" his tag, not on walls, but on commercial broadcasts) named Jerome: "Jerome saw Jerome: perceiving himself unreal. Jerome: scamming a transer, creating a presence via video graffiti. Thinking he was doing it for reasons of radical statement. Seeing, now, that he was doing it to make himself feel substantial, to superimpose himself on the Media Grid."[9]

Whether Baudrillard calls it *telematic culture* or science fiction writers call it *the Web, the Net, the Grid, the Matrix,* or, most pervasively, *cyberspace,*[10] there exists the pervasive recognition that a new and decentered spatiality has arisen that exists parallel to, but outside of, the geographic topography of experiential reality. As Vivian Sobchack explains: "Television, video cassettes, video tape recorder/players, video games and personal computers all form an encompassing electronic *system* whose various forms 'interface' to constitute an alternative and absolute world that uniquely *incorporates* the spectator/user in a spatially decentered, weakly temporalized and quasi-disembodied state."[11]

There are also the cybernetic systems which "incorporate" no "spectator/users" at all. The interfacing system of banking computers forms a complex global structure which is very nearly self-regulating.[12] Paris links to New York which connects, in its turn, to Tokyo: the money, or data, never sleeps and never stops its circulation within what Jameson has called "the bewildering world space of late multinational capital."[13] Jeremy Rifkin has noted in his dolorous *Time Wars* that the computer has also effectively superseded the human experience of *temporality.* "The new 'computime' represents the final abstraction of time and its complete separation from human experience and the rhythms of nature." Of course, the blame for the financial "crash" of October 1987 was placed upon the global computer that exists effectively beyond human control.

In both spatial and temporal terms, then, the bodily experience of the human is absented from the new reality, precipitating a legitimate cultural crisis which has some precedent in the upheavals of the late nineteenth century.[14] In this context the productions of postmodernism become comprehensible, even sensible: the labyrinthine and decentered forms, which respond to the loss of a readable cartography (Jameson) and the displacement of lived space; the withdrawal into an empty historicism, a simulacrum of the past, during a period in which the data bank has usurped historical analysis and in which the memory bank has usurped memory; the waning of ethical principles (indeed of subjectivity itself) as the possibilities of a moral center and the human as an agency of change seem to devolve to nothing; and the simultaneous over- and undervaluation of sign systems at a time when the sign *is* everything but *stands for* nothing. Particularly important, and intimately connected, are two frequently noted phenomena: the decline of the master-narratives which structure our understanding of the social structure and the rise of simulation as a prevalent form.

Narratives, those imaginary resolutions of real contradictions (as Lévi-Strauss described myth), are crucial conduits of ideological suppositions. Hayden White has demonstrated the importance of literary models of narration to the task of historical writing; it is the act of *emplotment* that permits "the real" to exist as a *meaningful* form of knowledge.[15] What narrative offers is a structure that provides connectives in the form of causal relations, sequentiality, and most importantly the teleological satisfaction of an ending, a final "steady state" through which all other elements will retroactively assume a full significance. Social hegemony operates in and through the master-narratives which organize all the rest: the narrative of scientific progress, for example, or class struggle (to cite but two).[16]

To argue, then, that the master-narratives have ceased to operate as privileged forms (or are no longer privileged in the same way) is thus to locate a potential upheaval in societal self-regulation. This is precisely what Jameson and Jean-François Lyotard once proposed as the case in postmodern culture. "I define *postmodern* as incredulity towards metanarratives," the latter wrote in *The Postmodern Condition,* noting that *legitimation* is no longer an automatic consequence of either narrative or linguistic acts.[17] (Recall the response to computer imaging as a loss of legitimation: "anyone" can construct—or deconstruct—reality.) The failure of the master-narrative is the result of the profound experiential and epistemological shift undergone by an increasingly technocratic and cybernetic culture: the regulation of the imploded society has passed beyond the spatio-temporal experience of its citizens (the loss of a *telos* renders even *entropy* empty as a structuring concept). Baudrillard is also engaged with the demise of master-narratives: "if it is possible at least to talk with such definitive understanding about power, sexuality, the body and discipline . . . it is because at some point *all this is here and now over with.*"[18]

Referentiality and legitimation are finished within Baudrillard's terminal fiction: there is no longer an unproblematic and empirically verifiable "real" to refer *to*. As a consequence, "the whole system [of representation] becomes weightless"[19]—a crucial metaphor which echoes Sobchack's "disembodied" electronic space. Quoting Debord, Sobchack notes that, "When 'everything that has been directly lived has moved away into a representation,' referentiality becomes *intertextuality*": the age of simulation has arrived.[20] Simulation becomes a function of telematic culture and the expansion of new technologies that substitute for experiential reality—the *digital* has replaced the *tactile*. (The relation between simulation and master-narratives will be discussed below.)

The simulations of terminal culture are encountered continuously: terminal space is entered through the panoply of computer games found in arcades, pizzerias, and the home, through the flight simulators used by the airline industry and the military, and through programs developed in the sciences to model realms heretofore invisible. Terminal space is the realm of virtual reality and real-time, interactive, computer-generated environments. It is the terrain of the special effects in *Brainstorm* (1983), *TRON, The Last Starfighter* (1984), *Terminator 2,* and Michael Jackson videos, and it is inhabited by artists such as computer-"painter" David Em and videomaker Max Almy. It invades "real" space via flashy, digitized graphics on TV: computer-generated geometries or processed images-within-images spinning across the field of the screen, voided of spatiotemporal context in a vertiginous display of their very depthlessness. While the functions differ, the aesthetic, with its commensurate phenomenological implications, remains.

An ontology of terminal culture may be derived through an ontology of its visual space: the images of a culture which constitutes itself *as* image. Here Sobchack's work has been invaluable. Discussing phenomenological distinctions among photographic, cinematic, and electronic "presences," she argues that the space of the last is precisely discrete, ahistoric, and disembodied. As Barthes and Metz have noted, the photograph is an object, a record of human vision and presence, a frozen moment of the past, while the cinema enacts a present-time *experience* of physical, bodily spatial reality. In considering electronic space, Sobchack moves beyond these notions, derived from Bazin and Comolli, to emphasize the temporal and spatial reductions characteristic of the computer-generated simulation: "Digital electronic technology atomizes and *abstractly schematizes* the analogic quality of the photographic and cinematic into discrete *pixels* and *bits* of information that are transmitted *serially,* each bit discontinuous, discontiguous, and absolute—each bit 'being-in-itself' even as it is part of a system."[21]

The photograph is discrete and immutable and so is very unlike the spatiotemporal malleability of the digital image. Merleau-Ponty has also noted the artificial discreteness of the photographic image: "The photograph keeps open the instants which the onrush of time closes up forthwith; it destroys the overtaking, the overlapping, the 'metamorphosis' [Rodin] of time."[22] Merleau-Ponty, though, is placing the photograph in relation to the more complex temporalism of painting. The painting's "grip upon space" and temporal "metamorphosis" has, as a result, a stronger sense of bodily investment than the photograph. The digital, processed graphics of electronic technology, on the other hand, produce a constant mutation divorced from the metamorphoses of human time and experience. The weakened representational function of these decorative and malleable images produce little sense of permanence, history, or bodily investment at all. Perhaps this is why, as Mihai Nadin has noted, despite the ostensible power of this massive technology, "electronic art seems to exhaust itself at the first encounter."[23] These images must "attract spectator interest at the surface," Sobchack writes. "Thus, electronic space constructs objective and superficial equivalents to depth, texture, and invested bodily movement. . . . [C]onstant action and 'busyness' replace the gravity which grounds and orients the movement of the lived-body with a purely spectacular, kinetically exciting, and often dizzying, sense of bodily freedom (and freedom from the body)."[24] The screen operates as the frontier between the two realities, physical and electronic. It is a space without center or ground, and with only a vector-graphic simulation of perspective (too crisp, too perfect) to guide a human eye that has suddenly become distinct from its corporeality, its spatiality, its temporality, and its subjectivity.[25]

The new dominance of the computer might comprise an unbearably depressing experience, and indeed for many observers, from Debord to Rifkin, it is exactly that. The human is lost in cyberspace, trapped within, but excluded from, the matrices of the terminal field, never to emerge intact. It is perhaps more provocative to rethink this Luddite posturing. One postulate of "the postmodern condition" is that terminal culture is too new, its impact too freshly felt, for any final judgments to be rendered upon it. Jameson notes that the new forms of the postmodern contain at least the *potential* to disrupt older forms of political dominances and inequities.[26] The computer has given new life to the sciences, to take one example, through *visualization,* permitting scientists to "see" what human senses cannot: the motion of subatomic particles, the intermingling of gases, the movement of geographic plates.[27] Technologies in mathematical modeling have led to the development of new sciences of chaos, studying nonlinear natural phenomena. The result is a fantastic new realm of images within new fractal dimensions, a new respect for the random—an extended, but valid, reconception of the "real." H.-O. Peitgen and P. H. Richter, the aestheticians of this movement, are rhapsodic regarding the computer's possibilities. The computer "can present us with imaginary worlds, put us into artificial landscapes, and cause us to forget the real world," but at the same time "this new medium is allowing us to see connections and meanings which were hidden until now."[28]

To engage with terminal culture means to somehow encompass it, but the means of doing so are not entirely apparent. In her book on electronic media and postmodern culture, Margot Lovejoy constructs a crisis of knowledge that is precisely a crisis of *vision:* "As yet, though we live in a culture in which images are the dominant currency of communication, we have been unable to form an adequate picture of the future. Despite the new electronic power to create instant image flow, the ability to see the more diffuse Postmodern connections . . . has become more difficult. . . . It is harder to visualize a multinational identity than a local entity. We can only see the world by forming a picture through various specialized mediations. . . . We now lack a convincing vision."[29] The lack of a vision adequate to the electronic datasphere has led to a set of allusive attempts to reconstitute the space of the computer in human—biological or physical—terms; in other words, *to permit terminal space to become phenomenal.*

In one attempt to *envision* the space of the computer, the Museum of Modern Art has hosted an exhibition called "Information Art: Diagram-

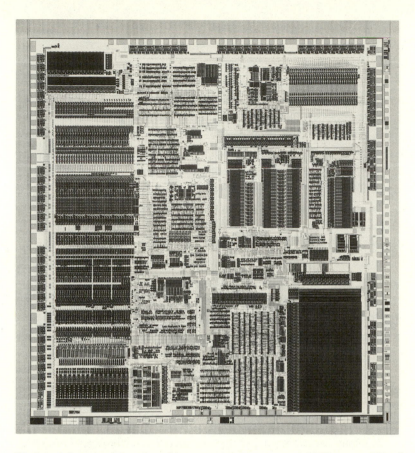

The inertial space of the microchip, or modernist masterwork? Diagram of "Intel 386™" (229,000 transistors). 1985. Computer-generated plot on paper, 84 × 79". Collection, The Museum of Modern Art, New York. Gift of Intel Corporation.

ming Microchips." Sponsored by INTEL, the show presented enlarge- ments of computer-produced diagrams reminiscent of an aerial view of urban sprawl (this resemblance is no coincidence—the chip, like the city, is designed for ease of circulation, constant flow, and a dense maximization of available space). At the same time their positioning on MOMA's walls inevitably suggested the modernist patterns of Piet Mon- drian and others.

Within the context of industrial design, the exhibition made perfect sense as an extension of the Bauhausian ideal of form following func- tion, but it was still unsettling to see well-heeled patrons of the arts scrutinizing these complex surfaces for hidden meanings, as though the chip, now susceptible to vision, was somehow also susceptible to knowledge. "Despite their ubiquity," the catalog read, "there is an element of mystery to integrated circuits. They are mysterious because they are sensorially inaccessible to us."[30] But the enlargement and aestheticization of the chip does not render it any *more* accessible. The exhibition became a celebration of the manifest inertia and inscrutability of the microchip, rather than a rationalist revelation of its function.

The modeling of three-dimensional, computational objects is another means of envisioning terminal space. What Timothy Binkley describes as "the virtual camera" becomes a means of representing and modeling the virtual spaces of abstract numbers and equations in forms similar to the tangible and perceptible objects of everyday life: "The virtual camera is an imaginary object ensconced in the abstract space of a hyperreal world whose features are described numerically using mathematical tools."[31] Electronic space thus projects a Cartesian ideal in the form of a perfectly coordinated and potentially infinite space, and objects within that space become functions of the coordinate structure. "[T]he 'image' is only a matrix of digital codes in a data space."[32]

A. K. Dewdney's column for *Scientific American* contained a number of programs and experiments designed to reveal and manipulate the parameters of this field. For example, mathematical modeling permitted the creation of hypercubes, which could only exist in the "purely mental construct of four-dimensional space."[33] Just as an illustration of a cube can "represent" a third dimension beyond the plane of the drawing surface, the non-Euclidean geometry of the hypercube could rotate and expand into an invisible, but nonetheless conceivable, *other space.* Cellular automata programs, of which the Vivarium represents the ultimate example, permit the simulation of population interactions in the ecosystem of the computer screen. *Life,* for one, is a set of simple equations for population behavior which can run indefinitely. *Wa-tor* is a program which permits a simulated "unfolding" of a toroidal shaped, oceanic planet populated by sharks and fish. The bounded field of the screen thus becomes a continuum (with fish exiting on one side and emerging on the other) that combines features of open and closed spaces, as well as a representation of an "impossible" space.

Core Wars simulates—in fact, *is*—combat between two computer programs vying for control of a memory bank. Legendary in hacker circles, Core Wars arose when a virus program was introduced into the computer banks of "a large computer research laboratory." The program commanded huge amounts of memory, slowing the system to a crawl until another programmer introduced another program to destroy the first. This was the first instance of the "computer virus" which has since figured in news reports, even gracing the cover of *Time* magazine

(Sept. 26, 1988), but it is also the genesis of the Core Wars clubs and tournaments. Invisible computer operations are granted a limited spatiality within the mock memory banks onscreen.

The concern induced by computer viruses led these spatializations from the specialized circles of hackers to a wider public. Explanations of the virus concept attempt to envision the inner dynamics of electronic space. *Time* in "Invasion of the Data Snatchers!" used comic strips to illustrate a viral "infection," complete with Dick Tracy-style labels and pointing arrows ("uninfected disk"). The process is narrated in a deliberately primitive manner to defuse the terrors of the invisible cybernetic realms within which the threat is instantiated.[34] It is obviously worth noting that the very term "computer virus" biologizes the operations of the machine, and many have noted the overlapping discourses around computer viruses and AIDS. Andrew Ross notes "the common use of terms like killer virus and epidemic, the focus on high-risk personal contact, . . . the obsession with defense, security and immunity, and the climate of suspicion generated around communitarian acts of sharing, whether private or public domain." The *Time* coverage "underscored the continuity of the media scare with those historical fears about bodily invasion, individual and national, that are often considered endemic to the paranoid style of American political culture."[35] The unknown realms of a cybernetic spatiality are thus mapped onto the familiar, albeit threatened, topography of the body or Cold War nation-state.

These attempts to envision the terminal realm intersect with the work of scientists studying chaos theory and fractal geometries. Scientists and mathematicians have proposed that there exists in nature a complex geometry characterized by similarity across scale. The line traced by a coastline, for example, exhibits an identical complexity at all magnifications. The natural order is not composed of the pristine Euclidean forms of trapezoid and ellipse, it is a corpus of intricate and infinite fragmentation. Magnify even an apparently smooth surface and discover the irregularities and complexities which become apparent at other scales of measurement. Dimensions are discovered which actually lie *between* the dimensions of human experience: *fractal* dimensions. Using the power of the computer to simulate and magnify, complexity at all levels becomes manifest: "a fractal is a way of seeing infinity."[36] Fractal geometry, as established by mathematician Benoit Mandelbrot, permits the modeling of chaos: complex, nonlinear systems. Complicated natural forms—the patterns of clouds, coastlines, or the global weather system—can be generated from simple, iterated, mathematical functions. Computer-generated maps of fractal topologies represent a kind of *terminal vision.* The scale of human perception and experience, already altered and augmented by telescope and microscope, no longer operates as an anchor for spatial exploration at all.

In science fiction films, fractal geometry has been used to generate simulations of realistic landscapes. The effects used in *Star Trek II* (1982) to illustrate the terraforming of a barren planet are an excellent example of "procedural graphics." Rather than laboriously inputting all of the visual elements, the computer is given a set of data and the appropriate parameters with which to manipulate it. The computer can then run the simulation on its own. Thus, "imaginary waves are actually breaking on an imaginary beach."[37] The Vivarium concept returns, but with an emphasis on graphics rather than organisms.

Of all the visualizations and representations of terminal space, none has the ubiquity of the Mandelbrot set. This fantastic informational "object" of infinite complexities is the result of iterating a relatively simple algorithm. By mapping the resultant set of points, a fringe region is revealed which retains an endless complexity of form upon subsequent magnifications. Shapes spiral about one another, forms repeat at every level, and new Mandelbrot sets lurk in every region, each surrounded by its own halo of complexity. This object, used to understand naturally occurring "chaotic" systems, has become the icon of fractal geometry and chaos sciences.[38] An underlying order has been revealed in the "random" phenomena of coastlines, snowflake patterns, and turbulence, and the technology of the supercomputer permits these revelations. The Mandelbrot set, as the archetype of both chaotic orderliness and the modeling power of the computer, has taken on an almost mystical significance—a cybernetic mandala, if you will.

A videotape produced by the Cornell Supercomputer Facility, *Nothing but Zooms,* presents a series of extended "zooms" (actually computerized magnifications) into different regions of the Mandelbrot set. The relentless forward probing, which brings about new levels of information and understanding, recapitulates the ontology of the forward tracking (or zoom) shot as experienced in *2001* and Michael Snow's *Wavelength* (1968), analyzed by Michelson.[39] In these films, narrative action is bound, visually, to the condition of phenomenological enquiry. An optical penetration of visual space exemplifies the epistemological core of narrative "movement" itself. In *Nothing but Zooms,* the choreography of optical elements permits the perception of an electronic cosmos where only the abstraction of indeterminate mathematical objects had lurked.

One is struck by the *immanence* of the Mandelbrot set. Everything is

A Mandelbrot set.

already there, and only the power of magnification is seemingly required
to bring it (or us) to light. The videotape enacts the most powerful of
cyberscopic gazes, as vision and object become functions of one another: the Mandelbrot set exists only to be seen and visually explored,
and the gaze in this nonnarrative tape exists solely to encounter and
explore the object. A vertiginous perceptual abyss opens before the
viewer (*abyss* is, perhaps, the wrong word: it is not an emptiness, for the
field is always filled, and the gaze is always renewed—but it is also the
very word to describe these mutable vortices and valleys). The imploded territories of terminal space are infinitesimal and infinitely vast.
In a sense the Mandelbrot set becomes a metaphor for the computer
itself—an object that is not an object, a bounded form which contains
the infinite.

Sobchack has noted a recuperative impulse behind chaos studies,
specifically in its obsession with the order which had eluded perception
but is now suddenly manifest in all things.[40] This is evident in the quasi-
mystical significance of *Nothing but Zooms,* revealed in its New Age
music and program notes ("A whole new world awaits you and personal
change you might not have expected is yours for the taking"). The
videotape becomes a visual rite of passage, a new means of centering
the self. The zoom provides an optical center by its very mechanics,
regardless of the objects photographed, and the sequences repeatedly

end where they began, on a newly located Mandelbrot set, for example. Circularity and symmetry thus become fundaments of the visual explorations, and the "chaos" of a disorderly, decentered reality is recontained within a framework of spiritual probing. (Sobchack points out that James Gleick's popular introduction to the field, *Chaos,* continually stresses the lonely, iconoclastic figures of the nonconformist, interdisciplinary avatars of chaos studies. Chaos is thus narrativized, personified, and granted the spiritual high ground—the terrifying limits of order are safely banished.)

Amygdala is a journal devoted to fractal forms in mathematics and in such natural objects as ferns and snowflakes. On occasion, fiction is included, such as "The First Encounter," by Ronald Lusk. In this short tale, a scientist is zapped into the imploded recesses of "the Object," and "In a very short time we were all making excursions into the Object, flying through its eddies and currents in a full-blown technicolor spectacular."[41] Though crude, the story demonstrates a desire to understand and experience electronic space in physical terms. The same desire is figured at Walt Disney World's Epcot Center, on the rides which penetrate and probe technological spaces, as well as in the Media Room at MIT's Media Lab, a room-sized interface with the computer's functions. The importance of an enveloping interface has also become increasingly evident in the public's fascination with virtual reality technologies (discussed in the next chapter). But it is science fiction, of course, which provides the most extensive evidence of the necessity of narrativizing and spatializing the electronic field, as well as the most sophisticated means of understanding the separateness of that space.

In an intelligent essay on cyberpunk science fiction, Istvan Csicsery-Ronay, Jr. argues that this concern with microcosmic spaces is partly a function of a cultural turning-inward—what Baudrillard has referred to as "a gigantic black hole . . . an implosive sphere, in which the curvature of spaces accelerates, in which all dimensions curve back on themselves and 'involve' to the point of annihilation."[42] Csicsery-Ronay writes of miniaturization, cybernetics, particle physics, communication systems, and the commensurate decrease of interest in space exploration, noting that "all these interests require the radical shrinking of focus onto microcosms, and all imply the impossibility of drawing clear boundaries among perceptual and cognitive, indeed even ontological, categories." *Implosive SF* is the narrative figuration of this.[43]

Implosive SF is figured, for example, in the flattened graphics of video, which represent a kind of cybernetic, simulated reality in such films as *20 Minutes into the Future, Explorers* (1985), and *THX-1138* (1971). This last was the debut feature of George Lucas, an expansion of his award-winning 1965 student film (*THX 1138 4EB*). Subtitled "Electronic Labyrinth," the diegesis of this earlier work was experienced entirely through the mediating sources of surveillance cameras and videophones, and presented an interiorized, imploded world. The adolescent narrative involves the title character rebelling against his totalitarian programming and asserting his individuality, but the aesthetic of the film works against its ostensible moral. Technology comprises and delimits the world without exception or respite. The space within the computer is dramatized by bold pans across microcircuits and flashing lights, but the actual mechanics are redundant against the film's white-on-white, NASA-inscribed environment. A cybernetic, computer-defined reality exists for the citizens, as overlaid graphics and low-resolution images present what Baudrillard calls "a hyperspace without atmosphere."[44]

Video artists have themselves sought to represent terminal space. Max Almy's *Leaving the 20th Century,* for example, sets its characters against a chromakeyed backdrop merging natural and cybernetic landscapes (her sophisticated image manipulations were noted in the previous chapter). Joan Jonas's effects are less controlled and less glossy than Almy's, and her *Double Lunar Dogs* (1984) is similar to Lucas's film in its relentless implosion and textural roughness. The setting is a lost starship which has been traveling toward an unknown terminus for generations (the work is very loosely based on Robert Heinlein's *Universe*)—still another monadic, technologically determined zone of imploded existence. Images are inset into the larger field, inverted and mirrored; footage is borrowed from NASA, Hiroshima, and SF film—all these are processes demonstrative of the mutability of data within this virtual reality. The insular and quietly implosive character of the tape creates a profound loss of place and loss of space. "There is no up, there is no down," the female protagonist says as she tries to maintain some connection to the history she has left far behind. Origins are forgotten and the future is inconceivable—we like it that way.

Despite Baudrillard's caveat that we require its prognostications no longer, science fiction still has a role to play. The genre has always been concerned to represent the present and not the future: *Star Trek* is a saga of the 1960s, not the twenty-third century. J. G. Ballard is far more knowing regarding the telos of science fiction when he notes that the writer's role has shifted to parallel the ontological redefinitions of the electronic era: "In addition, I feel that the balance between fiction and reality has changed significantly in the past decade. Increasingly their roles are reversed. We live in a world ruled by fictions of every kind. . . .

We live inside an enormous novel. For the writer in particular it is less and less necessary for him to invent the fictional content of his novel. The fiction is already there. The writer's task is to invent the reality."[45] Science fiction serves as the means to do precisely that.

Many theorists of SF have noted the privileged phenomenological status of the genre. In diverse works it is the interaction of space and perception which enables a tentative definition of being for both protagonist and reader-spectator. As Delany and deLauretis note, the process of reading science fiction *already* initiates a process of dislocation which resists the totalization of meaning, and this is redoubled in the thematic or phenomenal concern with spatial orientation and exploration (see chapter 1). A new phenomeno-logic is required by the "qualitatively new techno-logic" which we now inhabit,[46] and science fiction has become a crucial cognitive tool. Paradoxically, in many works science fiction produces a range of *narratives,* those explicatory semiotic mechanisms, about *simulation,* that phenomenon of the postreferential era. There is an ongoing attempt to explore and cognitively map the new terminal spaces, to establish a cartography within the paradigms of the simulated and the spectacular.

A phenomenology of science fiction helps us to understand the strategies of these works: specifically, their attempt to redefine the imperceptible (and therefore absent to consciousness) realms of the electronic era in terms of the physically and perceptually familiar. The motive is to render the electronic fields present to consciousness—to turn them into phenomena—and therefore susceptible to human intention. Husserl's "phenomenological reduction" shifts the philosopher's attention *toward* the cognitive processes of consciousness and *away* from the veracity of any given external conditions. "The universal *epoche* of the world as it becomes known in consciousness (the 'putting it in brackets') shuts out from the phenomenological field the world as it exists for the subject in simple absoluteness; its place is taken by the world as given in *consciousness.*"[47] An emphasis upon the activity of a guided consciousness, rather than upon the absolute reality of the world "in itself," has evident benefits in constructing a phenomenology of an abstract and nonphysical space such as that being defined here.

In order to constitute electronic space as a "noema" susceptible to an act of "noesis," writers such as Baudrillard or William Gibson rely on metaphors of human perception and mobility, which further suggests the specific "phenomenology of perception" elaborated by Merleau-Ponty. Merleau-Ponty's materialist and existentialist phenomenology grants the reality of the objective world, but continues to emphasize the interaction that occurs between perceptible, physical object and perceiving and motile subject, an interactivity that instantiates the very consciousness of the subject. Merleau-Ponty's preliminary emphasis on the primary activity of *perception* corresponds to the paradigmatic strategies of visualization which are shared by narrative, scientific, and philosophical elaborations of electronic space (in the next chapter, the significant place of the *body* as a "point of view on the world"[48] will be further considered, as the subject is inserted into the grids of electronic space).

Whether "cyberspace" is a real place or not, our experience of electronic space is a "real" experience. By distinguishing the constitution of being as an activity of interface, phenomenology suggests that the status of being is not an absolute condition, but one that changes relative to changes in the experience of the real.[49] And so Baudrillard, the students of chaos, the cyberpunks, and others *have* constructed a master-narrative, one grounded in the centrality of human intention and perception, which has the cumulative effect of inaugurating a new subject capable of inhabiting the bewildering and disembodied space of the electronic environment—*the virtual subject.* In contemporary science fiction, the ontologies of space and narrative combine and often contradict one another. In one sense, science fiction can be said to provide the referential dimension absented from the new electronic space: the function of the genre, then, is to compensate for the loss of the human in the labyrinth of telematic culture by simply transforming it into an arena susceptible to human control. This is a somewhat conservative, and even reactionary, response to the demands of these new spaces. Upon further examination, however, recent SF frequently posits a reconception of the human and the ability to interface with the new terminal experience—as in cyberpunk—and thus a uniquely terminal space becomes a fundamental part of human (or posthuman) redefinition. In either case, what is involved is a *projection* or *transmission* of the human into "the infinite datascape"[50] and the concurrent construction of a spatial simulacrum of the invisible circulation of information. These narratives literalize McLuhan's vision of a prosthetic extension of the human nervous system into the new fields of the electronic environment, granting the process an important spatiality *which represents a simultaneous grounding and dislocating of human bodily experience.*

CYBERSPACE

Instead of being made of natural materials, such as marble, granite, or other kinds of rock, the new monuments are made of artificial materials, plastic, chrome, and electric light. They are not built for the ages, but rather against the ages.—Robert Smithson ¶ If 'monuments' in fact exist today, they are no longer visible.—Paul Virilio ¶ Disk beginning to rotate, faster, becoming a sphere of paler gray. Expanding—And flowed, flowered for him, fluid neon origami trick, the unfolding of his distanceless home, his country, transparent 3D chessboard extending to infinity. Inner eye opening to the stepped scarlet pyramid of the Eastern Seaboard Fission Authority burning beyond the green cubes of Mitsubishi Bank of America, and high and very far away he saw the spiral arms of military systems, forever beyond his reach.—William Gibson

TERMINAL

SPACE

In the final citation above, William Gibson introduced the world to cyberspace, a vast, geometric, limitless field bisected by vector lines converging somewhere in infinity, permeated by the data systems of the world's corporations. Cyberspace is the new ground inscribed by the implosive forces of blip culture, but it is remarkably like the space predicted in 1966 by the sculptor Robert Smithson, who recognized a new monumentalism composed of the materials of contemporary culture (and what material is more pervasive, more plentiful, or more axiomatic of the era than data?). Paul Virilio correctly notes that these new monuments arc invisible to human senses, trapped as they are within the inert plastic shell of the computer terminal, but science fiction operates to reveal this monumental field. Case, the protagonist of *Neuromancer,* has been neurologically modified to experience the electronic field as a physical space, a cosmos open to his exploration. The space arrayed before him has dimension and depth, shape and substance; the new monuments, the coldly burning scarlet pyramids and green cubes, are displayed to his gaze.

Smithson, in his "Entropy and the New Monuments," described the advent of a new spatiotemporality in artistic practice. The sculptures of Donald Judd, Sol LeWitt, and the other minimalists are monuments to the dissipation of energy throughout the system of human activity— they represent, in a sense, a kind of negative monumentalism. In these works of chrome and plexiglass there is an absence of movement which implies a denial of space and time. These monuments reject any mimesis of the natural world, and instead enact the demise of past and future in favor of a timeless, spaceless, and finally inertial present. The works exhibit a profound absence of judgment as their status as *objects* is accentuated.

"Instead of causing us to remember the past like the old monuments," Smithson wrote, "the new monuments seem to cause us to forget the future. . . . They are not built for the ages, but rather against the ages."[51] Smithson is prescient in his anticipation, in 1966, of many of the ensuing cultural debates around the waning of history, of subjectivity, of cultural mapping. If the emergent zeitgeist is indeed one of "inverted millenarianism," as Jameson would have it, of "the end of this or that,"[52] then the new monuments are entirely appropriate to their era. It is the age of entropy, marked by the cessation of kinesis (it should also be noted that entropy is a term adopted within the model of cybernetics, where it signifies an inevitable loss of information).

The perceptual field which emerges from this "instantaneous ubiquity" (Virilio) is one of an infinity of surfaces and planes both seen and not seen. Time is reduced to an absolutely present, and therefore entirely inertial, space. In a metaphor drawn from Smithson's favorite source, science fiction, the artist describes this field as a "City of the Future:" a city constructed of "null structures and surfaces" which performs no function.[53] For this new monumentalism had not arrived fully conceived in a Greenwich Village art gallery; it had been forecast by the collapse of the older monument of the urban environment, although Smithson avoids a simplistic condemnation of the zero degree of architecture represented by the International Style. Again, it is a form axiomatic of its cultural moment. "There is something irresistible about such a place," Smithson remarks of the Union Carbide building, "something grand and empty."[54] No longer is the city the site of circulation, motion, *action:* if it retains a monumental status, it has become a monument to entropy.

The conceptual shift occurring around the figuration of the city also extended to science fiction, and Smithson's devotion to the writings of Ballard indicate his awareness of that. Yet while Ballard's writing evokes an entropic urbanism, a great deal of science fiction is marked by its trajectory of *implosion.* The operative modality is not the absence of motion or circulation, but rather their passage beyond the threshold of human sense. If the city is now figured as an inertial form, it is so because of this new arena of action that has usurped the urban function.

What is fascinating is the similarity of Gibson's description of the imploded field of cyberspace to the "new monuments" of Smithson's concern. Cyberspace, in its vectored perfection, its spaceless space, its scaleless scale and its timeless time, seems like an electronic facsimile of one of LeWitt's open modular cubes, but in Gibson's text this area is transformed into a *narrative* space, and one therefore explicitly defined as a site of action and circulation rather than that null space of which Smithson wrote. There is thus a profound contradiction operating through this conversion of an entropic space, as a new field of implosive activity arises that retains the very geometric forms which connote the subversion of human endeavor. It is a contradiction with important implications for understanding science fiction and postmodernism, and will be examined later in this chapter, but it is worth noticing the similarity that exists between the new monuments of minimalist art and the monumentalism which continues to pervade the cultural field, operating largely through the genre of science fiction.

The Cybernetic (City) State

While cyberspace is a new field, an alien terrain in the best science fiction tradition, it does have its precursors. The notion of a dark and crowded space broken by neon forms and corporate structures is surely not unfamiliar. Perhaps we can begin to learn about Gibson's cyberspace by learning from Las Vegas or Times Square or Tokyo for, on one level, cyberspace only represents an extension of the urban sector located at the intersection of postmodernism and science fiction. As was the case for Smithson, then, the alteration of urban space finds its echo within other cultural forms, other spaces.

Cyberspace arises at precisely the moment when the topos of the traditional city has been superseded. The city has changed: "this new realm is a city of simulations, television city, the city as theme park."[55] William Sharpe and Leonard Wallock have identified three major stages "in the evolution of the modern city."[56] Following the earlier two stages (the first marked by "population growth on an unprecedented scale and by the emergence of industrial capitalism" [16] and the second based upon the segregation represented by the shift to an impoverished center city surrounded by affluent suburbs), the present moment is characterized by a radical decentering of the urban environment. The rise of shopping malls, industrial plazas, cinema multiplexes, and numerous service operations has yielded a dispersed set of "metrocenters" (Eric Lampard's term), in which the functions of the urban environment are replicated, in miniature, along the highways. These new clusters, "edge cities" or "plug-in cities," remain connected to the larger cultural whole through "an intricate . . . and efficiently managed network of freeways, telephones, [and] radio and television outlets." As Sharpe and Wallock note, such descriptions of a new urbanism are validated by the 1983 report by the Federal Committee on Metropolitan Statistical Areas, which observed that "sprawling urban areas with no clearly defined center are the trend" (17).

Following the work of Melvin Webber, who described the city "as a social process operating in space,"[57] they conclude that there has arisen "a new conception of the urban no longer synonymous with locale" (17), but one rather defined by a continued participation in the circulation of information permitted by the new electronic technologies of telecommunications: "Our large urban nodes are, in their very nature, massive communication systems. In these intricately complex switchboards, men are actively involved in the business of producing and distributing the information that is the essential stuff of civilization" (86). Webber's metaphor is literalized in Bruce Sterling's 1985 cyberpunk novel *Schismatrix,* as an ancient character has himself wired into the computer network: " 'I'm the local stringer for Ceres Datacom network. I hold citizenship in it, though legally speaking it's sometimes more convenient to be treated as wholly owned depreciable hardware. Our life is information—even money is information. Our money and our life are one and the same' " (179). If the "home office" has not yet become a reality, then the replacement of a centralized "downtown" with the decentered sprawl of multiple metrocenters is now the defining fact of urban existence.

There has thus arisen a new and boundless urbanism, one which escapes the power of vision through its very dispersal. The "urban vocabulary, based on concepts of space and concentration, . . . is rapidly becoming outmoded" (23). Sharpe and Wallock (and the texts in their collection) devote their attention to the artistic representation of the city in classical and modernist modes, demonstrating an ongoing demand to produce a legibility from the chaos which characterizes the surface of urban existence. The recent and continued "decentering of the urban field" renders that urban experience increasingly illegible, finally yielding the entropic formations of Pynchon and Saul Bellow.

While Sharpe and Wallock have contributed extremely valuable work in outlining the history, not only of urban growth but of urban representation (from Baudelaire to Fritz Lang), there remains one startling elision in their survey. Science fiction, a genre which has—since its inception—assiduously produced an imaging of the city in stories, novels, films, comic books, and illustration, goes entirely unmentioned. This absence is especially highlighted in two ways. First, the authors are especially sensitive to the technological metaphors, derived from computers or space flight, which have arisen to characterize the new urbanism. They argue, for example, that Anthony Downs's term for this dispersal, "satellite spawl," is: "a mixed metaphor. This term combines the space-age symbol of high-technology and frontier exploration with the Victorian vision of disorderly and unplanned growth. In satellite sprawl we encounter a peculiar mixture of past and present to express an otherwise indescribable future" (34). Additionally, there is Jameson's observation that science fiction is defined by the display of a totalizing gaze which reveals the entire city (or planet or machine) in a single action of vision and description.[58] Science fiction is thus explicitly involved in a cognitive and phenomenological "writing" of new urban spaces. If, for example, the new "nonplace urban realm"[59] is invisible through its existence in and through the fields of information circulation, then *Neuromancer* will render that information field tangible, legible, and spatial. Cyberspace is precisely a *nonspace realm,* in Webber's sense of the term.

In both dystopian and utopian inscriptions, the city as a monumental form has been exhaustively mapped and remapped in science fiction. The rise of the genre remains bound up in the same technological revolutions which produced the complex industrial urban environment, with all the commensurate ambivalence toward the idea of progress that might imply. The city was most frequently projected as a negative entity, while utopian aspirations were focused instead upon an agrarian existence. In the late nineteenth century, beginning with Bellamy's *Look-*

ing Backward, the industrial utopia begins to gain prominence, a movement which reaches its apotheosis in the visual science fiction of the 1920s, including the superbly visualized cities of *Metropolis* (1926) and *Just Imagine* (1930), and especially in the pulp magazine artwork of Frank R. Paul: "Paul could not draw convincing human beings, but he could draw wonderful cities—and his images of the future permeated the early pulps quite irrespective of what was written in the stories."[60] These bulbous and rococo images of turbines and hovercraft, massive new engines for living and moving, define the utopian monumentalist impulses of the genre at that particular point in its existence more fully than any written text.

The alienation and dis-ease of American culture in the 1950s, coupled with the new movement away from the city as the dominant space of

The promise of a rational future: Fritz Lang's *Metropolis* (1926).

William Cameron Menzies's *Things to Come* (1936).

habitation, yields a science fiction in which the city is projected as claustrophobic and isolating, an outsized monadic structure sealed off from its surrounds. Asimov's *Foundation* (1951) begins on the planet Trantor, a planet-sized metropolis devoid of intrusive natural forms, while *The Caves of Steel* (1954) features an Earth population moved below ground, functioning in the catacombs of a metallic beehive. Brian Stableford correctly notes that the monumentalism of the city is as dominant here as in Paul's day, but that the meaning has entirely altered; one might say that it is the era of the International Style of science fiction urban design, as vast, featureless high-rises (or conapts, to use Phil Dick's term) replace the complex and ornamental spaces of earlier fictions.[61] Here begins the shift toward the more interiorized or imploded monuments of the contemporary period.

The redefinition of the city that occurred within the productions of postmodernism also affected the conception of the metropolis in recent science fiction.[62] From a plethora of texts, a remarkably consistent imagining/imaging of the city has emerged, one characterized in the first place by its boundlessness. The city is both micro- and macrocosm: even when it turns in upon itself, as it often does (Jameson's example is John Portman's Bonaventura Hotel), it both celebrates and denies its own interiority. The shopping mall is emblematic of this spatiality: it possesses a monadic self-sufficiency in which the outside world is denied (the mall has no windows and no weather, while points of egress are hidden off to the sides), but this is coupled with a recapitulation of forms that strongly connote *exteriority*—"streets" are lined with carefully planted and nurtured trees; a central "food court" mimics the piazzas and plazas of a more traditional urban space. This imploded urbanism, reconciling the irreconcilable differences between public and private, or inside and outside, is insistent upon its status as a "total space."[63]

The new urban space is directionless—coordinates are literally *valueless* when all directions lead to more of the same. For Paul Virilio, in an observation with real applicability for cyberspace, the city is now composed of "a synthetic space-time" that *simulates* the lost geophysical urban spaces of human habitation and circulation. Urban monumentalism has thus become false and spectacular (in Debord's sense): the walls are no longer so solid, nor so impermeable—"the appearance of surfaces hides a secret transparency." The new space is produced by the invisibly penetrating network of satellites and terminals. As Virilio puts it, "The exhaustion of natural relief and of temporal distances creates a telescoping of any localization, of any position. . . . The instantaneousness of ubiquity results in the atopia of a single interface."[64] *Atopia* might here be regarded as signaling a movement away from a physical topography, rather than a moral ambivalence. Positionality has lost its relevance in the "urban nonplace."

Now the city is constructed along all the axes of three-dimensional space: in hotels of the Bonaventura type, the main lobby is usually located on the fourth or fifth floor, rather than on street level. It is becoming increasingly common to find oneself *suspended* in a massive space, rather than trapped at its bottom; this refusal of directionality thus extends to a denial of gravity[65] (long an aspiration of Le Corbusier, the "sidewalk in the sky" has become a reality with the advent of the monadic shopping mall). The city is both monumental and without scale, in the sense that many of the same forms repeat at different

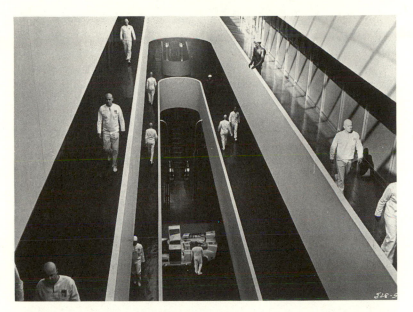

The nightmare of a rational future: George Lucas's *THX 1138,* 1971.
(Warner Bros.)

levels—the home television screen becomes the gigantic advertising sign of Times Square or Tokyo, for example—further contributing to this vectorless existence. As Raoul Vaneigem put it in 1963, "We are living in a space and time that are out of joint, deprived of any reference point or coordinate."[66]

Science fiction has long participated in precisely this ambiguous urban spatiality:

> *Noon-talk on Millionth Street:*
>   *"Sorry, these are the West millions. You want 9775335 East."*

Ballard's early story, "The Concentration City" (1957) rehearses the notion of a boundless city with considerable force.[67] In this consciously Kafkaesque tale, a young man (Franz M.) dreams of the free space which must exist somewhere.

> *"Dollar five a cubic foot? Sell!"*

The story transcends the overcrowded subgenre of metropolitan over-population. Ballard instead reconceives space as an analogue of time: the city is a continuum without beginning or end, a null field which extends to the limits of the three dimensions. That the space should end, that there should be something beyond the city, is as heretical as imagining a time before time began.

> *"Take a westbound express to 495th Avenue, cross over to a Redline elevator and go up a thousand levels to Plaza Terminal. Carry on south from there and you'll find it between 568th Avenue and 422nd Street."*

The city is without center and without beginning; a technological sprawl to the limits of infinity. Franz attempts to journey past those limits, only to find himself returned to where he began, spatially and temporally. The urban territory is marked by an infinity of space, a multiplicity of surfaces: time is displaced within a field of inaction and, ultimately, inertia as the city, the universe, circles back upon itself in a closed feedback loop: in the language of the Situationists, the city-state has become *the cybernetic state.*

The unbounded urbanism of Ballard's *metrocosm* is popular in the visual science fiction presented in numerous comic books of the 1970s and 1980s, including Britain's *Judge Dredd* series as well as Italy's *Ranxerox.*[68] The work of Moebius (Jean Giraud) is particularly sustained in its display of a complex urban space. In works such as "The Long Tomorrow" (1975–76) and *The Incal* (1981–88), Moebius builds images of cities which have profoundly influenced their representation in science fiction film and literature.[69]

"The Long Tomorrow" evokes Chandler and Spillane as Pete Club, a "confidential nose" (tomorrow's private eye) from the 97th level is summoned by a mysterious aristocrat who lives in a "snazzy conapt" all the way up on the 12th ("This is the upper crust!" he remarks). Club is sent to the depths of the city ("I kid you not, it was a dump, the 199th level") and eventually to the surface, via antigrav chute. The notion of the buried city where the privileged strata are those closest to the surface is axiomatic of the confused space (the "total space") of the metropolis, public but enclosed, expansive but claustrophobic. The street, once the central site of circulation and exchange, and around which urban space was once conceived, can now be located (only with difficulty) at the nearly invisible bottom of a narratively and spatially decentered environment.

The antigrav chute emphasizes the scale of the city while presenting it as a weightless space, an area of suspension and vertical boundlessness. In *The Incal,* the hero, John DiFool, is thrown from Suicide Alley and the full-page illustration provides a high-angle view of his vertiginous drop. The concentrated city fills the frame as we look down at

Concentrated cities: *The Incal* by Moebius and Alexander Jodorowsky.   (Marvel Comics)

level upon level of urban sprawl: the bottom is invisible in a diffused
cloud of white, and thus this is a city without top, without bottom,
without limits. DiFool is suspended above it, high in the frame, regarding the city, the people, and the birds below him. There is no logic or
order to the space which lies littered and cluttered, a morass of high
and low technologies, a chaos of intersecting lines. The only constant is
the drop, which serves as much to reveal the entire urban space in a
glance as to transform it into an environment of threat and spatial
dislocation (especially for poor DiFool).[70]

   This privileged vision of space illustrates Jameson's proposal that
much science fiction permits the existence of an impossible and totalizing gaze which functions through spatial description ("no normal human city or village can be 'taken in' in this way"[71]) rather than through
narrative action. In this way science fiction becomes part of a process of

"lateral perceptual renewal," which parallels works in the so-called high arts. Jameson's comments on Raymond Chandler are instructive in this regard:

> Chandler formally mobilized an "entertainment" genre to distract us in a very special sense: not from the real life of private and public worries in general, but very precisely from our own defense mechanisms against that reality. The excitement of the mystery story plot is, then, a blind, fixing our attention on its own ostensible but in reality quite trivial puzzles and suspense, in such a way that the intolerable space of Southern California can enter the eye laterally, with its intensity undiminished.[72]

Jameson proceeds to argue that science fiction performs an analogous function for history and temporality rather than space, but this is a position he has since modified.[73] While Jameson never quite reconciles defining two genres in the same terms of spatial exploration, one important difference seems to be that the landscape of Chandler's L.A. is as much a social and psychological space as a physical one; a moral field endemic to the genre of crime and mystery fiction. Science fiction is, by contrast, grounded in the new "intolerable spaces" of technological culture and the narrative exists to permit that space to exist in a manner now susceptible to human perception, comprehension, and intervention. The genre provides, as Ballard noted, "a philosophical and metaphysical frame."

Blade Runner and Fractal Geography

The apotheosis of this urban vision, as well as an effective synthesis of SF and Raymond Chandler, is *Blade Runner,* directed by Ridley Scott, based upon a novel by Philip K. Dick, and designed by Syd Mead and Lawrence G. Paull, with special effects by Douglas Trumbull. That the film can serve as an impressive guide to the precepts of the postmodern aesthetic as elaborated by Jencks, Jameson, and others is a concept which has been extensively explored elsewhere.[74] The film presents—*performs*—a decentered and boundless space dispersed, thanks to the hovercars and rooftop chases, across all three dimensions of the urban topography. Instead of the pristinely gleaming future cities of *Things to Come* or the Gernsbach era of pulp science fiction, *Blade Runner* displays a bold and disturbing extrapolation of current trends: it is a future built upon the detritus of a retrofitted past (our present) in which the city exists as a spectacular site; a future in which the nostalgia for a simulacrum of history in the forms of the *film noir* (narrationally) and

Concentrated cities: Ridley Scott's *Blade Runner,* 1982. (The Ladd Company)

forties fashion (diegetically) dominates; a future when the only visible monument is a corporate headquarters. Most urgently, it is a future in which subjectivity and emotional affect are the signs of the nonhuman.

In designing the architecture of this future Los Angeles, Paull has acknowledged the influence of Moebius and particularly the image of that 199th level in "The Long Tomorrow" that he encountered in *Heavy Metal* magazine. "We took certain elements of scale and density from some of the cities in the magazine," he stated. Syd Mead, who produced the vehicles and initiated the notion of a densely layered space, explained: "Once you get past one hundred floors you need a whole new highway system. That's why the street scenes are so impacted—because the streets are practically underground,"[75] much like the buried city approached at the start of the Moebius strip. In *Blade Runner* street level feels like the underworld.

"The Overexposed City," Paul Virilio's recent exploration of metro-cosmic space, is interesting in its applications to *Blade Runner,* as Eric Alliez and Michael Feher have demonstrated, in addition to tracing some of the implications of this radically reconceptualized environment. Virilio insists that the city has become a space of simultaneous dispersion, as public space loses its relevance, and concentration, due to the "synthetic" spatiotemporality of terminal culture (the false cohesion of the society of the spectacle; a synthesis of the images and texts which proliferate to create a "virtual" spatiotemporal cohesion). The new monument is no longer the substantial spatiality of the building, but the depthless surface of the screen. This is a transformation literalized in *Blade Runner* by the proliferation of walls which *are* screens, sites of projection now rather than inhabitation. Furthermore, many of these monumental surfaces exhort the citizen/viewer to a further dispersal in the form of emigration to the new suburbs, the off-world colonies.[76]

The design of the film offers a fine example of a spectacular hyperreality. Not since *2001* has there been a future so meticulously imaged and, like that earlier film, *Blade Runner* rewards the attentive (or repeat) viewer by presenting a complex but eminently readable space that exists in contrast to the decentering effects of the narrative structure. As Deckard approaches police headquarters, the viewer is presented with two spaces. The first is the superbly detailed urban space which dominates the film, an effect produced by a seamless blend of miniature vehicles, models of varying scales, computer controlled camerawork, and multiple layers of traveling mattes. The result of this precision is a cinematic analogue to John DiFool's dive from Suicide Alley (in the Moebius illustration), producing a totalizing gaze which attains an impossible clarity through the perception of a deep and detailed space in which everything is nevertheless visible. The scene provides, as does so much science fiction, a privileged tour of a richly layered futurity in a narrative moment which exists solely to present this urban space both bewildering and familiar. The city is sepia-toned and mist-enshrouded, a fully industrial and smog-bound expanse which yet retains, in this sequence at least, some semblance of a romantic utopian impulse (the score by Vangelis is helpful). The gaze which enables this powerful space is augmented by the existence of a second field defined by the controls and data screens of the hovercar. These images impose an order on the movement of the gliding vehicle shown to be traveling through a traffic corridor whose existence is invisible to the unaided eye. The effect is one of scopic and epistemological pleasure: the viewer sees and deduces how (not to mention *that*) the future works. One

Inverted cities: "The Long Tomorrow" by Moebius and Dan O'Bannon (Marvel Comics). A major influence on the design of *Blade Runner.*

perceives and participates in this temporary alliance between technology and poetry, this mechanical ballet.

As with much recent science fiction, much of the pleasure results from continual transformations of scale and perspective. Paull's comments regarding the density and scale of the work in *Heavy Metal* make it reasonable to assume that, in addition to the comic strips of Moebius, the powerful high-tech illustrations of Angus McKie had a formative impact. McKie, a British science fiction illustrator, produced a comic strip entitled, "So Beautiful and So Dangerous," which ran in *Heavy Metal* in the late 1970s.[77] His obsessively detailed spacecraft and cities, some the size of planets, are further rendered with airbrush effects to produce a sense of atmospheric haze: the effect is a stunning redefinition of scale which evokes and extends both the first sequence of *Star Wars* and the last sequence of *Close Encounters* (1977). The resemblance of the monadic headquarters of the Tyrell Corporation to McKie's work is undeniable, and identical in its production of an unprecedented monumentalism which exists entirely apart from the scale of the human. In McKie's work an immense alien spacecraft descends as a scientist "proves" that man exists alone in the universe: the huge illustration—clearly derived from *Close Encounters*—is designed to make a mockery of such anthropocentrism. (*Neuromancer* also owes something to *Heavy Metal,* and so cartoonists such as Moebius, Angus McKie, and Philippe Druillet provide essential touchstones for the dense visual style that still pervades SF literature and cinema.)

The attention to similarities across scale found in the study of fractal geometry also bears on the visual field displayed in *Blade Runner.* The German physicist Gert Eilenberger argues that aesthetically satisfying forms are those which hold elements of order and disorder in a delicate balance; "dynamical processes jelled into physical forms."[78] James Gleick, in his overview of chaos studies, notes that to Benoit Mandelbrot, "art that satisfies lacks scale, in the sense that it contains important elements at all sizes." A Beaux-Arts structure attracts the viewer at all distances, from the distant observer of its overall architecture to the proximate examiner of gargoyles and scrollwork, in a way that the Seagram Building doesn't.[79] The manner in which McKie's impossible shifts of scale serve to invalidate the learned spatiality of human orientation is also a good example of Mandelbrot's physics/aesthetics. Order and disorder, similarity across scale, a world of infinite detail and complexity; these are the hallmarks of the dynamical systems which constitute our world.

This is intriguing in its relation to the play with size and scale in *Blade Runner.* The visual complexity of the urban space nevertheless remains a function of the superbly synchronized special effects technology, thus providing that balance of order and disorder (*2001,* by contrast, offers a very different experience of *order* at all levels—a partial function, perhaps, of its theme of a controlling alien intelligence). *Blade Runner* also offers the city as a complex and changing form: a fractal environment, in a sense. The first view of the city is an extreme long shot which takes in the entire space through one totalizing glance that defines it as an undifferentiated and homogeneous site of industrial overgrowth. The next shot offers a fiery smokestack—the first monument to punctuate this diabolical space—and this followed by the city visible as a reflection in an unsituated and disembodied eye. That eye then begins to penetrate the space, moving forward over the metroscape to finally locate the massive structure of the Tyrrell corporate headquarters. In

Redefinitions of scale: *So Beautiful and So Dangerous* by Angus McKie. (Heavy Metal Communications)

the sequence which follows, the camera locates Deckard, the blade runner protagonist, by literally coming down to street level: the neon signs, futuristic attire, and lighted umbrella-handles now become available to perception and inspection. A streetside vendor uses an electron microscope, and the drama becomes molecular. The film traces a detailed path across scalar levels, with each pass revealing further complex forms.

In one of the most striking sequences of *Blade Runner,* the transgression of scalar perspective is dramatized. Deckard's electronic inspection of a photograph transforms its visual field, penetrating the surface of the image to reveal it as complex and multidimensional. This sequence represents the most hypnotic demonstration of cinematic suture and control in contemporary cinema. Deckard inserts a photograph into his electronic enhancer, and the inert object is thereby converted to the digitized and serialized bits and bytes of the electronic image. A grid is overlaid upon this field and measured coordinates now regulate and guide the eye's movement across the terrain of memory. Issuing verbal commands reminiscent of film direction ("Track right. . . . Now pull back . . ."), Deckard temporalizes the frozen moment of the photograph and a classic scene, the search of a room for clues, is played out in terminal form. The private eye becomes another telematic simulation, and the space of the photograph is transmuted into the temporal domain of narrative/cinema.

The human is inserted into the terminal space as a pure, totalizing, gaze. The boundaries of the screen are eradicated, and the cyberscopic field becomes fully phenomenal, susceptible to human vision and action. Through Deckard's instructions the "depthless surface of the screen" is probed, tested, and finally entered. The screen, that frontier separating terminal and physical realities, is rendered permeable, and the space behind it becomes tangible and controllable. The photoenhancing sequence serves as a graphic preamble to the cybernauts and terminal obsessions of *TRON* and *Neuromancer,* wherein humans are physically or neurologically inserted into the terminal reality. Here the photograph bridges the two realms, while vision becomes the force that can cross that bridge. As Merleau-Ponty writes, "Vision is not a certain mode of thought or presence of self, it is the means given me for being absent from myself, for being present at the fission of Being from the inside—the fission at whose termination, and not before, I come back to myself."[80] Vision permits an interface with the objects of the world, and thus the emergence of thought and the presence of the self is a function of the simultaneous projection and introjection that defines the act of vision. The visualization of electronic space thus acknowledges the reality of an other space—a *new* "other space"—that must be known in order for Being to arise. The representation of a metaphorical "terminal space" thus enacts first the fission of the subject and then the beginnings of its reconstitution as a *terminal* subject.

The photoscan sequence in *Blade Runner* is also an encounter with the drama of scale. "The composition changes as one approaches and new elements of the structure come into play," as Gleick remarked of the Paris Opera.[81] In *Blade Runner* a new fractal dimension is discovered somewhere between the two-dimensionality of the photograph and the three-dimensionality of experiential reality. We might in fact label this new fractal dimension the *cinematic,* for the cinema has always participated in this ambiguous and shifting dimensionality, this magnification of sight which produces new dimensions. That is what I take to be the essence of what filmmaker and theorist Jean Epstein called *photogenie* in the 1920s: the specificity of cinema lies, not in the emphatic dramaturgy of narrative temporality, but rather in a spatial exploration that complexly binds multiple perspectives and scalar shifts.[82]

Much of the effectiveness of *Blade Runner,* then, lies in its continual investigation of the various permutations of a complex and self-similar space (note the microchip design of the vast Tyrrell building) which finally becomes terminal. This passage is appropriate within the context of a similarity across scale for, as noted above, terminal space serves in many ways as an imploded version of the urbanism which has so dominated science fiction in both its literary and visual instances. *Blade Runner* represents a dynamic moment in which urban space begins to complete a trajectory toward terminal space.[83]

Cyberpunk

This trajectory has its correlate in the literary science fiction of the same period. In its concern with a particular (and particularly urban) representation of cybernetic culture, terminal space is the domain of *cyberpunk.* Cyberpunk proved to be a revitalizing force in science fiction, fusing the literary values and technological expertise which had previously been disported into separate subgenres. Although the movement ended almost as soon as it began, leaving a motley assortment of short stories and novels, its impact has been felt, and its techniques absorbed, across a range of media and cultural formations. Perhaps we should not regard this movement as a closed literary form, but rather as the site where a number of overdetermined discursive practices and cultural concerns were most clearly manifested and explicated. Cyberpunk's techno-surreal images and narrative strategies have added at least one new word to the lexicon (*cyberspace*) and have significantly altered the representation of electronic technology in narrative.[84] It is worth noting at the outset that the real advent of cyberpunk, with the publication of *Neuromancer* in 1984, was preceded by at least three films that, in varying ways, had a formative impact upon the cyberpunk aesthetic: *Videodrome, Blade Runner,* and *TRON* (all 1982).[85]

Cyberpunk was the inheritor of two traditions within SF: first, the so-called "hard" science fiction of vast technical detail and extrapolative power which dates from the 1930s and John W. Campbell's editorship of *Astounding Science Fiction*. Hard science fiction has always demonstrated a disdain for more traditional literary values, and certainly the "cardboard" characters peopling the works of Heinlein and Asimov are not only a part of their charm, but an important aspect of science fiction as a genre of philosophical, rather than psychological, concern. Paradoxically then, but perhaps inevitably, the other tradition from which cyberpunk derived its form was the openly experimental writing of the (again so-called) New Wave of science fiction writers which arose in the 1960s.

The New Wave, which includes such authors as Delany, Ballard, and Michael Moorcock emerged from the sociological science fiction of the 1950s (Sturgeon, Pohl and Kornbluth, and Sheckley, for example), but also from an awareness of contemporary literary production originating outside the genre. Writers like Barth, Vonnegut, and especially Pynchon and Burroughs, used the languages of technology and science fiction in highly reflexive and self-conscious reformulations. Moorcock's editorship of the British journal *New Worlds* provided a forum for a science fiction responsive to the forms of postmodern fiction, as did Harlan Ellison's *Dangerous Visions* anthologies in the United States. "SF was attractive," Moorcock wrote retrospectively, "because it was overlooked by the critics and it could be written unself-consciously."[86] The impact on the field of science fiction was incalculable, if only for the quality of writers that were attracted to a field which permitted literary experimentation within a somewhat commercial context.

Fred Pfeil, a critic and sometime science fiction writer, has offered an interesting reading of the New Wave and its cyberpunk descendents. Pfeil perceptively argues that what "the New Wave SF writers found . . . , either through Ballard's work or from some other prompting, is the aestheticizing principle itself as a way to work what we might, following Benjamin, call the 'allegorical ruin' of a now collapsed and bankrupt utopian/dystopian dialectic." The science fiction of the New Wave allegorized the exhaustion of "the real"—as represented by the dichotomous terms of redemption or damnation—through a baroque and overelaborate writing that emphasized a pure materiality.[87] This accounts for "the otherwise inexplicable, hothouse florescence and sudden significance of that whole host of autotelic language practices, experimental forms, and, strictly speaking, inadequately motivated but luxuriant image play which is the SF New Wave."[88]

The New Wave thus constituted a moment of Modernist compromise for Pfeil, caught as it was between an outmoded set of narrative strategies and thematics "and a 'new' which could not yet be born."[89] In cyberpunk and other science fiction of the 1980s, on the other hand, a new thematics emerged (one which I am calling *terminal identity*), along with a complex and heterogeneous set of ideolects to speak that new thematics. As Pfeil observes, the science fiction of the 1980s "is a very different thing from the New Wave SF of the 1960s; it is at one and the same time 'trashier,' 'pulpier,' and far more sophisticated, even more liberatory, than those earlier writings."[90]

I think that Pfeil's analysis of the accomplishments and limitations of the New Wave is correct, but there remain some significant continuities between the SF of the 1960s and the 1980s that require elaboration. Within the New Wave's transformation of the genre, the predilection of science fiction for the mapping of alternate worlds and reality became melded with an awareness of, and familiarity with, the experience of hallucinogens—trips of another kind. While the crystalline mutations of Ballard's environments demonstrate a clear fascination with the psychedelic modality, Brian Aldiss's *Barefoot in the Head* (1969), set in the years following the Acid Head War, is an explicit—although not isolated—attempt to stimulate a trip within a nonlinear narrative context. Michael Moorcock's series of novels and episodes starring proto-cyberpunk Jerry Cornelius, with their fluid and shifting urbanism and youth-culture entropy/exuberance, perhaps epitomize this generic moment better than any other works.

By the 1980s the free-form cultural movement built around the consumption of hallucinogens was no longer visible, and even the prophet of psychedelia had found a new drug: Timothy Leary proclaimed the computer to be the LSD of the 1980s. "Computers are the most subversive thing I've ever done," he said, adding that: "Computers are more addictive than heroin. . . . People need some way to activate, boot up, and change disks in their minds. In the 60s we needed LSD to expand reality and examine our stereotypes. With computers as our mirrors, LSD might not be as necessary now."[91] Mathemetician/cyberpunk/programmer Rudy Rucker quotes a hacker comrade who used to say, "Computers are to the eighties what LSD was to the sixties."[92] Indeed, some early researchers into hallucinogenic drugs were equally interested in other mind-expansion techniques, such as parapsychology and "electronic computing machines and the study of analogous brain mechanisms."[93] Such comments demonstrate a continuum between drug and terminal cultures, a continuum central to understanding cyberpunk. Hallucinogens provided an opportunity for the literary conception of radically different spatiotemporal orientations, an extension of the extant limits of the terrains of science fiction, and computers furnished a similar occasion (Gibson's "fluid neon origami trick").

It is interesting that in these more conservative times the probing of new spaces operates within the *hardware* of the computer, rather than in the *wetware* of the mind or spirit (Norman Spinrad has described a conflict between hackers and hippies).[94] The cyberscape is dominated by the pure Euclidean forms of pyramid and cube (albeit in scarlet and green). Cyberpunk returned the experimental wing of the genre to its technocratic roots. "Like punk music, cyberpunk is in some sense a return to roots," wrote Bruce Sterling, an important author, editor, and essayist of the movement: "The cyberpunks are perhaps the first SF generation to grow up not only within the literary tradition of science fiction but in a truly science-fictional world. For them, the techniques of classical 'hard SF'—extrapolation, technological literacy—are not just literary tools but an aid to daily life."[95] Larry McCaffery also puts the punk back in cyberpunk, noting the shared attitude, not simply of rebellion, but "of defiance towards cultural and aesthetic norms; an attitude of distrust towards rationalist language and all other forms of discourse required by legal, political, and consumer capitalism."[96] At this point, the accuracy of Pfeil's analysis becomes evident—there *is* a politically significant difference between a narrative model rooted in the alternate-reality experiences of a somewhat solipsistic youth subculture and another grounded in the transformation of quotidian existence by a proliferating set of global electronic technologies.

It should not be assumed that cyberpunk represents a co-optation of the experimentalism of the New Wave by the technologists of hard SF. Cyberpunk offered an important rejection of rationalist technocracy in favor of a science fiction set at street level. Sterling writes: "Science fiction . . . has always been about the impact of technology. But times have changed since the comfortable era of Hugo Gernsback, when Science was safely enshrined—and confined—in an ivory tower. The careless technophilia of those days belongs to a vanished, sluggish era, when authority still had a comfortable margin of control."[97] The protagonist of one William Gibson story hallucinates those very gleaming futures of the Gernsback era—now hopelessly old-fashioned—and only some sustained television viewing can return him happily to the disembodying and dispersed technologies of the present.[98] The measured forms of instrumental reason no longer dominate the technosphere which has slipped away from human control, as Baudrillard continually notes, and into an implosive and self-regulating state (some cyberpunk narratives feature corporate villains—thus revealing a nostalgia for human control and responsibility—while in other texts the dramatic conflicts are the product of "ghosts in the machine" [a literal, if electronic, deus ex machina]).

While the writers of the New Wave responded to the failure of social controls with a renewed emphasis on subjectivity and "inner space," the cyberpunks maintained a sometimes careful but often opportunistic ambivalence. The worlds they built are filled with name-brand debris of a fully industrialized and technologized culture: "They'd left the place littered with the abstract white forms of the foam packing units, with crumpled plastic film and hundreds of tiny foam beads. The Ono-Sendai [cyberspace deck]; next year's expensive Hosaka computer; a Sony monitor; a dozen disks of corporate-grade ice; a Braun coffeemaker" (*Neuromancer*, 46).

In Gibson's fiction, much of it set in the Sprawl—BAMA, the Boston-Atlanta Metroplex—the perspective is less street level than gutter level, as new technologies yield a new range of black markets and marketeers

rather than a gleaming, utopian vision of progress. Johnny Mnemonic, in another Gibson story, inhabits the demimonde of the Sprawl, renting the memory chips implanted in his head to gangsters needing secret

data storage space. This is far from the magnificent, streamlined towers of urban control on display in a film like *Things to Come* or the General Motors Futurama exhibit at the 1939 World's Fair.

This dark, pragmatic, and paranoid urbanism further links the subgenre to the forms of the *film noir* and private eye fiction: Jameson's comments on Chandler are profoundly applicable to Gibson. There is a pervasive and long-standing complementarity between science fiction and crime fiction, and this has only become more pronounced around cyberpunk and its obsessions with urbanism, the underworld, and social marginality.[99] As Brian McHale points out, and as will be discussed later in this chapter, the detective story is involved with the status of *knowing,* while science fiction's domain is the realm of *being.* That there should be a significant conflation of these two genres, then, is unsurprising but provocative, and it merits some consideration.

The detective story, as analyzed by Roland Barthes, is strongly oriented toward a play with what he called fiction's "hermeneutic code." In other words, the narrative sets up a central enigma which it is the task of the detective (and/or the reader) to explicate.[100] Dennis Porter has noted that the classic form of detective fiction involves opening "a logico-temporal gap" between the time of the crime's commission and the time of its telling. The task of the detective (and the fiction) is thus to close that gap and restore the logical temporal order.[101]

Science fiction detective stories have rarely enjoyed success, and it is probably true (as *The Science Fiction Encyclopedia* maintains) that the combination is difficult "because in sf the boundary between the possible and the impossible is so flexible."[102] In other words, the rules which govern the science fiction diegesis are often unknown, or unclear, or even inconsistent—complicating the already difficult task of problem-solving. Additionally, since the science fiction story is often predicated upon a technological innovation or extrapolation (a "novum," to use Darko Suvin's term), the "solution" to the mystery often involves an unforeseeable twist—a time machine, for example.[103]

But just as American crime fiction cannot be reduced to the model of the classic (often English) detective story, the confluence of science fiction and crime fiction is not exhausted by the cognitive puzzles of futuristic "locked-room" mysteries. *Blade Runner* and related works by Moebius and Gibson owe far more to the alienated spatialities of Chandler or Ross MacDonald than to the puzzles of John Dickson Carr or Agatha Christie. A set of motifs is shared by writers in both genres: a concern with models of social order and disorder; narrative structures based on perception and spatial exploration; and, most significantly, a mapping of compacted, decentered, highly complex urban spaces. *Blade Runner* is exemplary on all three points. The replicants pose a threat to the social order, raising questions regarding the status of being and the nature of state control. Deckard is the technologically enhanced detective/perceiver, seeing, reading, and exploring an unsettling and chaotic environment. Finally, the intricate urbanism of the film is the point at which the iconographies of science fiction and *film noir* thoroughly overlap.

Jameson has written that:

> the form of Chandler's books reflects an initial American separation of people from each other, their need to be linked by some external force (in this case the detective) if they are ever to be fitted together as parts of the same picture puzzle. And this separation is projected out onto space itself: no matter how crowded the street in question, the various solitudes never really merge into a collective experience[;] there is always distance between them. Each dingy office is separated from the next; each room in the rooming house from the one next to it; each dwelling from the pavement beyond it. This is why the most characteristic leitmotif of Chan-

dler's books is the figure standing, looking out of one world, peering vaguely or attentively across into another.[104]

These comments are equally apposite to *Blade Runner,* which extends Chandler's "separation of people from each other" into the distance between planets, between the human and the nonhuman, and even between physical and electronic environments. *Neuromancer* and its many imitators are equally involved in this generic crossover (although usually it is the thief, rather than the cop, who is engaged in the quest).

While the narrative produces a linkage between spaces, Jameson argues that the experience of spatial separation is, in fact, the true experience of the work (and surely Chandler's incoherent "solutions" lend credence to that view). The homology between the Chandler-*noir* axis of crime story and the street-level formations of cyberpunk is neither superficial nor coincidental, but is fundamentally connected to the experience of the "intolerable spaces" (now urban- *and* cyber-) that define contemporary existence. As with Chandler's fiction, the narrative estranges and grounds the reader by emphasizing the reality of alienation while still producing what Jameson has referred to as "an aesthetic of *cognitive mapping.*"[105] Although Chandler's L.A. was nearly as technologized as *Blade Runner's* L.A., Chandler's was grounded in visible technologies. Now the *noir* narrative is mapped onto the invisible but experientially real spaces of electronic culture.[106] The task of narrating this fundamental urban separation then, once exclusively the province of the detective genre, now falls to that hybrid of science fiction and urban crime narrative known as cyberpunk.

Cyberspace is an abstraction which, diegetically and extradiegetically, provides a narrative compensation for the loss of visibility in the world, the movement of power into the cybernetic matrices of the global computer banks, and the corresponding divestiture of power from the subject ("We no longer feel that we penetrate the future; futures now penetrate us"[107]). The planes of cyberspace enable the activity of spatial penetration and thus produce the subject's mastery of a global data system. Oddly, writing about cyberpunk often defines it as *dystopian,* marked by *noir*-ish excesses in extended inner cities. There are dystopian elements to be found, not least in cyberpunk's satirical approach to contemporary urbanism (see the novels of Jack Womack for examples), but to reduce the genre to one rhetorical mode seems misguided.

Andrew Ross has produced a typical reading of cyberpunk as urban dystopia in "Cyberpunk in Boystown." In some ways the essay is very useful: to grapple with cyberpunk, Ross considers Gibson, *Blade Runner* and its imitators, Frank Miller's comic book *Elektra Assassin,* and Steve Jackson's notorious cyberpunk role-playing game. He is right to note cyberpunk's dispersal beyond the field of the literary, but the plurality of texts serves a remarkably univocal reading. As his title suggests, Ross understands cyberpunk as an adolescent and masculinist genre. Responding to Bruce Sterling's assertion that cyberpunk is an expression of a contemporary zeitgeist, he observes that this particular zeitgeist ignores feminism, race politics, environmentalism, and other significant, contemporary, cultural forces. (This is not an incorrect position, *as far as it goes,* but Ross takes certain cyberpunk postures far too literally. It's also true that urban paranoia is a fashionable attitude, and cyberpunk at its weakest has reduced all of this to formula, as in the role-playing game.[108] There *is* an evident rock 'n' roll romanticism at work, riding atop the adolescent sensibility of most SF.)

Ross and others emphasize the image of urbanism that dominates the form. There is a surfeit of dystopian writings on the city in the latter half of the twentieth century, from Jane Jacobs's *Rise and Fall of the American City* to Mike Davis's *City of Quartz.* The city is in crisis, its superstructure decaying while its tax base relocates to less expensive edge cities and other dispersed metrocenters. As Webber and others suggest, the city has entered a new phase of existence as a decentered nongeographical entity. Cyberpunk is an important touchstone here: Davis's massive reading of Los Angeles refers frequently to *Blade Runner,* a future to which L.A. seems to consciously aspire; his book is adorned by a quote from Gibson, who suggests that Davis's work is more cyberpunk than his own. Perhaps the darkest chapters emphasize the rise of Los Angeles as a high-security state, a space of control and containment: "the 'fortress effect' emerges, not as an inadvertent failure of design, but as deliberate socio-spatial strategy."[109] The control of space is seen as a *strategy,* in Michel de Certeau's sense of the word (see chapter 3), but for Davis the only significant tactics of resistance, such as gang membership, have been demonized. Cyberpunk represents another set of tactics.

Ross finds it significant that most cyberpunk writers are suburbanites or nonurbanites (forgetting the power that the works have held over urban *readers* since their appearance nearly a decade ago). The nonurban perspective of the writers reveals itself in their hyperbolized versions of an inner city run riot. The protagonist, inevitably a white male, probes, negotiates, and penetrates this site of multicultural otherness, mastering it in the process (thus cyberpunk heroes inherit from the

Tarzan tradition—lords of the neo-urban jungle).[110] But the nonurban cyberpunk authors do not simply exist in some *other place*—in the era of the "non-place urban realm" all these spaces (urban, suburban, nonurban) connect.

Further, to dwell on cyberpunk's dystopian portrait of the city is to ignore the genre's narrative compensations (that move past the code of the great white hero). Much cyberpunk has been concerned with the phenomenologically relevant *other space* of information circulation and control. *Neuromancer* transformed terminal space by casting it in physical terms, rendering it susceptible to perception and control. David Tomas also argues that cyberspace represents a powerful space of accommodation to new technological forms: "there is reason to believe that these technologies might constitute the central phase in a postindustrial 'rite of passage' between organically human and cyberpsychically digital life-forms as reconfigured through computer software systems."[111] He understands cyberspace in explicitly anthropological terms as a *mythological* space (a far more productive approach than Ross's own paradigm of naturalism). And if the subgenre remains connected to its adolescent roots, well, rock 'n' roll has always represented a means of techno-social enfranchisement, and some sense of technological control can come through mastering an electric guitar as well as a computer. Even at its most conservative, cyberpunk thematizes an ambivalence regarding terminal existence. The works are *correctives* to the dystopian city-spaces of the present. Urban space and cyberspace become reciprocal metaphors—each enables an understanding and negotiation of the other.

I'm not suggesting that critics *couldn't* deal with the politics of cyberspace (exactly who *does* gain access to electronic space, in cyberpunk and in the "real world"?), simply that they don't. Of course Ross characterizes cyberpunk as *dystopian*—he has ignored its utopian spaces. Compare his view to that of Allucquere Rosanne Stone, who notes that for hackers, the technologically literate, and the socially disaffected, "Gibson's powerful vision provided . . . the imaginal public sphere and refigured discursive community that established the grounding for the possibility of a new kind of social interaction." While Ross downgrades adolescent cyberpunk gamers, Stone describes a more sophisticated *community* of readers and the reemergence of an electronic public space.[112] Paul Arthur has further linked this hypertechnologized space to the pastoral tradition, noting that cyberspace represents a new frontier, one that replaces an urban landscape desiccated by the pervasiveness of consumer dynamics.[113] So while cyberspace frequently recapitulates the complexities of the postmodern "urban nonplace," it frequently permits the subject a utopian and kinetic *liberation* from the very limits of urban existence.

Neuromancer

Cyberpunk at its best is not quite reducible to the work of William Gibson, but he is certainly both its most archetypal literary figure—with three novels, a hypertext project, and a collection of short stories to his credit, he is nearly a subgenre unto himself. (He has also collaborated on a novel with fellow cyberpunk Bruce Sterling.) In *Neuromancer,* Gibson coalesced an eclectic range of generic protocols, contemporary idiolects, and a pervasive technological eroticism combined with a future-shocking ambivalence. Aside from the old and new waves of science fiction, Gibson's prose and perspective owes much to the streetwise weariness of Chandler and the neologistic prowess of William Burroughs, which provide its underworld savvy and technoslang (the razor-girls of Night City or the meat puppets—lobotomized prostitutes[114]).

Another clear stylistic forerunner, and thus a major progenitor of cyberpunk fiction in general, is *Dispatches,* the journalistic account of the Vietnam war by Michael Herr. Jameson has written of this text that it "impersonally fuses a whole range of contemporary collective idiolects, most notably rock language and Black language,"[115] as does Gibson within an urban context. Herr breaks down traditional narrative paradigms in favor of a powerfully decentered spatiality.

> Helicopters and people jumping out of helicopters, people so in love they'd run to get on even when there wasn't any pressure. Choppers rising straight out of small cleared jungle spaces, wobbling down onto city rooftops, cartons of rations and ammunition thrown off, dead and wounded loaded on. Sometimes they were so plentiful and loose that you could touch down at five or six places in a day, look around, hear the talk, catch the next one out. There were installations as big as cities with 30,000 citizens, once we dropped in to feed supply to one man.[116]

Where are these places? What do they mean? The helicopter, like the hovercar of *Blade Runner,* adds verticality to the spaces of postmodern warfare, but the connections between places are lost in an orgy of motion. Jameson: "In this new machine which . . . does not represent motion, but which can only be represented *in motion,* something of the mystery of the new postmodernist space is concentrated."[117] The computer is the ultimate extension of the new machine, particularly through the dialectical tension maintained between its inert physical form and the megabytes of data circulating in nanoseconds of time, and it is put *in motion* in *Neuromancer*. One character in *Dispatches* is seen "coming out of some heavy heart of darkness trip, overloaded on the information, the input! The input!" (6)—a perfect cyberpunk credo.

Neuromancer was uncannily anticipated by Jameson's 1984 essay on postmodernism and is a remarkable consolidation of the themes and issues of terminal culture. The novel is set in the twenty-first century, when the world is dominated by the high-tech *zaibatsus* of Japan, Germany, and Switzerland. Fortunes are to be made in the illegal retrieval and sale of data, and Case (a closed object, a container, a hard case) works on the black market. Data is a protected commodity, and cybernetic security systems can only be circumvented by people like Case, a cyberspace cowboy, neurologically jacked into the world of the computer. Armed with the proper ICE (intrusive counter-electronics), Case can negotiate his way through the most elaborate systems. But Case had blown a job and his employers damaged his nervous system as revenge: he can no longer jack in. "For Case, who'd lived for the bodiless exultation of cyberspace, it was the Fall." Two years later, a small team of brutal specialists has appeared to fix the damage and bring Case back into cyberspace to penetrate the defenses of an AI (artificial intelligence) for unknown purposes.

In the action-adventure tradition of Ian Fleming, the action jumps from Japan's Chiba City to the Sprawl, then to Europe and up to Freeside, an orbital colony. The urbanism is insistent, even in outer space, where Freeside, a rotating habitat with centrifugal "gravity," is presented as an especially disorienting spatial environment: "it made no sense to his body" (123–24). Street directions within this imploded urban space recall Ballard's "Concentration City": "Rue Jules Verne was a circumferential avenue, looping the spindle's midpoint, while Desiderata ran its length, terminating at either end in the supports of the Lado-Acheson light pumps. If you turned right, off Desiderata, and followed Jules Verne far enough, you'd find yourself approaching Desiderata from the left" (151). Delany has noted that it is precisely such spaces and descriptions that frustrate readers unfamiliar with the genre who are unable or unwilling to accept the redefinition of bodily experience implied by this string of words. Gibson is masterful at this sort of dislocation; witness the opening sentence of his second novel, *Count Zero* (1986): "They set a slamhound on Turner's trail in New Delhi, slotted it to his pheromones and the color of his hair." This is a work which begins in medias res, and it is a world of professionals. (Thomas Disch notes that while *Neuromancer's* Case is a "Ulysses of cyberspace," the gentler *Mona Lisa Overdrive* [1988], the third book of the Cyberspace Trilogy, is peopled by "innocents and naifs," permitting a friendlier interface with readers.)[118]

The imploded urbanism of Freeside continues the movement toward containment of the metroscape and a bonding with electronic space. Simulated weather effects disguise the nature of this habitat, which hangs suspended within the nullity of outer space. Simulation melds with reality to preserve some sense of traditional spatial experience, but Freeside suggests nothing so much as the structures of cyberspace.

Gibson continually refers to the similarities between the matrices of the electronic and physical realities. The very first sentence of *Neuromancer* establishes the impossibility of a "real" space existing apart from its electronic analogue: "The sky above the port was the color of television, turned to a dead channel."[119] As on Freeside, the air of Chiba City is filled with simulations: "Under bright ghosts burning through a blue haze of cigarette smoke, holograms of Wizard's Castle, Tank War Europa, the New York skyline" (8). The real metroscape of New York becomes simply another simulation, reduced to data and transformed into the hyperreality of the hologram. As a veteran of cyberspace, Case is well aware of the overlapping. While being chased through Chiba city, he feels an adrenaline rush and realizes his pleasure: "Because in some weird and very approximate way, it was like a run in the matrix. Get just wasted enough, find yourself in some desperate but strangely arbitrary kind of trouble, and it was possible to see Ninsei as a field of data. . . . Then you could throw yourself into a high-speed drift and skid, totally engaged but set apart from it all, and all around you the dance of biz, information interacting, data made flesh in the mazes of the black market" (16).

Later, Molly, another member of the team, breaks into the headquarters of Sense/Net while Case performs a cyberspace run on the same target. Case is also jacked in to Molly's experience through the miracle of sim-stim—simulation-stimulation—and the narrative cuts from physical assault to cyberspace run, all the while remaining within the diegetically grounded perspective of Case, whose body remains in the hotel room: physical and electronic spaces are made equivalent, each an extension of the other.[120]

A physical unreality begins to pervade the metroscape, an expression of the disembodied and dislocating spaces of the postmodern city in which sign and spectacle dominate, in which reality seems usurped by its own simulacrum. The simultaneous dispersion and concentration characteristic of the "overexposed city," as Virilio calls it, finds its only adequate analogue and representation within the matrices of terminal space. It is a space that one is physically absent from, in that the space no longer permits any authentic bodily function or experience: cyberspace is thus the more honest spatial figuration in its open acknowledgment of the supersession of individual bodily experience.

Urban space becomes the metaphor for the electronic spaces of data circulation. Vivian Sobchack has noted: "The multinationals seem to determine our lives from some sort of ethereal 'other' or 'outer' space. This is a space that finds its most explicit figuration in the impossible towering beauty of *Blade Runner's* Tyrell Corporation Building—an awesome megastructure whose intricate facade also resembles a microchip."[121] In *Neuromancer,* the reader's first introduction to the Sprawl is in terms of data circulation and terminal representation:

> Program a map to display frequency of data exchange, every thousand megabytes a single pixel on a very large screen. Manhattan and Atlanta burn solid white. Then they start to pulse, the rate of traffic threatening to overload your simulation. Your map is about to go nova. Cool it down. Up your scale. Each pixel a million megabyes. At a hundred million megabytes per second, you begin to make out certain blocks in midtown Manhattan, outlines of hundred-year-old industrial parks ringing the old core of Atlanta. (43)

This is a most explicit mapping of terminal onto physical space and demonstrates the need for new cartographic strategies, as well as new sources of vision, to attain some comprehension of, and competence in, "the bewildering world space" of corporate activity, that "other space." Images of building exteriors, especially the glass corporate headquarters of the late modernist era, no longer reveal anything of their functions or purposes. Images of human exteriors also reveal nothing: they are no longer relevant to the new "real" space of terminal culture. But program a map to reveal data circulation and worlds of information are revealed. We are entering cyberspace.

Of course, Gibson is the best guide to this new arena of human activity, and *Neuromancer* provides its own definition (this is the narration from a children's program): "Cyberspace. A consensual hallucination experienced daily by billions of legitimate operators, in every nation, by children being taught mathematical concepts. . . . A graphic representation of data abstracted from the banks of every computer in the human system. Unthinkable complexity. Lines of light ranged in the nonspace of the mind, clusters and constellations of data. Like city lights, receding" (51). The concept of cyberspace is not much of an extrapolation beyond present realities of user interface. Here are the images which accompany the above narration: "a two-dimensional space war faded behind a forest of mathematically generated ferns, demonstrating the spacial possibilities of logarithmic spirals; cold blue military footage burned through, lab animals wired into test systems, helmets feeding into fire control circuits of tanks and war planes." Much of this is not extrapolation at all—the space wars of the video arcades, the fractal forms of fern "life" growing on a monitor screen, and the use of computers and simulation to aid in training military personnel as well as in developing new targeting technologies guided solely by the operator's vision have all been a part of terminal experience for decades.[122]

Certain other aspects of this "nonspace" need to be emphasized. Just as Chiba City, the Sprawl, and Freeside were endowed with some of the attributes of cyberspace, so cyberspace is characterized as a field "like city lights." Cyberspace is represented as an imploded urbanism—Blip City. During a run, Case is at the mercy of some advanced Kuang Grade Mark Eleven ICE (bad news):

> Headlong motion through walls of emerald green, milky jade, the sensation of speed beyond anything he'd known before in cyberspace. . . . The Tessier-Ashpool ice shattered, peeling away from the Chinese program's thrust, a worrying impression of solid fluidity, as though the shards of a broken mirror bent and elongated as they fell—"Christ," Case said, awestruck, as Kuang twisted and banked above the horizonless fields of the Tessier-Ashpool cores, an endless neon cityscape, complexity that cut the eye, jewel bright, sharp as razors. (256)

Again, the profoundly dislocating field of cyberspace, a field of "solid fluidity," "complexity that cuts the eye," and "horizonless" space is coupled with the image of the "neon cityscape." That the T-A cores, "a dozen identical towers of data," resemble the RCA building (assuredly *not* a glass box) endows the space with a faintly baroque familiarity.

The question is, does the imposition of the forms of the cityscape on the new datascape ground the image by rendering it with familiar strokes, or does it instead extend the dislocating power of the urban realm? A bit of both, it would seem, for cyberspace certainly hyperbolizes the space of the city, projecting the metroscape into an exaggerated representation that accentuates its bodiless vertigo, but it permits the existence of a powerful and controlling gaze. In Gibson's cyberspace, in fact, the disembodied metroscape achieves its fullest expression: in a simultaneous movement of dislocation and centering, the human now exists as *pure gaze* while the fragmented "nonplace urban realm" is translated into visual terms. Cyberspace becomes the instantiation of a truly postmodern urban language in which the density and proximity of the central, inner, city becomes the compensatory analogy for the spatially dispersed matrices of information circulation and overload.

In one sense, cyberspace is not really a space at all, but simply a construct occupied by the programs and data systems of the world. "In the nonspace of the matrix," Gibson writes, "the interior of a given data construct possessed unlimited subjective dimension; a child's toy calculator, accessed through Case's Sendai, would have presented limitless gulfs of nothingness hung with a few basic commands" (*Neuromancer*, 63). J. David Bolter has stressed that electronic space is, in many ways, simpler to understand than its physical or mathematical counterparts, precisely because it is "an artifact, a constructed space that must function in thoroughly predictable ways in order to serve its technological purpose."[123]

Bolter has defined mathematical conceptions of electronic space as amalgams of both Platonic and Cartesian spaces. For the Greeks, space was simply the sum of matter in the universe—there was no such thing as space without substance. Even the atomists, while acknowledging the existence of empty space, only went so far as positing the space in which matter (atoms) moved. The development of a coherent relation between the geometries of Euclid and the algebras of the Muslim world was the contribution of Descartes and led to a radical reconception of space as "an infinite set of dimensionless points."[124] Points, or objects, were now defined in terms of the space they occupied, rather than the space being defined around the objects. Newton, seizing upon the contributions made by the coordinate system of Cartesian analytic geometry, was thus able to describe, through physics, the forces of gravity and motion.

The interest of Gibsonian cyberspace derives from its status as a *phenomenal,* rather than a mathematical elaboration of electronic space. Cyberspace is generally regarded as finite, if virtual—a construct which serves the set of objects within it, as in ancient cosmologies. At the same time, though, it is a coordinate system of seeming limitlessness: Gibson continually stresses the endless *space* as well as the data contained within it. Following the strategies of computer-graphics researchers, Gibson has transformed the virtual field of the Cartesian coordinate system into the Newtonian spaces of concrete forces and forms (*TRON* performed a similar operation). This is no idle transformation; it reduces the infinite abstract void of electronic space to the definitions of bodily experience and physical cognition, grounding it in finite and assimilable terms. Merleau-Ponty once raised objections to the detachment of Cartesian coordinate space by noting that he is inside space, immersed in it; space cannot be reconstructed from an outside position.[125] Cyberspace, with its aesthetic of immersion, maintains the mathematical determinism of the coordinate system, but it superimposes the experiential realities of physical, phenomenal, space upon the abstractions of this Cartesian terrain.

The reductionism of cyberspace also extends to its definition as an *abstraction* of the data in all the computers within the human system, a reprogramming which reduces the complexity to avoid an overload and permit the assimilation by human perception (as in the map of the Sprawl: "Cool it down," Gibson advises): "Put the trodes on and they were out there, all the data in the world stacked up like one big neon city, so you could cruise around and have a kind of grip on it, visually anyway, because if you didn't, it was too complicated, trying to find your way to a particular piece of data you needed."[126] Here, in *Mona Lisa Overdrive,* Gibson makes his own project explicit. Cyberspace is a method of conceiving the inconceivable—an imaginary solution to the real contradictions of the Dataist Era. In this sense, *Neuromancer itself* represents a "consensual hallucination"—an abstraction and reduction of the complexities of cybernetic culture to a kind of reckless, but sensible, cognitive experience. Not everyone can read *Neuromancer:* its neologisms alienate the uninitiated reader—that's their function—while its unwavering intensity and the absence of traditional pacing exhaust even the dedicated. The work is best experienced as something other than narrative—poetry, perhaps—so that the images may perform their estranging, disembodying functions. The reader must jack into *Neuromancer*—it's a novel for would-be cyberspace cowboys.

Gibson has admitted that a primary influence on his conception of cyberspace were the comic book visualizations of *Heavy Metal,* already discussed in relation to *Blade Runner.*[127] Gibson's version of cyberspace is now the only possible model, and it has influenced comics in its turn. As the name implies, *Cyberpunk* by Scott Rockwell and Darryl Banks is a particularly clear homage: cyberspace is composed of intersecting planes and geometric forms (although the effect is like the beginning of a network movie-of-the-week). *Iron Man: CRASH,* written and illustrated

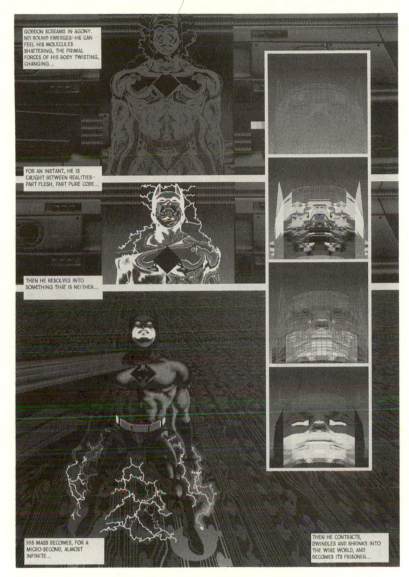

Batman in cyberspace: Pepe Moreno's 1990 *Digital Justice*, produced entirely on a Macintosh computer. (© 1990 DC Comics. All Rights Reserved.)

by Mike Saenz entirely on a computer, features elaborate 3-D modeling effects (Saenz has since designed an "adult" computer adventure called "Virtual Valerie"). Again vector lines and solid 3-D modeling combine to create the cybernetic realm; again Tokyo serves as the technological other. Undoubtedly the most sophisticated of the new "computer comics" is Pepe Moreno's cyberpunk Batman novel, *Digital Justice,* which features an electronic palette of sixteen million colors and the Joker as a malevolent computer virus. A comic's adaptation of *Neuromancer* serves as an interesting translation of the original (as Gibson himself notes in his introduction) and a closing of the representational circle (the rendering techniques employed by Bruce Jensen are more traditional than the computer-aided designs of Saenz or Moreno). These comics simplify the narrative elements of *Neuromancer,* but they also preserve the dense urbanism, romantic rebelliousness, and overall cybernetic overload. For the most part, in this case the medium has become more derivative than innovative.[128]

The Production of Cyberspace

Jameson's understanding of space as a structuring concept of the postmodernity connects to the work of Henri Lefebvre, whose remarkable book, *The Production of Space,* has only recently appeared in English. Lefebvre was strongly affected by a range of discourses in European culture. Situationism, with its emphasis on lived, urban reality set the terms for a debate in which Lefebvre and Michel de Certeau were very interested, despite their rejection of fundamental Situationist precepts and attitudes. Lefebvre combined principles of Marxism with phenomenology, Surrealism, and a host of other discourses to produce an original and powerful amalgam that seems remarkably appropriate to the 1990s.

In *The Production of Space,* Lefebvre condemns the quest for a "science of space," rejecting the loose metaphoricity in which *everything* has become a "space" (Foucault is the clear villain of this piece). Mere interpretations of spatiality overemphasize a symbolic "reading" of what is, primarily and always, a lived relation. He further argues that the fragmentation of space is the product of a mental "division of labor" that only sustains "the subjection" to state power. A more effective understanding of space would resist the fragmentation of this multitude of competing "spaces," while reinscribing the relationship between space, social organization, and modes of production. Lefebvre imagines what such a "science of space" might yield: aside from this reification of existing power relations, "it embodies at best a technological utopia, a sort of computer simulation of the future, or of the possible, within the framework of the real—the framework of the existing mode of production. . . . The technological utopia in question is a common feature not just of many science-fiction novels, but also of all kinds of projects concerned with space, be they those of architecture, urbanism or social planning."[129]

For Lefebvre the condition of space always exists in relation to the mode of production, and new modes produce new spaces. The rise of trade in Greece was bound to the emergence of urban space, which in turn supplied the conditions for the emergence of philosophy (14). The rationalist spaces of the industrial era worked invisibly to sustain an economic system (see Dickens's *Hard Times*). But that rationalism was no permanent condition: "The fact is that around 1910 a certain space was shattered. It was the space of common sense, of knowledge, of social practice, of political power . . . ; the space, too, of classical perspective and geometry, developed from the Renaissance onwards on the basis of the Greek tradition (Euclid, logic) and bodied forth in Western art and philosophy, as in the form of the city and town." Lefebvre concludes: "Euclidean and perspectivist space have disappeared as systems of reference, along with the other former 'commonplaces' such as the town, history, paternity, the tonal system in music, traditional morality, and so forth." The emergence of modernism was thus "truly a crucial moment" (25).

Two propositions of Lefebvre's are relevant to comprehending the spatiality of postmodernism: first, natural space is disappearing; despite frantic and belated efforts to protect it, it "is also becoming lost to *thought.*" One correlate is that society produces space, but Lefebvre goes further: "each society offers up its own peculiar space, as it were, as an 'object' for analysis and overall theoretical explication. I say each society, but it would be more accurate to say each mode of production" (31).

Lefebvre tells us that "the shift from one mode to another must entail the production of a new space" (46). A new spatiality connected to changes in the mode of production—we are ready to consider the new space of the present: "Cyberspace . . . a word, in fact, that gives a name to a new stage, a new and irresistible development in the elaboration of human culture and business under the sign of technology."[130] Cyberspace is clearly a *produced* space that defines the subject's relation to culture and politics. Like all such spaces, however, it does not simply exist to be inhabited; space implies position and negotiation. Lefebvre: "all 'subjects' are situated in a space in which they must either recognize themselves or lose themselves, a space which they may both enjoy and modify. In order to accede to this space, individuals (children, adolescents) who are, paradoxically, already within it, must pass tests" (35). Case, the cowboy, enjoys jacking in maybe a little too much ("And somewhere he was laughing, in a white-painted loft, distant fingers caressing the deck, tears of release streaking his face" [*Neuromancer,*

52]), and his job as a cybernaut (a pilot) involves constant feedback between self and space. Flynn, the hacker-hero of *TRON* may look like an adult, but he acts like an adolescent; he even owns a videogame parlor, a space almost ridiculously apposite to Lefebvre's analysis (and if the protagonists are adult, the *audience* is often adolescent). Michael Benedikt writes that "cyberspace's inherent immateriality and malleability of content provides the most tempting stage for the acting out of mythic realities."[131]

A standing joke about cyberspace is that, in an era of ATMs and global banking, *cyberspace is where your money is.* So cyberspace is a financial space, a space of capital; it is a social space; it is responsive; it can be modified; it is a place of testing and the arena for new technological rites of passage (Tomas). In these regards at least, cyberspace fulfills the conditions of spatiality as propounded by Lefebvre. Whether a real space or a "consensual hallucination," cyberspace produces a unified experience of spatiality, and thus social being, in a culture that has become impossibly fragmented. On the other hand, we should note that cyberspace is "a technological utopia, a sort of computer simulation of the future, or of the possible, within the framework of the real—the framework of the existing mode of production."

The passage of the subject into the pixels and bytes of "invisible" terminal space addresses the massive redeployment of power within telematic culture. In the context of a lost public sphere and an altered mode of production, cyberspace becomes the characteristic spatiality of a new era. In the context of cybernetic disembodiment, rooted in nanoseconds of time and imploded infinities of space, cyberspace addresses the overwhelming need to reconstitute a phenomenal being. This occurs first through a revelatory act of visualization, in a movement that both decenters and recenters the subject in a manner aptly described by Merleau-Ponty: "the proper essence of the visible is to have a layer of invisibility in the strict sense, which it makes present as a certain absence."[132] He has theorized that in every act of vision there remains something unseen, or which otherwise marks this vision as incomplete, and this marks the existence of an objectively "real" world that exists independent of perception and cognition. Thus the otherness of cyberspace abides as an ultimately *defining* metaphor, an attempt to recognize and overcome the technological estrangements of the electronic age, and a preliminary attempt to resituate the human as its fundamental force. "Vision alone makes us learn that beings that are different, 'exterior,' foreign to one another, are yet absolutely together, are 'simultaneity.' "[133]

PARASPACE   . . . The condition of hyperspace is itself insane.

—Barry Malzberg   ¶ Separations are proceeding. Each alternative Zone

speeds away from all the others, in fated acceleration, red-shifting, fleeing

the Center.—Thomas Pynchon

The Paraspaces of Science Fiction

Cyberspace is clearly a *paraspace,* as Samuel Delany has defined the
term. Writing and speaking somewhat informally about cyberpunk fiction, Delany has begun to develop a notion of a science fictional space
that exists parallel to the normal space of the diegesis—a rhetorically
heightened "other realm." A number of science fiction writers, he argues, "posit a normal world—a recognizable future—and then an alternate space, sometimes largely mental, but always materially manifested, that sits beside the real world, and in which language is raised
to an extraordinarily lyric level." Further, "conflicts that begin in ordinary space are resolved in this linguistically intensified paraspace."[134]
The construction of these spaces is not exclusive to cyberpunk; rather,
Delany locates a series of writers whose works are powerfully paraspatial. Indeed, the notion of a paraspace might be endemic to the genre of
science fiction, as even the earliest texts permit such a linguistic intensification directed toward the exotic spaces of, for example, *outer space*
or *the future.* The language in such works transcends the descriptive,
instead offering the reader an experience of explicit "otherness." "How
to describe the inherently indescribable," asks the narrator of Norman
Spinrad's *The Void Captain's Tale* (1983)—a tautology which has value in
defining the impetus behind the genre's foundational texts.

I will return to this conception of the paraspace as SF fundament
below. First, it is important to note that Delany is right: there are writers
whose texts make clear a separation between normal- and paraspaces,
writers whose literary practices enable such a division. The archetypal
figure in such a canon, as Delany notes, would be Alfred Bester, whose
two early novels, *The Demolished Man* (1953) and *The Stars My Destination* (1956), remain pinnacles of achievement in the genre. *The Demolished Man* is about telepaths, and Bester uses innovative typography to
portray the snaking and interconnecting thoughts of the telepathic
characters. This paraspace is invisible, but it is no less materially

manifested for that, and is defined by a linguistic concretization that centers attention on the materiality of the signifier in a manner almost unheard of within the boundaries of popular narrative. Only *The Stars My Destination* rivals it for boldness.[135]

Stars is set in a far future dominated by a form of limited teleportation called "jaunting."[136] The narrative centers on Gully Foyle, who thirsts for revenge against the starship NOMAD, which failed to rescue him from a drifting hulk in deep space. Foyle sees visions of an inexplicable "Burning Man" several times, but this remains unexplained until the climax. As Foyle faces certain death by explosive, he begins to flicker in and out of existence, jaunting in space and time (and thus he is his own apparition). The brute intensity of Bester's prose then demonstrates Foyle's overwhelming experience of sensory conflation and confusion known as synaesthesia: "Touch was taste to him . . . the feel of wood was acrid and chalky in his mouth, metal was salt, stone tasted sour-sweet to the touch of his fingers, and the feel of glass cloyed his palate like over-rich pastry. Smell was touch. . . . Hot stone smelled like velvet caressing his cheek. Smoke and ash were harsh tweeds rasping his skin, almost the feel of wet canvas. Molten metal smelled like blow [sic] hammering his heart, and the ionization of the PyrE explosion filled the air with ozone that smelled like water trickling through his fingers" (212–13). The very linearity of the text decomposes as Bester "envisions" the sounds of language (215):

> The Burning Man winced. "Stop!" he called, blinded by the noise. Again came the dazzling pattern of the echo:
>
>
>
> StOpStOpStOp
>
> OpStOpStOpStOp
>
> StOpStOpStOpStOp
>
> OpsStOpStOpStOpStOp
>
> OpStOpStOpStOpSt
>
> OpsStOpStOpStOp
>
> OpStOpStOpSt
>
>

Bester's concrete poetry was too idiosyncratic to be very influential, at least until the advent of the New Wave. Delany and Roger Zelazny both were evidently engaged with the pyrotechnical games Bester had brought to the genre.

A considerable number of Zelazny's writings engage with parallel spaces of one sort or another. Even his most popular work, the Chronicles of Amber series, is an extended visit to a paraspace. Amber is the one true Earth of which all others are but shadows, and Zelazny's chromatic prose emphasizes the transitory nature of all realities (although Amber does provide a Platonically idealist grounding for the ontological shifts). All the knowable spaces, the work seems to propose, are paraspaces.

In "He Who Shapes" (1964), the parallel space is the world of dreams (the psychoanalyst's virtual reality), which Render (!) the Shaper manipulates to bring his patients' conflicts into focus and encourage their resolution. The paraspace has moved inside the mind in a trajectory that typifies the "inner space" concerns of the New Wave writers: "Lovely as it was, with the blood and all, Render could sense that it was about to end. Therefore, each microsecond would be better off as a minute, he decided—and perhaps the temperature should be increased. . . . Somewhere, just at the periphery of everything, the darkness halted its constriction. Something, like a crescendo of subliminal thunders, was arrested at one raging note. That note was a distillate of shame and pain and fear. The Forum was stifling."[137] The story begins in paraspace; a dislocation for the reader commensurate with the geographical imprecision of the passage. Sound, temperature, and time flow, "givens" within the diegesis of any mundane tale, are invested here with both malleability and sensuality. There is the suggestion of a controlling force, but the enigmatic prose reveals only a deliberate insubstantiality. A constant elision of meaning occurs, so that characteristics are transmuted in a manner reminiscent of Foyle's synaesthesia—sounds are endowed with emotion; temperature has a bearing on darkness; subliminal forces rage. Only in the last sentence does the space become visually descriptive, although in an extremely weak form.

Delany points out that the story's original title, "The Ides of Octember," is "a figure of rhetorically distorted language" that refers to "a time whose possibility or impossibility we can only even talk about when we are in the dream space." The title substituted by the editor (and the title of the expanded version, *The Dream Master*) names an element of normal space rather than the "pertinent subspace." The earlier title was "a sign of a space in which language could be distorted in a certain way, giving us access to certain purely verbal constructs."[138]

Although Delany limits his precepts to the operations of literary texts, it is a simple matter to find analogues in other media. Narrative cinema is rife with such "heightened rhetoricity," especially in the paraspaces presented by the special effects work of the science fiction film. Annette Michelson has demonstrated the breakdown of linear narrative in favor of a spectacularity and sensuality of form in her extensive phenomenological analysis of *2001,* and it is her intent that much science fiction film operates in a similar (if less sustained) fashion.[139] An exemplary text in this regard is *The Incredible Shrinking Man* (1953) wherein Scott Carey begins a process of diminution after exposure to an odd combination of insecticides and radioactive materials.[140] The film first holds to an objective, eye-level schema that emphasizes the banality of Scott's suburban existence. As in Don Siegel's 1956 *Invasion of the Body Snatchers,* the deadpan banality emphasizes the horror by grounding it in the experiential familiarity of the everyday. As the shrinking continues for Scott, the style changes. A mysterious shot of Scott sitting amidst normally scaled furniture allows the viewer to momentarily believe that the process has been arrested. His wife appears on the stairs in the following shot, but a cut back to Scott reveals an empty staircase behind him. The disjunction of cinematic space is unsettling, literally *dislocating.* It becomes apparent that Scott is now inhabiting a dollhouse and that the filmmaker has crosscut between very different spatial scales.

Following an attack by his cat, Scott tumbles down to the basement, a masterpiece of cinematic spatial construction which Michelson has linked to the cinematic explorations of Stan Brakhage and the sculptures of Robert Morris.[141] The camerawork becomes radically subjective, as the familiar space of a suburban basement is transformed into a vast realm that resembles the postholocaust landscapes of such future-archaic films as *The Road Warrior* (aka *Mad Max II*) and Richard Lester's *The Bed-Sitting Room* (1969). The space is empty and open, littered with the detritus of everyday existence. (These spaces are products of *bricolage,* Lévi-Strauss's term for construction from "the means at hand"; Derrida adds that *bricolage* is "the necessity of borrowing one's concepts from the text of a heritage which is more or less coherent or ruined.") The camera movement is now slow and languorous as it describes the grain of the wooden stairs, the height of the space, and the distance to the farther walls. Objects are transformed here in the paraspace: pins become swords, matchboxes offer shelter from the storm, pencils serve as life rafts, spiders turn into hellish monsters. Commodities become objects—colorful and decorative objects at that—and if they retain a functionality, it has been altered. The large paint cans and matchboxes prefigure the mass culture borrowings of Pop and similarly recognize these products' imbrication in everyday life; an imbrication so full that the objects are no longer *seen.* Sobchack makes similar observations, arguing that "We, as viewers, are forced . . . to constantly reevaluate our responses to the ordinary and normal, to the animate and inanimate." The film is, "perhaps, paradigmatic in its ability to totally alienate us—and its protagonist—from a customary taken-for-granted environment."[142]

But, as Delany notes, the paraspace is not simply a separate sphere, but a site where the conflicts of the normal world are resolved, and the transformation of the basement serves this function. References to emasculation are rife, from the title onward. A climactic moment occurs when Scott's wedding ring falls from his shrunken finger (member), and Scott's delight in meeting a carnival woman shorter than himself says much about dominance and "normal" masculine functioning in the culture of the 1950s (anxieties which are played through in the other direction in Nicholas Ray's *Bigger Than Life* [1957]). Scott's sexual anxiety further reveals itself in confrontations with a cat (often linked to the female in popular myth—as a witch's familiar, for example) and a spider (not the Black Widow which might be expected for narrative *and* geographic reasons, but a hairy, Medusa-like tarantula), whose dripping maw lowers itself atop this hapless, helpless male. Fortunately, Scott is able to penetrate this orifice with his pin/sword, thereby realizing his power and his significance. The justly famous finale features Scott liberated from his basement prison, gazing at the stars as he realizes that he remains an important part of the cosmos.

Sketched in such Freudian-Proppian terms, the film is greatly reduced. But what is significant in understanding the film as *science fiction* is that the resolution of the psychosocial crisis of the male in suburban America occurs in the *paraspace,* characterized here by the rhetorical excessiveness of an exaggeratedly subjective camera placement and movement and a concern with estranging the viewer from familiar spatialities. The camerawork surpasses the requirements of narrative just as surely as did Bester's typographical play and similarly dislocates the spectator in the reading process, redirecting attention to the text's own rhetoricity.

Worlds in Collision

An interesting text to place alongside Delany's observations on the genre of science fiction is Brian McHale's *Postmodernist Fiction.* This work represents a serious—if incomplete—attempt to define recent changes in narrative structures and rhetoric and offers a continual engagement with both high and popular forms of literature. McHale borrows a categorization from the Prague school of linguistic and semiotic analysis—the concept of the dominant. As Roman Jakobson argues, "The dominant may be defined as the focusing component of a work of art: it rules, determines, and transforms the remaining components" (6).[143] Thus the dominant is not the sole characteristic of a text, but it exercises a determining influence over the rest; even in the case of a self-contradictory text, the dominant would serve to guarantee some structural integrity. In modernist fiction McHale defines the dominant as *epistemological*, as exemplified by the questions of narrator, narration, and knowledge that structure literary works as diverse as those of Faulkner, Nabokov, Henry James, and even early Pynchon. Modernism is organized around perception through shifting consciousnesses and unreliable narrators. Interpretation becomes a foregrounded and dominant activity for the reader of, and characters within, the modernist text.

The postmodern text replaces such an epistemological impulse with an *ontological* imperative. Knowledge is no longer emplaced as the structuring problematic; instead, Being is centered, as the status of the world and existence become defining issues. Postmodern fiction stages a dissolution of ontological boundaries, presenting a collision and shifting of worlds. *Gravity's Rainbow,* for example, is not bound by the perceptions or dementia of its major characters; the bizarre occurrences in and around London and Germany are not accounted for by reference to, say, Tyrone Slothrop's paranoia. The world itself has shifted, redefined itself, in a very real sense. The world *is* populated by film characters come to life; narrative paradigms *do* envelop and affect the characters, and with their full complicity. The world is no longer identical with itself in postmodern fiction; it exists no longer as a homogeneous site of fixed meaning. Entropy has seized the conditions of being. The ground is not as firm as it was; if the characters undergo mental disorder, it is as a result of the ontological slippage and not the reverse.

In Robert Coover's "The Phantom of the Movie Palace," the space of the movie theater is materially invaded by the specters of spectacles past, and conversely, the films projected are not immutable but subject to the editing whims of the projectionist: "He'll run a hero through all the episodes of a serial at once, letting him be burned, blasted, buried, drowned, shot, run down, hung up, splashed with acid or sliced in two, all at the same time, or he'll select a favorite ingenue and assault her with a thick impasto of pirates, sailors, bandits, gypsies, mummies, Nazis, vampires, Martians, and college boys, until the terrified expressions on their respective faces pale to a kind of blurred, mystical affirmation of the universe."[144] Certain paradigmatic tropes can be identified herein. The title of the story (and of the collection in which it is found, *A Night at the Movies*) is itself a reference to another text (or set of texts), defining the diegesis as metafictional. Like the cut-ups of William Burroughs, the text explicitly points to its own imbrication in a series of textual systems—the world *is* a text. The specific reference to cinema is also typical of postmodern literature—McHale notes that this is not an appropriation of cinematic forms of representation (as in the modernisms of Joyce, Proust, or the Futurists, for example), but instead represents an affinity for the tremendous phenomenological force, and resultant ontological weight, with which the cinematic apparatus endows its fictions. Often, a film within the text offers an opportunity for additional recursive, metafictional, structures, further emphasizing the inescapable processes of textuality.

Finally, Coover does not identify his projectionist as deluded in any way, nor is it surprising to any character that the world should behave this way. The ontological substitution of the text's world for ours is the very precondition of the fiction. Indeed, the bombardment of found images is directed as much at the reader as at the vampires and college boys of Coover's cinema, so that our own expressions might pale to a kind of mystical affirmation of the universe. The universes of postmodern fiction bring such affirmation with them. The ground on which they might be questioned simply ceased to exist. The oft-repeated motto of Hassan i Sabbah, Master Assassin of Burroughs's fiction, is exemplary: "Nothing is true. Everything is permitted."

McHale emphasizes the centrality, in postmodern fiction, of the *Zone,* and indeed it is difficult to ignore such a pervasive trope. The Zone is often the site of the ontological shifts which occur in these dieges es. The mysterious site of an alien visitation is called the Zone in Tarkovsky's *Stalker,* as is the segmented Germany through which Tyrone Slothrop wanders in Pynchon's *Gravity's Rainbow.* In William Burroughs's mythology for the space age, the region in which all was permitted and everything coexists was the Interzone. The city/cosmos of *Alphaville* is divided into zones.[145] Even when the name is absent, the function of the Zone remains central. McHale convincingly demonstrates how Latin America functions as an ontologically slippery zone in writings by Bartheleme ("Paraguay"), García Márquez, Cortázar, Fuentes, and others. Latin America is conceived as a heterotopian zone through its conceptualization as "Europe's other, its alien double," as well as through its own regional heterogeneities. Ohio serves as a Zone in fictions by Bartheleme, Guy Davenport, and Kenneth Patchen: here its very middle-American blandness is reincorporated into the myth of the frontier— that border between worlds (McHale, 49–53).

What the Zone permits is a collision between worlds and thus be-

tween different ontological states. In the Zone "a large number of fragmentary possible worlds coexist in an impossible space," and if that
space contains allusions to historical spaces (Ohio, Latin America,
occupied Germany), it "in fact is located nowhere but in the written text
itself." The principal method of zone building depends upon "introduc-
ing an alien space *within* a familiar space, or *between* two adjacent areas
of space where no such 'between' exists" (45–46). In *Gravity's Rainbow,*
Slothrop observes that "here in the Zone categories have been blurred
badly" (353).

The significant failing of McHale's analysis occurs in his all too convenient separation of ontology from epistemology, which is indicative of
the pervasive lack of historical grounding that characterizes his study.
That the subject should cease to function as the site of meaning and cohesion in the world is an extraordinarily significant change, but McHale
reacts as though such a shift had only literary-aesthetic significance.
But the ontological mutability of the postmodern text does not simply
exclude an epistemological position, but is fully a sign of *epistemological
surrender.* The world has lost visibility, corporeality, and comprehen-
sibility. New modes of experience have not yet fully arisen to ground
and explain the subject within these new realities, although some postmodern textual practices represent remarkable attempts at such new
mappings. Here is the point at which the subject disappears from our
fictions as coherent sites of exploration, to be replaced by worlds and
zones whose rules of functioning are precisely *not* to be determined.

Science fiction also stands as a significant cartographic mode. The
language of science fiction has been threatening to emerge numerous
times in this discussion of "worlds in collision," and McHale is fully cognizant of the genre's relevance to his understanding of postmodern
fiction. Unlike David Porush, whose book on cybernetic fictions fails to
address the genre at all,[146] McHale finds much to value in SF: "Science
fiction, like postmodernist fiction, is governed by the ontological dominant. Indeed, it is perhaps *the* ontological genre *par excellence.* We
can think of science fiction as postmodernism's noncanonized or 'low
art' double, its sister-genre in the same sense that the popular detective thriller is modernist fiction's sister-genre" (59). The "cognitive estrangement" which Darko Suvin has defined as central to the genre
foregrounds the ontological status of the world in ways fully assimilable
to McHale's terms.[147] "World" becomes literalized in tales which are
about different stars and planets, and by playing the structures of
different worlds against each other (as in Ursula Le Guin's *The Dispossessed*), these ontological structures and their meanings are tex-

tually foregrounded. Even in much of the genre's most banal output, the universe is a heterotopic space.

Samuel Delany's introduction to *Empire,* a comic book scripted by Delany and illustrated by Howard Chaykin, contains this sense of SF as an ontologically significant, heterotopic discourse (it is also remarkably similar to comments by Joanna Russ—see the Introduction):

> But it is just that multiplicity of worlds, each careening in its particular orbit about the vast sweep of interstellar night, which may be the subtlest, most pervasive, and finally the most valuable thing in s-f. . . . It's a basic image which, if you let it, can almost totally revise the gravity-bound, upper/lower organization which holds up (or holds down) so much of our thinking. . . . The whole concept of an endless, linear, vertical measure, ever mounting and with no ceiling, has given way to the concept of relative, unfixed centers, different worlds, different points of view related only by direction, distance and trajectory. . . . This experience of constant de-centered de-centeredness, each decentering on a vaster and vaster scale, has a venerable name among people who talk about science fiction: "the sense of wonder."[148]

The "de-centered de-centeredness" of science fiction came to inform the language strategies of many postmodern novelists.

In a provocative moment McHale goes so far as to compare Philip José Farmer's Riverworld series with Samuel Beckett's *The Lost Ones.* In each fiction the world is figured as a giant machine, with a limited set of invariable rules; a closed cybernetic system, in other words. Both involve transitory limbolike spaces, although Farmer's is macrocosmic— a planet large enough to hold all the Earth's resurrected dead—while Beckett's is a cylinder only fifty meters wide and sixteen meters high. McHale demonstrates the narrative imperatives that structure the popular Farmer text but which are rejected by Beckett, and thus genre and literature are posited as finally separate in practice.[149] It can be argued that McHale underestimates Farmer and Dick; nevertheless, he remains one of the few critics to recognize *the influence of the genre on postmodernism* as well as the concurrent impact of postmodernism on the genre.[150]

Urban Zones and Cyber Zones

It is now possible to return to Delany's discussion of science fiction paraspaces, with the new recognition that these spaces are identical to the Zones of McHale's analysis. Paraspaces similarly involve an ontological shift, as they redefine and extend the realms of experience and human definition in contradistinction to the possibilities inherent in normal space. "Fragmentary possible worlds coexist," as McHale stated. What is demolished in paraspace and zone is any vision of fixed space, subjectivity, or language, as these new, and radically mutating, ontologies emerge. "More and more," writes cyberpunk theorist Istvan Csicsery-Ronay, Jr., "SF treats hallucination as an object in the world," as a result of "the impossibility of drawing clear boundaries around perceptual and cognitive, indeed even ontological, categories."[151]

These manipulations of cinematic and literary language, at once poetic and ludic, help to situate the "fluid neon origami trick" of Gibson's cyberspace. The imploded regions of cyberspace recall the hallucinatory excesses of the New Wave, but with a greater physicality. "His mouth filled with an aching taste of blue," Gibson writes in a knowing appropriation of Bester's synaesthetic trope: "The cold was the taste of lemons." Rhetoricity is connected to technology—that "other space" is always materially, technologically, constituted—in fact, Delany claims that rhetoricity *allegorizes* technology (the implications of which are discussed below). This is nowhere truer than it is of cyberspace, for that "consensual hallucination" is the designated space where access is permitted to the invisible power structures and data linkages of the Information Era. That cyberspace is an hallucination, an artificially induced visualization of the global data system, enhances its allegorical function—its poetic excess is precisely the point. The human remains reduced by this interface with a complex other space in which the world's most significant activities occur. In ordinary space, Delany states, "characters are likely to forget that technological contouring" which surrounds them in both real- and cyberspaces.[152] In cyberspace the rhetorical intensity foregrounds the estrangement of technology for both character and reader, even while it permits a limited interface.

Csicsery-Ronay finds in cyberpunk's weary technological hipness the very apotheosis of postmodernism, while Jameson's volume on postmodernism cites Gibson on the first page and calls cyberpunk "the supreme *literary* expression if not of postmodernism, then of late capitalism itself."[153] McHale's more recent writings understand cyberpunk in a more precise relationship to postmodern fiction, noting, for example, extensive overlaps between Pynchon's fiction and certain cyberpunk tropes.[154] He claims that "part of cyberpunk's significance derives from the changing relationship between SF and 'mainstream' fiction in recent decades" (312). This marks a shift from earlier periods, when New Wave SF borrowed from older modernist models while mainstream fiction claimed "classic" SF tropes for its own use. Now "postmodernized SF mingl[es] with postmodernism: here we see just how tight the feedback loop has become" (318). If Gibson borrows from Burroughs and Pynchon, then Kathy Acker and Don Delillo are poised to reappropriate that appropriation. McHale goes so far as to define cyberpunk as "a convenient name for the kind of writing that springs up where the converging trajectories of SF poetics and postmodernist poetics finally cross."[155]

While modernism began to problematize the status of the self, these "centrifugal tendencies" were "never brought to full fruition . . . until the emergence of a postmodern poetics that explores and problematizes the ontologies of worlds and texts."[156] Postmodern fiction stages the breakdown of the self figuratively, through discursive strategies, while cyberpunk constructs diegetic objects that stage the formation of a new "centrifugal self" and ground the linguistic deformations. Because of its literalness, therefore, cyberpunk does not represent the same rejection of high/low (or other) boundaries in culture as postmodern fiction. Concentrating on Gibson, cyberpunk's premiere rhetorician, McHale observes that juxtaposition is Gibson's primary rhetorical tactic. Gibson admits as much: "Assembled word *cyberspace* from small and readily available components of language. Neologic spasm: the primal act of pop poetics. Preceded any concept whatever. Slick and hollow—awaiting received meaning."[157] McHale further notes that Gibson depends upon *incongruous* juxtapositions: "Gibson's fiction functions at every level, even down to the 'micro' structures of phrases and neologisms, on the principle of incongruous juxtaposition—juxtapositions of American culture with Japanese culture, of high technology with the subcultures of the 'street' and the underworld and so on. The term 'cyberpunk' itself has been constructed according to this incongruity principle" (310). These "incongruous juxtapositions" or "mongrelizations" don't *elide* cultural hierarchies, they *revel* in them: "The effect of incongruity here and elsewhere in Gibson's writing obviously depends on the persistence of hierarchical cultural categories" and not on their dissolution (310).

McHale makes a valuable point, one crucial to his sense that there *is* a difference between "postmodernized SF" and postmodernist fiction. That these are presented in cyberpunk as *threatened* boundaries, and sites of deep anxiety, is nevertheless incontestable. Veronica Hollinger is more attuned to the ambiguities of cyberpunk when she describes the "conflictual framework of realist literary conventions played out in the postmodernist field" as characteristic of cyberpunk fiction.[158] In her model each literary tradition undermines the other, producing a hugely self-conscious rhetorical system. If Hollinger seems, in her turn, overly optimistic regarding cyberpunk's radical potentials, her major argument is very useful.

As I have shown, the specific phenomenological space that cyberspace constructs is imbricated with the rise of minimalism as well as the prevalence of a dislocating urbanism. The phenomenological and sociological impact of urban space has led to a commensurate rhetorical intensification in the pages of postmodern, as well as science, fiction. McHale's interesting distinction between epistemological and ontological dominants offers a more complete understanding of the differences between the often identical strategies of modernist and postmodernist representation. For example, Sharpe and Wallock note that: "The city is the locus of Modernism, and each aspect of city life seems to generate or demonstrate a characteristic of this artistic movement—multiplicity of meaning, loss of sequential or causal connection, breakdown of signification, and dissolution of community. For artists and writers the modern city has come to mean as much a style, a fractured syntax, a paratactic sign system, as a physical construct with certain demonstrable boundaries" (11). The language in this passage inevitably recalls the terms Jameson used in his elaboration of the "cultural dominant" of postmodernism.[159] What, then, has changed in the transition from the condition of modernity to postmodernity? Quite simply, through the shift in the experience and definition of the city from centralized place to dispersed "nonspace," the city has passed beyond the sensory powers of the individual, and thus the same literary-artistic systems represent a different reality. While the epistemological dominant of modernism produced a fragmented and pluralistic set of representational systems to encompass the perceptual engagement with the urban environment, this has yielded to a related set of representational systems that write the passage of the city beyond the parameters of perception itself.

The city has therefore become a Zone, in which categories have indeed been blurred badly. *New Worlds* editor Michael Moorcock has thoroughly mapped the urban zone of London; first in the extended explorations of the uncertainties of Pop-era London in the Jerry Cornelius novels, "the Cornelius adventures were a dark comedy set not just in space and time, but in all spaces and all times; . . . in Moorcock's all-connecting 'Multiverse,' that realm of infinite possibilities"[160] and later in such broader historical fictions as *Mother London* (1988).

In an interview with Delany, Takayuki Tatsumi points out that the paraspaces of Delany's own fiction are *social,* rather than simply technological.[161] The postmodern city has indeed become a paraspace. The absence of coordinates and boundaries, combined with a paradoxical depthlessness, creates a space that is no space, no place. The spaces of Delany's cities—especially Bellona in the massive *Dhalgren* (1975)—are perfect examples of McHale's zones. Bellona has suffered an unspecified cataclysm, and the populace has largely fled. For those who have remained, and for those who have even migrated *to* the wounded city, Bellona is a site of social and subjective redefinition. Apocalyptic visions of double suns abound, to be briefly marveled at by the populace. Such impossible cities, be they designed by Calvino, Moebius, Pynchon, or Delany, alter without reason. As those other city planners, the Situationists, noted, "Any sign or word is susceptible to being converted into something else," a formula that acknowledges the ontological instabilities of contemporary urbanism. The subject is neither the causative agent nor the epistemological center of these shifting realities. There *is* no center.

The Situationists' division of the city echoes the psychologist's topology of the brain. "The districts . . . could correspond to the whole spectrum of diverse feelings that one encounters *by chance* in everyday life," Ivan Chtcheglov proposes, listing the Bizarre and Happy Quarters as examples.[162] The city is linked to the condition of subjectivity, but in these later cities of postmodern representation, it is the subject that is formed in response to the conditions of existence—the world can be understood as a subjective projection no longer. In Delany's *Triton* (1978) the city includes an "unlicensed sector" of permitted anarchy—a classic zone. A similar anarchic sector appears in Sterling's *The Artificial Kid* (1980). The Ninsei sector in *Neuromancer* is another: Case reflects that "burgeoning technologies require outlaw zones. . . . Night City wasn't there for its inhabitants, but as a deliberately unsupervised playground for technology itself" (11). These zones represent the libido of the technocratic city (although in *Neuromancer* the libido is carefully monitored and controlled). To map the city through the language of psychoanalysis might indicate its status as subjective projection, or— and this seems more accurate—it might represent the very usurpation of subjectivity by the urban configuration.

Urban space becomes a space of performance in the unlicensed zones, as it has for many subcultures, and the stylistic and rhetorical excesses of rock and roll undergrounds since the 1950s demonstrates that more than just an attitude is shared by punk and cyberpunk; they overlap in their urbanism as well. John Clute's introduction to Moorcock's Jerry Cornelius series, an important precursor of cyberpunk, locates the city as a spectacular space that obviates the very existence of a fixed subjectivity: "identity in the city is a costume drama. The presentation of self in everyday life in the inner city is a form of theatre, where identity is role and where entropy is high, for time is passing." Jonathan Raban writes: "in the city we can change our identities at will, as Dickens triumphantly proved over and over again in his fiction; its discontinuity favours both instant heroes and instant villains impartially."[163] The Cornelius novels (something of a cross between Dickens and Burroughs) have presented a desperate vaudeville of urban deformations: "Jerry Cornelius is the paradigmatic native of the inner city," Clute continues. "His constant failures are the failures of the city."[164] The condition of the city and the condition of the subject become identical.

A remarkable comic book, *Mr. X,* depicts another urban failure that encapsulates many dominant postmodern figures—*Blade Runner* filtered through Gabriel García Márquez.[165] Mr. X, the designer of Somnopolis, aka Radiant City, returns to destroy his corrupted creation. The city was constructed according to the principles of *psychetecture:* "the theory that the very shape and size of a room could alter a person's mood or neurosis" (here the Situationist *psychogeography* is combined with Le Corbusier's Radiant City). But his city has been altered. The flat, cartoony artwork of Jaime and Gilbert Hernandez depicts an ontologically uncertain zone of competing anachronisms where no two clocks agree, figures perpetually fling themselves to the ground below, humans and robots coexist in a purposeless *ennui.* Mr. X is devastated ("The subtleties of my psychetecture . . . *destroyed*"). Dreams of efficient control are over, and the "artist-hero of the machine age, the industrial designer"[166] is an insomniac, endlessly cataloging the casualties of his designs. The rationality of urban planning is now an outmoded vehicle of megalomaniacal control; a misguided attempt to impose a center on a chaotic, surreal, existence. Mr. X (also known as, variously, Walter Eichmann, Santos, and Michael) marks a shift from controlling center to shifting subject. Mr. X is *sous rature,* as his name(s) implies and so is the city.

By mapping cyberspace onto just this sort of entropic urbanism and slippery subjectivity, Gibson blurs the separation between normal- and paraspaces: a tricky maneuver with important implications. The neon spaces of *Neuromancer,* explicable in science fiction terms as a "consensual hallucination" of the "infinite datascape," *allude* to the shifting opalescences of postmodern representation, while the distance produced by that allusion allows the text to resist the reassuring certainty of postmodernism's predictable *un*-certainties. Here undecidability operates in full force, as the constitution of cyberspace becomes a site of ontological break *and* continuity.

As noted, the rhetorical effects of *Neuromancer* depend upon the thick fusion of idiolects which Gibson, the genre's premier *bricoleur,* deploys. If cyberspace is "like film compiled from random frames," then so is the language of the novel (here, for example, he alludes to Burroughs). Gibson's prose is built, like the Cornell boxes which figure in *Count Zero,* upon the detritus of other arts, other fields; like the space of a Cornell box, it is densely allusive and profoundly mysterious. The space of the text is deeply cultural in origin, explicitly contoured by other writers, genres, and voices. Language becomes the site of the origin of the subject, a site of identity. The heavily referential space of the text thus removes that origin to a site *outside* the subject and *inside* the technologies of information.

Reflexively textual in its rhetorical excess as well as its definition as, literally, *embodied data,* cyberspace allegorizes electronic technology and the reading process. In cyberspace, data (text) becomes physical space in a manner commensurate with the ontological and literary mutations of the postmodern literary text. The subject (character and reader) is redefined, or at least realigned, within a new experiential reality. Thus *Neuromancer* itself comprises a compacted, imploded, data space, a paraspace that sacrifices the referentiality of traditional narrative for a resonant representation of terminal *experience.* The readers' experiential realities (the realities of cities, television, computers, shopping malls, and other imploded fields) are impacted, condensed, abstracted, and returned to their gaze:

> It came on, again, gradually, a flickering, non-linear flood of fact and sensory data, a kind of narrative conveyed in surreal jumpcuts and juxtapositions. It was vaguely like riding a rollercoaster that phased in and out of existence at random, impossibly rapid intervals, changing altitude, attack, and direction with each pulse of nothingness, except that the shifts had nothing to do with any physical orientation, but rather with lightning alternations in paradigm and symbol-system. The data had never been intended for human input.[167]

Here, in *Count Zero,* the paradigms of postmodern art are distilled to their phenomenological essence. In *Mona Lisa Overdrive,* Angela might stand in for the ideal reader *after* reading Gibson's cyberspace trilogy:

"Angela Mitchell comprehends this room and its inhabitants through shifting data planes that represent viewpoints, though of whom or what, she is in most cases in doubt. There is a considerable degree of overlap, of contradiction."[168]

Jameson noted of Herr's writing in *Dispatches* that: "The first terrible postmodernist war cannot be told in any of the traditional paradigms. . . . [I]ndeed that breakdown of all previous narrative paradigms is, along with the breakdown of any shared language through which a veteran might convey such experience, among the principal subjects of the book."[169] Cyberspace constitutes the first terrible postmodernist *battleground,* formed by "this new and virtually unimaginable quantum leap in technological alienation." The cyberspace cowboys are those veterans whose experience of technological fusion is literally ecstatic. Through the introduction of a densely impacted idiolect, language becomes both a means of speaking this "technological alienation" and of accommodating oneself to it. The language inscribes the mastery of the subject over the technology and its space. This "ecstasy of communication" (or information) is what Jameson fails to see in Herr's prose, and what Coppola and Kubrick captured in collaborations with Herr (*Apocalypse Now* [1979]; *Full Metal Jacket* [1987]). Mere alienation is no longer permissible, no longer useful, no longer interesting, no longer *relevant.* The technological space demands a new cognition. Of course, Gibson's narrative paradigm includes a strong, central hero whose abilities and knowledge put him beyond the reach of mortal men, rather than Herr's weary and disoriented journalist, but the language retains the dislocations of syntagmatic breakdown. The result is neither ecstasy nor alienation, but some deeply ambivalent entwining of the two.

Return to Paraspace (Into the Quanta)

The ontological refiguration which permeates science fiction and postmodernism is not solely the product of decadent late-capitalist sensibilities, but derives in part from the radical redefinition of objective phenomena which has taken place in a world governed by the laws of quantum mechanics. This arcane branch of physics has enjoyed a boom period in the age of postmodernism, due to a spate of popular texts which revel in the "violently acausal" models of occurrence which hold at the submicroscopic level of quanta. To the realm of quantum physics belongs Heisenberg's Principle of Indeterminism, which holds that the observer cannot help but affect the thing observed. The status of the quanta, and whether it behaves as a particle or a wave, is determined solely by the method and period of observation. Perception, then, determines ontology to a provocative degree. The universe becomes a randomly oscillating subset of all possible states, and there may be multiple, and perhaps infinite, universes flickering into existence at all given moments. Without hyperbole, standard notions of linearity, causality, temporality, and ontology have been thrown into disarray in the face of a mechanical model predicated on the notion that, at some point, all empirical evidence is worthless.[170]

It is surely not within my capabilities to validate this current worldview, but a familiarity with the basic principles has gained wide currency at the end of the 1980s, from the arcana of Douglas R. Hofstadter's *Gödel, Escher, Bach* and Stephen Hawking's *A Brief History of Time* to lighter fare such as Fred Wolf's *Taking the Quantum Leap* and *SPY* magazine's article on quantum mechanics and time travel.[171] The "spin," or interpretation, which these different commentators place upon the new uncertainties of existence is interesting. Timothy Ferris, in his *Coming of Age in the Milky Way,* is able to fit quantum mechanics into an overall cosmogeny which has always seemed somewhat heretical and which was always able to be overturned on the basis of new evidence and methods of perception and measurement. In other words, Ferris's broad perspective enables him to gracefully assimilate the apparent discontinuities of the quantum field to the continuity of the history of radical science. *SPY* magazine, which has been at times emblematic of both the best and worst tendencies of a postmodern zeitgeist, emphasizes the liberating effects of an acausality which permits us to fully co-opt the past and future to our own trivial pursuits. And Fred Alan Wolf (whose book for the lay reader frequently begins sentences with "And") reassuringly posits the disjunctive findings of quantum mechanics as an empowerment of the observer who unproblematically grounds reality: "Perhaps the order of the universe may be the order of our own minds," he writes.

On some level, quantum mechanics represents an overturning, not just of Newtonian physics, but of Einsteinian spatiotemporality as well. Einstein is a paradigmatic modernist figure: principles of relativity were not predicated upon the denial of causality, but notions of absolute knowledge were disavowed because the position of the observer was relative to the thing observed. Einstein stopped short of embracing a thorough relativism; he was unable to accept the postulate that *everything* was relative. His model of the universe still contained immutable laws of motion, temporality, and causality. In the world of quantum physics, on the other hand, the observer fundamentally *determines* events. The universe is cast as a field of possibilities devoid of absolute causation. Fred Alan Wolf writes, "Our perceptions of reality will, consequently, appear somewhat contradictory, dualistic, and paradoxical. The instantaneous experience of the reality of Now will not appear paradoxical at all. It is only when we observers attempt to construct a history of our perceptions that reality seems paradoxical."[172] The postmodern repercussions are obvious. The task of history is doomed in the absence of a model that can avoid paradox, and paradoxically, it is the desire for order and explanation that brings paradox into existence in the first place.

At the subatomic level, then, we find the ultimate paraspace, an imploded and "violently acausal" realm in which the ontological status of subject and universe is opened to question and positioned for redefinition. Small wonder, then, that science fiction has gained new prominence as a narrative and phenomenological paradigm. Quantum mechanics and postmodernism become metaphors for each other in their mutual privileging of uncertainty, indeterminism, acausality, and nonlinearity, while science fiction anchors these unsettling phenomena within the relative familiarity of its narrative structures. Within a quantum world, science fiction both privileges the estrangement of subject and world and grounds them in a deterministic, if shifting, structure.

The SF Text as Paraspace

Barry Malzberg's *Galaxies* allegorizes the relation between new physics and new narrative most effectively.[173] Malzberg has constructed an elegant modern novel about the impossibility of narration, and science fiction, with its impossible spaces and times, becomes emblematic of the futility of the narrative act. The subjectivity of the author dominates the events and subsumes characters and actions in a thorough erasure of their very claims to reality. "[T]his will not be a novel so much as a series of notes for one," he begins.

Yet science fiction, in keeping with McHale's observations of the genre's practices, alters Malzberg's modernist paradigm in ways he might not have anticipated. The drama of the starship being dragged into the maw of a black hole provides a metaphor for the breakdown of narrative causality and sequence, but the reverse is also true, as the breakdown of the signifying chains of narrative find their analogue in a physical reality that obliterates experience, causality, history, and, consequently, the definition of the subject. Malzberg's subjectivity takes a new position within the indeterminate, post-Einsteinian fields of faster-than-light "tachyon drives" and collapsed neutron stars. There is a mapping of the epistemological uncertainties of modernism onto the ontological indeterminism of quantum science and science fiction. The crisis of subjectivity is repositioned as an ontological crisis, rather than simply as an epistemological one.

The language of paraspace allegorizes technology, according to Delany. Paul de Man has written that "allegory designates primarily a distance in relation to its own origin, and, renouncing the nostalgia and the desire to coincide, it establishes its language in the void of this temporal difference." The space constructed in these zones and paraspaces is a function of literary or cinematic syntagms and thus is inherently temporal as well as spatial. A profound crisis of *time* arises in these zones to accompany the spatial crisis, an event that, to de Man, "corresponds to the unveiling of an authentically temporal destiny"; in other words, to the inevitability of the death of the subject and the existence of a nonself. Allegory "prevents the self from an illusory identification with the non-self, which is now fully, though painfully, recognized as a non-self."[174] The figures of allegory break the transparency of language and institute instead a metafigural zone of problematic identifications (an apt description of Malzberg's project in *Galaxies*). The mutability of language in the zones and paraspaces of postmodern science fiction coincide with this allegorical impulse (although the exigencies of narrative often recontain the paraspatial excess).

Delany's definition of the science fiction paraspace as a zone of heightened rhetoricity and linguistic defamiliarization ultimately demands comparison with his more general theories of the functioning of language within the genre. Delany has argued that the language of science fiction enacts a continual defamiliarization of language. The value of the genre may be found in the operations it performs on its readers, when, for instance, figural language becomes literalized by the text ("Then her world exploded," is a favorite Delany example) or a range of possible meanings becomes expanded ("He turned on his left side"). Therefore: "We must think of literature and science fiction not as two different sets of labeled texts, but as two different sets of values, two different ways of response, two different ways of making texts make sense, two different ways of reading. . . . The encounter, then, is between two discourses, science fiction and literature."[175] It could be argued that, for Delany, the genre of science fiction *itself* comprises a kind of paraspace—a site of ontological confrontation characterized by an intensified engagement with the structures of language and experienced by the reader as being in collision with mundane reality. The genre is already defined by such an intensification, and thus his conception of the paraspace seems redundant in its dependence upon a heightened heightening. There are some differences, though, that make the para-space crucial to understanding the contemporary importance of the genre.

The major difference, of course, is that the different ontological realm of the paraspace is experienced by the *characters* within the diegesis, such as the unfortunate captain of the starship *Skipstone* in *Galaxies*. When *Neuromancer's* Case frequents the arcades and clubs of Chiba City, the technologism of his environment eludes him. But his return to the hypertechnologized arenas of cyberspace is marked by a rhetorical excess which describes—enacts—his own experience. When we first meet Gully Foyle, he is adrift in "a weightless emptiness of blinding sun and jet shadow, frozen and silent," but it is the synaesthesia which truly dislocates Foyle, the character, from his ontological sphere. Delany states: "Ordinary space is just as technologically contoured as any of these technologically constituted paraspaces. . . . But ordinary space (like ordinary language) is the place where the characters are likely to forget that technological contouring, just as characters, enmeshed in ordinary language, are likely to lose the sense of its rhetoricity."[176] The paraspace is always constituted as an other space for the characters and exerts tangible effects upon them. It is the space in which the *character's* language, rationality, and subjectivity are broken down and deconstructed. That is precisely the function of rhetoric, according to de Man: "Rhetoric radically suspends logic and opens up vertiginous possibilities of referential aberration," and these aberrations have profound implications for any subsequent discussions of being and ontology.[177]

Merleau-Ponty has written that perception occurs with the entire body, and not simply according to a set of discrete sensory apparatuses. The emphatic nature of sense perception is a relative rarity. Within his phenomenology, synaesthesia represents a confrontation with a totalized, rather than compartmentalized, activity of perception: "Synaesthetic perception is the rule, and we are unaware of it only because scientific knowledge shifts the centre of gravity of experience, so that we have unlearned how to see, hear, and generally speaking, feel, in order to deduce, from our bodily organization and the world as the physicist conceives it, what we are to see, hear and feel."[178] This is remarkably close to Delany's paraspaces, which reveal the technological contouring usually ignored, forgotten, or "unlearned." The rhetorical deconstruction of science fiction thus doubles its operations as a narrative form of phenomenal exploration and definition, while synaesthesia represents the overlap of rhetorical and perceptual recontouring. Further, if the paraspace represents a new field *within* the diegesis, then the ontological shifts of postmodern fiction are now grounded and explicated. The representation of the alternative space is linguistically heightened to connote the overloading or estranging of the characters' sensory apparatus. Language thus regains a mimetic function. For Delany, presumably, this would be an example of the undecidability of language in SF, and so it exemplifies the metafigural discourse that recommends the genre.

Perhaps the axiomatic paraspace occurs in the penultimate scenes of *2001,* in what was once known as the "trip sequence." In this sublime and psychedelic display, an already intensified cinematic rhetoric is taken still further. The film permits its special effects an almost languid spectacularity, as the widescreen camera lingers in a series of long takes.[179] Shot/reverse shot structures are similarly distended in time and space, and narrative is displaced by technological choreography. In the trip sequence, all these tropes are exaggerated. The effects become less definitively representational and take on that undecidability to which Delany refers. The viewer cannot know if these images are mimetic (they might be, but mimetic of *what?*), so representational and figurative languages are condensed. The close-ups of the astronaut are reduced to tinted, still-frame insertions of a single eye, underscoring the inadequacy of his perceptual-cognitive apparatus and transforming the perceiver into an object to be perceived. Finally, the causative structures of narrative, already underemphasized, are entirely elided.[180]

The sequence initiates a foregrounding of perception, representation, and cognition in both Dave and the viewer. Annette Michelson writes, "Experience as Vision ends in the exploration of seeing," which she locates as the film's reflexive strategy.[181] It is not coincidental that this is all preparation for an evolutionary journey beyond the individual and beyond the human. The finale, when the Starchild returns to Earth, signifies a passage beyond the strictures of a familiar ontology. Logic is suspended, and "vertiginous possibilities" emerge through referential aberrations. The intensification of this paraspatial sequence performs an ontological deconstruction *within the diegesis* as well as for the film viewer. These emphatic figurations operate for reader and character. One result is that the character becomes an infradiegetic surrogate for the reader, and the paraspace becomes what de Man termed an allegory of reading.

While no other narrative film quite approaches the destabilizing levels of *2001,* an interesting example is Douglas Trumbull's 1983 film, *Brainstorm.* The narrative is predicated upon the invention of a sensory recording/playback apparatus which will permit the encoding of all sensory information. Rooms full of people test the equipment, each nodding in stimulated bliss, while inserts reveal what they are experiencing: an auto race, a horse ride, a bacchanal. The military (of course) seeks to co-opt the technology by using tapes of psychotic breakdowns as brainwashing tools. Trumbull originally wished to present the experiences relayed by the invention by projecting those sequences at sixty frames per second, but finally had to settle for using a wider-screen ratio to connote the sensory recordings. What is at stake here is a "realer than real" experience in the insert sequences, an extension of what André Bazin called "the myth of total cinema." The allusion to an enhanced sensory engagement with the apparatus is created by an intensification of the cinematic rhetoric (heightened resolution, boosted sound, enlarged screen, exaggerated kinesis). For a special effects technician such as Trumbull, the yearning for a totalistic experience of cinema is palpable, and the characters in the film become surrogates for the cinematic creators and spectators.[182] The film's most effective sequence shows the process of dying being recorded and later played back. The image pulls back from the body of the lifeless woman, and the image becomes a bubble amongst millions of others: a cosmos of memories. The spirit continues to rise, joining others wafting toward the infinite. Once again the paraspace does not simply hyperbolize rhetoric, but brings as its consequence the death of the subject in the physical *and* referential sense. (Of course, God is held out as the ultimate signified, even if direct experience remains impossible.)

Even more to the point of de Man's analysis of rhetoric as a metafigural device is Norman Spinrad's 1983 novel, *The Void Captain's Tale,* due to the self-consciousness of its prose and the close imbrication of language, narrative and dramatic theme. First, Spinrad's text is deeply dislocating to the reader throughout, as the future which it posits features a polyglot language comprised of old Earth tongues, including German, French, and Japanese, and so the novel is always engaged in a particularly heightened rhetoricity—a fine example of text *as* paraspace. Further, mythological allusions are explicit (the captain writes that "one tale-telling mode would have me recite my exploits and adventures") as is their function. The "void" to which the title refers is the vast distance between the stars, a region described by the captain in paraspatial terms: "For the merest instant, the purest augenblick, the great latticework tunnel blurred into the apparent solidity of tremendous relative motion, the stars in the central circle dopplered through blue into violet and beyond, as we seemed to hurtle forward into an unreal universe of ultraviolet pinpricks through black velvet keening into eye-killing transvisibility."[183] Ideas of blurring, unreality, and perceptual failure are raised in this brief excerpt. The void arouses primal fears, and elaborate rituals hide its existence from the starship passengers. Simulation chambers can replicate any environment: thus fiction masks the terrors of the void.

Even the role of the captain is based in fiction; he is merely a psychologically necessary simulacrum of a controlling persona; on this occasion, he is unable to forget "that the drama of conning my ship as the starfield eased gracefully into new configuration was illusion, that we were moving along a ballistically inevitable curve as beyond my control as kismet" (26). The same is true of the elaborate shipboard rituals: "In those bygone days when starfaring meant generations spent in a single voyage, it was soon learned that only ships large enough to be worlds entire could sanely convey their human cargo from star to star, indeed that further, only carefully crafted shipboard cultures would prove viable: those in which rite, art, festival, entertainment, indeed interior architecture itself, were all designed to concentrate consciousness on the world inside, and to avoid excessive true awareness of the absolute reality without" (33). The textual system of the novel is thus marked by two heightened paraspaces—the dark abyss of interstellar space and the colorful, busy, simulated spaces aboard ship.

A (somewhat existential) allegory of reading is clearly established among these intersecting rhetorical constructs. The fictions of ritual and myth are a mode of coping with, assimilating, the technological conditions and limits of existence. The paraspace of the void is the site of human limits, the boundaries of being and the death of the subject. The shipboard myths are substituted for the void—simulation substitutes for narrative as a mode of emplotment, and grounds the unknown in the terms and rhetoric of the familiar. That the language of *The Void Captain's Tale* should be so overburdened alludes to the desperation of denial that language enacts against the "unveiling of an authentically temporal destiny" (de Man). The mask of language is both excessive and inadequate. Language cannot, finally, produce its object. The void remains.

If the rituals played out aboard ship function as a means of technological adaptation and denial, then it is a simple matter to read the novel as an allegorization, not just of technology and science, but of science fiction as well. The decadent passengers are readers, and sometimes tellers, of tales. The mythic forms of shipboard existence ground human experience as effectively as the technological imagination of science fiction, and similarly endow the alienating forces of invisible technologies with a phenomenal familiarity and a vulnerability to human control. The figural excesses of the diegetic shipboard dramas recenter the subject as the agent of cause and meaning, while Spinrad's own metafigural excesses reveal the subject as a rhetorical effect. Spinrad's prose permits the reader a cognition of narrative's purpose and an understanding of the specific functioning of the science fiction text. In a later essay McHale draws identical conclusions to my own: "The paraspace motif . . . not only serves to bring into view the 'worldness' of world; it also offers the possibility of reflecting on world making itself, and on science fiction worldmaking in particular. Paraspace is, at least potentially, a scale model of the fictional world itself, a fictional-world-within-the-fictional-world."[184]

Science fiction restores to the zones of postmodernism their radical mutability and restores to the reader the uncertainties of rhetorical and technological engagement. Cyberspace, further, grounds its phenomenology in ontology—the historically specific ontology of the Dataist Era, the Information Age. Subject dislocation is enacted by a movement through an excruciatingly technological, decentering spatiality. The site of origin of the subject passes first outside the body and then inside the terminal. But cyberspace is also fully situated within the general paraspatial configurations of the genre of science fiction, wherein the rhetoric of the genre deconstructs the transparent figurations of language and so refuses the subject a fixed site of identification. Such a deconstruction does not point to an *annihilation* of subjectivity, but rather to the limits of the existing paradigms. The subject is deconstructed through the interrelated synaesthetic operations of technology, narrative, and language. Phenomenologically and rhetorically, then, the subject is *broken down* in the zones of cyberspatial simulation, there to await its reconstitution amidst these fields of data.

Coda—Baudrillard in the Zone

For reasons that should now be apparent, much contemporary philosophy has come to roost in the technologically manifested paraspaces of science fiction. Donna Haraway, Paul Virilio, Deleuze and Guattari all occupy a niche that Istvan Csicsery-Ronay, Jr., has called "the science fiction of theory," but Baudrillard occupies a privileged niche. I regard Baudrillard not as a techno-prophet in the Toffler mode, and still less as a philosopher sharing kinship with, say, Bataille or Foucault, but rather as the producer of a particular language that shares everything with the hypertechnologized languages of the science fictional paraspace. Baudrillard produces a discourse in which our technological contours are emphasized through a rhetorical heightening. The result is a synaesthesia not dissimilar to the displacing rhetorics of Bester, Dick, or Zelazny.

We are the characters in a science fiction by Jean Baudrillard that could be subtitled (with a nod to Robert Heinlein) "If this goes on . . . ," and his synaesthetic collapse is directed at us. His calculated retreat to a strategy of evocation seems an appropriate method of modeling the electronic deluge: "Today it is the very space of habitation that is conceived as both receiver and distributor, as the space of both reception and operations, the control screen and terminal which as such may be endowed with telematic power—that is, with the capability of regulating everything from a distance. . . . Simulators of leisure or of vacations in the home—like flight simulators for airplane pilots—become conceivable. Here we are far from the living room and close to science fiction."[185] This is philosophy as a computer game: "What I advance here is an exercise in simulation": "I am no longer in a state to 'reflect' on something, I can only push hypotheses to their limits, snatch them from their critical zones of reference, take them beyond a point of no return. I also take theory into the hyper-space of simulation—in which it loses all objective validity, but perhaps it gains in coherence, that is, in a real affinity with the system which surrounds us."[186] In these writings Baudrillard seeks recourse in the language and extrapolative techniques of SF to construct a new *space* for philosophy, one far removed from those "critical zones of reference" which belong to another era, not to the epoch of implosion. Evoking Bataille, Baudrillard writes that theory "must become excessive and sacrificial to speak about excess and sacrifice. . . . It is not enough for theory to describe and analyse, it must itself be an event in the universe it describes."[187] The theorist is no longer permitted "critical distance," for the theorist is also "in the zone," also an event in the universe to be described. This is a position Baudrillard tenaciously developed in the early 1980s. Whatever Baudrillard's limitations as a philosopher, and they are undoubtedly legion, his paraspatial strategies nevertheless seem eminently defensible.

Baudrillard is a cyborg writer, superimposing a technologism—that always exceeds rationalist bounds—upon the familiarity of what we continue to call "direct experience." Baudrillard's own "master-narrative" is thus a science fiction that repeatedly (and obsessively) narrates the loss of narration, and builds its coherence from the evocation of *in-*coherence. He notes: "It is thus not necessary to write science fiction" because we are in it.[188] Like the hacker hero of *TRON,* Baudrillard is irresistibly drawn into the terminal (para)space of simulation, the grids and matrices of the Master Computer.

TERMINAL

SPACE

3 TERMINAL PENETRATION

NARRATIVE AND VIRTUAL REALITIES   In their

imaginations they saw the cinema as a total and complete representation of

reality; they saw in a trice the reconstruction of a perfect illusion of the out-

side world in sound, color and relief.—André Bazin, 1946   ¶ But in the com-

puter country, they dream of eliminating the interface, of breaking down the

barrier of the screen and eliminating the distinctions made between this side

and that side.—Karrie Jacobs, 1990

By now the image is becoming familiar—but not quite. A figure stands in
a kind of high-tech bondage. Wires and cables snake from gloves and
sensors to a pair of hard-crunching computers off to the side. The head
is enshrouded by an elaborate apparatus that blocks the subject's eyes
and ears. The figure stands in an uneasy crouch, reaching out to grasp
the invisible air. This is not, however, some sensory deprivation night-

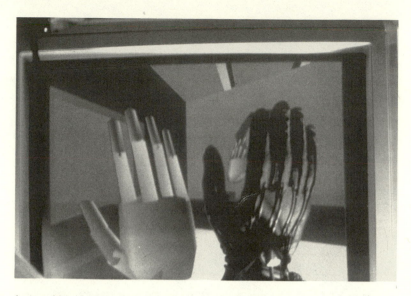

A virtual hand and its real world counterpart. Dataglove™ and virtual world by VPL Research.

mare. The subject is comfortably ensconced in *virtual reality,* a cyber-netic paraspace comprised of real-time interactive data. The cables are connected to sensors, providing a computer with information regarding the subject's bodily orientation. The helmet apparatus feeds the sub-ject visual and auditory information about the virtual environment. In addition to 360° sound, the helmet contains two miniature color moni-tors (called Eyephones), in order to produce stereopsis through a simulated parallax. Sensors in the helmet respond to head (and even eye) movement: "the user can enjoy the illusion of scanning an artificial panorama as he turns his head."[1] With the addition of the Dataglove, which translates hand movements into electric signals, the user can grasp and manipulate the objects in the virtual environment.[2] Voice recognition completes the interface. The subject can thus hear a sound behind her, turn to see its source, walk toward it, and even (with the aid of a Dataglove) pick it up, while to an outside observer, of course, nothing is there.

"Workers . . . have constructed several artificial realities for use in this system," reports *Scientific American.*[3] Marvin Minsky, a cofounder of MIT's Artificial Intelligence Laboratory, muses—somewhat alarmingly—that wires inserted into the nerves would allow the sensation of touch. For the ex-hippie Timothy Leary, this virtual realm represents the ultimate way to "tune in"—as one developer notes, "The computer literally knows where your head's at."[4]

Virtual reality significantly extends the sensory address of existent media to provide an alternate and manipulable space. Multiple users can enter the same virtual reality and play virtual catch or otherwise interact on this virtual plane. They can appear to each other in different forms, or as different species or genders—a simulated, but powerful, polymorphism is at work here. To be installed into such an apparatus would be to exist on two planes at once: while one's objective body would remain in the real world, one's *phenomenal body* would be projected into the terminal reality. In an ecstatic exaggeration of Merleau-Ponty's phenomenological model, world and body comprise a continually modifying feedback loop, producing a terminal identity without the terminal—a *cybersubject.*

Virtual reality technologies have attracted much attention at the beginning of the 1990s, and it is evident that the age of simulation, endlessly explored by cultural theorists, is far from over. A surfeit of articles have appeared discussing the new virtual reality technologies, ranging from the relative sobriety of *Scientific American* to the more popular speculations regarding virtual sexual relations ("teledildonics"). Much print is devoted to outlining the entirely feasible and practical applications for virtual reality systems. Article after article declaims the seemingly limitless potentialities of virtual existence—applicability seems to be no problem. Derived as it is from simulations technologies, virtual reality provides an ideal training environment for pilots or drivers. Astronauts can experiment in "weightless" conditions, while aspiring surgeons can practice their craft on virtual corpses (also known as electronic cadavers). Scientists can walk around inside a complex protein molecule, observing the intricacies of its structure or manipulating its components to simulate a chemical reaction. NASA has long been at the forefront of simulations technology, and NASA's Scott Fisher writes of *telepresence,* a robot controlled by a distant user (SF author Robert Heinlein called them "waldos") whose sensorium is wired into the phenomenological experience of the robot. Even the complexities of information management can be "navigated" by a "Virtual Environment Workstation," where data and control options could coexist in the same space as the user.[5] Early "artificial reality" designer Myron Krueger has also proposed such a "computer without a screen": "A computer presence will permeate the workplace and the home, available whenever a need is felt."[6] Back in the real world, architects are using Jaron Lanier's

VPL virtual reality technology to design buildings and take clients on walk-throughs before any construction has begun. And there is surely no difficulty in extrapolating the entertainment possibilities for this new medium.

At this point the discourse surrounding the immersive interface of virtual reality far outstrips the achievement (as almost every writer feels compelled to point out). The VR apparatus is still bulky and inconvenient—far from the desired ideal of a transparent interface technology. At the same time, the computational requirements are so intense as to put the experience out of reach for all but the wealthiest clients (design firms or the government, for example). There is every reason to believe that the technology will improve to the point of widespread feasibility within a decade. Yet the mere existence of *virtual reality* makes possible a new interrogation of some issues crucial to human and social existence. In his book-length study Howard Rheingold demonstrates that VR represents an incredible fusion of simulations technologies (including television, computer-graphics, real-time computer processing, and others).[7] Using *cyberspace* as a common synonym for the simulated spaces of *virtual reality*, Rheingold writes that "cyberspace feels like one of those developments that come along unexpectedly and radically alter everyone's outlook forever after."[8] Michael Heim has called cyberspace "a tool for examining our very sense of reality."[9] Such ontological and epistemological issues as the nature of the human, the real, experience, sensation, cognition, identity, and gender are all placed, if not under erasure, then certainly in question around the discursive object of virtual reality and the postulated existence of perfect, simulated, environments. Virtual reality has become the very embodiment of postmodern *disembodiment*.

Jonathan Crary, writing about the technology of the camera obscura, argues that it "is what Gilles Deleuze would call an assemblage," and the same must also be true of the immersive technological environment of virtual reality: "an object about which something is said and at the same time an object that is used. . . . [It] cannot be reduced either to a technological or a discursive object: it was a complex social amalgam in which its existence as a textual figure was never separable from its machinic uses."[10] The polymorphous possibilities of VR have produced a range of responses, from the merely prurient to the unabashedly utopian (Michael Benedikt notes the "almost irrational enthusiasm" that surrounds the topic).[11] As a number of journals, including *OMNI, The Whole Earth Review,* and *MONDO 2000,* devote continuing attention to the VR phenomenon, some discursive patterns are beginning to emerge (terminal identity fictions that I call, while admitting my own potential culpability, *cyberdrool*). Vivian Sobchack asks, in *Artforum,* what fantasies are being fulfilled by this "new subculture" which is "busy mutating—'downloading' its consciousness into the computer, leaving its obsolete body behind, and inhabiting the datascape as new age cyborgs." Sobchack is correct to isolate "a peculiar oxymoronic cosmology" at work, "which explicitly links high technophilia, 'new age' animism, spiritualism, and hedonism, and Sixties counter-cultural 'guerilla' political consciousness."[12]

One sign of this emergent subculture must be the reemergence of Dr. Timothy Leary. Leary, whom we have already encountered in the shift from psychedelics to software (see chapter 2) may not be the most reliable spokesperson, but he does exemplify the terminal fiction of what Sobchack has termed these "New Age Mutant Ninja Hackers." For Leary, computer technology in general and virtual reality simulations in particular offer a path to self-knowledge, self-realization, and self-empowerment: "Software of the future, and the interfaces between individuals and the Matrix, will be designed for people to interact with their own minds and with one another."[13] Leary's pronouncements are even more hyperbolic than Baudrillard's and are even possessed of some of the same paranoia about the operations of power, but Leary lacks any of Baudrillard's irony (or, for that matter, Gibson's). The rhetoric, dense with allusions to science fiction, circles around itself, cyberpunk-style, but this time in a vain attempt to describe real objects and real operations: "The screen is where the perceptual wetware groks the informational output of the cyberware [*man*]."[14]

Other proponents of cyberdrool demonstrate more restraint than Leary, but reveal identical fantasies of subject-empowerment: "Cyberspace," writes Howard Rheingold, "is a human-computer interface, but it is also a mind-space, the way mathematics and music and myth are mind-spaces—mind-space you can walk around in and grab by the handles."[15] Note, within Rheingold's alliterative list, the simultaneous positioning of cyberspace as coextensive with (or at least analogous to) the discourses of Enlightenment rationalism, high art, and folk culture.

Cyberdrool is at its most egregious in Brenda Laurel's "Art and Activism in VR," an article about political responsibility and *activism* that avoids any mention of a political agenda. There is an expressed desire to enrich the spirit, to forge "new connections between body and imagination and spirit." In an age of large-scale ecological Armageddon, AIDS, the assault on civil liberties, and the decline of the urban industrial superstructure, Laurel's use of the word "activism" to describe the

VPL Eyephones™ and
Dataglove™. Technology
becomes you . . .

exploration of a new medium is, at best, an act of startling hubris.[16] Cyberdrool is almost blind to ideology: "What we call reality," writes Nicole Stenger, "was only a temporary consensus anyway."[17] There is little understanding of social process or political understanding revealed in these writings, just an obsolete and naive liberalism that believes that if we all just *thought about it like reasonable human beings,* societal inequities and the drive for power would evaporate. Hence Laurel's conclusion, in which she calls for a vigorous commitment toward the advancement of a more humanist technological agenda for VR. "Conscience and heart," she writes, "can make all the difference." Can they?

Sobchack argues that this ostensible expansion of the parameters of reality is actually more of a withdrawal. "In an age in which there is too much perceived risk in living and too much information for both body and mind to contain and survive, need we wonder at the desire to transcend and escape where and who we are?" She further cites the "doubled desire" described by philosopher Don Ihde in relation to technological culture: "Both utopian and dystopian, self-preservational and self-exterminating, the 'new age mutant ninja hackers' articulate a simultaneous and contradictory desire: they 'want the transformation that technology allows,' but they 'want it in such a way that it becomes' them." Ihde continues: "Such a desire both secretly *rejects* what technologies are and overlooks the transformational effects which are necessarily tied to human-technological relations. This illusory desire belongs equally to pro- and antitechnology interpretations of technology."[18] Thus, the "new age mutant ninja hacker" seeks to merge with technology, but with subjectivity not only intact but essentially unchanged. This electronic solipsism clearly derives from the compelling but ultimately naive prognostications of Marshall McLuhan, and it is marked by the same refusal to acknowledge the political reality of power and its operations.[19]

Most of the journalistic accounts (from beyond the fringe as well as within the mainstream), and even some of the pronouncements of affiliated scientists and technicians, tend to stress the fundamental newness of the VR experience, and yet its precursors are clear, from videogames to graphical computer interfaces to, of course, the movies. *Scientific American,* reporting on the technological developments around "virtual reality," describes the target in terms familiar to theorists and students of the cinema—as a quest for realism. *Brainstorm* notwithstanding, cinema has nothing to rival the reality systems of contemporary electronics. In fact, one is frequently reminded, in studying the VR sensation, of the meditations of André Bazin on "the myth of total cinema." The prehistory of cinema was dominated by a desire for "a total and complete representation of reality," he wrote. The inventors of the medium, those other scientists and technicians, "saw in a trice the reconstruction of a perfect illusion of the outside world in sound, color and relief." By such standards the silent cinema, the monochromatic cinema, and the flat cinema represent a set of compromises with what the medium ought to be. "In short"—Bazin proclaims—from within this perspective, "cinema has not yet been invented."[20]

Virtual reality—or "artificial reality" to use Myron Krueger's original term—describes "a computer interface that seemingly surrounds the individual."[21] The developmental history of computers is almost synonymous with the history of the interface. Howard Rheingold reports that "the focus of attention has shifted from the way computers work to the way computers are designed to be used by people—*the human-computer interface.*"[22] In common parlance the interface is the tool that permits the user to input or receive information from the computer. Keyboards and punchcards represent two approaches to inputting information, while the computer's translation of machine language into English and its display on a monitor enables the user to understand and utilize the data. The attempt to increase computer literacy has resulted in increasingly "intuitive" interfaces; systems that operate in already familiar ways. Virtual reality represents an attempt to eliminate the interface between user and information—by "transforming data into environment," as Karrie Jacobs put it.[23] The interaction with information takes on a "direct" sensory quality that makes it "the ultimate interface" (Rheingold). Thus, the intensified spatial experience of virtual reality, with its simulated immersion into an interactive and non-narrative alternate space (with a promise of simulated touch and odor to follow) can be easily assimilated to the same dream that Bazin isolated in 1946, the dream of total cinema.

The dictionary provocatively defines an interface as "the boundary of two bodies or spaces." The human-computer interface can certainly be described as existing between a body *and* a space. At the same time, the very rise of the communication and information technologies embodied in the computer have given rise to pervasive notions that such boundaries, if they exist at all, are almost infinitely malleable. The blurred interface between human and electronic technology is perhaps the trope that most effectively defines the concerns of postmodern culture, in otherwise diverse works ranging from Nam June Paik's TV Penis through Godard's *Alphaville* to Pynchon's cybernetic paranoia: "Maybe there is a machine that will take us away, take us completely, suck us out through the electrodes out of the skull 'n' into the Machine and live there forever with all the other souls it's got stored there."[24] In *Gravity's Rainbow* the technology puts everyone under the shadow of the bomb (V-2 and, by extension, nuclear): "Each will have his personal Rocket. Stored in its target-seeker will be the heretic's EEG, the spikes and susurrations of heartbeat, the ghost-blossomings of personal infrared, each Rocket will know its intended and hunt him."[25] Perhaps nuclear destruction, like the apocalyptic car collisions of J. G. Ballard's *Crash,* represents the ultimate interface with the realities of a technologized existence.

The interface has thus become a crucial site, a significantly ambiguous boundary between human and technology. The interface relocates the human, in fact *redefines* the human as part of a cybernetic system of information circulation and management. The more invisible the interface, the more perfect the fiction of a total imbrication with the force fields of a new reality.

One expects the release of a wave of virtual reality fiction, in which a host of anachronistic fantasies are played out within virtual worlds (as on the holodeck in *Star Trek: The Next Generation*), but so far there has been hardly a trickle. In Gibson's *Count Zero* the young protagonist's mother is addicted to simstim soap operas on Sense/Net: she would "just go straight over and jack into the Hitachi, soap her brains out good for six solid hours. Her eyes would unfocus, and sometimes, if it was a really good episode, she'd drool a little" (44). But Gibson does not bring the reader into these virtual worlds—their passivity is too removed from the kinetic antics of his cyberspace cowboys. One recent fiction that does attempt to construct the kind of electronic "habitats" that VR enthusiasts anticipate is Neal Stephenson's *Snow Crash* (1992). The most appealing aspect of the novel is his conception of the Street: a public cyberspace, or virtual reality. The Street features new developments of offshooting "side streets," private domains hidden inside "buildings," and public "boulevards" where virtual denizens circulate to exchange information or to just be seen. Stephenson's world seems to spring from Benedikt's description of cyberspace: "Cyberspace: a new universe, a parallel universe created and sustained by the world's computers and communication lines. A world in which the global traffic of knowledge, secrets, measurements, indicators, entertainments, and alter-human agency takes on form: sights, sounds, presences never

seen on the surface of the earth blossoming in a vast electronic night."[26] In *Snow Crash,* Hiro Protagonist reminisces about negotiating the Street in the old days: "When Hiro first saw this place, ten years ago, the monorail hadn't been written yet; he and his buddies had to write car and motorcycle software in order to get around. They would take their software out and race it in the black desert of the electronic night."[27]

Stephenson is adept at envisioning a data space as a site of *social* interaction and interactivity, and his conception of the human in the electronic realm is memorable. Users can jack in from elaborate, high-res, customized hardware setups or simply dial up from public access lines. Naturally, their mode of access is reflected in the appearance of their "avatars," which include "stunningly beautiful women, computer-airbrushed and retouched at seventy-two frames a second," plus "Wild looking abstracts, tornadoes of gyrating light," and a "liberal sprinkling of black and white people . . . rendered in jerky, grainy" fashion that is less frequently updated. This mode of interface is hardly invisible. "Talking to a black-and-white on the Street is like talking to a person who has his face stuck in a xerox machine, repeatedly pounding the copy button, while you stand by the output tray pulling the sheets out one at a time and looking at them."[28] While Stephenson acknowledges a reflexivity of interface, there is a "realist" hierarchy at work, and black-and-whites are low on the scale. At the apex are "the avatars of Nipponese businessmen, exquisitely rendered by their fancy equipment, but utterly reserved and boring in their suits." The Street is an appealingly plausible portrait of a heterogeneous space that has everything and nothing in common with more traditional public spheres.

Two interesting fictions predate the technologies of virtual reality, but anticipate its tropes. One work with some relevance to the relationship between cinematic narrative and virtual reality is Michael Crichton's 1973 film *Westworld*. The central, memorable, concept concerns a fabulous theme park where visitors can interact with lifelike simulacra. In Westworld you can pick a gunfight with Yul Brynner, while jousting and other debaucheries are available over in Medievalworld or Romanworld (only Westworld is at all convincing—probably because of the familiarity of the Western cinematic tradition, not to mention the familiarity of its backlot sets).

Westworld's central notion of an electronically simulated, interactive environment anticipates the advent of virtual reality systems but, without the aesthetic or political contexts of cyberpunk, *Westworld* lacks an effective visual language. Where it should revel in the hyperreal, the film unfortunately settles for the banality of an overlit, TV aesthetic (only Yul Brynner's performance produces the essential feeling of surrender to a cinematic fantasy).[29] The plot, predictably enough, involves a failure of the "foolproof" technology, as the renegade robots slaughter the hapless guests. A similar dystopian vision marks Ray Bradbury's "The Veldt" (1950) in which a nursery offers a range of simulated environments to amuse the children. The children trap their parents in a "simulated" African veldt and leave them to be devoured by the all-too-real "simulated" lions. In these cautionary tales the subject is actually devoured by the "reality" of simulations technologies.

Perhaps an explanation for the relative paucity of virtual reality fictions lies in the fact that narrative *already* functions to construct an enveloping, simulated existence—narrative *is* a virtual reality. Reality, as writers such as Baudrillard and Ballard continually argue, is becoming fiction, and "the writer's task is to invent the reality." As Ballard reminded us, "We live inside an enormous novel." (Baudrillard's remarks about Disneyland are equally apposite to VR: virtual reality is thus a simulation whose function is to make the real world seem *more real*.)[30]

The virtual reality of narrative can thus operate as a real interface between human and technologized culture, revealing or providing a continuity between subject and machine. Science fiction is most explicit in narrating (and thus, in a sense, *producing*) such a continuum, but the discourses of non-SF writers like Pynchon and DeLillo, and techno-visionaries like Toffler and Baudrillard, perform a similar function of representing the human and technological as always-already coextensive. In the hands of many writers, the text becomes a machine itself, or a machine-product, such as the writing machine in Raymond Roussel's *Locus Solus* or the machinery of William Burroughs's cut-ups. These automatic texts are not indicative of the writer's unconscious, but rather of their own cybernetic origins.[31] David Porush writes, "Cybernetic fiction is a means for the author to present himself or his literature as a soft machine, a cybernaut-like hybrid device."[32] *Soft machine* is appropriated from Burroughs and aptly designates the site of interface or *interzone* (to make my own appropriation).

The urgency of developing a cyberscopic vision of the exotic electronic paraspace was discussed in the previous chapter, but now the human is "ready for something new" (*Videodrome*). The body must somehow be *inserted* into this newly revealed plane and granted the mobility and embodied presence which is the next step toward control.[33] The paradox is revealed by cyberpunk John Shirley, writing of a video vandal that he was "creating a presence via video graffiti . . . to make himself feel substantial, to superimpose himself on the Media Grid."[34] To become substantial, one must become insubstantial: one must enter the cyberspatial realm.

This chapter will detail a range of experiences—encountered in literature, cinema, games, and theme parks—that permit the intricate activity of interface that is increasingly indispensable. One further distinction needs to be made among these interfaces with the electronic world that are produced through different media. We must distinguish between an interface that incorporates some form of *direct sensory engagement* (games and theme parks, for example) and an interface that operates through an action of *narrativization* (literature). These represent two distinct modes of subject address, although—and this is essential—they often occur in tandem. The cinema itself combines them, incorporating its phenomenology of vision with the guidance, *telos,* and closure of narrative. Computer games almost inevitably combine narrative progression with "virtual" sensory pleasures. Repeatedly, the operations of narrative will be shown to constrain the effects of a new mode of sensory address, and so the fascination with the rise of virtual reality systems might represent a possible passage beyond narrative into a new range of spatial metaphors. The richer the sensory interface, the more reduced is the function of narrative. In this context, the SF film *TRON* becomes a fascinating cyborg object poised between the demands of narrative and the "pure" spatiality generated by virtual reality systems.

Following a brief overview of the world of computer games, the chapter will trace a trajectory from the narrated terminal penetrations of

Vernor Vinge's "True Names" and William Gibson's *Neuromancer* through the hybrid electronic/cinematic experience of *TRON* to the direct bodily engagement of a visit to Disneyworld. This trajectory, more conceptual than chronological (its objects are roughly, although not precisely, contemporaneous), reveals the emphatic tension between an interface constituted by the operations of narrative and one constructed through direct bodily engagement. The illusion of subject empowerment depends upon the invisibility of the apparatus, and when electronic reality appears to permit a direct incursion by the terminal subject, then what functions can narrative retain?

FUN IN CYBERSPACE

It is almost impossible to draw a neat line between the serious and the playful in computer art. The ambivalence about what is play and what is serious recalls similar ambivalence in modern physics, in Dada, and in the work of Oulipo.—O. B. Hardison, Jr. ¶

Tomorrow learning space will be just as useful as learning to drive a car.

—Wernher von Braun

The Data Glove is only one of the virtual environment tools offered up by the technology of the computer. Most prevalent are the games which line the shelves of every computer store. When Case jacks in to cyberspace in *Neuromancer,* he enters a realm which "has its roots in primitive arcade games" (51). In Steven Levy's history of the minicomputer, *Hackers,* games are very significant. "Games were the programs which took greatest advantage of the machine's power—put the user in control of the machine—made him the god of the bits and bytes inside the box." After buying a new game, a kid could "go home for what was the essential interface with the Apple [Computer]. Playing games."[35] Levy's glibness does not hide the validity of his observation. Games are far more than an idle recreation for many "users;" they in fact represent the most complete symbiosis generally available between human and computer—a fusion of spaces, goals, options, and perspectives. "To see tomorrow's computer systems, go to the video game parlors!" proclaims the acclaimed systems designer Ted Nelson.[36] Games literally test the user, and in more than just eye-hand coordination.

The first computer game, developed by hackers in 1962, was Spacewar, a simulation that presented flat outlines of starships doing battle by spitting small pixels at each other while vying for position around a gravitationally powerful "sun." The next was Adventure, a text game which described surroundings and action. The adventurer could, by typing simple instructions ("GO NORTH"), move in different directions, examine a range of objects, learn secret words, and interact with other characters. Howard Rheingold correctly observes that "Adventure is a virtual world in a conceptual," rather than a sensory, way.[37] Both games remain paradigmatic of computer gaming, and the most intriguing games have combined the kinesis of Spacewar with the interactive narrative format of Adventure. Players solve puzzles (and sometimes those puzzles are bugs in the design of the game which have to be recognized and worked around). Games become metaphors for hacking itself—the process of experimenting with computer structures in a nonformal and often intuitive manner. Some games have made the hacking/gaming relation obvious: in *Hacker,* for example, players find themselves in an unfamiliar computer system and must experiment to learn about their environment and locate themselves in the system in a kind of electronic cartography. Inevitably, there is even a computer game version of Gibson's *Neuromancer.*

The *Neuromancer* game was ardently backed by cyber-enthusiast Timothy Leary. "[T]he great thing is that you are a hacker playing it. That's the key to the whole game," he comments. It is an attractively packaged product, with a beautifully synthesized photo on the front, a soundtrack by cyberpunks-*avant-la-lettre* DEVO, and a great deal of Gibson's original prose. The game operates in both first- and third-person modes: the player guides the Case character through Chiba City, but takes on first-person perspective in cyberspace. Again, Adventure serves as the template for the interactive narrative adventure, while Spacewar-honed reflexes are demanded in the cyberspace sequences. The problem is that the gaming environment is, in many ways, *more* linear—or at least more narrative—than Gibson's own reckless creation: the ambivalence of the original work is lost in the psychedelic display onscreen. This is part of a more general problem with computer gaming, in which the player's interactive control is often more potential than actuality.

Falcon and *Shuttle* offer real-time, sophisticated simulations of jet and space shuttle control. *Dungeon Master* permits the player a first-person point of view of the labyrinthine corridors of a multileveled dungeon replete with secret doors, animated fiends, and, possibly, a final triumph. *Neuromancer* and *Police Quest* shift from first- to third-person perspectives, but substitute more complex narratives. The range of simulations available to the player is thus not quite as simple as the word might first suggest. Some games allow the player to shift the rate of temporal passage, so a night can pass in moments. As bleary gamers can attest, the spatiotemporal malleability of the computer world can seem to cross over to the physical world, just as Jeremy Rifkin noted in *Time Wars,* replacing the fixed rhythms of real life.

There was, and is, a *ludic* quality encouraged by hacking away in the minicomputer universe, since the computer provides a realm in which all things are possible, and with minimal risk. Seymour Papert's research on computers and education stresses the computer environment as a closed, formal system, separate from the everyday world.[38] This is uncannily close to Johan Huizinga's definition of *play* from his philosophical treatise *Homo Ludens:* "a free activity standing quite consciously outside 'ordinary' life as being 'not serious,' but at the same time absorbing the player intensely and utterly . . . It proceeds within its own proper boundaries of time and space according to fixed rules and in an orderly manner."[39] *Cosmic Osmo* provides an interactive, animated environment where children (and adults) can wander, Alice-like, through an unfamiliar landscape, playing games, talking to characters, recording their own sounds (and playing them back); all without risk to anyone (including the computer system).[40] The game fosters experimentation with the virtual objects in its world, while the forking paths of the nonlinear experience replace the traditional syntagmatic structure of the story. Although restricted to the space of the screen, "games" such as *Cosmic Osmo* point toward the more enveloping alternate worlds of virtual reality systems. Jaron Lanier's company, VPL, has developed a virtual world derived from the Mad Hatter's tea party. A user can follow the instructions to "Eat me" or "Drink me" with the same sudden scalar disruptions once experienced by Alice alone, or one can "play" any other character.

Games thus present a range of options for players and hence offer a range of subject positions. With every advance, the imbrication becomes more total; the symbiosis more emphatic. Through the translation of percept into movement, the players' thoughts (to paraphrase

Merleau-Ponty) are given their place in the world. Through play a kinetic interaction is established between subject and object: the perceiving body becomes a phenomenal body.

The exploratory environment and the intuitive interface are at the heart of the Macintosh computer, perhaps the most important design in minicomputers since their inception. The goal at Apple was to empower the individual against the forces of corporate power and central control. Their *1984* commercial, directed by Ridley Scott, featured a most spectacular projection of the Orwellian vision, but now the proles were controlled by the "Big Blue," IBM (unnamed): "The idea was to portray a totalitarian state that didn't work, like East Germany in 1953, and to give it the air of the dank and leaky spacecraft in *Alien*. The sets were modeled after those used to create Everytown, the art-moderne 'city of the future' in the 1936 science fiction classic *Things to Come*."[41] In the commercial the proles gather in an enormous meeting hall, as a blonde, young, female athlete with a sledge-hammer runs in and smashes Big Brother's screen. Apple was unveiling its Macintosh, the announcer said. Personal computing, with a friendly interface, was "why 1984 won't be like *1984*."

"Instead of merely receiving our mental model of reality, we are now compelled to invent it and continually reinvent it. This places an enormous burden on us. But it also leads toward greater individuality, a de-massification of personality as well as culture."[42] That this "de-massification" might itself be an ideological operation, an act of covert mythologizing, never occurs to Alvin Toffler. Toffler's formative vision, emblematic of the quasi-mystical attitudes of the Macintosh division, might be labeled *hippie-hacker*.[43] Telematic power would be anticorporate, decentralized, *personal*: such was the mythos.[44]

Thus, in the 1980s two techno-myths arose: *cyberpunk* and *hippie-hacker*. Both were opposed to technocratic mythologies of centralized control—Down With Radiant City and other Corbusierian fantasies. While hippie/hacker substitutes an ethos of personal control and individual empowerment through the simple mastery of the benign interface, cyberpunk enacts the end of controls—depicting a world where technology circulates more or less freely and, where, as is the case in *Neuromancer,* technology has its own agenda. Baudrillard is quintessential cyberpunk, while VR prophets Brenda Laurel, Jaron Lanier, and Howard Rheingold preserve the hippie-hacker ambition. Both acknowledge our inevitable imbrication with the new state of things in *blip culture*.

As each article on the burgeoning VR phenomenon is published, the scientists and researchers who comprise the virtual reality community frequently "gather" electronically on the WELL (the Whole Earth 'Lectronic Link—an electronic message exchange system) to discuss the implications of the latest coverage. Articles stressing the long-term implications and overall seriousness of the project are praised, while rampant speculations about virtual war games and virtual orgies are viewed with suspicion. What frequently, although not always, eludes the professionals is precisely the ludic attraction of cyberspace and the "seriousness" of such play and playful speculation. On at least one level, virtual reality is a ludic engagement with the space of the computer that refigures it as a perceivable and physical environment. Many of the designers of NASA's virtual reality system had, as a matter of fact, once worked as game designers for Atari.[45]

Virtual reality represents an immersion in a computer-constructed space that obviously holds a strong appeal (although one anticipates a strong Luddite backlash from critics who reify the "natural" qualities of contemporary reality and worry about becoming "lost in cyberspace"), and it might be possible to regard the desire to play in the virtual playground as a simple desire for escape, for an alternative environment without the daily pressures of life in "the real world." Yet just as the desire for cinematic pleasure bears deeper psychosexual and political implications, so the fascination with virtual reality reveals something more complex. As with the early cinema, the major fascination now lies with the technology itself, rather than with the specific fantasies/realities generated therein. I would therefore contend that virtual reality speaks to the desire to *see* the space of the computer (as discussed in the previous chapter), and to further figure it as a space one can *move through* and thereby comprehend.

This desire forms the basis for much of the science fiction of the 1980s. Computer games are at the center of numerous science fiction narratives. In *Ender's Game,* by Orson Scott Card, and *The Last Starfighter,* the technological expertise of gaming is mapped onto real-universe conflicts, and only the power of the hacker can save the cosmos. Vernor Vinge's "True Names," a significant precursor to *Neuromancer,* features a game designer who joins other hackers in a cybernetic otherworld: "The basic game was a distant relative of the ancient Adventure that had been played on computer systems for more than forty years" (more on this tale below). The teenage hacker of *Wargames* (1983) enters a Pentagon computer system. "Do you want to play a game?" it asks. Repeatedly, the computer game player-designer is sentimentally posited as *other* to this world, but integral to the integrated circuits of the next.

Terminal space becomes phenomenal in the discourse of science fiction, a *narrative* compensation for the loss of visibility in an electronically defined world. The character is inserted into the cybernetic field, transforming perception into subject mobility. The human is granted its own spatiality, and consequently a control, over these new vectored fields. "If 'actions' are invisible," writes John Clute, "then our fates are likewise beyond our grasp."[46] If this is true, then to project the human into the nonvisible spaces within the computer is to transform that space into a dramatic arena: no idle transformation. For to dramatize the terminal realm means to somehow insert the figure of the human into that space to experience it *for us,* to affect it *for us,* and to be affected by it *for us.* Much recent science fiction, then, stages and restages a confrontation between figure and ground, constructing new human forms to interface with the other space of cybernetic reality (see chapter 4). This chapter, however, is still concerned with the human: the superhackers, or cyberspace cowboys, or perhaps they should be called the *cybernauts.*

JACKING IN
Now I am light, now I fly, now I see myself beneath myself, now a god dances through me!—Friedrich Nietzsche ¶ Speed is the cry of our era, and greater speed one of the goals of tomorrow.—Norman Bel Geddes ¶ "Concrete is radical. Concrete is the future. You don't cry about it man, you skate on it."—Lewis Shiner, SLAM

True Names
Vernor Vinge's novella, "True Names," originally published in 1981—prior to the appearances of *Blade Runner, TRON,* or *Neuromancer*—is an adept exploration of cybernetic spatiality and interface.[47] Its extrapolation of a physical space derived from the abstractions of computer operations and gaming protocols is at once strikingly original and comfortably familiar. Here, the global data net becomes a literal extension of

one of the characters. In the future, computer users gather in illegal cybernetic enclaves disguised in their self-defined alteregos. Some of these groups engage in harmless hacker vandalism, like the phone phreaks of the 1960s who wired themselves into AT&T's electronic system (some of whom were to develop strong ties to computer hacking)— penetrating data banks and leaving vivid signs of their feats, for example.

The existence of this other realm is more than a diegetic convenience. Vinge recognizes the relation between games and narrative, and their dual metaphorical relation to the interface between subject and terminal: "Mr. Slippery had often speculated just how the simple notion of using high-resolution EEGs as input/output devices had caused the development of the 'magical world' representation of data space. The Limey and Erythrina argued that sprites, reincarnation, spells, and castles were the natural tools here, more natural than the atomistic twentieth-century notions of data structures, programs, files and communications protocols" (81). As in *Neuromancer,* the digital information of the Other Realm is recast in the form of a simulated universe now "perceivable analogically" (94). Vinge's characters even speculate, with true hacker allegiance, that their computational power outstrips that of the government precisely because of their reliance upon the metaphorical interface of fantasy narrative. The best interface, then, is no interface, or rather the illusion of direct insertion into the computer's virtual spaces. The recourse to magic is, of course, quite clever, in that it preserves the invisible manipulations of cybernetic power while grounding that invisibility in the familiar guise of individual power.

In attempting to stop a renegade hacker whose access to military and economic data threatens global stability, Mr. Slippery (aka Roger Pollack) and Erythrina (real identity unknown) are given unprecedented access to the world's data through their synaesthetic interfaces:

> —but they were experiencing what no human had ever known before, a sensory bandwidth thousands of times normal. For seconds that seemed without end, their minds were filled with a jumble verging on pain, data that was not information and information that was not knowledge. To hear ten million simultaneous phone conversations, to see the continent's entire video output, should have been a white noise. Instead it was a tidal wave of detail rammed through the tiny aperture of their minds . . . He controlled more than raw data now; if he could master them, the continent's computers could process this avalanche, much the way parts of

the human brain preprocess their input. More seconds passed, but now with a sense of time, as he struggled to distribute his very consciousness through the System. (95–96)

Vinge is familiar with computer operations in a way that Gibson isn't, and so his language is less hyperbolic and more logical. Still, this lengthy passage remains quintessential cyberpunk (despite the fact that Vinge's sympathies are clearly hippie-hacker) and is emblematic of the concerns of postmodern media culture as well. The white noise of the Information Age is granted a sensory reality as the human is interfaced to the electronic. Like Baudrillard, Vinge's cyberhackers are overwhelmed by the Dataist Era and recognize the paradox of the present—"information is not knowledge." Unlike Baudrillard, Vinge's fiction postulates a new telematic existence which recenters the human, who is now able to process data through an expanded sensory field. Computers become adjuncts of the human brain once more, as a centralized consciousness organizes the processing of this avalanche of data. "More than three hundred million lives swept before what his senses had become," Mr. Slippery reflects (96). Pain becomes ecstasy as the human is empowered by this translation onto the fields of information.

In this fiction it is a specific type of individual that is empowered. "True Names" is an interesting distillation of hacker culture, interactive fiction, role-playing games such as Dungeons & Dragons (and the fervent cult of players which surrounds such games), the "other realm" of science fiction conventions, populated by the subculture of science fiction fandom, and the countercultural techno-shenanigans of the early phone phreaks. The peripheral figures associated with these activities, perennial outsiders, are granted centrality and invisible power in "True Names." As Norman Spinrad notes of Orson Scott Card's extremely popular novel *Ender's Game,* the hero and the reader are linked in an especially close identification: "the identification figures *are* the audience's fantasy images of themselves."[48] This is surely true of the puckish videogame hacker in *TRON,* as well as the Romantic, *noir*-ish outsider Case in *Neuromancer.*

"True Names" offers, within a cybernetically determined existence, a vision of transcendence and overwhelming power reminiscent of Clarke's *Childhood's End* or the finale of Clarke and Kubrick's *2001.* In the latter work the infant superhuman returns to Earth—"a glittering toy no Star-Child could resist." The perspective of the planet is global; *2001*'s Star-Child represents the apotheosis of the all-encompassing gaze that Jameson defined as emblematic of science fiction narrative. The Star-

Child's first action ("he put forth his will") is to detonate all the orbiting nuclear weapons in a casual gesture of absolute control. In "True Names" the perceptual transcendence, with its implications of cosmic power, is similar, but grounded in the encompassing network of electronic information systems. Mr. Slippery is possessed of "millions of perceptors" (111) permitting a "microscopic yet global scrutiny" (99–100): "Every ship in the seas, every aircraft now making for safe landing, every one of the loans, the payments, the meals of an entire race registered clearly on some part of his consciousness. With perception came power; almost everything he saw, he could alter, destroy or enhance" (112). Finally, Mr. Slippery and Erythrina voluntarily reject the position of God and withdraw from the consciousness of the global data net. This is a nostalgic decision comprehensible only within an ideology in which the human subject is *already constructed* as unique, controlling, and transcendent.

In an introduction, Vinge presents some speculations about the subject in science fiction, noting that the genre often posits an intelligence superior to ours. When this encounter actually occurs, "human history will have reached a kind of singularity—a place where extrapolation breaks down and new models must be applied—and the world will pass beyond our understanding. . . . The best we writers can do is creep up on the singularity, and hang ten at its edge" (47). The language of science fiction stages its own aporia. Vinge's hackers construct a narrative field of heroic fantasy to ground and empower their cybernetic interface, just as Vinge himself constructs a science fiction narrative to reveal the implications of the global electronic network that might comprise some sort of transcendental intelligence; that might ultimately produce the singularity that renders all representational forms obsolete. Vinge's narrative is an analogical convenience—a means of accommodating the reader to telematic reality—but he is unusually self-aware of his function as a narrator of the unfamiliar.[49]

Cyberspace Cowboys—Kinetic Urban Subjects

Neuromancer continues the translation of percept into kinesis and control initiated by "True Names" and *Blade Runner's* photoscan sequence (see chapter 2). Deckard's control of the computerized image and the verbal/optical interface which permits this detective to operate in terminal mode are extended by the EEG/computer linkup called "jacking in." Case is further empowered by his entry into a digitized environment that is perceivable analogically; its smooth geometries are analogues for the realm's fully digital existence. *Neuromancer* is the most phenomenologically significant science fiction text since *2001:* Case's projection into the "infinite datascape" gives him the direct control of the data in that virtual world, so it is not surprising, then, that his entry into cyberspace is strikingly kinetic (in fact, turbulent and discontinuous):

> And in the bloodlit dark behind his eyes, silver phosphenes pour-
> ing in from the edge of space, hypnagogic images jerking past
> like film compiled from random frames. Symbols, figures, faces, a
> blurred, fragmented mandala of visual information.
> Please, he prayed, *now—*
> A gray disk, the color of Chiba sky.
> *Now—*
> Disk beginning to rotate, faster, becoming a sphere of paler gray.
> Expanding—And flowed, flowered for him, fluid neon origami trick.
> (52)[50]

What this sequence narrates is actually the passage from discontinuous experience to the glissades of datascape mastery. At first cyberspace is characterized by the chaos of boiling light and indiscriminate montage (an image cut-out of Burroughs's novels and screenplays). Transcendence follows; a zen-like, natural communion designated by references to origami and flower blossoms. But, fluent or turbulent, kinesis distinguishes the interface. (Gibson has praised the comic book adaptation of his novel by saying that it *moves* right—the self-similarity of kinesis defines the trajectory of *Neuromancer* at all levels.)[51]

Merleau-Ponty has, of course, written on the significance of subject mobility:

> The translation of percept into movement is effected via the ex-
> press meanings of language, whereas the normal subject pene-
> trates into the object by perception, assimilating its structure
> into his substance, and through this body the object directly regu-
> lates his movements. This subject-object dialogue, this drawing
> together, by the subject, of the meaning diffused through the ob-
> ject, and, by the object, of the subject's intentions—a process
> which is physiognomic perception—arranges round the subject a
> world which speaks to him of himself, and gives his own thoughts
> their place in the world.[52]

The relevance of this passage to *Neuromancer* is clear and extensive. It is the state of "the normal subject" (as distinct from those sufferers of apraxia or agnosia to whom Merleau-Ponty refers at the outset) to penetrate the object via an act of perception that reciprocally endows the subject with bodily presence. Intentions and meaning are translated into activity in a world defined by that very subject-object interface. In *Neuromancer,* cyberspace exists as an analogic environment that permits the subject to "assimilate its structure into his substance." In so doing the subject experiences "a world which speaks to him of himself." Further, "his own thoughts" are granted "their place in the world." (What isn't provided in Merleau-Ponty's model is the possibility of a world, such as cyberspace, that exists solely to permit this subject-object imbrication.)

The negotiation of cyberspace always emphasizes motion. Gibson: "Headlong motion through walls of emerald green, milky jade, the sensation of speed beyond anything he'd known before cyberspace" (256). Merleau-Ponty: "for us to be able to conceive space, it is in the first place necessary that we should have been thrust into it by our body, and that it should have provided us with the first model of those transpositions, equivalents and identifications which make space into an objective system and allow our experience to be one of objects, opening out on and 'in itself.' "[53] The spatiality of *Neuromancer* exists to permit bodily mobility and, hence, subject definition. The human becomes the dramatic center, the active agent in a spatiotemporal reality from which he—and it is always a "he"—has been rigorously excluded. From a description of the subject's passage through the world, a pas-·sage marked by continuous processes of orientation and adaptation, the phenomenology of perception is transformed into a transcendent valuation of human experience and its "logical" consequent, human control. This is a danger of which Merleau-Ponty seems cognizant when he writes: "Mobility, then, is not, as it were, a handmaid of consciousness, transporting the body to that point in space of which we have formed a representation beforehand. In order that we may be able to move our body towards an object, the object must first exist for it, our body must not belong to the realm of the 'in-itself.' "[54] The physical engagement of the body, then, yields a *simultaneous* construction of subject and world. Neither preexists the other—neither subject nor body are "givens."

Unlike *2001,* which emphasizes the alienation that accompanies the action of subject reorientation and redefinition, *Neuromancer* stresses only the alienation that follows the *removal* from this other space—"For Case, who'd lived for the bodiless exultation of cyberspace, it was the Fall"—normal space is now the site of alienation. The reader should not be misled by the reference to "bodiless exultation," by the way, for the

Citizen of cyberspace: Iron Man as man/machine/vehicle in the computer comic *Iron Man: Crash* by Mike Saenz, of Virtual Valerie Fame. (Marvel Comics)

subject in cyberspace is granted perception and mobility, conditions predicated upon a lived-body; a new body, perhaps, but a body nonetheless. Yet the reader of *Neuromancer* is kept in the dark regarding the form of that body—the subject in cyberspace never examines *himself*. I have always envisioned the character as one geometric form among others, distinguished more as a vehicle than a human form and, in fact, this is how Case is depicted in the comic book adaptation, propelled along on *TRON*-like beams of light. In Mike Saenz's CAD (Computer Aided Design) production, *Iron Man: Crash,* the computer drawings transform the real world into cyberspace—technologized, de-individuated, vectored space. Within such a realm Iron Man is an appropriate citizen: already half-human, half-machine, as much vehicle as driver. Bruce Jensen's art for the *Neuromancer* adaptation depicts Case sitting at his desk as though poised behind the wheel of a Ferrari—static, yet suggestive of a powerful kinesis.

1. Cyberspace and the Omnipotence of Thoughts
Thus, the duality between mind and body is superseded in a new formation that presents the mind as itself *embodied.* The body, here, exists *only* in phenomenological terms: it perceives and it moves (a reductive and utopian version of Merleau-Ponty's model of subject-construction, which eliminates the mortal limitations of a physical body). Through the construction of the computer itself, there arises the possibility of a mind independent of the biology of bodies, a mind released from the mortal limitations of the flesh. Unlike the robot forms of the modernist era, wherein a mechanical body substituted for the organic, the invisible processes of cybernetic information circulation and electronic technology construct a body at once material and immaterial—a fundamental oxymoron, perhaps, of postmodernity.

The redefinition of the subject under the conditions of electronic culture is a response to the fear that the human has become obsolete, last year's model. Faced with the possibility of its own extinction, or at least its new irrelevance, the human subject has produced a range of representations of itself as melded with the matrices of terminal existence. The human proudly takes up a position within the machine, but almost always from a position of mastery, so that by entering the machine, the machine becomes a part of the human. The subject is, and is not, afraid to leave its body behind. The computer can become a new body, with its electronic sensorium extending far beyond human capacities. And yet, some residual form of the body is retained in almost every instance (and sometimes, as in *TRON* or "Overdrawn at the Memory Bank," the narrative centers upon the recovery of the protagonist's "meat" body).

If there is an ambivalence regarding the status of the body, however, no such hesitation marks the attitude toward the mind. Cyberspace is a celebration of spirit, as the disembodied consciousness leaps and dances with unparalleled freedom. It is a realm in which the mind is freed from bodily limitations, a place for the return of *the omnipotence of thoughts*.

In *Totem and Taboo,* Freud quotes Frazer's *The Golden Bough* on the subject of magic: "Men mistook the order of their ideas for the order of nature, and hence imagined that the control which they have, or seem to have, over their thoughts, permitted them to exercise a correspond- ing control over things." For Freud, there is at the heart of magic a desire to believe in the omnipotence of thoughts and the power of will: "A general overvaluation has thus come about of all mental processes— an attitude towards the world, that is, which, in view of our knowledge of the relation between reality and thought, cannot fail to strike *us* as an overvaluation of the latter."[55]

To illustrate the phenomenon of the omnipotence of thoughts, Freud refers to "the evolution of human views of the universe": "At the animis- tic stage men ascribe omnipotence to *themselves.* At the religious stage they transfer it to the gods but do not seriously abandon it themselves, for they reserve the power of influencing the gods in a variety of ways according to their wishes. The scientific view of the universe no longer affords any room for human omnipotence; men have acknowledged their smallness and submitted resignedly to death and to the other necessities of nature." "None the less," he adds, "some of the primitive belief in omnipotence still survives in men's faith in the power of the human mind, taking account, as it does, of the laws of reality."[56] One cannot help but note that Freud's anthropology has imposed a model of psychological development on the process of cultural change. The "evolution" that he describes is fully analogous to the growth of the infant through childhood: the original belief in the power of will (which, in fact, predates the full emergence of the ego), the surrender of power to the parents (who may still be influenced "in a variety of ways"), and the final (albeit provisional) acceptance of the reality principle.

Freud notes that "Primitive men and neurotics . . . attach a high valuation—in our eyes an *over*-valuation—to psychical acts" (89), and here we must observe the prevalence of narratives about "psychical acts" that occur in the genres of science fiction and fantasy. Within a worldview now dominated by the "scientific" paradigm, thoughts are reinvested with their originary omnipotence. In her essay, "The Plea- sure of the Interface," Claudia Springer writes, "Rather than portraying human fusion with electronic technology as terrifying, popular culture frequently represents it as a pleasurable experience. The pleasure of the interface, in Lacanian terms, results from the computer's offer to lead us into a microelectronic Imaginary where our bodies are obliterated and our consciousness integrated into the matrix."[57]

Cyberspace represents the return of the animistic view of the universe *within* the scientific paradigm. Consciousness becomes separated from the body—it becomes a body *itself*—as its power spreads throughout the global electronic space of terminal culture. In this sense, then, cyberspace is a refusal of the reality principle and of any limits on subject power. The power of the will is now hardwired into the Net. If I have described the subject in cyberspace as a purely perceptive and kinetic subject, then I should also note that Freud has discussed "the animistic soul" in terms of "its volatile and mobile quality, its power of leaving the body and of taking possession, temporarily or permanently, of another body." All of these are "characteristics which remind us unmistakably of the nature of consciousness" (94). Thus the penetration of consciousness into the cyberspatial matrix is an extension of the power of the will which recalls the "animistic" conception of the universe that precedes the emergence of the mature ego.[58] Gibson seems aware of this: witness the emergence of voodoo mythology as another paradigm for cyberspatial existence in *Count Zero* and *Mona Lisa Overdrive* (see below).

2. A Tactics of Kinesis
These narratives and graphic representations function as *tactics of accommodation* to a new mode of existence. As Michel Certeau notes in the pages of *The Practice of Everyday Life,* in another passage with fascinating implications regarding *Neuromancer,* it is a question of "the status of the individual *in technical systems,*" because "the involvement of the subject diminishes in proportion to the technocratic expansion of these systems."[59] The involvement of the subject in modern life is crucial to Certeau's analysis, and rather than lament (or celebrate) the disappearance of the subject, as Baudrillard is wont to do, Certeau conducts a series of microanalyses (an appropriate form to this imploded era) to demonstrate the tactics by which subjects interpose themselves into the technocratic systems of power which hold sway in the present.

Tactics, in Certeau's system, are opposed to *strategies,* which Certeau defines as follows: "I call a *strategy* the calculation (or manipulation) of power relationships that becomes possible as soon as a subject with will and power (a business, an army, a city, a scientific institution) can be isolated. It postulates a *place* that can be delimited as its *own* and serve as the base from which relations with an *exteriority* composed of targets or threats . . . can be managed" (35–36). Strategies are thus associated with space, and specifically with those spaces which are owned and operated by powerful dominant forces. Strategies operate in space, consolidating power over others who impinge on that space. The glittering geometric shapes of cyberspace, for example, represent the control of space by corporations and military systems; these are protected by ICE—Intrusion Countermeasure Electronics—thus preventing unwanted incursions (the acronym is fictional, the concept is surely not). The information is inside/behind the structures of ICE, while the exteriority of these defense systems operate against any perceived "targets or threats."

Against such strategies must be seen the *tactics* of the cyberspace cowboys: "I call a 'tactic,' on the other hand, a calculus which cannot count on a 'proper' (a spatial or institutional localization), nor thus on a borderline distinguishing the other as a visible totality. The place of a tactic belongs to the other. A tactic insinuates itself into the other's place, fragmentarily, without taking it over in its entirety, without being able to keep it at a distance" (xix). For Certeau, "*tactics*" refer to the set of practices performed by subjects upon and within these controlled fields. A tactic is equivalent to a speech act, which "is at the same time a use *of* language and an operation performed *on* it" (33). It is temporal, a trajectory across the spaces of strategic control which uses that space as its foundation. The phone phreaks, accessing free telephone service from AT&T, were engaged in a tactical, piecemeal, appropriation of the monopoly's resources. The result is not the overthrow of a system recognized as massive and monolithic, but instead a nibbling at the edges of power and thus an elision of control.

The same is true of Gibson's cyberspace cowboys. "A thief, he'd worked for other, wealthier thieves, employers who provided the exotic software required to penetrate the bright walls of corporate systems, opening windows into rich fields of data" (5). Tom de Haven's script for the comic book adaptation is even more explicit: "His employer had provided the exotic software to crack industrial banks and corporate libraries. . . . But it was Case who penetrated the systems and snatched information."[60] The adaptation stresses the power of Case in going his employers one better—employers whose status as thieves blurs with their status as capitalists. Case becomes the tactician in opposition to all parties, corporations and "employers" both.

Foucault's theories of disciplinary technologies figure prominently in Certeau's model, but Certeau rejects the monolithic structures of power that serve as Foucault's foundation. Arguing that Foucault has abstracted the strategic manipulations of power from the broader matrix of power relations and resistances, Certeau restores a more heterogeneous practice than is inscribed in Foucault, while still preserving the most valuable parts of Foucault's model. Certeau lists the synonyms Foucault employed in evoking the maneuvers of the strategists of power: "'apparatuses' ('*dispositifs*'), 'instrumentalities,' 'techniques,' 'mechanisms,' 'machineries,' etc." (45). With reference to Certeau, cyberpunk fiction can be understood as a narrative of tactics: corporations and the military control cyber*space,* so that the cowboys become infiltrators, deceivers, and tricksters. Cyberpunk narratives construct trickster tactics within the "machineries" of cybernetic culture.

Certeau is eloquent on the new spaces of cultural practice. "There is no longer an elsewhere," he writes. "Consumers are transformed into immigrants. The system in which they move about is too vast to be able to fix them in one place, but too constraining for them ever to be able to escape from it" (40). Unlike Baudrillard, for whom this totality of cybernetic control is fundamentally irresistible, Certeau finds the limits of control in its very totalization: "the strategic model is also transformed, as if defeated by its own success." The notion of a protected, strategic, space is predicated upon a separation between this space and others. When the "proper," or proprietary, space becomes the "whole" space, then:

> little by little [the strategic model] will exhaust its capacity to transform itself and constitute only the space . . . in which a cybernetic society will arise, the scene of the Brownian movements of invisible and innumerable tactics. One would thus have a proliferation of aleatory and indeterminable manipulations within an immense framework of socioeconomic constraints and securities: myriads of almost invisible movements, playing on the more and more refined texture of a place that is even, continuous, and constitutes a proper place for all people.

This last might even be more than illusion—Certeau argues that narrativity has an important function: "A theory of narration is indissociable from a theory of practices, as its condition as well as its production." Far from existing apart from the tactical struggle, narrative is fully embroiled in the articulation of resistance. The novel is, for him (as well as for Bakhtin), a set of heterogeneous discourses marked by contradiction and simple coincidence. Narratives produce heterogeneity and resistance. "The story does not express a practice. It does not limit itself to telling about a movement. It *makes* it" (81). Narrative produces (a) movement—the kinesis of tactical resistance. More than mere articulators of meaning, narratives "say exactly what they do." This is consistent with Certeau's larger argument that microresistance occurs everywhere, even within the supposedly monolithic structures of language.

For Certeau the function of narrative is to demarcate boundaries; precisely to locate a space which may not be geographic. "What the map cuts up, the story cuts across" (129). Frontiers and bridges also function as part of the narrative, serving as the sites of exteriority and the space "in-between": in other words, they represent the other spaces against which the space of the story emerges. The passage into the frontier lands, or other spaces, and the subsequent return to one's "proper" space, comprise an archetypal narrative structure for Certeau which frequently reveals the ambiguity of the "proper" space itself: "Within the frontiers, the alien is already there" (128). Case's forays into cyberspace in *Neuromancer,* and Flynn's translation into data in *TRON,* represent similar forays across the "bridge" and into the cybernetic "frontier." Cyberspace provides the key to understanding and controlling the alien spaces of home.

In the sequels to *Neuromancer, Count Zero,* and *Mona Lisa Overdrive* (1989), a cyberspace counterculture emerges, dominated by figures of voodoo. Certeau notes that the high-tech tactics of resistance often hearken to earlier archetypes, as the term "trickster" might imply: "Increasingly constrained, yet less and less concerned with these vast frameworks, the individual detaches himself from them without being able to escape them and can henceforth only try to outwit them, to pull tricks on them, to rediscover, within an electonicized and computerized megalopolis, the 'art' of the hunters and rural folk of earlier days." William Gibson describes voodoo in the pragmatic terms of the tactician:

> "Vodou . . . isn't concerned with notions of salvation and transcendence. What it's about is getting things *done.* You follow me? In our system, there are *many* gods, spirits. Part of one big family, with all the virtues, all the vices. There's a ritual tradition of communal manifestation, you dig? . . . Come on, man, you know how this works, it's *street* religion. . . . Vodou's like the street. Some duster chops out your sister, you don't go camp on the Yakuza's doorstep, do you? No way. You go to somebody, though, who can get the thing *done.* Right?"[61]

Voodoo is conceived as a *kinetic* system of empowerment, a religion explicitly involved with the tactics of the street (it also evokes the kinesis of the animistic spirit, as discussed above). Voodoo is also presented, like cyberspace itself, as an alternative method of conceptualizing the system: " 'Think of Danbala, who some people call the snake, as a program. Say as an icebreaker. Danbala slots into the Jackie deck, Jackie cuts ice. That's all.' 'Okay,' Bobby said, getting the hang of it, 'then what's the matrix? If she's a deck, and Danbala's a program, what's cyberspace?' 'The world,' Lucas said."[62]

Later in *Count Zero,* Bobby wonders whether the "spirits" he encounters are real: " 'I don't think I can swallow them being a bunch of Haitian voodoo gods, but who knows? . . . Could be, they're virus programs that have gotten loose in the matrix and replicated, and gotten really smart.' "[63] Bobby's mention of virus programs is interesting: some regard virus hackers as heroically battling the monolithic structures of financial and military power and information control—viruses are seen as a particularly insidious tactic of resistance, feeding upon the very spaces of strategic control. What is also interesting is how the latter two books in Gibson's Cyberspace Trilogy largely forego the cybernetically inflected idiolect of *Neuromancer* in favor of the "street" lingo of voodoo. Case begins to seem like an anachronism, more a part of the strategic system than of the tactical resistance. These "stories of miracles create another space, which coexists with that of an experience deprived of illusions." Further, these narratives separate themselves from technocratic, instrumental reason: "They exist alongside the analysis of facts, as the equivalent of what a political ideology introduces into that analysis. . . . They re-employ a system that, far from being their own, has been constructed and spread by others, and they mark this reemployment by 'superstitions,' excrescences of this belief in miracles which civil and religious authorities have always correctly suspected of putting in question the 'reason' behind power and knowledge hierarchies" (17–18). The interface of voodoo superstition with cybernetic certainty has a literally subversive effect upon the rational, geometric perfection of cyberspace. The modernist "mythology" of rationality, the mechanisms of instrumental reason, are undermined by a new set of postmodern tactical incursions. The data is reappropriated in the name of an appropriated religion as the *loas* of disembodied intelligences circulate through the instrumental spaces of information.

Unquestionably, Certeau's analysis of tactics, superstitions, and narratives has extraordinary relevance for an understanding, not just of *Neuromancer,* but also of the later variations Gibson has worked upon the theme. The relationships between narrative and tactical resistance and narrative and spatial appropriation tell us much about the tactics of

William Gibson, whose prose is rife with appropriations from literature, rock & roll, and surrealist art. It is no coincidence that *Count Zero* refers to that other master of appropriation and microspaces, Joseph Cornell (perhaps cyberspace should be rechristened the "Gibson box"). Gibson's found prose, his electronic idiolect, constructs a narrative of tactical appropriation, as his breakneck prose constructs an experience of kinesis and hyper-cyber-mobility. The ramifications of the subject's insertion into the RAM spaces of the information era are extended and grounded within social systems of power and resistance, strategies and tactics.

TRON—Cinema in Cyberspace

Neuromancer resembles *Blade Runner* in its bleak, impacted urbanism and in the density of its informational system, but it is *TRON* that represents the most sustained cinematic attempt at mapping cyberspace. The film predates cyberpunk, and its Disney ethos seem so at odds with the dominant attitudes of the subgenre that it remains largely unassimilated, even unremarked, in accounts of cyberpunk fiction. *TRON* exists in a kind of cybernetic vacuum, yet remains a deeply consequential gesture toward accepting and cognizing the existence of cyberspace and toward endowing its existence with phenomenological significance. If its narrative is often incoherent, and its characters lack "substance," then these flaws can perhaps be regarded as indicative of the film's struggle to define a new space; its failures then become symptomatic of the very ambiguities and uncertainties that cyberspace represents.

In films as different as *Scanners, Wargames* (1983), *Brainstorm,* and *TRON,* climactic scenes feature a character engaged in a frantic quest for information or control through the computer terminal. That the hurried and hushed pecking of fingers on keyboards lacks the visual interest of car chases and special effects pyrotechnics is evident. Jameson's comments regarding the representation of these instruments of reproduction, cited in connection with Philip Dick in chapter 1, are also interesting in this context: "they make very different demands on our capacity for aesthetic representation than did the relatively mimetic idolatry of the older machinery of the futurist movement. . . . Here we have less to do with kinetic energy than with all kinds of new reproductive processes; and in the weaker productions of postmodernism the aesthetic embodiment of such processes often tends to slip back more comfortably into a mere thematic representation of content."[64] What Jameson misses here is the significance of the transformation of these reproductive environments of data storage, circulation, and retrieval into dramatic and kinetic environments of cybernetic accommodation. "Weaker productions" these might be, but in their insistence upon envisioning and entering these spaces of reproduction, they are clearly significant and are something more than "mere thematic representations." The various forms of cyberspace permit the reintroduction of the "kinetic energy" which had disappeared into electronic space. Cronenberg, in *Scanners,* tracks his camera across a circuit board before his telepathic protagonist instigates a spectacular meltdown—the computer becomes a physical body for Cronenberg, and thus a space of mutation. In *Brainstorm,* tense terminal intercutting gives way to an after-death cybernetic experience.

TRON's narrative, like *Neuromancer's,* involves a further penetration of the terminal frontier as Flynn, the hacker protagonist, finds himself translated into the virtual space that exists within the master computer. The film begins, as do *The Andromeda Strain* (1970), *Brainstorm, Explorers,* and others, with floating electronic graphics and numbers (the *floating signifiers* of cybernetic culture?). The camera probes the amorphous graphics and tracks across computer-generated circuitry, a perspective from above which dissolves to a vision of a real cityscape: urban and cybernetic spaces are again overlapped and interchanged. In the tradition of cinematic science fiction populism, *TRON* is a saga of man vs. machine and individual vs. corporation. The urban landscape therefore represents an a priori arena of capitalist domination and control, while the infraterminal spaces demonstrate the shift of corporate power to electronic fields. The employees of ENCOM work in small cubicles and the matte-painted background shows these cubicles extending back to an apparent infinity. Later, in cyberspace, the cells that Master Control uses to hold uncooperative, anthropomorphized computer programs are displayed in a similar shot: the panoptic powers of the corporation exist at all levels.

The attention that *TRON* received upon initial release was due to its special effects: it was the first commercial film to include entirely computer-generated sequences. Although much of the film is only computer-*enhanced,* sixteen minutes of footage represented the state of the art of computer animation techniques (circa 1982). These processes do not require any physical models or drawings—everything can be generated, including effects of depth, light, shadow, and movement, by the computer. The procedures remain powerfully labor-intensive, but computer power and time is the issue, not the man-hours of traditional animation processes.

Syd Mead, designer of the vehicles and street scenes in *Blade Runner,*

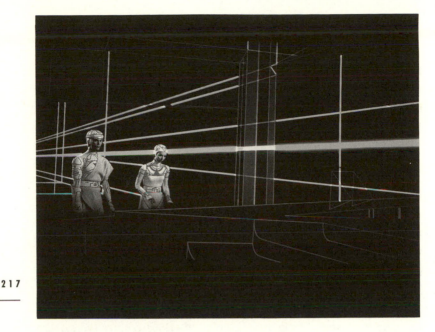

TERMINAL Computer-generated backgrounds in *TRON*'s cyberspace.
(Walt Disney Productions)

PENETRATION performed similar tasks for *TRON*. While the *Blade Runner* hovercars were constructed of a maze of jutting wheels, realistic dials, and endless details, both ornamental and functional, the vehicles of *TRON* are smooth and modular, almost featureless and boldly monochromatic. "Our visual vocabulary is made up of familiar objects, each of which has a recognizable form," Mead has written. "The tank featured in *TRON* started as a quick review of the images which instantly say 'tank.' "[65] It is certainly interesting that the object-based MAGI Synthavision database used to animate these forms permitted constructions built up from a collection of previously defined "primitive" geometric shapes—precisely the method Mead used in designing his vehicles.[66] The Euclidean perfection of the tanks, lightcycles, and carriers of *TRON* speaks to the conditions of their cybernetically pristine origin.

The disengagement from the physical body of the referent also extends to a new mobility. The computer-controlled camera brought an unimagined exactitude of cinematic movement and enabled the swooping maneuvers along the canyons of the Death Star in Lucas's *Star Wars,* but the precision of the computer-generated image inscribes a precision of perspective which eludes the ordinary eye. In addition, the simulated objects of this unreal world are presented through a camera movement that is itself a simulation. The apparent point of view can begin at an encompassing angle high above the action, then move smoothly down, ease beneath it, and rotate and track to follow a hurtling vehicle toward its destination. This is not a trajectory associated with the physical experience of a human perspective and represents a kind of ecstatic terminal vision, a kinetic transcendence of bodily limitations. The human appropriates the space through the exercise of a powerful, nearly omnipotent gaze.

To understand the significance of *TRON*, two cornerstones of film theory should be introduced, albeit in extremely abbreviated fashion. First, the motion picture camera has frequently, almost invariably, been linked to subjective vision. As one textbook states, "it is usually impossible not to see camera movement as a substitute for *our* movement."[67] Writers on the cinema, in its early history as well as its contemporary manifestations, have often written of a camera/eye equivalence. For some theorists the camera's function is precisely to reproduce the spatiotemporal unities of human perception (see works by Siegfried Kracauer and André Bazin, for example). In other writings the camera constructs an entirely new kind of vision, *extending* the power of the human eye (Dziga Vertov and Stan Brakhage are exemplary of this mode) and thus the experience of consciousness itself. In cinematic practice, as Christian Metz has punned, there are some "objective (*objectif*) preconditions:" lens choices tend toward the 50mm "normal" lens, for example, so called because it most effectively simulates the spatial relations produced by lens of the human eye. Theorists and filmmakers from Hugo Münsterberg to Maya Deren and beyond have demonstrated how cinematic structures allude to states of consciousness—the close-up, for example, is analogous to the phenomenon of attention, while the flashback replicates the functions of memory in a particularly sensible form.[68]

Almost equally pervasive, although less remarked, has been the linking of cinematic vision to the technologies of modernity. Reflexive gestures toward the power of the medium itself fall into this category, including the knockabout comedy of early films like *Uncle Josh at the Picture Show* (1902), the sublimity of Keaton's *Sherlock Jr.,* and René Clair's *Paris Qui Dort* (both 1924) and the thoroughgoing analysis of the medium performed in Vertov's *Man With a Movie Camera* (1929), not to mention the entire history of the New American and Godardian cinemas. The technology of the cinema is often combined with *other* technologies. When the operators of Hale's Tours mounted the camera on the front of a locomotive, audiences experienced a powerful synthetic kinesis which was a function of the camera as well as the engine's new mobility through a redefined landscape. The films of Hale's Tours might present nearly pristine landscapes, but tours of new metropolises were equally popular—the exoticism of new locales coupled with the exoticism of new technologized spaces.

In Clair's avant-garde crane shot in *Paris Qui Dort,* the camera, now mounted on one of the elevators in the Eiffel Tower, shows us the intricacy of that monument to modernity as nothing else could. Annette Michelson has produced a number of texts around the relationship between film and the industrial technologies of the modern period. She writes, "Clair not only exploits the tower's mobile potential but also brings into play its subjective functions, its framing, focusing, viewfinding capacities. The tower had been décor and actor. By transforming it into a complex optical instrument, a filmic apparatus, Clair makes it a camera." She also notes that the use of the tower as a cinematic vantage dates back to the Lumiéres.[69] Michelson has also written about Eisenstein's appropriation of a factory conveyor in *Strike* (1925) and his creation of a space at once phenomenal and polemical: "a sumptuous movement of the camera through that factory's space, inspired, no doubt, in a way characteristic of him, by the concrete structure of the space and its industrial cranes."[70] Here she refers to Eisenstein's "propulsion into cinema," but one might extend this to include the spectator's analogous propulsion into cinema and simultaneous propulsion into the newly technologized world of which cinema is only one emblem (in her essay on *2001,* the propulsion of the spectator into the cinematic field becomes an explicit theme).[71]

This brief review should at least indicate that cinema often provides coincident analogues of subjective *interiority* and technological *exteriority.* Almost from its inception, cinema is a cyborg apparatus. So that when Christian Metz declares that the fundamental identification which the spectator has is "with the camera," the historical significance of this ought to be understood. The "double movement" of projection and introjection, presented by Metz in primarily phenomenological terms,[72] can also be seen in terms of the *projection* of a purposive human consciousness, but the *introjection* is of a particularly technologized space, a space which the camera mediates and assimilates to the terms of vision. The crisis of the subject in postmodern electronic space, then, is a crisis represented in terms of an ambiguous subjective vision, presented effectively in Cronenberg's *Videodrome* (see chapter 1).

The introduction of computer-generated graphics into the cinematic presentation of films like *TRON* or *The Last Starfighter* therefore poses no particular analytical difficulties. Cinema has traditionally been interlaced with new technologies of vision and mobility, and thus with extensions of consciousness and subjective empowerment. The cinema *already* constructs a space of accommodation to unfamiliar technologies. As Walter Benjamin observed, cinema's development corresponds to profound changes in the apperceptive apparatus. *TRON* utilizes computer-generation techniques to signify the activity inside the computer, and so there is something both mimetic and symbolic in these representations. Light is made tangible, and as it is used both to define space and indicate levels of power, light comes to signify existence itself.

TRON's game grid is black until activated, whereupon thin rays of light circumscribe the playing field and boundaries. As in *Neuromancer,* this is an infinite, *potential* space that does not exist until it is occupied and thereby delimited. *TRON* makes extensive use of vector graphics to generate backgrounds and cyberscapes. These spaces extend in three-dimensions and are defined around the inevitable structure of the grid, with vectors meeting at a virtual horizon in the depthless distance. *Neuromancer's* original book cover featured a similar design, and in fact such grids have become a ubiquitous part of cyberspatial representations, recalling the grids that marked so many modernist movements: "The grid functions to declare the modernity of modern art," Rosalind Krauss writes, and it states "the autonomy of the realm of art" from the realms of nature and mimesis. The space demarcated by the grid constitutes its own sufficient reality. Krauss argues that the grid further announces the temporality of modernism because it is "the form that is ubiquitous in the art of *our* century" alone. The grid therefore serves as a doubled sign of modernity—as it represented the present, "everything else was declared to be the past."[73] The "new monuments" of cyberspace, constructed of chrome and light, still adhere to the principles of modernity in their abjection of nature, their rational autonomy, and their insistence upon a present that has transcended its own history.

The three-dimensional grids that structure electronic space recall Sol LeWitt's open modular cubes, and *TRON* contains what must be a direct quotation in the laboratory where Flynn is digitized, a space dominated by a large, white scaffolding within an overall cubic array. The overlap between physical and terminal spaces is foreshadowed, but a phantom minimalism arises as well. Elsewhere, Krauss has described the project of minimalist sculpture in terms that are strikingly appropriate to the cyberspatial representations of *TRON:* "The significance of the art that emerged in this country in the early 1960s is that it staked everything on the accuracy of a model of meaning severed from the legitimizing claims of a private self. . . . The ambition of minimalism was, then, to relocate the origins of a sculpture's meaning to the outside, no longer modeling its structure on the privacy of psychological space but on the public, conventional nature of what might be called cultural space."[74] "Conventional systems of ordering" were summoned "to determine composition," most notably, the regular geometric angles and intersections of the cube and the grid. The "cultural space" of contemporary existence is predicated upon an interrogation of the body and its space of inhabitation. The translation of this imploded monumentalism (Smithson's term for the products of minimalism) into the cyber-fictions of *TRON* and *Neuromancer* thus represents a significant popularization of the forms and rhetoric of avant-garde practice. On the other hand, it represents a mapping of a three-dimensional sculptural space onto the flat terrain of the cinema or video screen, which drastically changes the bodily integration with that space. The body must now appropriate the space as a *perceiving* body, just as Deckard engaged with the terminal space of the photoscanner in *Blade Runner.*

TRON begins with a complex trajectory among phenomenal spatialities before settling into a sustained presentation of life in cyberspace. Computer forms coalesce into a humanoid figure, there is an electronic flash, and the film's title is revealed. The camera probes the title, revealing the floating geometries of cyberspace. Subjective camera movement again heralds the problem of a new subjectivity. Cyberspace gives way to the more familiar urban grid as the viewer is reintroduced to the real world, in the form of a teenager playing a videogame. The action shuttles between human and cyberspace perspectives, as videogame blips are transformed into "living," "breathing" entities with their own personalities.

"Meanwhile," as a title reads, "in the real world . . . ," the head-hacker at this videogame emporium, Flynn, is introduced, seated at his terminal in an attempt to break into his old employer's computer to prove that his game programs were stolen by the new company president. Flynn is already imbricated in the cybernetic realm; he is already a part of the machine, like Case, who is incomplete when not jacked in. He also resembles Edison Carter from *20 Minutes into the Future,* introduced wielding his videocamera while existing as little more than a video image himself. These characters are coextensive with a new electronic technology that utterly defines them, even before their literal entries into the space of the machine. The pervasive overlap of urban- and cyberspace is now met by the first movements in the trajectory toward a new humanity; cyborg spaces must be inhabited by cyborg beings.

The shots of Flynn's physical presence before the alphanumeric terminal display, engaged in a rhetorical dialogue with his icebreaking program, are succeeded by an aerial tracking in across cyberspace. The camera moves down into the matrix to reveal the smooth form of a cyber-tank. Now the computerized Flynn (Flynn's "program") sits at the controls. Before it, on yet another screen, a wireframe display of a computer landscape stretches onward, while the control station rotates within its nested setting of counter-rotating wheels. A shot over the program's shoulder to the vector display puts the program "in" cyberspace. The static scene of invisible information processing (in both human brain and computer bank) has been transformed into the hyperkinetic vocabulary of the war film. The space is thus grounded for the viewer in three ways: by the narrative, through the genre of the war movie, and by the evocation of a video game. Flynn types frantically in the "real world," until the terminal reads that his illegal code "has been deleted from the system" (an interlude in cyberspace demonstrates just how painful such deletions can be).

As the sequence continues, the film intercuts with increasing speed among the three spaces: Flynn in the so-called real world, Flynn's computer-analogue at the high-tech controls of its cybernetic tank, and the smooth, computer-generated chase between the tank and pursuing security vehicles. Three levels of action are thus introduced, each with its own distinct phenomenal quality. The first and third levels, representing physical and cybernetic spaces, are already familiar from the analysis of *Neuromancer,* but the middle level, featuring the Flynn-program, offers something else, namely, the Disney stock-in-trade, anthropomorphism. In the Disney universe, actuarial programs are as boring as the insurance salesmen who use them, and all programs engage in debates regarding the existence of the "users"—those mythic beings in another realm. "If there aren't any users, then who wrote me?" asks one theologically inclined computer program. The problem of configuring the space of electronic culture for human appropriation and assimilation is largely sidestepped by a narrative which avoids any hint of "otherness." Gravity holds within this electronic system; and if jubilation exists, then it is far from the "bodiless exultation" in which Case rejoices. Computer programs are human—in fact, computer programs seem to be white, heterosexual, and chaste.[75] Other functions are, like R2D2 and C3PO of *Star Wars,* more like pets, such as the animated "Bit" (or, in Epcot Center, "I/O"). Electronic space is a fully bodied space—a space of denial, appropriation of the crudest sort.

Visually, though, *TRON* almost decimates its own crude anthropocentrism. First, the film is unrelentingly flat. Mead's vehicles and light-cycle arena and the costumes by Moebius emphasize the flatness of the cybernetic space—the costumes are only detailed with a latticework of thin lines suggestive of microcircuitry, for example. A comparison of Mead's work on *Blade Runner* and *TRON* is instructive. Where *Blade Runner* presented a bewilderingly complex urbanism, a site of dislocation through density, *TRON's* spaces are monotonously barren. The Panavision screen often features a single character in a grey costume, circuit lines glowing dully red, standing against a grey background, broken perhaps by a blue line which extends offscreen to further emphasize the emptiness of the horizontal expanse (at the end of the film, when the "good" programs are triumphant, warmer colors spread over the cyberscape—again, the cold functionalism of the corporation leaves its mark on the cybernetic realm).

In addition, computer-generated effects, such as those found here or in *The Last Starfighter,* are characteristically too perfect to be taken as acceptable facsimiles of the real world. The surfaces are too smooth and undetailed, reflections too perfectly focused, movements too unswerving and noninertial. As Sobchack has written, "electronic space constructs objective and superficial equivalents to depth, texture and invested bodily movement."[76] The new "depthlessness" that Jameson has proclaimed as characteristic of postmodernism receives its surest (but least critical) figuration in these translations, abstractions, and reductions of the real world. The body, with its analogic imperfections, is exempted from the digital world—this is precisely a *disembodied space.*

Finally, there is no reassuring intercutting to the stability and familiarity of the aforementioned "real world" once Flynn has been translated into the memory banks of the computer. Sobchack writes that the deflated space of *TRON* therefore: "presents this new electronic subjectivity and terminal space as nearly 'absolute'. For most of the film almost everything and everyone have mutated into a simulation, and the category of the 'real' (that narrative 'real world' mainframing the computer program world) is short-circuited and loses power. Simulation seems the *only* mode and space of being."[77] She further notes that the film exemplifies Baudrillard's proclamation that the medium no longer exists in its strictest sense, because everywhere there is only immixture.[78]

Metz argued that cinematic identification is primarily with the filmic apparatus itself—specifically with the camera. This identification is frequently disguised by the operations of narrative and the spectator's concomitant secondary involvement with his or her screen surrogate, but in many films the power and presence of the camera is nevertheless displayed, however fleetingly. *TRON's* cyberkinesis, radically distinct from bodily movement, hyperbolizes the identification with the camera—although, in this case, the "camera" is a fiction—it's a virtual camera, moving about in a virtual world. In *TRON* and other computer-generated works, the space *is* the fiction. Still, the "camera" gives the viewer *a place* in this virtual world, a place defined almost solely in terms of spatial penetration and kinetic achievement. If Merleau-Ponty is right, and the ability to conceive space depends upon our being "thrust into it by our body," then *TRON's* cinematic kinesis constructs an effective space of accommodation. More directly than even *Neuromancer's* breathless prose, *TRON* "thrusts" its viewers into a once-inconceivable space. As explicitly as in the early history of film, the viewer identifies with a hyperomniscient camera, now associated with the virtual realities of postmodern technology.

On the other hand, *TRON* certainly never attains the thorough destabilization of space and spectator that one associates with *2001* or the raising of the bridges in Eisenstein's *October*. A useful film to compare to *TRON* is probably Michael Snow's epic *La Région Centrale* (1971). Here, Snow permits a remote-controlled camera to reconstruct the physical landscape and the spectator's perception. As in *TRON,* the camera attains a freedom of movement (about its own axes) "which can mechanically perform more motions than the subtlest of film-makers, holding it by hand," could ever achieve. The world depicted, as P. Adams Sitney notes, is a function of the camera's own technology: "The whole visible scene, the hemisphere of the sky and the ground extending from the camera mount (whose shadow is visible) to the horizon, becomes the inner circumference of a sphere whose center is the other central region: the camera and the space of its self."[79] Like the tundra-space of Snow's film, *TRON* produces an epic representation of a space which alludes to the invisible technology through which that space is constituted. But *La Région Centrale* forces the viewer into radical modes of perceptual engagement, and without the reassuring presence of the human in the landscape to act as the spectator's reifying surrogate. Like *2001* and *October,* Snow's film presents a technological space in which the horizon is thrown out of balance, a decentering and *cinematic* space perceptually different than physical reality. *TRON* is not quite so extraordinary.

Vivian Sobchack argues that the "deflation of deep space" in films like *TRON* is "presented not as a loss of dimension, but rather as an excess of surface. The hyperspace of these films is proudly two-dimensional."[80] This excess of surface is a sign of what Jameson regards as the waning of the subject, of interiority, in its traditional form, and it finds a figuration within this "alternative and absolute world" of "discrete pixels and bits of information that are transmitted *serially,* each bit discontinuous, discontiguous, and absolute."[81] What is constructed is a new space which does not so much annihilate, as require the *refiguring* of, the subject.

In strikingly analogous terms, Rosalind Krauss has analyze the "radical developments" of minimalist sculpture. On one level, minimalism continued what Rodin and Brancusi initiated by relocating the "point of origin of the body's meaning" from "its inner core to its surface:" "[T]he sculpture of our own time continues this project of decentering. . . . The abstractness of minimalism makes it less easy to recognize the human body in these works and therefore less easy to project ourselves into the space of that sculpture with all of our settled prejudices left intact. Yet our bodies and our experience of our bodies continue to be the subject of this sculpture—even when a work is made of several hundred tons of earth."[82] While it might seem a bit silly to apply such terms to a Disney film, some comparisons do suggest themselves. Cyberspace is precisely noncorporeal, and so it is precisely nonsubjective. If it is an interiorized space, then this is not the interiority of psychologized subjectivity, but rather of a fully technologized (cultural) space which overlaps and restates the vocabularies of a postmodern urbanism. In the terms that Krauss offers, the radical aspect of *TRON* might be located in its "relocation of the point of origin of the body's meaning" from a *psychological* essentialism to the parameters of a *techno-cultural* configuration. Even when the work is "made of" millions of bytes of information within the banks of a computer's memory, "our bodies and our experience of our bodies continue to be the subject" of that work.

The excess of surface apparent in *TRON's* paraspace emphasizes a terminal decentering of human experience and definition. As Jameson wrote, in the days *before Neuromancer,* "this latest mutation in space—postmodern hyperspace—has finally succeeded in transcending the capacities of the individual human body to locate itself, to organize its immediate surroundings perceptually, and cognitively to map its position in a mappable external world."[83] The point of origin of the subject is relocated, away from an a priori interiority and toward the modes of a technologically produced cybernetic culture.

The subject must be reinterpreted, must reinterpret *itself,* to project itself into that space—the literally unsettling spatiality creates the conditions for that reinterpretation. The cyberspatial explorations of *TRON* and the cyberpunks are attempts to encode "our bodies and our experience of our bodies," even if the abstractness of their spaces make it "less easy to recognize the human body . . . and therefore less easy to project ourselves into the space." Krauss's understanding of sculpture, an art form of bodily engagement with a spatiotemporal object, reveals an underlying narrative impulse that now becomes explicit in the cyberfictions of *Neuromancer* and *TRON* (where the surrogate experience of narrative *replaces* bodily engagement).

TRON wavers between narrative and spectatorial dominants, creating a provocative aesthetic countertension. The film also oscillates between the familiar, character-centered structures of "classical" Hollywood cinema and a nonsubjective terminal identity generated by the hyperbolic trajectories of a computer-simulated camera that exists apart from the narrative in a giddy display of its own cybernetic power. I have noted that many of these works presented narratives *about* simulation, and now the function becomes clear. The narrative marks the dislocation of the human in the terminal nonspace, but it also represents the means of encoding that space as a possible site of human projection. In *Neuromancer* and *TRON,* the breakdown of the syntagmatic chains of narrative (deliberate in *Neuromancer* but clearly accidental in *TRON*) underscores the self-sufficiency of the spatialities being projected. Both rely on familiar generic paradigms to ground their spaces, but neither narrative quite succeeds *as narrative.* Narrative ultimately narrates its own failure and supersession by the overwhelming phenomenological imperatives of terminal space.[84]

Finally, then, *TRON* exists as cyborg cinema; part "organic," part "cybernetic;" partly destabilizing, partly reassuring. The computerized effects fill the cinema screen, mingling digital and analogic technologies of reproduction. The ambiguous status of this *TRON*-object extends to the representation of terminal space: the subjectivity established there is *analogous* to Flynn's, in that the viewer is also propelled into cyberspace, but it is hardly *identical* to Flynn's—the viewer's experience is bounded by the purely visual engagement with a two-dimensional screen. The *narrative* thus encourages an identification with Flynn to enhance the phenomenological impact of the *film's* electronic spatiality.

The narrative serves as an almost literal analogy for the viewer's perception of the terminal space. Perhaps this very redundancy obviates the imperatives of narrative, leaving it as a formal structure without conviction. In its narrative, its special effects, and its camera aesthetic, *TRON* operates as a provisional form, an interface between different cinematic functions and varying subjectivities. In its kinesis it provides an elegant example of Merleau-Ponty's "physiognomic perception," that subject-object interface; while its narrative, with its anthropomorphic assimilations, serves the ostensibly similar—if redundant—function of speaking "to him of himself," giving "his own thoughts their place in the [new] world."

But, finally, the narrative of *TRON* promises no *need* for accommodation to a new reality. Rather, the diegesis posits cyberspace as coextensive, and indeed *synonymous,* with physical reality—simulation replaces reality, yes, but the banality of both realms makes the experience moot. In *Neuromancer* a hypertechnologized everyday reality requires all the trickster skills of the cybernetic tactician just to survive: the headlong kinesis of cyberspace is only the literalization of an already cyberneticized existence, while in *TRON* cyberspace is a theme park just as comfortable as the adolescent, Disneyfied "real world." The narrative denies the need for accommodation and finally denies that the world has changed at all, while the film's special effects construct an undeniably new and important space into which it thrusts its viewers, propelling them toward a perceptual accommodation with the demands of a terminal reality.

There's Always . . . *Tomorrowland*

TRON is not the Disney empire's sole engagement with the technological spaces of the electronic age, as the cyberspaces of Disneyland and Walt Disney World demonstrate. Referring to the 1939 World's Fair, H. Bruce Franklin has correctly noted that, "A fair billing itself as the World of Tomorrow may be considered just as much a work of science fiction as a short story or a novel, a comic book or a movie."[85] This must also be true of such exhibitions as Future World or Tomorrowland. These disneyworlds bear an interesting relation to works of contemporary science fiction literature and cinema in which the ontologies of space and narrative intertwine.

The theme parks operate as deeply ambivalent experiences; but Tomorrowland and Future World speak eloquently to the anxieties of the present era. The pervasive fear which underlies the decade just past is a consequence of recognizing that *we are in the future*. The future

is no longer a harmless fiction, a sacred age which, by its very definition, will never arrive; it is upon us with a vengeance. The disembodying
spaces of the terminal era exist independently of human experience or
control, and thus our presence in the future has initiated a seemingly
inexhaustible period of mega-nostalgia, an obsessive recycling of yesteryear. Even futures past are exhumed and aired, their quaint fantasies
simultaneously mocked and yearned for. A perusal of *Popular Mechanics*
magazines from the 1930s through the 1950s would demonstrate the
promise of an abundant, machine-aided existence where the satisfied
citizen would calmly smoke his pipe amidst an array of vacuum-tubed
Rube Goldberg devices tirelessly servicing his every desire. The comic
book character Zot! lived in one of the wonderfully bulbous cities
designed by Frank R. Paul for the cover of any issue of *Amazing Stories.*
"SF futures are moments of our past," Jameson states.[86]

These are reveries of progress based upon *visibility,* recalling Clute's
description of the crisis in science fiction: "No longer has information
any tangible, kinetic analogue in the world of the senses. . . . Gone are
the great arrays of vacuum tubes."[87] Technological change has moved
into the terminal spaces of the computer, the video screen, and the
fiber-optic cable. The return to the retro-futures of the 1920s through
the 1950s speaks to a perceived loss of subjective comprehension of,
or control over, the invisible cyberhistories and cyberspaces of the
present.

This taming of temporal progress and these projections of fantasies
of an innocent technological mastery bring us to the gates of the Magic
Kingdom of Tomorrowland and to Walt Disney World's EPCOT Center.
EPCOT—which finally opened in 1982, years after his demise—was Disney's dream of an Experimental Prototype Community of Tomorrow:
real futures, brought to you by real corporations. In practice, it is more
like an extension of the more traditional world's fair/amusement park
ambience of the original Tomorrowland.

Tomorrowland grows more wonderful with the passage of every year,
as its parabolic, populuxe stylings give a full and nostalgic voice to the
aspirations of the New Frontier (although its concrete expanses also
suggest a down-at-heels airport). The extroversion of its boomerang-
inflected balustrades stands in contrast to the imploded and anonymous mall structures of EPCOT's Future World. In Tomorrowland, each
aerodynamically turned, turquoise-and-white-colored detail enshrines
a visible yearning for flight, a thrusting beyond limits, and the hope and
confidence in an unambivalently better tomorrow. It unintentionally
becomes the most charming of retro-futures—even the name bespeaks

a casual colloquialism. *Tomorrow* is, after all, not so far away, while *land* suggests the whimsicality of the fairy tale (it is an all-important suffix in conveying a childlike innocence or nostalgia). Its extension at EPCOT, however, is something more than an exercise in self-similarity—*Future World* is a state of mind rather than a make-believe location, a corporate symbol of monadic inclusiveness. The *future* is indefinite and permanent; the *world* is equally inescapable and essentially boundless.[88] Tomorrowland is a promise, while Future World sounds more like a threat. The expansiveness of the missions to Mars and exploration beneath the sea is replaced by the concern with the imploded cybernetic spaces of information management. This latter-day ode to tomorrow could as well be any corporate plaza in the outskirts of any urban area. Its immaculate commons, mirrored facades, and soaring fountains stand in proud affirmation of nothing in particular.

Disney's contemporary future is dominated by a benign corporate sponsorship providing effective population control, abundant consumer goods, and the guarantee of technological infallibility. Of course, Disneyland and Disney World exemplify this future vision better than any other site on Spaceship Earth. These theme parks have long aroused admiration for their skillfully designed spaces. Urban planner James Rouse declared that "The greatest piece of urban design in the US today is Disneyland. Think of its performance in relation to its purpose." Michael Sorkin has proposed, not altogether admiringly, that Disneyland is "the place where the ephemeral reality of the cinema is concretized into the stuff of the city." And Margaret King argues that the Disney parks humanize their technology through architecture: "The Disney town is a kind of stage based on architectural symbols for romanticized, stylized human interaction. . . . The example of the parks may provide an alternative vision of what people seek in urban environments: everyday life as an art form, with entertainment, fantasy, playacting, role-playing and the reinstatement of some of the values which have been lost in the megalopolis."[89] These lost values also find their way into the ludic urban topography of the Situationists: "In each of its experimental cities unitary urbanism will act by way of a certain number of force fields, which we can designate by the classic term 'quarter.' Each quarter will tend toward a specific harmony, divided off from neighboring harmonies; or else will play on a maximum breaking up of internal harmony.[90] The Situationist division of the city (see chapter 2) is a paraspace that echoes the topology of the brain. The maps of Disneyland also suggest such a model: the different-colored lands echo the diagrams of cerebral lobes, while Main Street mimics the stalk of the central nervous system leading into the central hub (the *corpus calossum*), which links these different regions. One might take this idea further—it's surely interesting that the rough-and-ready macho pragmatism represented by Frontierland and Adventureland are located in the "left brain," while the whimsy of Fantasyland and the fantastic science fiction of Tomorrowland are strictly right brain "functions." This layout is identical in all versions of the Magic Kingdom.[91]

The Situationists demanded a revolution of everyday life—the communist/capitalist reliance upon labor was refused for a more total liberation of the individual against the repressive reason of the state. Situations were designed to provoke a recognition of alienation and permit the perception of the reifications of spectacle. The division of urban space would produce maximal harmonies and disharmonies, a notion exploited in SF (in the anarchic, libidinal, unlicensed zone of Delany's *Triton,* theatre groups abruptly perform for "micro-audiences" of one). Can one perceive, in these Situationist texts of 1953–58 (Disneyland opened in 1955), an impulse toward a politicized Disneyland, the theme park as Situation and unitary urban field? "That which changes our way of seeing the streets is more important than what changes our way of seeing painting. . . . It is necessary to throw new forces into the *battle of leisure.*"[92]

Still, the corporately controlled Magic Kingdom as it exists is the antithesis of the anarchic urbanism enshrined in the Situationist texts (and what might they have made of Euro-Disney?). The Disney empire is a strategic space, one that seems particularly susceptible to the trickster tactics of its visitors. But this apparent accommodation actually masks an ongoing activity of containment. One early Tomorrowland concept was the *Autopia,* where youngsters could drive actual, though miniature, automobiles. It was Disney's intent that they would learn traffic safety at an early age and would thereby be prepared to enter the L.A. freeway system. Unfortunately, the children took "demented delight" in crashing the cars, and the ride had to be put on tracks.[93] One can hardly blame the kids for resisting the immaculately conceived guidance that dominated the park at all turns, but the Disney ethos could never tolerate these signs of technological breakdown. When Disneyland opened, its designers waited to see where people actually walked before the layout of paths and park areas was finalized. Thus, the parks actually *assimilate* the tactical trajectories of its visitors, returning them in the form of strategies. Walking across the grass loses its subversive appeal—it's easier and more efficient to keep to the walkways. Subversion is rendered pointless or even, as in the case of the Autopia, impossible. Thus, what one finds at Disneyland, or Disney World, are *simulations* of tactics: simulations of the *dérive,* that aimless passage across the complexities of urban space so cherished by the Situationists, and simulations of *walking,* in the specific sense of inscribing oneself upon the territories of strategic power.

The "guests" circulate through the "lands" of the Magic Kingdom—Adventureland, Frontierland, Tomorrowland, Fantasyland—or the "worlds" of EPCOT Center—Future World, the World Showcase. When Disneyland first opened, there was no analogue for this aimless travel, this *dérive,* but now the shopping mall endows these environments with a phenomenological and sociological familiarity. Malls aspire to the same monadism as the Disney worlds, and their designs echo that of the parks with varying explicitness. Parking is relegated to vast outside areas, leaving the "real world" invisible beyond the boundaries of the

The future according to Futurama. Designed by Norman Bel Geddes for the General Motors Pavilion at the 1939 World's Fair. (Courtesy Photofest)

commercial kingdoms (recall Baudrillard's wonderful caveat that the real world only *seems* real against the background of Disneyland's explicit simulations). Perhaps, as in the immense and hypertotalizing mall in Edmonton, Alberta, there is even an amusement park. The spectacle has even come full circle: the national shopping pavilions and restaurants of the World Showcase (opened in 1982), recall the kiosks and "food courts" of countless suburban malls. The World Showcase represents a peculiar implosion of American tourism: foreign lands are further reduced and domesticated, rendered safe while remaining absurdly picturesque (including *actual natives*). The global village of McLuhan's dreams has been supplanted by the global *mall.*

William Kowinski proposes that strolling through a mall is a visual, blip culture experience: "It's TV that you walk around in."[94] One chooses from among an abundance of selections (stores::channels), solicited by an array of colorful enticements and standardized slickness, overwhelmed by the overall electronic *buzz.* Arthur Kroker makes the same comparison, but in postcyberpunk language: "Shopping malls are liquid TVs for the end of the twentieth century. . . . Shopping malls call forth the same psychological position as TV watching: voyeurism. . . . Rather than flicking the dial, you take a walk from channel to channel as the neon stores slick by. And not just watching either, but shopping malls have this big advantage over TV, they play every sense. . . . A whole image-repertoire which, when successful, splays the body into a multiplicity of organs, all demanding to be filled."[95] The body implodes within the cyberspace of the shopping mall in yet another manifestation of terminal identity. Kowinski: "[I]t's worth noting that Disneyland and the first enclosed malls were being built at about the same time."[96]

The nexus of mall/television/Disneyland is further enriched by the historical significance of Disney's response to television. At a time when every other movie studio regarded television as dire competition, Disney was to become the first producer to successfully exploit the new medium. *Disneyland* was a gigantic promotional piece for this new park: the behind-the-scenes footage, old films, and new productions were all geared toward selling the new attraction (Richard Schickel argues that Disneyland represented a uniquely new medium). ABC even financed the new park by buying over one third of the shares of Disneyland, Inc.[97] The mutually reinforcing symbiosis of the Disney-land/world/mall and the implosive reality of television is thus not coincidental, but designed. William Thompson, calling the park a "technological cathedral," noted in 1971 that "Disneyland itself is a kind of television set."[98] The theme parks represent an extension of the already-imploded spaces of TV set and shopping mall. Perhaps that consumerist nexus accounts for the park's architectural eclecticism. As Thomas Hine explains, "Disneyland offered a choice between Frontierland and Tomorrowland. So did the American Suburban house. The kitchen was futuristic, the dining room early American. Nobody paid much attention to the inconsistency."[99]

The World of Motion (presented by General Motors) tour concludes with an immense model of a future city replete with gleaming white spires, pneumatic transport, hovercars, and an overall expansiveness which never, ever, sprawls—an updated version of GM's Futurama, a sensation at the 1939 World's Fair. A vision of the future still survives at Epcot Center, then, based on central management, urban planning, and continuing technological progress. Disney World becomes a final haven for a purely technocratic projection of the future—the last bastion of instrumental reason. Perhaps the Disneyzone[100] is Le Corbusier's Radiant City. Like Disneyland, Radiant City enshrined a "value-neutral" dedication to the technologies of rationalism. This is precisely the future that cyberpunk has rebelled against. William Gibson's "The Gernsback Continuum" (1981) is about *the end of the future*. A photographer engaged to capture images of the Utopian architectures of Frank Lloyd Wright and other 1930s and 1940s futurists enters one of those Zones endemic to postmodern fiction ("Ever so gently, I went over the Edge"). In a giant ontological shift, he finds himself within this imaged, imagined, but never created retro-future. Now it exists, inhabited by an equally Utopian population. Gibson's description perfectly evokes the aspirations of another age, but it also sounds like a trip to Disneyland:

> They were white, blond, and they probably had blue eyes. They were American. Dialta had said that the Future had come to America first, but had finally passed it by. But not here, in the heart of the Dream. Here, we'd gone on and on, in a dream logic that knew nothing of pollution, the finite bounds of fossil fuel, of foreign wars it was possible to lose. They were smug, happy, and utterly content with themselves and their world. And in the Dream, it was *their* world. Behind me, the illuminated city: Searchlights swept the sky for the sheer joy of it. I imagined them thronging the plazas of white marble, orderly and alert, their bright eyes shining with enthusiasm for their floodlit avenues and silver cars.[101]

To exorcise these "semiotic ghosts," he watches television until they go away.

Bodies in cyberpunk fiction and performance (hell, *existence*) are invested in technology at street/skin level. "For the cyberpunks," author/editor Bruce Sterling writes, "technology is visceral. . . . [I]t is pervasive, utterly intimate. Not outside us, but next to us. Under our skin; often, inside our minds."[102] In gentler language, cyberpunk is "about how our increasingly intimate feedback relationship with the technosphere we are creating has been, is, and will be, altering our definition of what it means to be human itself."[103] The body is inscribed and defined, paradoxically extended and delimited by these pervasive, invasive technologies.

Brooks Landon astutely notes that cyberpunk, ostensibly a literary subgenre, is non- or even antinarrative in its practice (literature is simply not phenomenologically *intense* enough for cyberpunk).[104] The compression of *20 Minutes into the Future,* the cityscapes of *Blade Runner,* the industrial noise of SPK and Skinny Puppy, the autodestructive robots of Mark Pauline's frenzied Survival Research Laboratory, the bodily transformations of Stelarc, the fragmentary voicings of Burroughs and the comics of Howard Chaykin are where the cyberpunk impulse reaches its fruition. In the best, most urgent, cyberpunk, narrative is reduced and seemingly impoverished (Gibson has become a better novelist but a weaker cyberpunk). The rides of Disneyland, however, for all their technological sophistication, retain a narrative drive inscribed by overdetermined and overlapping teleologies.

"Disneyland," Thomas Hine observes in *Populuxe,* "was the first place ever conceived simultaneously with a TV series," and the park is indeed notable for its overall narrative character. The Magic Kingdom was designed, not by architects, but by filmmakers, Hine continues; not as a group of buildings, but as an experience. It was "a movie that could be walked into."[105] One is led along Main Street USA toward the pinnacle of Fantasyland's castles. At the central square, towering Starjets lead to Tomorrowland, while other monuments lead to further adventures. Phillip Johnson stated that the park's architecture was dedicated, not to the design of space, but to "the organization of procession."[106] A general *telos* operates whether one concentrates on the overall structure of the entire park, the features of the various lands, or the details on each of the buildings—as Hine says, the experience is of a sequence of establishing shots, medium shots, and close-ups. Several writers have observed how the rides mimic the linear and anticipatory structures of narrative: "Each car is wired for stereophonic sound and turns electronically so that the occupant sees only what the designer has intended . . . exactly the way the movie camera sees."[107] The rides are intensely narrative as well—Peter Pan's Flight recapitulates the entire narrative of the film, encounters with giant plastic sea creatures in

20,000 Leagues Under the Sea are narrated by an ersatz James Mason, and the famed Jungle Cruise provides a human guide pretending to steer the vessel while interacting with the real flora and pseudo-fauna. Even the roller coaster, whose raison d'être is purely kinetic sensation, is narrativized in the Magic Kingdom. Space Mountain and Thunder Mountain are geographically specific simulated experiences (a space flight, a runaway train) which arguably add little to the pleasures of gravity.

It is not a startling innovation, this commingling of kinesis and narrative—as Raymond Fielding pointed out in 1957, Disney's Trip to the Moon is only an updating of the Hale's Tours exhibits which were popular between 1904 and 1906.[108] Audiences for Hale's Tours boarded a mock train carriage, and while a film of exotic locales played up ahead, the coach would be rocked and a breeze might even play over them. Now retitled Mission to Mars, the Disney attraction features a preflight area, seats which move in a simulacrum of gravitational effects, a film view of the exotic Martian landscape through upper and lower "windows," and even a fictitious crisis for dramatic effect. This combination of simulation and transportation, as noted, was a fundament of the park's conception. The WEDway (as in Walter E. Disney) People Mover has the distinction of being a ride with no purpose beyond demonstrating its own transport technology (it remains one of the most relaxing attractions at the park). Referring to the world's fairs of the nineteenth century, Michael Sorkin argues that

> as the scope of the fairs grew, the ordering and connection of elements assumed paramount importance. Reaching the scale and density of small cities, the fairs also became models, adopted visionary urbanism as an aspect of their agendas, both offering themselves as models of urban organization and providing, within their pavilions, panoramic visions of even more advanced cities to come. The crucial role played by movement systems within the enlarging fairs was not simply a product of necessity but a paradigm for physical relations in the modern city.[109]

Transportation becomes a pragmatic necessity, but also an augury of things to come. What comes most pervasively narrativized at these world's fairs is the mastery of technology, and primarily the high-concentration, high-circulation, high-technologies of the urban field. In the Disneyzone a utopian alternative to contemporary urbanism still prevails, but now the urban spatial negotiation becomes the paradigm for negotiating the newly pervasive *non*-spaces of terminal culture

(Sorkin: "Disneyzone . . . is a cartoon utopia, an urbanism for the electronic age"[110]).

The comfortable environments of the Disney parks represent the highest degree of user-friendliness in a human-technology interface, but ironically these are situated within an enormous, centrally controlled apparatus—in Certeau's terms, strategic space. In its structure and geography the park suggests a spatialization of computer functions. The park is, in fact, a giant computer, complexly programmed and constantly self-monitoring.[111] An exhibit at Communi-Core offers a limited view of the gigantic inert masses of computers which help to run "the show." There, for example, is the ominous MACS—Monitoring and Control System (pronounced "MAX"[112]). The uninteresting computer shells and human caretakers are enlivened by a holographic (but cute) anthropomorphized computer function: I/O ("eye-oh," computerese for "input/output"), permitting an apperception of invisible cybernetic operations.

The theme parks are themselves remarkably effective, albeit less explicit, visible projections of terminal space. The Disneyzone parallels the computer's program. The rides and attractions—files—are gathered into the subdivisions of the different Lands—folders. "Utilities" punctuate the array in the form of food and service kiosks. The pervasive transportation systems (monorail, horse-carriage, railroad, paddleboat, double-decker bus, WEDway People Mover) shuttle "guests"/ users from function to function, comprising an extremely efficient operating system. All the technology remains hidden behind the tropical plants and architectural facades, just as the ubiquitous beige shell of the personal computer disguises the microcircuitry within. Finally, the blips being processed and circulated within this cybernetic paraspace are—us. The computer becomes a site of bodily habitation and experience in the Disney theme parks—a technological interface so effective that most users are unaware of the interface at all.

All of the architectural, landscaping, and narrative strategies employed at the parks exist to reassure the visitor. Disneyland began as a park where Disney could extend his miniature train set in a surrounding of realistic landscape effects. A fascination with Americana also informed the project from an early point, and dioramas depicting historical events and eras (much like the tableaux of early film history) were placed along the train's route in a "coherent sequence." Finally, a desire to construct a safe and clean environment, thoroughly distinct from the chaos and boorishness of the traditional amusement park, contributed to the design. The result was an America reduced, frozen, and sanitized—a fortress against the dis-ease of 1950s society. Disney announced that, "Disneyland is going to be a place where you can't get lost."[113]

This evocation of a pseudo-Americana has distracted attention from the function of the technological. While Margaret King argues that Disneyland presents "traditional values in a futuristic form," she has missed the more interesting notion that the park prepares its "guests" for the future, and technologies to come, by grounding them in heavily *traditional forms.* The sophistication of the audioanimatrons presents singing bears and presidential simulacra; anthropomorphism is as prevalent as in any Disney film, and the narrative *telos* of architecture and rides further acclimates the subjects to the technologies around them. The entrance to the park is crucial: "Main Street is not an end in itself but the entryway into other less familiar realms."[114] The process of accommodation is heightened in Future World, where rides narrate the histories of the technologies of communication, transportation, and electricity.

But the rides do even more than this. The combination of simulation and transportation is an urgent part of the agenda. The body is put *in motion* in Disneyland—real movement of the subject's actual body occurs. Inevitably, though, this is supplemented by a further, *simulated* kinesis. The wraparound movie screens inevitably feature helicopter drops into the Grand Canyon (handrails are provided for queasy participants). In the Horizons ride the four-person vehicle moves laterally across an enormous IMAX screen. As a whirling molecular shape rotates outward to apparently engulf the visitors, the car tilts against the direction of the vortex. The kinesthesia is intense and effective, enhanced (as in Hale's Tours) by the "horizon" of the vehicle. The World of Motion propels its cars through a tunnel of frantically surging, projected images which includes the vertiginous passage into cyberspace originally used in *TRON.*[115] In the meantime, artificial breezes, sounds, and even smells extend the sensory address (the Universe of Energy's dinosaur presentation includes a change in humidity).

Tom Gunning has asserted that such technological attractions as Hale's Tours give "a reassuring context to this experience. . . . The desire to provide a place for the spectator related to the movement within the spectacle reveals the enjoyable anxiety the audience felt before the illusion of motion."[116] Lynne Kirby notes that this anxiety is hardly innocent, and she has convincingly argued that Hale's Tours was a symptomatic response to an urban-induced "hysteria" and that the simulated transport served to equip its audience with an illusion of mastery over, or at least accommodation to, the mighty technological forces which were being increasingly deployed.[117] She refers to Benjamin on the role of cinema: "The film is the art form that is in keeping with the increased threat to his life which modern man has to face. Man's need to expose himself to shock effects is his adjustment to the dangers threatening him. The film corresponds to profound changes in the apperceptive apparatus."[118] The same is true for the hypercinematic simulations of Tomorrowland and Future World.[119]

In the preceding chapter, I argued that contemporary science fiction produces two distinct ontological frames of reference—those of space and narrative. Science fiction provides the referential dimension absent from these new, disembodied, electronic spaces; the function of the genre is to compensate for the loss of the human by transforming these spaces into arenas susceptible to human perception. Recent SF further reconceives the subject and its ability to interface with the new terminal paraspace. Cyberpunk acknowledges the supersession of individual bodily experience in its hyperbolic, overdetermined prose, but the decentering of the human subject performed in the presentation of *other spaces* existing beyond human intervention is undermined by the transformation of these spaces into arenas of dramatic, human action. Cyberspace is entered by the cyberspace cowboys, and thus human will and determination are brought to bear upon this terminal realm. At its best a symbiosis is proposed, but in practice the ultimate *recentering* of the human subject within the cybernetic cosmology is beyond dispute.

In a similar manner, what finally occurs through all of the intensification of sensory experience on the rides of Tomorrowland and Future World is nothing less than an inscription *of* the body, *on* the body. These journeys into technologically complex zones ultimately serve to guarantee the continuing presence and relevance of the subject. You have a body, the rides announce; you exist. The body (the subject) penetrates these impossible spaces, finally to merge with them in a state of kinetic, sensory pleasure. The visitor is thus *projected* into the datascape and is *incorporated* by the technology (and by the narration of the technology) quite as fully as the cyberspace cowboys of Gibson's *Neuromancer*. The inscription on the body announces the human-machine interface, and technology thereby creates the conditions for its own acceptance. The Disney version is thus not so different from cyberpunk fiction in its presentation of a technological and overwhelming cyberspatiality physically *penetrated* by the body of the subject. Future World dazzles its guests with dislocating *other spaces* in the manner of a science fiction text, and augmented by a bodily address these rides locate and center the human, further reifying a perceived power.

In more banal fashion, therefore, Disney finds himself aligned with the cyberpunks at last. All this occurs within the most centralized and technocratic of environments, finally bearing out some of Baudrillard's darkest pronouncements. In Future World, technology indeed seems to possess its own agenda and engages in an endless process of writing itself on the bodies of its "guests" to permit those illusions of assimilation and mastery. The enormous, paraspatial, and cybernetic realm of Walt Disney World thus comprises a massive and self-regulating interface in which an illusory terminal space is rendered visible, controllable, and perhaps even adorable.[120]

The trajectory through the cyberspaces of this section, from the narrative metaphors of *Neuromancer* and *TRON* through the ludic explorations experienced through computer games, Disneyzones, and virtual reality technologies, traces the path of an increasingly direct interface operating between technology and body. Despite the headlong *rush* of Gibson's prose in *Neuromancer,* the reader's body nevertheless remains distinct from the techno-surrealist evocations of another reality that is uncomfortably like our own (the player of the *Neuromancer* game can engage with the diegesis more directly). In *TRON* the viewer is thrust into a technologically and phenomenologically distinct space through the synaesthetic effects of cinematic kinesis, but this radical maneuver is contained, explained, and grounded by the operations of a particularly conventional narrativity. Finally, in the imploded science fiction environments of EPCOT Center and virtual "cyberspace" the body is directly addressed by a provocative combination of kinesis and its simulation. Ultimately, narrative itself comes to seem a kind of clunky and intrusive interface, an anachronism from an earlier era of terminal identity.

The replacement of narrative by the sensory engagements of virtual reality represents the culmination of a fantasized form of representation that no longer seems representational. In this sense, virtual reality becomes the fulfillment of that drive toward Bazin's "myth of total cinema," a cinema without boundaries. All the senses are engaged by a perfect simulacrum of reality which denies its own technological origins. While Bazin emphasizes the impossibility of this long-standing fantasy of a total cinema, it can still be acknowledged that the promise of virtual reality does—to some degree—obviate the need for the narrative paradigm that has heretofore permitted the exploration of space by the spectator's screen-surrogate.[121] The body in virtual reality transcends the need for a surrogate character to experience the diegesis *for* him or her, or for a narrative to ground the exploration of an unfamiliar space. Instead, an illusion of direct, immediate (and seemingly *nonmediated*) engagement is produced, while spatial exploration is at last acknowledged as an experiential end in itself.

Virtual reality (in its present, primitive form, and as anticipated by Gibson's kinetic, frenetic cyberspace) thus effectively models the phenomenology of Merleau-Ponty as it continues the quest for total cinema that Bazin describes. Within these spaces of accommodation, narrative and virtual, the body moves toward its symbiosis with the electronic. The next stages of terminal identity, explored in the following chapter, map the cyborg superimpositions in which the human becomes fully inscribed, defined, and delimited by the forces of electronic culture.

TERMINAL

PENETRATION

4   TERMINAL FLESH

INTRODUCTION

Street boys of the green with cruel idiot smiles and translucent amber flesh, aromatic jasmine excrement, pubic hairs that cut needles of pleasure—serving insect pleasures of the spine— alternate terminal flesh when the egg cracks.—William Burroughs

With the appearance of *Neuromancer's* Case and *TRON's* Flynn, the state of terminal identity, the thorough imbrication of human being and electronic technology, is nearly complete. The body of the subject, and thus the subject itself, has been encoded and decoded, penetrating the terminal to discover, as a character in *Schismatrix* finds, that "there's a whole world behind this screen."[1] These subjects move between urbanand cyberspaces while retaining and even extending those qualities that mark them as human.

In contemporary fiction and philosophy the body has been successively—if not simultaneously—addicted to, infected by and wired into the cybernetic system. The imploded arenas of the datascape become the new phenomenal ground for bodily awareness. It is the experience of the body that operates to center the subject, which is why the body must serve as the locus for any interface with terminal reality (the narrator of Bernard Wolfe's *Limbo* muses, "The human skin is an artificial boundary: the world wanders into it and the self wanders out of it").[2] So far, the body has remained largely protected, a boundary that might be transgressed, but a boundary and limit point nevertheless. Yet, within these discourses, the body is hardly inviolate—it is instead a site of almost endless dissolution. From here the language of terminal identity becomes increasingly de-forming of the human, as the subject is simulated, morphed, modified, retooled, genetically engineered, and even dissolved.

Under postmodernity, science fiction emphasizes the *uncertainty of depth.* In Rudy Rucker's novel *Software,* a character's mind is transplanted into a robot body. "The whole process of changing bodies felt miraculous," he reflects. "Had he proved that the soul is real . . . or that it isn't?"[3] Good question, and one that science fiction is no longer afraid to ask. If SF narrates the body, it is no longer to privilege an eternal soul. The narratives of terminal flesh, whether SF or related tales of horror, offer up a series of provisional conclusions to the problem of human definition. The subject is the *body,* mutable and mutated. The subject is the *mind,* thinking and cognizing. The subject is its *memory,* recalling history and experience. The body in science fiction can be read symbolically, but it is a transparent symbol (as well as a symbol of its own transparent status), an immanent object, signifying nothing beyond itself. It is literally objectified; everything is written upon its surface. In the era of terminal identity, the body has become a machine, a machine that no longer exists in dichotomous opposition to the "natural" and unmediated existence of the subject. What is at stake in science fiction is no longer the fusion of beings and the immortality of the soul, but the fusion of being and electronic technology in a new, hard-wired subjectivity.

None of this is to suggest that science fiction has somehow negotiated or resolved the dilemmas of the subject and the body-machine. The very proliferation of narrative solutions, and the parallel explorations being performed in horror, reveals pervasive cultural anxieties and contradictions. The ecstatic dissolution of the body is counterbalanced by the recuperative strategies of narrative and generic structure within which the subject maintains his autonomy and power ("*her*" autonomy and power is another question). Hard SF writer Gregory Benford speaks for the genre's conservatism when he writes, without irony, that "*Neuromancer* lacks heft finally because it admits no more than a surface reading"—of course *Neuromancer,* of all recent science fiction texts, best exemplifies the notion of *infinite surfaces.*[4] Yet *Neuromancer,* too, retains its solitary male hero and the macho postures of several genres. These are significant compromises, mediating between dissolution and a centered subject.

The mode of accommodating to the immanence of the body is what Baudrillard has termed the tactic of *seduction.*[5] Mark Poster writes that "Seduction plays upon the surface thereby challenging theories that 'go beyond' the manifest to the latent" and that it stands as a prologue to Baudrillard's later notions of simulation and hyperreality.[6] Seduction stands against those theories that "privilege forms of rationality." Much postmodern science fiction deserves the label through the continual passage, often both diegetic and structural, beyond the categories and resolved dialectics of the rational. The cut-ups of Burroughs, the techno-surreal transmutations of Ballard, the paranoid alternate realities of Philip Dick, the voyage "beyond the infinite" in *2001,* the paraspatial vertigo of Gibson's cyberspace, the (literal) dissolution of the body in the films of David Cronenberg—all make manifest a confrontation with the end of meaning; all effect a critique of a fully technologized instrumental reason—from a position *within,* rather than opposed to, the seductive, commercial surfaces of contemporary mass culture.

The dominant image is the cybernetic cyborg, a figure of indeterminate interface. The body is dissolved: malleable as data and more ephemeral than its own stored image. Even sexuality is distilled to the meaninglessness of transparency and surface—"The genitalia is but a special effect" (Baudrillard),[7] and as with all special effects, the viewer's fascination is precisely with the spectacle of a surface. Sexuality, in its heavily commodified and telematic multiplicity, can be regarded as the epitome of this movement outward from subject to body. "In this cybernetic peripetia of the body, passions have disappeared."[8] The disappearance of the body is the disappearance of desire (more than the manifestation of the self, here the body represents the terrain of a desire now replaced by its own simulacrum), a symptom of surrender to the desireless rationality of the cybernetic state.

For the Krokers the body becomes a floating signifier of crisis—what they call *panic bodies:* "an inscribed surface onto which are projected all the grisly symptoms of culture burnout as the high five-sign of the late 1980s."[9] The hysteria around physical fitness, civil liberties, AIDS treatment, the right to life, the right to death, eating disorders, the war on drugs, surveillance in the workplace, steroids in pro sports, and the sexual exploits of public figures are all symptoms of this hyper-rhetoricized body, as though its presence *in discourse* will somehow guarantee its continued relevance *in the world.* To Baudrillard and the Krokers, the debates that inscribe the body at the center of the discourse on power are so many red herrings, misdirecting the public and preventing the realization that the forces of power have bypassed them entirely. It is as Baudrillard said: if we can talk about these things, it's because they no longer matter.[10]

Baudrillard's prose mutates the body into a device fully assimilated to the modalities of the telematic interface. The body is no longer metaphor or symbol; nothing lurks below the flesh. The body is now an infinite set of surfaces—a *fractal subject*—an object among objects (*Ecstasy*, 40). Neurophysiology replaces the Freudian model of *the soul* (or *psyche*) with "an operation definition in terms of the genetic code (DNA) and cerebral organization (the informational code and billions of neurons)" (50). The discourse of science transforms subject to object, human to machine. The baroque hyperbole of some of the best (and worst) postmodern writing models the crisis of the subject, as the simultaneity that once characterized modernist temporal experience now takes on spatiality as a body opened to a scrutiny that denies its meaning and depth. Baudrillard: "We are looking for a reduction into partial objects and the fulfillment of desire in the technical sophistication of the body. In itself changed by sexual liberation, the body has been reduced to a division of surfaces, a proliferation of multiple objects wherein its finitude, its desirable representation, its seduction are lost. It is a metastatic body, a fractal body which can no longer hope for resurrection" (44). There can be no resurrection, for "what body shall one resurrect?" The reduction to a pseudo-continuum of surfaces demolishes the possibility of regaining the deeper continuities (religion, history) that underlie existence.

The dissolution of boundaries, the "end of borders and frontiers" (*The Fly*), the waning of affect, the erosion of meaning and representation, the rise of spectacle and simulacra, and the demise of history—all of these familiar tropes are played out upon the physical manifestation of the subject—the body. The Krokers' compendium of postmodern bodily travails, *Body Invaders: Panic Sex in America,* presents a quintessential narrative of terminal identity, densely packed with allusions to artworks, philosophers, and cultural phenomena:

> *Semiotically,* the body is tattooed, a floating sign processed through the double imperatives of the cultural politics of advanced capitalism: the *exteriorization* of all the body organs as the key telemetry of a system that depends on the *outering* of the body functions (computers as the externalization of memory; *in vitro* fertilization as the alienation of the womb; Sony Walkmans as ablated ears;

computer generated imagery as *virtual perspective* of the hyper-
modern kind; body scanners as the intensive care unit of the exteri-
orization of the central nervous system); and the *interiorization* of
ersatz subjectivity as a prepackaged ideological receptor for the
pulsations of the desiring-machine of the fashion scene.[11]

The Krokers create a science fiction of conflation in which Walkmen,
artificial insemination, computer functions, and body scanners *are*
all operating at once upon the same body. As with Baudrillard, all meanings are imploded; all social practices are equal and equally dispersed
throughout the technocultural system. The crisis of the body is posed
as a crisis of meaning and definition. The relationship of the subject to
his or her own body is opened to debate, extrapolation, and legislation.
If the narration of dissolution often seems ecstatic in tone and promise,
it also frequently ignores the real-world politics of new bodily technologies. It has fallen to feminist and gay forces to confront the politics
of reproductive technologies and viral containment, while postmodern
metaphors and discourses madly multiply around them. The real bodies at stake are often forgotten while consuming Baudrillard or the
Krokers (in the Semiotext[e] editions, Baudrillard is especially consum-
able: their sexy, slender, black profiles suggest little cyberdecks or
Nintendo cartridges). What status should be granted to "real" bodies in
a "real" world? And if the body disappears into a Baudrillardian or
Krokeresque rhetorical abyss, should that be read as a sign of discursive contention and redefinition or as an obfuscated surrender to the
irresistible forces of telematic culture?

The body must become a cyborg to retain its presence in the world,
resituated in technological space and refigured in technological terms.
Whether this represents a continuation, a sacrifice, a transcendence, or
a surrender of "the subject" is not certain. Elements of all three pertain,
but in works as otherwise diverse as *Neuromancer* or *Max Headroom*,
Blood Music or *Videodrome,* the condition of being is presently listed as
terminal.

LIFESTYLES OF THE ELECTRONICALLY EN-

HANCED   Where we might expect greater resistance to mechan-

ical replacements of vital and intimate organs, we find that what sounds like the ultimate philosophical question, "Am I human or machine?" is an-

swered by many people, "I don't care, as long as I am."—Myron Krueger ¶

Since he felt excluded from the circle of humanity, he plugged himself into

another circle that nourished—the electrical circuit.—Bruno Bettelheim ¶

"I'm wired to the ass. . . ."—Bruce Sterling, *Schismatrix*

The Persistence of Memory

Cyberspace cowboys are specialists and image addicts are underground figures, but in other science fiction, interface is a mainstream
activity. Much SF is concerned with the status and commodification of
memory, which seems to produce an ersatz humanity. Trumbull's *Brainstorm* features the marketing of sensory experience—the consumer can
jack in to any of a range of phenomenologically intense virtual activities
(one user gets hooked on an orgasm loop). When its inventor discovers
that it can also record memories, he prepares a "tape" for his estranged
wife. "What is it?" she asks, and he answers simply, "Me." Philip Dick's
1965 short story, "We Can Remember It for You Wholesale" also features
entrepreneurs engaged in the commerce of memories; ersatz experiences for the masses. A disenchanted bureaucrat visits REKAL, INC. to
buy the memory of an exciting espionage adventure on Mars (cheaper
than the real thing, and safer too). When it turns out to be his own
memory, eliminated from his own mind, reader and protagonist are left
to ponder the suddenly manifold relations of mind, memory, and being.[12] Giuliana Bruno has argued for the centrality of memory in the
construction of the self in *Blade Runner* (based on a novel by Dick), in
which the replicants are programmed with artificial memories (and
their visual totems, photographs) to make them indistinguishable from
humans.[13] To have memory is to have history; it is also to develop
empathy. The distinction between human and android produces an
ontology grounded in *morality* and not *biology,* as Spinrad noted of
Philip Dick's universe.[14] The tangibility of the photograph creates an
ersatz history and a frame of reference that belies the androids' electronic origins.

Memory is thus constitutive of the self in these fictions. In an era of bodily transformation, change, and dissolution, the mere (and ahistorical) *fact* of physical existence is no longer a guarantor of truth or selfhood. John Varley has been most concerned with questions of memory in a few interconnected tales. As the title "Overdrawn at the Memory Bank" suggests, citizens in Varley's future can have the sum total of their memories recorded and stored as a hedge against future catastrophe. Should the body meet with an accident, a new body can be constructed and the recorded memories installed. The continuity of memory thus implies a kind of immortality, in which the vicissitudes of the flesh become irrelevant. Of course, as he notes in "The Phantom of Kansas," the experience produces an anxiety that "comes from the common misapprehension that one will wake up from the recording to discover that one has died."[15]

Varley's narrator argues that the recording does not constitute another *you:* "looked at from a fourth-dimensional standpoint, what memory recording does is to graft a new person onto your lifeline at a point in the past. You do not retrace that lifeline and magically become that new person."[16] In "The Phantom of Kansas," the protagonist must find out who keeps killing her, without ever gaining the new knowledge/ memory to help her solve the case. Varley returned to the memory theme in 1989 with the epistolary, "Just Another Perfect Day": a single, long letter from the protagonist to himself, because he awakens each day with no memories of the past twenty-two years (and counting). The letter reveals the existence of everything from alien invaders to true love, all to be experienced afresh by the reader of the letter with every new morning. Varley's memory play continually stages a rebirth, in which memory and reality are subtly at odds.

"Overdrawn at the Memory Bank" stages a temporary loss of the body and its replacement by a cybernetically reconstituted memory *as* consciousness. Fingal has come for a vacation at the Kenya disneyland—a virtual holiday in the "body" of a powerful lioness. Problems ensue when Fingal's body is accidentally scrapped. As the hunt for his body continues, Fingal begins a new "life" within the data banks of the system computer. An outside operator communicates with him via "supernatural" manifestations—ghostly hands write messages on the "wall"—a sign of Fingal's struggle to "normalize" the phenomena he experiences and thereby reduce the sense of ontological displacement. As his handler explains in a convenient brochure: "Life in a computer is not the sort of thing you could just jump into and hope to retain the world-picture compatibility so necessary for sane functioning in this complex society. . . . Since you can't just become aware in the baffling, on-and-off world that passes for reality in a data system, your mind, in cooperation with an analogizing program I've given the computer, interprets things in ways that seem safe and comfortable to it."[17]

In his imaginary cyberspace, Fingal puts himself through computer school and learns to interface directly with the system. After years of study, he graduates and finally emerges from the dataspace (his body has been found) to discover that only six hours have elapsed. As with *Blade Runner, 20 Minutes into the Future,* and the writings of the cyberpunks, Varley's text wavers between defining the human as consciousness or body. If the unitary truth of the Cartesian *cogito* is insufficient in grounding the experience of the human, as Merleau-Ponty maintains,[18] then this insufficiency is even more pronounced under the terms of a postmodern reality. In the age of terminal identity, there are a myriad of selves and a multitude of realities.

Cyberpunks with a Plan

In the late 1970s and early 1980s, on the fringes of the contemporary music industry in Europe and America, a set of performers pushed punk rock in uncompromising directions: "Punk's implicit concentration, in its purest form, on situationist theory . . . had left the door open for an even more comprehensive investigation of capitalism's decay."[19] A concern with industrial (and commercial) culture linked these bands as a somewhat cohesive subunit, and Jon Savage has argued that musicians as diverse as DEVO, Throbbing Gristle, Kraftwerk, SPK, Brian Eno, Cabaret Voltaire, and The Residents had some underlying relations—their independent position within an information society in which access to correct or alternative information was largely impossible. Many relied on synthesizers and industrial sounds, and nearly all incorporated extramusical texts into their performance.

Although neither the most inventive nor the most subversive of the industrial culture bands, DEVO lasted over fifteen years as a cult phenomenon with some real commercial sensibilities. This dance on the edge of mass acceptance endows their pose with the ambivalence that seems crucial to the postmodern formations of popular culture. DEVO's song lyrics played to a subhumanism that defined both them and their culture ("He was a mongoloid/One chromosome too many/And it determined what he could see"). Mankind was in a state of de-evolution, moving backward away from its own humanity. The music was rhythmic and repetitive, with odd percussions and spastic twitches throughout; the vocals were strangulated, whiny, yet impassioned. The human was a construction of this electronic machinery and also its prisoner, while the lyrics both celebrated and resisted the movement toward de-evolution.

DEVO's music videos were actually produced on video instead of film (a rarity), and many make extensive use of chromakey, dislocating the band from any "real" spatiality. This anticipation of the malleable modalities of virtual reality even extends to a precyberpunk evocation of cyberspace, as the band is "inserted" into a field of computer generated images and effects ("The Day My Baby Gave Me a Surprize," 1981). "Freedom of Choice" (1980) participates in the same evocation of electronic consumerism and illusory "choice" that marks Max Almy's *Perfect Leader*. (DEVO is not only funnier than Almy, they are more interestingly positioned in relation to dominant culture.) DEVO always incorporated video into their concerts: their 1984 tour was performed with synchronized video effects. The live space of performance was transformed into an analogue of electronic (TV) space.

Before DEVO, the German synthesizer group Kraftwerk had been having notable success with their own "glossy cyberpop."[20] Kraftwerk forged insistent, immutable rhythms with electronic instruments that announced their own robotic predictability. Onstage automata figured prominently in their "live" act, and their 1991 tour used "android likenesses" as "frontmen" ("We'll see if we can get them to improvise," founder Ralf Hutter said). Their sounds were sampled by hip-hop groups, giving their music new relevance and an increasing urban credibility. Mark Dery, writing in the *New York Times,* reports that "Mr. Hutter sees no irony in the fact that Kraftwerk's cold, cerebral robo-rock has inspired so much bumping and grinding. 'We have always been great dance fanatics,' he says. 'To us, machines are funky.' "[21]

Terminal identity fictions move beyond the boundaries of the book and into a range of popular media (Brooks Landon argues that these nonliterary forms are where cyberpunk reaches fruition). While the odd-yet-cuddly DEVO and the male-model mannequins of Kraftwerk produce no real transgression, they surely deserve mention for their forays into a *terminal performance*. Real negotiations of a cyberneticized existence are thought, in a playful version of what Fred Pfeil called the "tryings-on of a new, cybernetic sense of identity."[22]

Terminal Cyborgs

If the notion of the *spectacle* as a surrogate, self-contained form of reality, a notion elaborated by commentators as different as Daniel Boorstin and Guy Debord in the early 1960s, gained currency in the 1980s, then it was largely due to the televisual extravaganza that defined

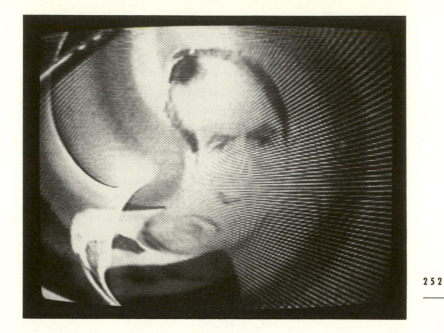

Deconstructing the spectacle of politics: Nam June Paik's *Global Groove* (1973). Poised between Burroughs cut-ups and the mass media figure of Max Headroom. (Courtesy Electronic Arts Intermix)

the Reagan presidency. Kennedy was the first president to benefit from the medium of television, but Ronald Reagan was the first to master it. As many commentators observed, the ex-actor and his advisers transformed the office into its own simulation, within which problems never existed, or were magically solved. While this phildickian spectacular bore little resemblance to the experiences of real citizens (most of whom didn't vote), this disjunction seemed an irrelevance, as the president retained an unprecedented popularity almost through his last days in power. The simulacrum of America over which Reagan presided permitted no scandal, no divisiveness, and little direct engagement with the press or the people. By the end of the 1988 election campaign, the mainstream media had begun to recognize the extent of their own complicity in the process of creating a *terminal politics*.[23] As historian Arthur Schlesinger, Jr., commented in the *New York Times,* "The rise of the electronic media has had an effect on draining content out of campaigns."[24]

Mark Crispin Miller, a perceptive, if dyspeptic, analyst of television and television culture, is savage in his discussion of Reagan's television presidency. While avoiding the apocalyptic language of Baudrillard, or the Frankfurt School rhetoric of Debord, Miller's analysis is fully in accord with their propositions. He concludes by noting that: "Television has reduced our political culture to a succession of gestures, postures, automatic faces. . . . Our candidates will continue to flash by between commercials, seeming to inhabit no real space, offering nothing but a short performance; and so we'll watch as we watch everything, not bothering to participate, because participation won't be needed. The show, we'll figure numbly, most go on."[25] If Miller does not locate the apathy of the public as a form of positive social resistance, as Baudrillard does in *In the Shadow of the Silent Majorities,* then neither does he exhort the citizens to "do their part" and vote. In Miller's writing, as in Debord's and Baudrillard's, the power of the media is very nearly absolute and irresistible.

Science fiction had long described this "politics by simulacrum," literalizing the metaphor.[26] Philip Dick's short story, "If There Were No Benny Cemoli" (1963), features a revolutionary leader who is purely a creation of the radical media. *Reported* reality supplants *experienced* reality as Cemoli's "activities" turn the tide of the revolution. The leader in *The Simulacra* is an artificial creation. A political speechwriter in Dick's *The Penultimate Truth* (1964) discovers that the state of war is a lie, and the leader is a "sim." Thomas Disch writes that the moral is clear: "Government is a conspiracy against the people, and it is maintained by the illusion of a permanent crisis that exists, for the most part, as a media event."[27] The figure of an electronic president reflects a forty year anxiety regarding the power of the media over the voters. Just as Dick's simulations are a response to the first great television president, John F. Kennedy, so are more recent versions by Shirley and others unavoidably read against the background of the Reagan years: "the phrase 'Reagan's image' is redundant."[28]

The continuing infusion of the spectacle into the parameters of "real life" continues unabated. The ultimate embodiment (or *dis*-embodiment) of terminal identity is the electronically enhanced simulation of a human. Miller cites a researcher for Grey Advertising who states: "All things considered, it's not so surprising that after years of exposure to electronic heroes, the average UltraConsumer wants to be one."[29] From the citizens of Baudrillard's America to Max Headroom and beyond, subjectivity and simulation are first mutually referential (Debord), then mutually defining (Baudrillard), and finally conflated (Headroom). The physical reality of the body is no longer a requisite for the existence of the subject. "Where's your body?" a wirehead is asked in *Schismatrix*. The answer: "I had it scrapped" (187).

In Sterling's Shaper/Mechanist stories, whose task it is to narrate the range of prosthetic extensions available to the posthuman order, *video* is a pervasive interface and an option. The "real world" is defined for one character as "lines on a screen." A resourceful Mechanist is a partial cyborg. "Chip grafts along the optic nerves. . . . I suffer a little from video burn. I have trouble seeing anything not on scan lines" (25). He later achieves wirehead status, explaining that "there's a whole world behind this screen." He continues: "It all becomes a matter of input, you see. Data. Systems" (179; see below for more on Sterling's Shaper/Mech fictions).

Scan lines connote a technologized, cyborg vision, a trope that has wide currency in contemporary cinema (and not only in SF cinema, either—see, for example, *Sex, Lies and Videotape* [1989]). A switch from film to video signals the onset of a mediated vision or even a mediated subjectivity. As has been amply demonstrated, television is axiomatic of the processes of superimposition and simultaneity (it's already a cut-up, remember?). Time is collapsed in video—superimposed on itself—creating an eternal present disconnected from experienced temporality (this is what Jane Feuer has called television's ideology of live-ness).[30]

Robocop synthesizes the diachronic narrative model of the cinema with the synchronic informational mode of video in a way that strongly suggests the overloading of Chaykin's *American Flagg!*[31] In a Detroit beleaguered by inner-city ethnic "others," an assassinated policeman is resurrected as a superhumanly powerful cyborg. The perceptual apparatus of this cybernetic law enforcer is a video camera, and overlaid images and videotex represent the figure's data banks. Video imagery thus denotes Robocop's point of view while it connotes his cyborg (read: hybrid, simultaneous, superimposed) status.

The film is itself punctuated by the forms of television: videotaped news broadcasts, sitcoms, and commercials interrupt (and only occasionally advance) the narrative. The media become a synecdoche for the culture at large, and the puerility of the programming in Robocop's world suggests that society mirrors the televisual reality in a gesture of implosion. Additionally, the intercutting between film and video images (although not as developed as in *20 Minutes into the Future*) creates a hybrid form—the citizens are themselves already cyborgs: blips within the blip culture. As the narrative proceeds, the programmed perfection of Robocop, a character of pure fascist functionalism devoid of the temporal experience of the human subject, delivers order to the "chaos" of

Robocop, a subjec-
tivity mediated
through video. (Orion
Pictures)

near-future Detroit. Unexpectedly, of course, the subjectivity of the
dead policeman resurfaces. When Robocop revisits his/its old suburban home, the real-time images of the deserted middle-class house are
overlaid with video images of the recalled family life pulled from Robocop's memory banks. Video ironically marks the temporal rift between
Robocop's human memories and inhuman status, while it movingly
transmits the character's disjunction from the continuity of human
existence.

Todd Gitlin has written that car commercials feature a blank and enigmatic New Man, helpless and incomplete without his high-technology
toy, and Robocop is the ultimate such toy.[32] *Robocop* even resembles a
car ad in its road-level camera placement. While Gitlin's proposition
well describes both the aesthetic and protagonist of *Robocop* (a literally
half-faceless figure) and Case's "fall" from cyberspace, it also evokes the
world of *20 Minutes into the Future*. Edison Carter is defined in and
through the tools of video production: he is never without the camera
that strikingly resembles Robocop's hyper-phallicized weaponry. Edison and his ubiquitous video camera supplement one another, but the
technologization of Carter functions still more deeply. In the world
which exists twenty minutes into the future, video-reporters are linked
to "controllers" at network headquarters. The controller, a computer-

jockey, locates potential stories, accesses relevant data, and steers the reporter with the aid of numerous surveillance systems. Edison Carter, the hero, thus becomes an object himself, another piece of sophisticated video technology (foreshadowing his replication *cum* resurrection as Max Headroom).

That Carter is already a part of the machine, and that lived and spectacular realities are all one is made evident when Carter and his controller, Theora Jones, break into the secure levels of Network 23 to uncover the truth about Blipverts. Rapid intercutting between the silent corridors of power and the computer displays and readouts graphically matches physical space with cyberspace: a superimposition that demonstrates their equivalence and sustained imbrication (it also recalls the sim-stim break-in sequence in *Neuromancer*). In the context of the ensuing chase scene, Carter effectively becomes the blip on a video-game screen. The future Max Headroom is *already* instantiated and controlled by the spectacle.

The translation of Edison into Max opens the world behind the screen as a space of habitation and as the site for the emergence of an ersatz subjectivity marked by its profound separation from the world of human experience. This is also the territory of "Pretty Boy Crossover," a short story by Pat Cadigan that neatly addresses this dichotomy in its depiction of a postpunk world of video celebrity.[33] Pretty Boys, dance club denizens, are "crossing over" into a purely digital existence where they will never age and never lose their place on the video dancefloor. The nameless Pretty Boy protagonist is offered the chance to digitize, to become S.A.D. ("Self-Aware Data"). "There may be no more exalted form of existence than to live as sentient information," he is told by the slightly sinister scientists behind the project. Cadigan's protagonist finally turns them down: "As long as they don't have him, he makes a difference. As long as he has flesh to shake and flaunt and feel with, he makes a pretty goddamn big difference to *them*." Cadigan reprises the flesh/subject, terminal/ object split, but the subject already exists in a world largely defined and delimited by the scan lines of terminal reality: "First you see video. Then you wear video. Then you eat video. Then you *be* video."

Edison Carter also gets to "*be*" video. When he gets too close to the truth of Blipverts, Bryce, the network hacker/scientist, has him killed by forcing him into a collision with a computer-controlled barrier that reads "MAX HEADROOM 2.3 M." Bryce subsequently rescues the body and tapes Carter's memories in order to produce a computer-generated simulacrum, reasoning that since Carter is so highly rated a newscaster,

"Then you *be* video": Edison Carter (Matt Frewer) and his computer-generated alter-ego. (Lorimar)

an effective electronic analogue might be able to continue appearing in profitable broadcasts even after the real Carter's demise. The imperfect duplicate, "Max Headroom" (to quote his first garbled utterance), was of course a literalization of television's talking heads—he consisted of only head and shoulders, usually seen against a shifting electronic pattern or against a few computer-generated props. At the same time, he embodies the notion of an electronically constituted culture. Unlike Brian O'Blivion, who only *appears* on television, Max only *exists* through television.

Max is clearly the perfect celebrity, within Debord's definition of celebrity as "the spectacular representation of a living human being" (Thesis 60). "The agent of the spectacle placed on stage as a star is the opposite of the individual, the enemy of the individual" (Thesis 56). The collapse of real and spectacle is also figured in *American Flagg!*, in which a videostar is replaced by a *tromplographic*™ simulation constructed from a computer's memory bank. "*I* get cancelled," he complains, "but the *show* goes on." Through the magic of Tromplography, a step beyond Disney's Audioanimatronics, the spectacularly insubstantial nature of the celebrity is made manifest. The hero is a hologram.

The ironic gloss provided by Max Headroom in his several manifestations was found in Max's pervasive sarcasm, that "old computer-generated *swagger*," which permitted him to mock the very medium that determined his existence. Guests on his talk show were mercilessly ridiculed, the American sponsors were mocked, and even the viewers came in for their share of abuse. In the diegesis of *20 Minutes,* Max could appear on any television, at any time, to speak directly to viewers about the drivel being broadcast. First in England, and then in America, Max caught on as a technological folk hero, serving as both the parody and the exemplar of spectacular culture. "Max Headroom is not merely *on* television," wrote one critic, "he *is* television." Max appeared with other celebrities and even recorded a single with synthesizer group The Art of Noise. A future conceived as science fiction now becomes a tromp-lographic™ reality. Rather than undermining the medium, as some left and even mainstream commentators would have had it, the Max Headroom phenomenon seems to demonstrate that the society of the spectacle no longer needs to hide behind its facade of cultural beneficence. Max was the spectacle personified more completely than Debord could have dreamed.[34] If the cyborg, the interpenetration of human and machine, is a frightening figure, an embodiment of technological anxieties with its implied loss of humanity, a loss frequently signaled by the disappearance of erotic desire, then Max Headroom, ostensibly an image of parodic resistance, instead incarnated a new countermyth, as the cyborg became reassuringly sexualized (if not downright debonair), and thus refreshingly human.[35]

One of the unintentional puzzles of *20 Minutes* concerns the survival of Edison Carter. The viewer (this viewer, at any rate) is led to expect that Carter will survive his Network-engineered traffic accident only by his translation into the electronic form of Max Headroom. Yet Carter effects a miraculous escape from the body bank where his body has been dumped and slowly makes his way back to Theora and his job with Network 23. When the film ends, and throughout the American TV series, Carter and his electronic double share the screen: as Max digs for information in the various information banks of the electronic culture, Carter negotiates more physical spaces. Carter seems redundant— Max seems to have been designed as his electronic resurrection and not just as his cybernetic twin.

But perhaps Carter serves a deeper function. All of the cybrid protagonists of the electronic age, including Robocop, Brian O'Blivion, *Neuromancer's* Case, and *TRON's* Flynn, retain a *meat component.* The flesh continues to exist to ground the subjectivity of the character. To let go of the flesh, then, is to surrender the subject. "This is the future," Max's creator declares: "people translated as data." This act of translation actually marks the end of subjectivity.[36] The televisual existence is, in most of these works, an existence as an *object* rather than as a *subject:* there is no point of view, no indication of subjective experience. This is why Edison Carter must survive: Edison is a subject; Max, despite his simulated sexuality, is only an object. The "meat"—the body—is always retained by the subject in cyberpunk (Fingal's strictly cybernetic existence in "Overdrawn at the Memory Bank" was only temporary).[37] Thus, the ideologically *radical* moment of *20 Minutes into the Future* consists of the creation of Max Headroom, a new figurehead for the electronic generation. But the *reactionary* moment is found in the retention of Edison Carter, a figure that preserves, against all odds, a traditional subjectivity. In one way or another, every work of cyberpunk produces the same radical and reactionary formation.[38]

As much as Max "himself," Reagan seemed fully a creation of electronic technology. Mark Crispin Miller, after noting, as all analysts have, Reagan's background as a Hollywood performer, observes: "His film career was undistinguished, because his celluloid image was basically too dim and vacuous to withstand the competition of more vivid presences. But this very emptiness has made him perfect for TV, which thrives on mundane types, demanding a pseudohomely style that Reagan puts on easily."[39]

In 1956 the opening ceremonies of Disneyland were telecast live; among the hosts was Ronald Reagan, who would one day be represented by a simulacrum therein.[40]

INTO THE PLASMA POOL. "It's weird and pissed off,

whatever it is."—*The Thing*

The Extrusion of the Flesh

The superimposition of technology on the human is dramatized in all its effects throughout science fiction: this is its function. The computer alone is narrated as a prosthetic extension, as an addictive substance, as a space to enter, as a technological intrusion into human genetic structures, and finally as a replacement for the human in a posthuman world (the computer is *juxtaposed* to the human; it is *superimposed* upon the human, and it ultimately *supersedes* the human). As in performance art, the body becomes the site of exploration, a site in which the implications of postmodern dissolution are inscribed and hypostatized. The body is already an interface between mind and experience; Merleau-Ponty writes of the body as a medium that permits a consciousness of the world. The subject "is [the] body and [the] body is the potentiality of a certain world."[41] The obsessive restaging of the alteration of the body is also a constant refiguring or redefinition of the subject through biotechnological apparatuses.

The cyborg performance art of Stelarc exemplifies these concerns with an explicitly surrealist sense of transgression, and with an immediate emphasis upon the flesh—as paradigmatic a postmodern landscape as cyberspace itself. Stelarc, an Australian performance artist living in Japan, has filmed his bodily interior, amplified its functions, enhanced its abilities, and worked toward "the body's transcendence of all conventional boundaries." As cyberpunk John Shirley has written, "All the signposts direct us to him."[42]

Through the sonic amplification of his bodily functions, Stelarc transforms his body into "an acoustical landscape"—an array of beats, beeps, and gurgles. The subject is replaced into the continuity of biological process, but this fusion is only performed through a symbiosis with electronic technology. Stelarc's more recent work has moved from mapping the body to extending and enhancing its capabilities. "Event for Amplified Body, Laser Eyes, and Third Hand," featured a third hand activated by his abdominal and thigh muscles. His real left arm was "controlled" by the random electrical impulses of a muscle stimulator. Stelarc has bounced laser beams off mirrored contact lenses, "drawing" with the beams that emanate from his eyes.

The Krokers note that Stelarc "makes of his own body its own horizon of sometimes repulsive, sometimes fascinating, possibilities."[43] He has explored and experimented with the "architecture" of the body, treating the body as an environment which needs to be made more adaptable. Shirley quotes Stelarc as stating, "We're at the time now where we have to start redesigning the human body to match the technology we've created. . . . [We] are confronted by the end of the human form as we know it." As Shirley points out, this is strikingly similar to "ideas explored by Bruce Sterling in *Schismatrix* and Samuel Delany in *Nova*."[44]

A concern with biological interface and dissolution pervades not only science fiction, but horror as well. One SF author wrote, "I have recently launched full-tilt into the deep end of Horror, THE coming venue for speculative fiction."[45] Cyberpunks K. W. Jeter and John Shirley have also shifted their attention to splatterpunk horror. Mass-market bookstores have instituted horror fiction sections; horror novels regularly appear on bestseller lists; horror films remain among the most durable of film genres; horror comics, primarily aimed toward an adult and subcultural market, have made their most significant appearance since the 1950s; heavy metal rock is dominated by images derived from horror; and the field is characterized by a dynamic interchange of talents.[46] *LOCUS,* the SF industry newspaper, now includes a section on "Horror/Dark Fantasy."

Just as the anxieties regarding technology and the Other have produced complex responses within science fiction, so the horror genre has produced a wide range of textual strategies, most of which center upon an extensive hyperbolization of the body and its (dys)functions. The works of science fiction that have been considered here have evidenced an increasing "subjectlessness" in their rhetorical effects and strategies. The threats in the horror film to the subject's health and well-being are, perhaps, excessive attempts at a recuperative mission. The task of the horror film might therefore be to rescue the body, and thus the subject, from the vicissitudes of modern urban, cybernetic, and viral existences;[47] in other words, from the interface with those exterior forces that threaten the subject's hegemony. But while horror has become ever more dedicated to an obsessive centering upon the *body* of the subject, this does not necessarily mark a return to the *terms* of the subject. The return of the body could actually be understood as an obsession with the *surface* of the body. While the interior organs are externalized or revealed to the viewer's fascinated gaze, the "depth" of subjectivity continues to be denied. The subject continues to be displaced in horror fiction, while the body is hyperbolized—opened up, as it were—as an infinite set of surfaces (Baudrillard's *fractal subject*).

The concern with defining the limits of the human finds expression in several science fiction/horror films of the 1980s that were organized around the phenomenon of "shape-shifting." The continually metamorphosing Alien in the film of the same name is anticipated and echoed in the return of the human simulacra in *The Invasion of the Body Snatchers* (1978), in the degenerating scientist of *The Fly,* and, perhaps most disturbingly, in the impressively mimetic alien invader of *The Thing.* All these were remakes of earlier works—even *Alien* bears its own gothic associations (e.g., James Whale's 1932 *The Old Dark House*). While the originals teased the audience with hints of the hideous transformations that occurred shrouded in fog or perhaps just off-screen, the remakes rewrite the originals by lingering on the lurid biomechanics with an almost affectionate disgust. The elaborate special effects of Rick Baker (*The Thing, Videodrome*), Rob Bottin (*Total Recall* [1990]), and Carlo Rimbaldi (*Alien, E.T.* [1982]), emphasizing complex facial reactions and muscular responses, renders the alien body in hyperreal, hyper-biologized terms. The Other, which can look exactly like ourselves, is endowed with the status of pure flesh.

Alien

In this context the importance of *Alien* cannot be overemphasized. The film is located at the juncture between science fiction and horror films, and an analysis of its strategies reveals much about the conditions of those genres. *Alien* presents the return of the repressed—the body—to the *space* of the science fiction film.

One first wants to note the film's extraordinary opening sequence, which presents the revelation of a fully realized world from which people are absent. The space-faring tugboat *Nostromo,* with a vast refinery in tow, cruises past the viewer amidst the silent voids of interplanetary space. The film then cuts to a series of languorous interior tracking shots that reveal the complex detail of empty corridors and control rooms. This introductory maneuver is a significant trope of the science fiction film, restaged in, for example, the African landscapes that open *2001* or the panavision cityscapes of *Blade Runner* or even the cosmic montages (often by astronomical artist Chesley Bonestell) that open such 1950s films as *The War of the Worlds.* Such an evacuation of the human from these richly detailed visions of existence surely complements the pervasive diminution of the human figure that occurs in science fiction set design, epitomized here through the scalar exaggerations of the monstrous *Nostromo.* As in *2001,* the ship is autonomous—a self-sustaining cybernetic organism that simply obviates the need for a human presence.

Suddenly, aboard the *Nostromo,* fluorescent lights flicker to life and the irresistible clatter of computer printouts swamps the soundtrack. A closeup of an activated console reveals the first sign of human habitation—a plastic coffee cup which clutters the surface. This intrusion of a particularly casual, nonrational, and unsystematized version of the human has the effect of separating *Alien* from the pristinely rational spaces and spacemen of *2001*'s earlier odyssey. Interestingly, the cluttered spaces of the *Nostromo* recall most clearly the fateful nuclear bomber of Kubrick's *Dr. Strangelove,* and that film is further evoked during a later crash-landing sequence that recalls the bomber fire through identical near-documentary camerawork and editing. This occasional documentary filmic style, especially when coupled with the improvisational acting styles of the cast, emphasizes a quotidian reality at odds with the deep-space setting. From the outset of *Alien,* then, the future has become exactly like the present.[48]

The iconography of *Alien* is thus largely familiar to viewers of the science fiction film, but the spaceship, the ringed planet, the urban industrialized space represented by this floating factory, the astronauts (whose suits evoke memories of Jules Verne and Captain Nemo), the android, the alien—each of these generic icons is filtered through the heterogeneous referential systems of postmodernity. The coffee cups on the console are the first sign of a space which belies the utopian technologism of most space exploration films. *Alien* uses several designers—Ron Cobb and Chris Foss for the Nostromo, Jean (Moebius) Giraud for the spacesuits, H. R. Giger for the alien and alien vessel, Michael Seymour and Ridley Scott for the overall production design— and the result is a fascinating mismatch of styles. The crew members possess no history and no real psychology—like the android, Ash, they are fully functional simulacra. And, of course, the alien itself is a creature of continual transformation—the very trope of an organic-technological malleability. The viewer is prepared—carefully prepared—for the complex phenomenology of science fiction cinema, with its surfeit of complex spaces all demanding to be read and comprehended.

Like the creature of the title, however, the film has one further metamorphosis to perform. At one very clearly marked point in the narrative, *Alien* definitively shifts its generic dominant from science fiction to horror. From the moment that the embryonic alien bursts forth from Kane's stomach, the carefully elaborated politically and economically credible future epoch with its detailed social hierarchy becomes the merest background to the new narrative task, which is simply to hunt down and kill the alien intruder—the monster. The rationality of computer directives and planetary scans is replaced by the irrational behaviors of frightened crew members hunting, inevitably alone, for the cat. At the same time, the complicated, but readable spaces of the ship succumb to the frantic pulsations of some inexplicably placed strobe lights. In short, a chaos engulfs the film—narratively and stylistically— not simply the chaos of a misplaced coffee cup, but a new and apocalyptic chaos that leads to the destruction of nearly all that we have seen.

This disjunction, which might mark the film's failure, can be productively read to understand the film's undeniable significance. Vivian Sobchack has written eloquently about what she calls "the virginity of astronauts" in SF cinema: "More than any other American film genre, then, science fiction denies human eroticism and libido a traditional

H. R. Giger's design for the adult *Alien*—the very trope of an organic-technological malleability. (20th Century Fox; illustration courtesy of Morpheus International)

narrative representation and expression. Sex and the science fiction film is, therefore, a negative topic": "The virginal astronauts of the science fiction film are a sign of penetration and impregnation without biology, without sex, and without the opposite, different, sex. They signify a conquering, potent, masculine and autonomous technology which values production over reproduction, which creates rather than procreates."[49] The splattering "birth" of the alien from the stomach of the male crew member Kane, then, represents the end of such "immaculate conceptions." The denial of sexuality, which is everywhere in the mainstream science fiction cinema, here reaches its limits. This is the return of the repressed, with a vengeance.

If science fiction cinema denies the body, displacing its attention instead onto the cool mechanics of telematic viewscreens, phallic spaceships, and androgynous androids, then, by contrast, horror is all *about* the body. The threat in the horror film is externalized; it almost always takes a physical form. This is neatly literalized in *Forbidden Planet,* wherein the murderous creatures are "monsters from the id." In the last two decades the horror film has presented a further hyperbole of the body—a meticulous lingering upon the destruction or transformation of the human body (a physicality divorced from any significant subjectivity).

One notes the massive feminization of the body that occurs in contemporary science fiction and horror, best represented in *Alien's* sets as well as its monstrous delivery. This grotesque parody of birth, and the slit that appears on Max Renn's stomach in *Videodrome,* confront the male subject with a proximate organicism at odds with male "rationality," "technologism," and "civilization." The male is positioned at the mercy of a banished biological nature in which not even the body provides that "halo of protection" that Baudrillard once referred to.

Thus the hyperbolization of the body must be read as both a confrontation with and a denial of the limits of the rational.[50] Barbara Creed notes a pervasive interest in the maternal body within what she calls the "science fiction horror film." In *Alien,* for example, "virtually all aspects

of the *mise-en-scène* are designed to signify the female: womb-like interiors, fallopian tube corridors, small claustrophobic spaces."[51] Sobchack concurs: "Nearly all of Alien's imagery is organic and/or sexual,"

she writes, "whereas the humans are not—except for Ripley's climactic emergence as female toward the end of the narrative."[52] The importance of the set designs by Swiss painter H. R. Giger cannot be overemphasized: sections of the film privilege a thoroughly sculptural space of techno-organic corridors, tunnels, and biological designs. The rationalist space of the spaceship becomes an embodied, and specifically feminine, space. The extruded organic forms, black fibreglass aesthetic and arrayed irregular, translucent egg-shapes suggest the sculptures of Eva Hesse more than a little, with her latent eroticism now made manifest.

Creed further argues that Alice Jardine's conception of "gynesis," in which the feminine comes to represent the arena over which our master-narratives have lost control, finds extensive figuration in the science fiction film. "[T]he body, particularly the woman's body, has come to signify the unknown, the terrifying, the monstrous."[53] Thus the dissolution of boundaries that seems endemic to the postmodern text is coded onto the body, the body that "becomes woman" through pervasive metamorphoses. It is therefore not surprising that many writings on *Alien* have concentrated upon the sexual anxiety that underlies the film's narrative and design. Although the film presents the viewer with a seeming rarity in this genre, namely a strong and competent female protagonist, it is clear that anxiety about feminism is displaced onto the figure of the alien Other (furthermore, in *Alien,* as in much science fiction, anxiety about *race* is equally predominant and equally inscribed in the design of the monster).

In *The Philosophy of Horror,* Noël Carroll maintains that the two simultaneous responses which define the work of horror are fear and disgust. Following anthropologist Mary Douglas, Carroll notes that we are afraid of and disgusted by the "impure": those things which violate or transgress our fundamental cultural categorizations.[54] When considering the evident metamorphosis of *Alien* from a work of science fiction to one primarily engaged with the structures and stylistics of the horror film, it might be worth asking what interstitial categories are embodied by the alien. For example, although Ash, the android, notes that he "admires its purity," the alien is actually very *im*pure. It is humanoid, but not human. It is simultaneously male and female, as many commentators have noted: "The alien, which is fond of womb-like and vagina-like spaces, is distinctly phallic, and it attacks Ripley, like a fantasy rapist, while she is undressing. But the alien is also equipped with a rather impressive set of vaginal teeth. It is born of eggs, and it continually gives birth to itself."[55] It is at once organic and inorganic, and this dichotomy structures much of the film. The android, Ash, is both organic and inorganic as well, and "his" destruction is marked by the gushing forth of the milky fluids which constitute "his" "blood." The ship on which the alien is found (the product of another alien race) is a masterpiece of organic machinery—a technological space that is also a body. Ash's comments notwithstanding, then, we may admire the alien for its interstitial *im*purity.

The separation of (rational) technology and (slimy) biology is very nearly a structuring principle of the science fiction film, and thus the transgression represented by *Alien's* alien is unquestionably important. The organic, almost intestinal, spaces of both the alien craft and the corridors of the Nostromo are invaded by a silicon-based life form that blends easily with the pipes and protrusions of human machinery. The blasting steam in the engine room and the condensed water that drips from high ceilings foreshadow the onslaught of fluids that characterize later sections of the film. Kane gives "birth," first with a splatter, and then with a gushing, of blood. The alien's dripping blood corrodes metal on three decks. Ash's milky fluids drench his still-functioning robot body. And in grotesque closeup, the alien's metallic teeth extrude while liquids spray about its mouth. More than anything else, it is this flood of bodily fluids that separates *Alien* from the antiseptic and virginal spaces of the science fiction cinema, so brilliantly epitomized and parodied in *2001* (for more on fluidity, see chapter 5). The pronounced, indeed hyperbolic, transition from science fiction to horror actually marks a profound moment in the history of the genre: *Alien* is the film in which *the body* invades the pristine and sexless rational spaces of the science fiction film. The genre hasn't been the same since.

The Fly

The term "body horror" situates the dominant realm of excess in American cinema of the 1980s. "Visions of excess are visions of the body and visions of death," Andrew Haase has noted of Bataille's writings, arguing that his concepts "possess the ability to take us directly to the limits of the body."[56] At a time when the comprehensible sense of continuity represented by history or religion or instrumental reason has given way to the sole remaining continuity of the physical, visible body, these films reveal the anxiety that accompanies this hyperbole of the flesh. The only continuity within these films seems to be the radical *discontinuity* of endless transformation and decay (what will the Thing look like *this* time?). The numberless permutations of which Alien and Thing seem capable repeatedly challenge the rationality of a body that has been the fundament of social and political being.

Thus the body becomes an elaborate fiction; a paraspace represented through the spectacularity of the special effect, presenting the death of the Subject through an obsessive play of simulation, replacement, and degeneration. The recurrent deconstruction of the body actually supports the subject's inviolability as the "place" of the subject shifts from the pure physicality of the body to the mind, the computer, or some other cyborg formation. The shifting experiential spaces described in the last chapters here meets a new uncertainty of bodily definition and subject knowledge through the immixture of 1950s "scifi" paranoia about the infiltration of the Other and the growing sense that we have indeed met the Other, and it is us. "I know I'm human," the protagonist of *The Thing* rationalizes, but this has become a hollow, and even a useless, knowledge.

These concerns are also relevant to Cronenberg's *The Fly.* Seth Brundle is a scientist with a teleportation device that he promises will "end all concepts of borders and frontiers, time and space." A subject is encoded as computer data at one point and is decoded at another; the genetic data is the same, but the physical being is newly constructed." ("Is it live or Memorex?" is Brundle's savvy quip.) The dissolution of geographic boundaries yields before the breakdown of genetic and bodily hegemony. Brundle had previously been incapable of grasping the uniqueness of the organic—"the flesh," an explicit reference to Burroughs—and his teleporter was attuned solely to the sterility of the inorganic. His education in the pleasures of the flesh leads to success, but the experiment goes awry due to a random mishap as an errant fly is encoded with Brundle as *part* of Brundle. Following his bizarre transformation, he at first believes the device to have improved him: "*You might think you were the one to teach me about the flesh, but you only know society's straight line about the flesh. . . . I'm talking PENETRATION beyond the veil of the flesh, a deep penetrating dive into the plasma pool!*" The languages of Burroughs and Cronenberg commingle as the "improved" Brundle calls for a transcendence. In this film "the (anti)hero starts out trying to breach the divide between man and machine, self and object," Manohla Dargis points out.[57] While Brundle's euphoria is misplaced, a similar yearning cuts across Cronenberg's body of work (work of the body): a desire for dissolution always accompanied by a fear of the void. Long live the new flesh.

The Brundle-fly ultimately fuses with the metallic transporter itself. Self and other, human and nonhuman, subject and object all become jumbled and dissolved within a universe grown increasingly malleable, decentered, and cryptic. There is no "resistance," "no halo of private protection, not even [one's] own body, to protect [us] anymore" (Baudrillard). Viruses and parasites demonstrate the vulnerability of the body to invasion from without; telepathy and physical projection break down the dichotomy between public and private; subjectivity and temporality collapse; man merges with machine: we have arrived in a zone without borders.

Blood Music

While the xenophobia and technological paranoia of SF and horror overlap, it has fallen to science fiction to narrate—and therefore produce—the human/machine interface in all its potential complexities.[58] Greg Bear's novel *Blood Music,* and his earlier novella of the same name, are highly effective hard-science narratives that perform some significant revisions of familiar 1950s horror film tropes.[59] Like *The Fly,* which it sometimes resembles, *Blood Music* combines the bodily obsession of horror with the technological otherness of science fiction. *Blood Music* is an exemplary narrative of implosion, viral contamination, mutation, organic/technological interface, the disappearance of the body, and the end of the subject. In its two versions, novella and novel, Bear succeeded in condensing a range of concerns that were endemic to SF in the 1980s. Although his other fiction lacks its resonance, *Blood Music* was recognized as a foundational cyberpunk text, despite the hard-SF trappings that remain untainted by any street sensibility.

The tale is set within the nascent biochip (or nanotechnology) industry—"the incorporation of protein molecular circuitry with silicon electronics."[60] Dr. Vergil Ulam of Genetron has constructed Medically Applicable Biochips—"Microscopic logic circuits. You inject them into the human body, they set up shop where they're told and troubleshoot."[61] Ulam has already injected these, now modified to randomly develop (or evolve), into his own blood stream. Soon the molecules have aggregated into complex microorganisms with their own behaviors, their own societies, and their own agendas. Their complexity is enormous; these organisms exist as almost pure genetic information. The resultant evolution is surprising, as he explains: " 'Something is happening inside me. They talk to each other with proteins and nucleic acids, through the fluids, through membranes. They tailor something—viruses, maybe—to carry long messages or personality traits or biologic. Plasmid-like structures. That makes sense. Those are some of the ways I programmed them. Maybe that's what your machine calls infection—all the new information in my blood. Chatter. Tastes of other individuals. Peers. Superiors. Subordinates' " (71). Viral infection marks the pervasive dissolution of the human and the passage to a posthuman order.

Here, then, is an amusing inversion of the premises of Theodore Sturgeon's "Microcosmic God," as the scientist invents a race and becomes a deity, but now is himself transformed by his creations. The new microbodies reconstruct Ulam's body, demonstrating a thorough mastery of their environment. Gradually, they become aware that Ulam is not the universe: " 'They're trying to understand what space is. That's tough for them. They break distances down into concentrations of chemicals. For them, space is a range of taste intensities.' " The narrator finds Ulam in a bathtub, surrounded by pinkish water that isn't bubble bath: " 'It's coming from my skin. They're not telling me everything, but I think they're sending out scouts. Hey! Astronauts! Yeah.' " From there it is only a matter of time before the "noocytes" transgress the boundary of the flesh and infect the world. Edward Milligan and his wife, Gail, are the next to dissolve: "They fell quiet and simply reveled in each other's company. What Edward sensed nearby was not the physical form of Gail, not even his own picture of her personality, but something more convincing, with all the grit and detail of reality, but not as he had ever experienced her before. . . . Edward and Gail grew together on the bed, substance passing through clothes, skin joining where they embraced and lips where they touched" (102–3).

Blood Music first seems only another installment of the alien invasion narrative, a paradigm perhaps best represented by *Invasion of the Body Snatchers*. The human is threatened by outside forces that are antithetical to "the human": that is, they are not mammalian; they are "clusters" rather than "individuals"; and they have no emotions (clearly the defining human quality in traditional SF: *never* do humans encounter *more* emotional creatures than themselves). If the only variation here was to substitute an *internal* threat for the more familiar external one, Bear's work would merit attention only as an AIDS-era update of a Cold War theme.[62] What he does, however, is to present the passage beyond the flesh—beyond the human—as a significant and legitimate evolutionary step. The human is not reified as an unchanging and finished product; instead, the work is concerned most exclusively with metamorphosis, transformation, development, and evolution. The characters in *Blood Music* may face the future with trepidation, but they face it.

Like *Videodrome*, *Blood Music* attempts to narrate a passage beyond the body, beyond the flesh, in hyper-bodily terms. Here, for example, is a quintessentially postmodern narration of the disconnection of the body from the world, one reminiscent of Stelarc's audio-body performance pieces:

> *Truly, you WISH to journey among us, be among us?*
> —I do.
> He stares at the red and green and blue on the VDT. The figures lose all meaning for the moment, as if he is a new born child. Then the screen, the table it rests on, the lavatory curtain beyond and the walls of the containment chamber are replaced by a silvery null. Michael Bernard is crossing an interface.
> He is encoded.
> No longer conscious of all the sensations of being in a body. No more automatic listenings and responses to the slide of muscles past one another, the bubbling of fluids in the abdomen, the push and roar of blood and pounding of the heart. He no longer balances, tenses or relaxes. It is like suddenly moving from the city into the heart of a quiet cave. (188)

This is one of the most physical passages in science fiction, reminiscent of Cronenberg not only in its viral intimacy, but also in its simultaneous sense of a transcendence of, and attachment to, the body. It is also emblematic of Delany's paraspace, in the rhetorical heightening which enacts the death of the subject (in science fiction "the subject" is often humanity itself). In its poetic brevity and repetition, the passage even recalls the "death" of HAL in *2001* ("My mind is going. My mind is going. I can feel it").

The noosphere is another dataplane, still another visualization of information circulation and control. On the molecular-cybernetic level, information is again perceptible and malleable. Another scientist is given a tour of a noocyte cluster, a passage through a biological cyberspace:

> [He] stood alone in the noosphere, surrounded by options he hardly knew how to take advantage of. He held his hand out toward the surrounding information. It rippled all around him, waves of light spreading from nadir to zenith. Ranks of information exchanged priorities and his memories stacked up around him like towers of cards, each represented by a line of light.
> The lines cascaded.
> He had been thinking. (204)

The human has become a computer while retaining and even augmenting a biological "nature." The narrative represents, and thus produces, the subject as, indeed, a soft machine. In Shirley's *Eclipse Corona,* languages of electronics and biology collapse onto one another:

> Jerome's chip communicating with his brain via an interface of rhodopsin protein; the ribosomes burrowing neurohumoral transmitters from the brain's blood supply, re-ordering the transmitters so that they carried a programmed pattern of ion releases for transmission across synaptic gaps to the brain's neuronal dendrites; the chip using magnetic resonance holography to collate with brain-stored memories and psychological trends. Declaiming to itself the mythology of the brain; reenacting on its silicon stage the personal Legends of his subjective world history.[63]

That the brain is like a computer, or even that the brain *is* a computer, finds expression in countless narratives about artificial intelligence, where the brain is figured as only so much programmable software, well-suited for duplication and even simulation. In Rudy Rucker's comic, proto-cyberpunk novel, *Software,* the inventor of the robots ("boppers") is about to receive their "gift of immortality:" "The mind . . . memories, habits, opinion, skills . . . is all software. The boppers had extracted Cobb's software and put it in control of this robot body."[64] Rucker, Michael Swanwick, and Bruce Sterling feature the term "wetware" in their writings: "As the cell divided, the bopper software would replicate along with the human DNA wetware. But the final step of building the bopper software into the human wetware had yet to be made."[65] Here is another cyborg term, connoting organicism ("wet") and technology ("ware"). Rucker, a computer programmer as well as a writer, is possessed of an eerie acceptance of the terminal future: "One could legitimately regard the sequence human-bopper-meatbop as a curious but inevitable zigzag in evolution's mighty stream."[66] Rucker's burlesque and distinctly subcultural voice endows these potentially paranoid projections with a kind of loopy charm.

Something intelligent and unsentimental is at work in these novels. Vernor Vinge, the author of "True Names" (see chapter 3), has praised *Blood Music* for its narration of transcendence. Vinge observed that SF edges up on this moment in which our own models will no longer be applicable, but for obvious reasons this is where the narrative must break down. That Bear actually "illustrates this wonderful/terrifying possibility" of the end of the human, the dissolution of the subject, is remarkable (that diacritical slash in Vinge's writing neatly condenses the ambivalence, multiple meanings, and representational limits of the language of science fiction).[67] Although there is no grand transcendent gesture in Rucker's fictions, these also produce a "remarkable" dissolution of the "natural" human position. "Soon," the narrator of "Blood Music" notes, "there will be no need for centralization."[68]

Schismatrix—Living in the Posthuman Solar System

A character in *Schismatrix* observes that the old categories are a bit outmoded and are breaking up. Technologies are more prevalent but less centralized; we are already cyborgs. Instrumental reason has been superseded by a culture that seems increasingly dispersed and in the process of a fundamental transformation. Cyberpunk remains the literary form most centrally concerned with the rhetorical production of a complex imbrication between human subject and the electronically defined realities of the Dataist Era. The deeply influential fiction of William Gibson has already been considered at length, and reference has been made to Swanwick, Rucker, Effinger, and Williams, but a consideration of the movement's other "leader," Bruce Sterling, reveals the operation of some very different strategies. Sterling has occupied the center of cyberpunk territory since the advent of the movement, and he continues to serve as the form's most valuable spokesperson, editor, and polemicist. The volume of cyberpunk writings edited by Sterling, *Mirrorshades,* has contributed more to the general acceptance of cyberpunk than any text besides *Neuromancer,* and Sterling's authorial collaborations with Gibson, Lewis Shiner, and Rudy Rucker have all produced fundamental texts. The coherence of cyberpunk as a movement is, to a large degree, attributable to Sterling's persistence and ubiquity.

Much of Sterling's writing is similar to Gibson's in its dense, hyperbolized appropriation of technical languages and in the clear recognition and acceptance of the conditions of the Information Age. As in *Neuromancer,* corporations and cartels serve as the ruling power; nations have ceased to exist. Computers, data screens, and terminals dominate Sterling's fiction as much as Gibson's, although video is more prevalent in Sterling's diegesis, both as fact and as paradigm. These similarities are evident, but there are equally apparent differences between the two authors that undermines the stylistic consistency implied by the "cyberpunk" label. Sterling's narrative structures are less derivative of other genres, and there is little of the literary quality of Gibson's prose, which is replete with echoes of his literary antecedents and popculture forebears. His impact has also been less overtly marked; it is difficult to think of another writer who is emulating Sterling's textual formations, formations that are significantly more dense and perhaps slightly less profound (at least on the surface) than those of Gibson.

In the writings that have been most characteristically cyberpunk, his Shaper/Mechanist series, Sterling remains entirely within the physical universe: the rhetorical and phenomenological freedoms of cyberspace are not to be had (by contrast, Walter Jon Williams, Joan D. Vinge, William T. Quick, Mike Saenz, Pepe Moreno, and Dan Simmons have all availed themselves of Gibson's cyberspace—it is nearly a defining trope of the subgenre).[69] Without the euphoric possibilities inherent in that particular paraspace there is, in Sterling's work, an even more pronounced ambivalence in its negotiation of the electronic and cybernetic datascape.

The Shaper/Mechanist series consists of five short stories—"Swarm" and "Spider Rose" (both 1982), "Cicada Queen" (1983), "Sunken Gardens" (1984), and "Twenty Evocations" (1984)—as well as the novel, *Schismatrix.*[70] This postulated future is set in a "posthuman solar system" of asteroid mines, orbital colonies, alien traders, and an anachronistic (and unvisited) Earth, in which different versions of humanity's successors struggle for dominance. Sterling's reflexive tactic is to play two different SF futures against each other. The Shapers are genetically "reshaped" beings whose enhanced biology provides amplified intelligence, disease-free bodies, and unprecedented muscular control. Their adversaries are the Mechanists, cyborgs whose posthuman abilities are a function of comprehensive mechanical augmentation (prosthetic body parts and the like). While the Shapers are confident of the imminent demise of the Mechanists ("They may totter on for whole centuries. But they will be cut off. They'll be cybernetic, not living flesh. That's a dead end, because there's no will behind it. No imperatives. Only programming. No imagination" [139]), the Mechanists find their increasingly cybernetic existence to be strikingly empowering. Witness this McLuhanesque epiphany: " 'With the loss of mobility comes extension of the senses. If I want I can switch out to a probe in Mercurian orbit. . . . Suddenly I'm there, just as fully as I'm ever anywhere these days. The mind isn't what you think, Mr. Dze. When you grip it with wires, it tends to flow. Data seem to bubble up from some deep layer of the mind. This is not exactly living, but it has its advantages' " (179).

The prose that presents this posthumanist future is axiomatic of Delany's theories concerning language in science fiction. Sterling's language is dense and jargon-ridden, at times difficult to decipher.[71] Each chapter begins with a statement of location and date, traditionally a helpful means of orienting the reader:

The Mare Tranquillitatis People's Circumlunar Zaibatsu: 27-12-'15

Where are we? If *Mare Tranquillitatis* suggests a lunar locale, then that deduction is unseated by *Circumlunar.* The word *zaibatsu* signifies a generic location (that is, in a cyberpunk novel) more than a spatial concept. The reader might finally deduce that the action is set in a corporate-built colony in orbit around the moon, and Sterling does explain that "There were ten of these worlds, named for the lunar mares and craters that had provided their raw materials" (13). Nevertheless, in order to "visualize scenes on the astronomical level," as Delany states, the reader must be extraordinarily attentive to the machinations of the text.[72] In Sterling's novel, though, even a more attentive reader could be gulled into believing that the setting was the Sea of Tranquility. Finally, note the vagueness of the date, which not only lists day before month (in distinction to the American style), but which leaves the *century* unspecified. The lunar setting night suggests a near-future 2015, except that the ensuing history reveals that far more time has passed.

Later, Lindsay Abelard, a modified human, surveys another space station. As in *Neuromancer,* an orbiting colony becomes the occasion for presenting a complex urban nonplace: "The grapelike cluster of cheap inflatables was hooked to an interurban tube road. He floated at once down the lacquered corridor and emerged through a filament doorway into the swollen transparent nexus of crossroads. Below was Goldreich-Tremaine, with its Besetzny and Patterson Wheels spinning in slow majesty; with the molecule-like links and knobs of other suburbs shining purple, gold, and green, surrounding the city like beaded yarn. At least he was still in G-T. He headed at once for home" (158). This baroque prose is far from Sterling's only style. He has a talent for pastiche, and several of his fantasy stories have mimicked oral and Asiatic narrative voices. His most recent solo novel, the near-future *Islands in the Net* (1988), is written in a comparatively straightforward manner. One can therefore deduce that the paraspatial density of the Shaper/Mechanist fiction is a strategy designed to produce specific effects in the reader.

The compression increases from story to story—not until "Cicada Queen" does the style approach what *Schismatrix* will offer. In his analysis of the Shaper/Mechanist fictions, Tom Maddox has noted that "Swarm" and "Spider Rose" "use the Shaper/Mechanist context as the ground for rather traditional SF." It is in the following story that the thematic concerns of the series are foregrounded: "With 'Cicada Queen,' the trope of posthumanism acquires symbolic depth, and the Mechanist/Shaper series its own higher level of complexity."[73] Maddox is primarily referring to the concepts Sterling deploys, but his observations hold true for the *language* of the narrative as well. There is, in fact, a strong correlation between "the trope of posthumanism" and the rhetorical density of the Shaper/Mech series.

Sterling is engaged in the production of a unique textual matrix that emerges from a web (or "net") of discourses; economics, politics, history, technology, and narrative all intersect to produce an idiolect that, at times, is hardly *narrative* at all. Instead, the effect is of a carefully developed semiotics of the future. The works crawl with a sensory overload—colors, textures, and odors are part of every description (the attention to color is especially reminiscent of Delany and Zelazny). Abelard has been trained as a diplomat by the shapers, and so he is overtly aware of the meaning behind every gesture (the protagonist of Delany's *Stars in My Pocket Like Grains of Sand* is also a diplomat—in postmodern SF, the diplomat becomes an explicit cultural semiotician). The body is qualified by its signifying function, as in this observation of an alien Investor: "In civilized Investor life [the frills] were a relic, like the human eyebrow, which had evolved to deflect sweat. Like the eyebrow, their social use was now paramount" (166).

The Shaper/Mech writing almost demands a deconstructive engagement through its willfully contradictory metaphors, signs, and terms.

As noted, the language exemplifies Delany's and deLauretis's analyses of science fiction's rhetorical maneuvers. When a character in *Schismatrix* says, "I'm wired to the ass," the phrase is meant to be taken literally on at least one level—the character is technologically augmented to a maximal degree (today, the phrase implies a purely figurative sense of intoxication, while yet another reading might be possible in, for example, a text by William Burroughs, in which the anatomical details would be made more explicit). Sterling's very title is oxymoronic, a *schismatrix* that inscribes an entirely contradictory tension between the *schism,* or gap, and the *matrix,* or connective network (as in a mathematical matrix). Also, in this tale of diplomacy, betrayal, and commerce, it's difficult not to read the title as a pun on *schismatic:* one who promotes or exploits schism. Finally, the term is perfect for the status of the information society in the Dataist Era—physically dissolute, yet coversely bound more closely together than at any other moment in history.

Most strikingly, Sterling's prose is marked by an obsessive deployment of technological and biological metaphors; each is nearly always described in terms of the other. It is this tropological system, at once contradictory and appropriate, that distinguishes the paraspatial quality of the Shaper/Mechanist discourse. This imbrication of human and machine is first signaled by a deployment of insect metaphors;[74] indeed, the first three Shaper/Mechanist stories, "Swarm," "Spider Rose," and "Cicada Queen," incorporate such metaphors into their very titles. In "Sunken Gardens" machines are described in insectoid (and arachnoid) terms: "The crawler lurched as its six picklike feet scrabbled down the slopes of a deflation pit" (81). "The crawler ran spiderlike along the crater's snowy rim" (83). "The black crawler was crouched with its periscoped head sunk downward, as if ready to pounce. Its swollen belly was marked with a red hourglass and the corporate logos of its faction" (85). In these examples the modeling of machine upon insect/arachnid is obvious and diegetic, but note also that Sterling emphasizes a certain mechanical autonomy: "The crawler worked its way up the striated channel of an empty glacier bed" (82). The story presents rival factions working to create a viable biosphere on a terraformed Mars; that these scrabbling mechanical spiders and mantises should engineer such metamorphoses is typical of Sterling's textual deformations. Life—the flora and fauna deployed by the crawlers—seems more like an infection spread by cybernetic carriers. Insect forms also recur in *Schismatrix* in the form of trained killer butterflies, and the ubiquitous multicolored roaches that have accompanied humanity into space, feeding upon its detritus. "If it weren't for the roaches, the *Red Consensus* would eventually smother in a moldy detritus of cast-off skin and built-up layers of sweated and exhaled effluvia" (68).

Insects are only the most evident metaphorical process conflating a number of irreconcilable terms such as life/nonlife, biology/technology, human/machine. Throughout the Shaper/Mech fictions, Sterling's tropological systems become more complex, as the operations of science fiction's syntax produce an emergent synthesis of the organic and the cybernetic—a soft machine. For example, in this description of an asteroid mining colony in *Schismatrix,* rock, biotics, and technology intersect: "Trade secrets were secure within Dembowska's bowels, snug beneath kilometers of rock. Life had forced itself like putty into the fracture in this minor planet: dug out its inert heart and filled it with engines" (181). None of the metaphors Sterling uses here is particularly original, but in their aggregate, the effect is, I think, notable. When Abelard visits a Shaper, they watch images on a videowall: "She switched scenes. A craggy landscape appeared; enormous pits next to a blasted, flaking area cut by two huge crevasses. 'This is erotica,' she said. 'Skin at twenty thousand times life size. One of my favorites' " (177). Alien recording tape *might* be alive: "Slowly, a memory, either biological or cybernetic, took hold of it. It began to bunch and crumple into a new form" (188).

The confusion between literal and figurative languages is thus fundamental to the experience of *Schismatrix,* forcing the reader to negotiate among dichotomies that are no longer dichotomous: "Lindsay ran his mechanical hand over his coils of gray hair. The steel knuckles glittered with inlaid seed-gems; the wire tendons sparkled with interwoven strands of fiberoptics" (142). "Wire tendons" is to be taken literally, but then what ought the reader to do with the "coils" of hair? The Shaper/Mechanist system is oxymoronic, its coherence and plausibility guaranteed only by the binding structures of language; specifically, the language of science fiction. Sterling often achieves a kind of cyborg poetry: "And there it was: the outside world. There was not much to it: words and pictures, lines on a screen. She ran her fingertips gently over the scalding pain in her knee" (122).

There is, in Sterling's writing, a profound acceptance of the human as a complex network of biological, political, technological, economic, and even aesthetic forces. To some degree, Sterling locates the technological as the determinant structure in defining the range of cultural systems. Even the central political struggle in the Shaper/Mechanist stories is technologically determined, as a character tells Abelard: " 'The Shapers, the Mechanists—those aren't philosophies, they're technologies made into politics. . . . Science tore the human race to bits. When anarchy hit, people struggled for community. The politicians chose enemies so that they could bind their followers with hate and terror. Community isn't enough when a thousand new ways of life beckon from every circuit and test tube'" (185). If Sterling subscribes to a model of technological determinism, then that model is always tempered by the recognition of technology's imbrication with other mutually affecting forces. In the last analysis, technology may exercise a determining power, but "the last analysis" is simply an abstraction that removes technology from its real conditions of existence.

By unfolding two versions of a posthuman future, "Shaper" and "Mechanist," both so familiar to readers of science fiction, Sterling has produced a deeply reflexive set of texts. What at first seems to be a dichotomy or even a dialectic ultimately stands as something much more like a Derridean *supplement*—as though the idea of the *posthuman* guaranteed the existence of a stable and clear definition of the *human*. If there was ever an "essential" human nature, then surely there is no longer. Neither does Sterling lament its passage, and thereby turn the Shaper/Mechanist future into a cautionary parable about the evils of unchecked technological development. Instead the series offers a consistent acknowledgment of the conditional status of human definition. "Maybe technology eventually turns them into something you wouldn't call human. But that's a choice they make—a rational choice" (53). By the end of *Schismatrix,* even its own central dichotomy is passing: "The old categories, Mechanist and Shaper—they're a bit outmoded these days, aren't they? Life moves in clades. . . . A clade is a daughter species, a related descendent. It's happened to other successful animals, and now it's humanity's turn. The factions still struggle, but the categories are breaking up. No faction can claim the one true destiny for mankind. Mankind no longer exists" (183).

BATAILLE AND THE NEW FLESH   Poetry leads to

the same place as all forms of eroticism—to the blending and fusion of

separate objects. It leads us to eternity, it leads us to death, and through

death to continuity.—Georges Bataille   ¶ "There's no going back, no start-

ing over. That's a game for those who still have flesh."—Bruce Sterling,

Schismatrix ¶ **I want to be a machine.—Andy Warhol**

Cosmic Continuity

In his introduction to *Erotism: Death and Sensuality,* Georges Bataille deals with the dissolution of the subject within what he terms "the crisis of existence."[75] The Christian, Western tradition Bataille describes defines the human subject through difference—difference from the inert objects in the world and difference from all the other objects that are possessed of their own subjectivity (other people). This difference is what we have learned to refer to as a "sense of self." The self is centered and self-knowing, continuous within itself, but discontinuous with the world it occupies—"even a vague feeling of self belongs to a discontinuous being," Bataille writes (102). Thus, to construct a sense of self, to become a subject, is to deprive oneself of the continuity that is a part of every being's existence: "Between one being and another, there is a gulf, a discontinuity. This gulf exists, for instance, between you, listening to me, and me, speaking to you. We are attempting to communicate, but no communication between us can abolish our fundamental difference. If you die, it is not my death" (12).

"We yearn for our lost continuity" (15). Bataille recognizes two means by which we overcome the discontinuity we experience as subjects. The biological imperatives of sexual reproduction demand an act of fusion with another being, and thus the ritualistic structures of eroticism signify one path toward a lost continuity. The second involves the process of rejoining the continuum of existence that occurs with death. In death the body decays, its putrescence marking not simply the dissolution of the individual, but the proliferation of life that arises in the very place of that demise. Death is also the obverse of reproduction, part of a cycle that implies the continuity which extends from one generation to the next.

Sexuality and death have therefore become heavily coded systems in all cultures, replete with rituals, taboos, and transgressions. Sacrifice and eroticism are rituals of continuity: " 'What I want to emphasize is that death does not affect the continuity of existence, since in existence itself all separate existences originate; continuity of existence is independent of death and *is even proved by death*. This I think is the way to interpret religious sacrifices, with which I suggest that erotic activity can be compared' " (21–22). Sexuality and death both deny, or even destroy, the sense of self that must be preserved, but both reconnect the subject to the larger continuities that are always present, albeit forcefully repressed. Sex and death produce a dissolution of the subject on one level, but produce a synthesis on another. This is the paradox, and thus the crisis, of existence.

Bataille's own philosophy does not aspire to the simple transcendence of the physical through which the discontinuity of being shall be miraculously effaced. His target is the entire civilization of renunciation that installs an instrumental rationality as its guiding principle.[76] Rather than an aspiration toward an Hegelian "Absolute Spirit"—and rather than a mere denial of that aspiration—Bataille's writings push toward a full evocation of the physical and the animal. At the end of man's "spiritual" or "rational" evolution, Allan Stoekl writes of Bataille's *oeuvre*, "at the *end* of reason, at the *end* of man, at the *end* of the Cartesian pineal gland (the supposed seat of consciousness) there is only orgasm and a simultaneous fall, a simultaneous death. Death and perversion do not take place in splendid isolation; instead, they are at the endpoint of the human."[77] Annette Michelson notes that this philosophy, which is also a sociology, is finally a cosmology, dominated by the image of a burning and endlessly radiating sun: "It is, indeed, the sun's incessant, untrammeled expenditure of energy which is its glory and which offers man the paradigm of social formation—for both the general economy and its consummation in the ritual of sacrifice. More than that, however, expenditure, destruction, and loss have ontological status; their limits are those of being."[78] Expenditure, sacrifice, mutilation, madness— Bataille's *excremental unreason* demolishes the prospect of a guiding rationality that withholds, that renounces, and that ultimately fails to conscribe what is human within the artificial confines of *a self*. "The one who sacrifices is free," Bataille writes, "free to throw himself suddenly *outside of himself.*"[79]

Bataille's evocative model of the virtues and limits of the flesh has real relevance for understanding SF and horror.[80] As in science fiction, Bataille's own language continually eschews the perspective of the individual for an evolutionary, anthropological, and even cosmological discourse on the nature of human existence. In an earlier essay, Bataille develops his model of economic expenditure (that exists in contradistinction to economic models based on use- and exchange-values). In deliciously cosmic terms, he advocates behaviors for human bodies akin to those powerful radiating forces of celestial bodies: "Through loss man can regain the free movement of the universe, he can dance and swirl in the full rapture of those great swarms of stars. But he must, in the violent expenditure of self, perceive that he breathes in the power of death."[81] Bataille writes the drama of the subject within frankly nonpsychologized terms, and science fiction is defined by such displacements of individual subjectivity (either willed or serendipitous).

But while most SF narrates the transcendence and dissolution of the individual, it is certainly *not* within the terms of a Bataillean discourse. Bataille maintains that "it is only at the boundary of death that laceration, which constitutes the very nature of the immensely free *me,* transcending 'that which exists,' is revealed *with violence,*"[82] but rare is the science fiction text that produces "death" through an explicitly physical (or textual) violence (horror fiction, on the other hand, might be another story). Science fiction more fully participates in strategies of denial; Bataille's introduction to *Erotism* allows the quasi-religious underpinnings of the genre to emerge: "Faced with a precarious discontinuity of the personality, the human spirit reacts in two ways which in Christianity coalesce. The first responds to the desire to find that lost continuity which we are stubbornly convinced is the essence of being. With the second, mankind tries to avoid the terms set to individual discontinuity, death, and invents a discontinuity unassailable by death— that is, the immortality of discontinuous beings" (119). Both methods of coping with the discontinuity of being have analogues within SF, and they frequently coalesce, as in Christianity. In science fiction the death of the subject is continually acted out in a form that yields a rebirth on another plane, producing a strengthened continuity. This frequently occurs within the linguistic concentrations of a "paraspace" (see chapter 2) that is ever-concerned with the death of the Subject. The rhetorical excesses that comprise the climactic scenes of *The Stars My Destination, 2001,* and *Neuromancer,* to take but three examples, both dissolve and reshape the human subject. The paraspace is "a negation that carries us to the farthest bounds of possibility," which happens to be Bataille's phrase describing the experience of death (24).

Eroticism and death are both encoded within science fiction's generic protocols. On one level, it is tempting to observe that SF deals directly with the notion of continuity since it is often so overtly about the continuity of the human species, but this directness often involves a transcendence of the very realm of the *physical.* The tension of the erotic, suspended as it is between the contradictory yearnings for the discontinuous and the continuous, is a tension of the flesh, of the physical being; this physicality is often elided in the heavily coded sexualities of science fiction. The erotic is disguised by a set of displaced alternatives, as we shall see.

Theodore Sturgeon's *More Than Human* (1952) occupies a provocative intersection with Bataille's thesis regarding the crisis of existence. The novel features mutant children who are marked as "different," and thus their status as discontinuous beings, and the concomitant sense of loss, is emphasized. One character, nearly an adult, is severely retarded, although this "fabulous idiot" displays telepathic ability. When he finally learns to speak, he names himself "Lone." Lone's telepathy first reveals the underlying continuity of existence, while separating him from that continuum: "Impression, depression, dialogue. Radiations of fear, tense fields of awareness, discontent. Murmuring, sending, speaking, sharing, from hundreds, from thousands of voices. None, though, for the idiot."[83] His mind finally touches a receptive subject, a girl who has been raised by her psychopathic father and who has never seen her own unclothed body. She has no knowledge of sexuality or the erotic. But bodily awareness is elided in her telepathic communion with Lone—the fusion of beings precedes physical contact: "Silently they lived in each other and then she bent and touched him, touched his face and shaggy hair" (11). "She did not know what a kiss was and any he might have seen had no significance to him. But they had a better thing" (12). The physical fusion of the erotic is displaced onto a mental plane (is this a higher plane?).[84]

Ultimately, a group being comes into existence from this collection of mutant beings, a new entity that calls itself Homo Gestalt. If Bataille has narrated the progress from animal to man, then Sturgeon has moved from man to superman. It is easy to perhaps dismiss the Sturgeon novel for its tentative physicality and its denial of erotic desire in favor of a purely mental intercourse. But in its narration of agonistic discontinuity that yields a transcendence to an existence predicated upon the most intimate continuity, Sturgeon has, with great delicacy, postulated the existence of being without ego, of a movement beyond the borders of a unified self. Within the limitations of the genre's conservatism (only beginning to erode in the 1950s, thanks in part to the editorial policies of Herbert Gold in *Galaxy* magazine, which published these tales), Sturgeon's text broaches some radical questions of being.[85] Indeed, telepathy clearly represents a kind of "flow" of the type described by Deleuze and Guattari and venerated by Klaus Theweleit: "Desire constantly couples continuous flows and partial objects that are by nature fragmentary and fragmented. Desire causes the current to flow."[86]

While Sturgeon's text recodes the erotic onto a mental plane, other science fiction texts grapple directly with the subject's death and subsequent rebirth in a new existential continuum. *2001* treats its remaining human subject, David Poole, as a synecdoche for the human species. In the penultimate sequence of the film, Poole is seen to age in discrete stages until reaching a state of severe decreptitude. He raises his arm to point at the monolith, whether in accusation or acknowledgment is unclear. The camera tracks in to the abyssal black absence at the core of the monolith. Clarke's novel is more explicit at this point (as at all others), as the Starchild prepares to return to Earth across the void of the universe: "Unwittingly, he had crossed it once; now he must cross it again—this time, of his own volition. The thought filled him with a sudden, freezing terror, so that for a moment he was wholly disoriented, and his new vision of the universe trembled and threatened to shatter into a thousand fragments. . . . Then he remembered that he would never be alone, and his panic slowly ebbed."[87] In a trope familiar throughout this study, the passage to a new level of being is marked by an enhanced perceptual ability. The Starchild's perception of the universe is whole and coherent, although the threat of discontinuity still looms.

In the film the track in to the monolith is followed by an abrupt return to the more familiar space of Earth orbit. A baby floats nearby, seemingly as large as the planet itself. The human has been taken to its evolutionary limit, to the very point of human obsolescence, but death is only the prelude to the triumphant rebirth heralded by the same Richard Strauss theme that was heard earlier as the ape picked up a bone to use as a tool (a weapon). The passage of humanoid to human is thus recapitualted at the finale of *2001* by a passage from human to more-than-human, a new state of being that clearly exists on a level of cosmic awareness denied the human subjects who are barely functional within the oppressive isolation of Kubrick's banal future. Here the evolutionary perspective is more marked, as is the sense of the transcendence of the discontinuities of human definition and a passage beyond the body (the "Starchild" is more ethereal and celestial than physical).[88]

Thus the fusion of sexuality is displaced into an ecstatic transcendence of the physical, just as the fact of death is elided through a cosmic, evolutionary perspective. Physicality, in the form of direct sexuality, is abolished (at least until the writings of the New Wave), and the putrescence of the body in death is displaced even further. While other genres, including war fiction, detective fiction, and (naturally) horror have reveled in the description of the rictus and contortions of dead bodies, science fiction has none of that, even as it appropriates narrative and narrational tropes from these very genres. Recent works (including *Blade Runner* and *Neuromancer*) have borrowed heavily from hard-boiled detective fiction, but without all the corpses. However, one must note that the city in recent science fiction is frequently presented as a decaying body—the decrepit buildings, the fetid effluvia of litter and assorted debris, the wet streets flowing with sewage from backed-up plumbing. The physical is again staged in displaced terms. The function of the detective is to reveal this urban body, to lay open its obsolescent, decaying form to our gaze.[89]

Panic Subjects in the Machine Civilization

Not all science fiction readily surrenders the status of being to the uncertain ambiguities of a new "terminal" identity—even cyberpunk manages to retain the body as the (empty) sign of an unchanged, nonterminal condition. While most SF fails to fully engage with terminal realities, some mainstream work effectively encapsulates a range of techno-organic anxieties. Norman Spinrad notes a newly prominent theme in science fiction: the rise of vast "machine-civilizations" that "dominate in the galaxy and, moreover, are engaged in the general extermination of organic sapients."[90] While acknowledging the "hard science plausibility" of such civilizations, Spinrad further observes that "the notion that such high machine civilizations would seek to exterminate lower organic forms seems to owe more to the anthropomorphic projection of our own unfortunate xenophobic imperialism."[91] The technophobia is evident as human Luddism is disguised as a kind of cybernetic reverse-Luddism, with disgruntled machines reacting violently to the "imperfection" of organic existence.

Advocates for the existence of machine-civs (including the popular science writer Timothy Ferris) argue that temperatures in the universe are more favorable to silicon-based lifeforms and that their virtual immortality would permit them to exist on a galactic, rather than merely a solar, level. "And sooner or later," Spinrad adds, "high organic civilizations will produce self-replicating, self-programming machines who will supersede them." These machine-civs, then, are our progeny, our successors, boldly going where no *man* has gone before. In some sense, these hypothetical civilizations represent the fruition of the human drive for immortality, but immortality is accompanied by (is predicated upon) the complete supercession of sexuality and decay—the supercession of our very organicism.

1. Buttonheads, Wireheads, and Charge Addicts

The machinery of the brain and the machinery of industrial and electronic cultures become coextensive in the postmodern science fiction of the body. Case is neurologically modified to jack into his state-of-the-art cyberdeck in *Neuromancer's* hacker-as-rock-star fantasy. But jacking in has its dangers. The deadly, hivelike Borg, the machine-civ on *Star Trek: The Next Generation,* enslave humans and augment their bodies with (punk-style) cybernetic modifications to turn them into drones of their central mind. Humans become prisoners of the interface. Case's own painful withdrawal from the ecstatic conditions of cyberspace reveals his status as prisoner: he is literally addicted to the Cartesian vectors of cyberspace. Science fiction often presents a similar, but more limited form of dependency in the form of the electrical addict. In Crichton's *The Terminal Man,* an experiment to control a patient's psychotic rages goes awry when the patient becomes an "elad" (electrical addict), which has a real history in neurological science.[92] Kingsley Amis, for example, refers to a 1956 *Scientific American* article ("Pleasure Centers in the Brain") and notes the birth of a new anxiety: "the fear of a pleasure so overmastering that it can break down the sense of reality or at least the pattern of active life."[93]

The idea of being literally *addicted* to technology has real durability in science fiction. The advent of these plug-in cyborgs, these techno-addicts who are physically wired into the computer system, indicates that human and machine have indeed become coextensive, but addiction is presented as neither positive nor unavoidable; it is described from the seemingly exempt position of the nonaddict. For these writers, and perhaps for much of the discourse on addiction as well, the *addict* is constructed as the opposite of the *subject.* The subject is defined through a mythos of self-reliance, free will, and nondependency. Novels by George Alec Effinger and Walter Jon Williams feature characters who refuse to surrender to buttonhead status. Effinger's Marîd tales are set in a Middle Eastern inner city where personality modification is de rigueur. Marîd tries to retain his individuality in the face of easy and thorough plasticity. "You will change your mind on Monday," he is told, and true to Delany's analysis of SF language, the phrase takes on a frightening duality: "No, I thought, it won't be me; it will be Friedlander Bey and his surgeons who will change my mind."[94]

Such characters attempt to preserve their free will, even within the dataspace that defines and delimits the major arena of social control. To merge with the data, then, is acceptable only as long as the subject remains the locus of control. While the *subject* is thus defined as a willed and (relatively) autonomous force, the *addict* (as elad, buttonhead, wirehead, or "persona bum") is portrayed as radically *de*-centered— passively buffeted by the data rather than remaining proudly (if only partially) resistant to its lures. (If this is explicit in Williams's *Hardwired,* it is already present in *Neuromancer* and *TRON.* Despite that similarity, neither the books by Effinger nor Williams construct the dense para-spaces of Gibson or *TRON,* so the coherence of the subject is retained by reader and characters. The radical movement of language around the boundaries of representation never occurs, although cyberpunk rhetoric is clearly evoked, especially by Williams.)[95]

The techno-addict returns in Spinrad's *The Void Captain's Tale,* one of a number of novels featuring cyborg-controlled spaceships. The pilot is jacked into the ship's sensors and systems; the ship thus becomes an extension of the human sensorium. In the earliest of these novels, Anne McCaffrey's *The Ship Who Sang,* the ship's "brain" is that of a human paraplegic. Delany's *Nova* opens as a derelict "cyborg-stud" staggers into a tavern, his senses literally *burned-out* by his ship's encounter with a nova. But Spinrad develops the idea most thoroughly: "In functional terms, the Pilot is the human component of the Jump Circuit, the organic element of our star drive, who, cyborged to the Jump Drive navigates the ship through the space-time discontinuity of the Jump and out the other side the requisite number of light-years in the right direction" (8) (in less functional terms, the job is more "orgasmic" than "organic"). Not everyone can be a pilot: it is among those women who have failed to discover a sense of self, and who now inhabit the "demi-mondes" and margins of society, that recruits are found. The "terminal addict" can fuse with the machine and guide it through the nonspace of the Jump, but this subject is more of an object, and the ability to interface with the void of nonreality provides scant consolation.

2. Antibodies

For the most part the putrescent body has been excluded from science fiction and has found its most prominent niche in horror. Bataille casti-gates Western civilization for its repression of the bodily in favor of a celebration of Man's eternal, rational "spirit." The animality of the human is denied. Stoekl explains that, "In Bataille's view, the bourgeois individuals—like Nietzsche or Breton—who foster a desire to revolt by soaring 'above' are destined for a fall, and in a way *want* to fall. Icarian revolt (as opposed to base subversion) is the only pathology Bataille will condemn; it is the pathological refusal to embrace stinking decom-position—an embrace that, from the point of view of any dialectic of the cure, must itself be pathological."[96] The body is figured as incomplete and inadequate; the rational is betrayed by the physical (buttonhead philosophy). This "pathology," *Alien* demonstrates, underlies much SF and is extensively explored in David Skal's *Antibodies,* a canny novel by a sometime critic that is all-too-aware of recent trends in art and cultural theory.[97] The work evokes Andy Warhol's machine-aesthetic, reflected in the foil walls of the Factory and his own oft-quoted desire to be a machine[98] (*Antibodies* also makes reference to, among other things, feminist SF journals, Survival Research Laboratories, the computer imaging of Nancy Burson, *Alien, TRON,* and *Robocop*). A cult has developed called the Cybernetic Temple, based on a disavowal of the animality of the flesh. The flesh rots, the flesh decays, as Diandra, a commercial artist, suddenly realizes: "—*mindbody meatbody deathbody stinking sagging shitting fetus bursting organs hanging buried alive in a coffin of blood oh god not me don't let it be me got to get out of this bucket of tripe it's sucking me down throwing me up take it away this pulsing writhing spurting spinning body-go-round, BODY*—" (25). To be mechanical, to be electronic, this is to be forever—"the only lasting reality." Diandra dreams of Disneyland's audioanimatrons (177). Bruno Bettelheim remarked of his case study of "Joey," who also believed that he was a machine, that "Joey's story might also be viewed as a cautionary tale," because it indicates "both our hopes and our fears of what machines may do for us, or to us."[99] What Bettelheim finally discovers is that the fantasy of machine control is a very *reassuring* fantasy for Joey, reflecting as it does a complete faith in the infallibility of technology: "It jeopardized his life when machines went awry."[100] As Bataille has noted, the putrescence of the flesh marks the horrifying, transitory experience of the individual, a horror that must be forcibly repressed.

Antibodies resembles some of the work of Philip Dick in its comically paranoid extrapolation of contemporary concerns, but it connects to the themes developed in feminist science fiction around pathologies of body image (see below). A cult "deprogrammer" explains the rise of the Temple: "America's morbid obsession with antisepsis has done its share to create this problem" (35). The denial of the flesh signaled by contemporary concerns with hygiene, cosmetic surgery, and eating disorders represents a desire to transcend the animalistic cycles of birth, life, and death. The hyperbole of the body is another sign of denial, to be found in the stardom of Stallone and Schwarzenegger, as well as in the panoply of grueling workout tapes for sale (of course, in these cases the body is already transformed into a kind of machine). Under the conditions of postmodernity, the comforting belief in the eternity of afterlife has yielded to the anxieties surrounding a fear of nonexistence. Spirit is denied, the body is denied—all that remains is the rational and the mechanical. The translation to data, or to mechanism, becomes a means of merging with the sole remaining continuum: telematic existence.

Still, the surrender of the flesh does signal the end of subjectivity and the status of *the self*. The true "antibodies" become objects, devoid of fleshly emotions and desires and their discontents ("The other passengers didn't bother her much today; she was beyond all that now" [p. 13]). The desire to become a cyborg connects to the new "eternal cycle" of consumerism and product circulation; one character predicts that, "In the future, shopping will become a major form of entertainment" (75). Obviously, this future is now, as afternoons at the mall and *The Price Is Right* and *The Home Shopping Network* make abundantly clear. The only transcendence offered in *Antibodies* is a transcendence of the flesh, unaccompanied by the illusive ecstasies of any larger cosmic continuum. Far from an actual transcendence, the antibodies represent the final triumph of the technocratic power of instrumental reason, as a functional, mechanical existence becomes the very signifier of high fashion.

Boys' Toys from Hell

Mark Pauline and his performance group, Survival Research Laboratories, have constructed a series of elaborate posthuman entertainments that put a different spin on a similar range of phenomena. SRL has constructed dozens of mechanical artifacts programmed only to destroy themselves or the other machines; spectacular performances that partly parody the popular "monster car" arena events. Pauline and his associates build robot flamethrowers, mechanical scorpions (insects again), catapults, and ram cars. In performance their creations assault one another, as machine sounds and lighting effects add to "the show." Human operators scramble to pull recalcitrant machines into position or to fire missles or control wayward vehicles. Pauline's first show, "Machine Sex," was held in the parking lot of a Chevron station.

Cyberpunk author Richard Kadrey has noted the black humor of an SRL show, in which machine behavior is controlled by the movements of Pauline's guinea pig, Stu (for Stupid): "SRL works hard to create a complex and wildly destructive device, only to sabotage it by leaving its control in the hands (or feet) of a rodent with the IQ of dirt. Here we see that power is mindless, as well as absurd."[101] There is clearly something satirical in these steamrollers running amok like something from a Roadrunner cartoon or a Jerry Lewis/Frank Tashlin comedy.

Comics editor Lou Stathis reported on a performance in Shea Stadium's parking lot: "It went on like that for about an hour, smashing and chasing, rolling and burning, crawling and flying, smelling and crushing, until just about everything was destroyed." Stathis further noted the disappointment among the thrill-seekers: "This crowd wanted a million-dollar fireworks show, full of dazzling pyrotechnics and multiple-orgasm climaxes, and all they got was a bunch of scruffy junkyard scavengers staging an improvised event." It's also relevant that the show avoided those traditional narrative structures that would have imbued the destruction with morality and meaning.[102]

Media coverage was always a part of the event. Pauline has noted that the media are *prisoners* of the Spectacle: "the media can never deny coverage to a good spectacle. No matter how ridiculous, absurd, insane or illogical something is, if it achieves a certain identity as a spectacle, the media has [sic] to deal with it. They have no choice. They're hamstrung by their own needs, to the extent they're like a puppet in the face of such events."[103] The SRL shows have been well-documented from the beginning on video and film, but video changes the nature of the performance. While a live spectator could never forget the human crew scrambling to set off explosives and put out fires, the video can exclude the human presence for long periods. The video presents a more romantic and more narrative performance, executed by automata that have magically become autonomous. One video features an amazingly beautiful slow-motion shot of an animal carcass, suspended on cables, slowly being pulled in half. The camera zooms in, and the shot is thrown slightly out of focus. Flamethrowers are visible in the background, in vivid colors that create a video burn. The camera pulls back as the carcass rips in two—and the viewer knows that this is war, this is hell, this is the apocalypse, this is madness.[104]

Meat and machinery merge in Pauline's art: a mechanism animates the corpse of a dead rabbit, making it walk backward; pig body parts are attached to a robot that shakes and vibrates. Animal remains are mounted on the front of combative, massive robot vehicles (suggesting a remake of *The Road Warrior* by Pasolini). Robots are thus invested with many attributes of their fleshly counterparts (animality, aggression, and a predilection for sacrificial [auto]mutilation) in a reversal of the "antibody" aspirations in Skal's novel. SRL's display has an aesthetic precedent in the image and sound tracks to David Lynch's darkly techno-organic *Eraserhead* (1978), where electronic, organic, and mechanical forms combined to create an effective cyborg ambience. In Pauline's work the precise technologism of science fiction and the organic transgression of horror integrate as the audience is spattered by diesel fuel and blood.

Mark Pauline's Survival Research Laboratory at work: an assault on technological rationalism. (6th Street Studio)

As in *Alien,* the machine is invested with the "bodily" fluids of a nascent organicism. Pauline and his associates stage an assault on mythologies of technological rationalism and the antisepsis of media culture. The work of SRL produces a dense network that resonates with history. There is something Hellenic about these catapults and other machines of war, and the performances also evidence a nostalgia for the mechanical, for a time when technology was still subject to workshop tinkering.

In the later shows the machines get larger and more gesturally rich (they shake with rage, raise their arms in triumph, and crawl pathetically). The street-level technology is cyberpunk, as is the sense of apocalyptic pleasure, but the machinery is electrical and mechanical, rather than electronic. And where cyberpunk narrative reveals a penchant for surrealism, the clearest precursor for a Survival Research Laboratories performance is dada, in all its antirationalist, technoterrorist tactical glory. After all, the notion of an out-of-control technology that reduces all human attempts at understanding to the level of the absurd and irrelevant, is hardly without precedent in the twentieth century. In fact, the "meaning" of the "meaningless" destruction in SRL performances is entirely clear in its assault on the convergence of technology, consumerism, militarism, and commodification.

A more negative assessment of the SRL phenomenon is supplied by Jim Pomeroy, who likens the events to such spectacles as female mud wrestling and monster truck rallies: "Playing to the pit and dancing on the edge, SRL begs many questions, offers few answers, and moves off the stage leaving smoldering ruins and tinny ears in its smoky wake. SRL is boys' toys from hell, cynically realizing the masculinist fantasies of J. G. Ballard and William Burroughs."[105] There is something to this, (though he makes no allowance for *irony* from performers or audience). Yet SRL is not a reasoned response to technological alienation, it is a *terminal fiction* that stages a nightmare version of future recreation. SRL is entertainment in a cyberpunk novel, today.

Crash

"The true marriage of human form and technology is death," Pauline has said, and it is no accident that the automobile should be the paradigmatic machine of alienation for SRL. To Pauline the car is a

potential, and frequently actual, murder weapon.[106] To celebrate the

Car crashes and insectoid machinery by SRL. (6th Street Studio)

publication of a RE/SEARCH issue devoted to J. G. Ballard, SRL staged a small homage to *Crash* by sending a ramcar—almost a cross section of a car—to plow into piles of junked cars with smashed and bloodied windshields. While *2001* and *Blood Music* offer up the human as a sacrifice to a greater cosmic connectedness, it is *Crash* that narrates most obsessively a sacrificial violence that empties the human experience of any transcendent meaning.[107]

Crash is a brilliantly ironic work, set in a postindustrial landscape of highways and automobiles, high rises and airports, television sets and billboards. It is a landscape in which the erotic is denied, repressed, and paved over by layers of concrete, tarmac, and chrome. Vaughan, the "hero" of *Crash,* fantasizes his death in a headlong collision with Elizabeth Taylor. The narrator, "Ballard," is ever-increasingly drawn toward Vaughan's vision of transcendent sex and violence. Vaughan has reinvested the de-eroticized landscape with the passion of desire: "The same unseen sexuality hovered over the queues of passengers moving through airport terminals. . . . Two months before my accident, during a journey to Paris, I had become so excited by the conjunction of an air hostess's fawn gabardine skirt on the escalator in front of me and the distant fuselages of the aircraft, each inclined like a silver penis towards her natal cleft, that I had involuntarily touched her left buttock" (40–41). The geometrical alignment of escalator, woman's hip, and distant airplane become urgently sexualized, but in the precise language of the engineer. Eroticism becomes a question of mathematics, of alignment. Ballard mocks the functionalist understanding of the human as a single component in a rational system—while both driver and automobile are defined in dispassionate terms as problems in engineering, both are also endowed and imbued with the irrationalities of erotic desire and violence.

By contrast, the setting of Michael Crichton's *The Terminal Man* is a Los Angeles in which Vaughan would feel much at home, but these characters are merely alienated by California car culture: "there was something inhuman about living inside a cocoon of tinted glass and stainless steel, air-conditioned, carpeted, stereophonic tape-decked, power-optioned, isolated. It thwarted some deep human need to congregate, to be together, to see and be seen" (158). "Inhuman" is, of course, a purely pejorative term here—compare this to the more complex ambivalence of *Crash:* "As I watched the packed concrete decks of the motorway from our veranda while Catherine prepared our first evening drinks, I was convinced that the key to this immense metallized landscape lay somewhere within these constant and unchanging traffic patterns" (65). For "Ballard" the freeways are the sign of a new system of meaning, while for Crichton's narrator they only mark the negation of the human (there is, nevertheless, in *The Terminal Man* some recognition that we have all, to some degree, achieved a terminal status; we have become cyborgs).

Ballard's achievement in *Crash,* to read it through Bataille, has been to narrate a profoundly isolating contemporary environment, within which Vaughan seeks a joyful synthesis with precisely those objects that distance the subjects, the very objects that reinforce the discontinuous experience of being. Bataille writes that "the movement that pushes a man in certain cases to give himself (in other words, to destroy himself) not only partially but completely, so that a bloody death ensues, can only be compared, in its irresistible and hideous nature, to the blinding flashes of lightning that transform the most withering storm into transports of joy."[108] In *Crash,* tragedy becomes consummation: "Vaughan dreamed endlessly of the deaths of the famous, inventing imaginary crashes for them. Around the deaths of James Dean and Albert Camus, Jayne Mansfield and John Kennedy he had woven elaborate fantasies" (15). Vaughan's dreamt-of crash into a movie-star's limousine becomes an act of sacrifice, an *automutilation,* that reestablishes his continuity with the world by literally crashing through the separations—both physical and spectacular—to achieve the complete fusion of a technologically eroticized and *violent* death. Ballard simultaneously mocks and evokes the "drive" toward transcendence and continuity. Few works of science fiction, indeed of literature itself, have been so transgressive.[109]

Limbo

Skal's "antibodies," as well as the electrically addicted buttonheads, are anticipated by what is perhaps the only science fiction novel to appropriate Bataille's notion of sacrificial mutilation. Bernard Wolfe's *Limbo,* first published in 1952, is an extraordinary anomaly, deriving imagery from Bataille while anticipating the cybernetic paranoia of Pynchon.[110] It is a dense, philosophical novel set in a postapocalyptic world dominated by the functionalist cybernetic paradigms of Norbert Wiener (whose theory of cybernetics provided, in the 1950s, "simultaneously a theory of communication and a promising technology of control").[111] The narrator, Doctor Martine, reflects that, "People, cowed by the machines that had grown bigger than themselves, could no longer think except in mechanical terms" (51). Wolfe is explicit about the power of a "managerial revolution" in a cybernetically defined society (that in-

293

TERMINAL

FLESH

cludes both American and Soviet cultures)[112] and the need to construct a mass culture "welded together into a tight, quickly mobilized monolithic unit whose nerve centers were the lightning quick mass media" (135).

In the postwar environment that Martine tours, societies perform lobotomies and amputations on their citizens, not only to prevent the possibility of war, but in order to move closer to the immobile perfections of a machine-like status ("the machine is the brain's dream of fulfillment"): "After the agony of the Third, the war in which the dream of perfection became a steamrollering nightmare, this brain has finally discovered how to link itself to its own projected vision—it has lopped off its animalistic tails. It has suddenly made the breathtaking discovery that the perfection of EMSIAC and other robot brains lies in the fact that they are sheer brain with no irrelevancies, no arms and legs, just lines of communication and feedbacks—and it has begun to overhaul itself in the image of the robot" (143). In *Limbo,* sacrificial mutilation is performed in the *service* of an instrumental, managerial reason, and not—as in Bataille's examples—as a sign of the suspension or transcendence of the rational. Wolfe brilliantly demonstrates the power of the technocratic society to co-opt and assimilate the most apparently subversive doctrines and behaviors. Thus the philosophy of "Immob:" "Immob is the cyber-cyto dialectic—the dwindling distance between cybernetics and cytoarchitectonics. The bridging of the gap between the mechanical and the human—the discovery of the Hyphen between machine and man—thus enabling man finally to triumph over the machine because it's *man* who has the Hyphen and not the machine" (142). Here is religious ecstasy and fusion—here is a terminal identity that is purely a surrender to the cybernetic predictability of the machine.

It is tempting to equate the cyberpunks (or their protagonists) and the Immobs, since both are imbricated in a technological sublime that substitutes the invisible cybernetic flow of the computer for the physical mobility of the human (*Schismatrix:* "With the loss of mobility comes extension of the senses"—recalling *Limbo's* automutilated Immobs). Just as the Immobs operate in service to a machine-driven economy, so the cyberpunks ultimately serve the increasing penetration of the machine into all aspects of quotidian existence. Vaughan's transgressive car crashes have been superseded by the kinetic appropriation of cyberspace. There is no irony, in *Neuromancer,* when Case is presented with his brand new, brand name cyberdeck. In *Neuromancer* the drive is all; the crash is nothing. Amputation and lobotomy are the analogies when Case is *unable* to jack in to the computer space.

Techno-Surrealism

Bataille's work, then, illuminates the strategies employed by the most subversive and excessive works on the *margins* of science fiction (Burroughs, Ballard, Wolfe, SRL), at the same time that it reveals the conservative impulses that underlie the genre itself (denying the animality of the human). A more delicate ambivalence is maintained in the field of cyberpunk, however, that lies somewhere outside the terms of Bataille's discourse. We speak no longer of flesh and the discontinuity of beings, but now of *terminal flesh* and the fusion of biology with electronics. Bataille has observed that the transcendence attained through religious eroticism represents "the fusion of being with a world beyond everyday reality," and a fusion with electronic reality, a reality that exists beyond our perceptual experience, is surely another example of the same phenomenon. "Jacking in" is precisely the means of disguising the discontinuity of a purely human existence by entering the *flow* of data in cyberspace—the subject is dissolved in the swirls of cybernetic

A *bricolage* of found objects: SRL's brand of Techno-Surrealism. (6th Street Studio)

information, but is at the same time further empowered through an extension of motility and spatial possession. Here, then, are the paradoxically simultaneous experiences of death and immortality that are fundamental to religious practice.

But it would be a mistake to focus on these romantic aspects of *Neuromancer* while ignoring its pervasive bricolage, its hallucinatory prose, its denial of narrative, its transformation of reality. What the cyberpunks share as a group, and what cyberpunk shares with the horror genre, is a surrealist perspective that reveals in the deformation and destruction, the resurrection and reformation, of the human. Taking their cues from Burroughs and Pynchon, as well as from Bataille and Breton and Dali and Man Ray, the techno-tactics of cyberpunk transform the rational structures of technological discourse to produce instead a highly poeticized, dreamlike liberation. The languages of science and technology are inverted by a metaphorical system of language that effaces the borders between conscious and unconscious, physical and phenomenal realities, subject and object, individual and group, reality and simulacrum, life and death, body and subject, future and present. The Shaper/Mechanist and cyberspace fictions construct collages, placing the subject in urbanesque cyberspaces or within insect mechanisms in alien habitats. The human is emplaced within the machine; the human becomes an adjunct to the machine—the cyborg is a cut-up, a juxtaposition, a *bricolage* of found objects.

If Gibson or Sterling fail to provide the surrealistically scatological pleasures of Bataille or Bunuel, much less Burroughs or Pynchon, then this should be read in terms of their intricate relation to the genre of science fiction. Unlike the more overtly literary mannerisms of the SF produced by the New Wave or Dangerous Visions groups in the 1960s and 1970s, fiction with far more evident connections to the surrealist and beat movements, the cyberpunk writings are not presented as subversive of the genre. These are *science fiction texts* that seek to *exploit,* and not to *exceed,* the language and protocols of the genre to which they belong. If 1980s SF is "more liberatory," as Fred Pfeil would have it, it is precisely because of its real engagement with lived experience and its "frenzied tryings-on of a new, cybernetic sense of identity."[113] The sustained inscription of a spectacular discourse *of the body* in cyberpunk is conspicuous and remarkable.[114]

It is even possible to regard the "shocking" erotic contents and stylistic tricks of the New Wave writers as more derivative and dated. As Debord wrote in 1957, "We now know that the unconscious imagination is poor, that automatic writing is monotonous, and that the whole genre

"Necronom IV" by H. R. Giger. The painting that inspired the look of *Alien*. (Morpheus International)

of ostentatious surrealist 'weirdness' has ceased to be very surprising."[115] Little that occurred after the psychedelic rediscovery of surrealism would necessitate revising that assessment. Still, cyberpunk's *technological* imagination, cut-up structures and cybernetic "weirdness" does succeed in "catalyzing for a certain time the desires of an era." In these more positive terms, cyberpunk "endeavor[s] to define the terrain of a constructive action on the basis of the spirit of revolt and the extreme depreciation of traditional means of communication," which is how Debord characterized the emergence of surrealism (note that cyberpunk also avoids "Futurism's puerile technological optimism").[116] I am far from arguing for the superiority of cyberpunk over the libidinal excesses of the surrealist movement, but I *would* propose that cyberpunk constitutes a discourse within which the concerns and techniques of surrealism again become relevant.

Henri Lefebvre is also convinced that surrealism retains a relevance for contemporary culture that has eluded most critics. "The leading surrealists sought to decode inner space and illuminate the nature of the transition from this subjective space to the material realm of the body and the outside world, and thence to social life."[117] He notes the failure of "surrealism's poetic project," however, arguing that "their poetry succeeded only in producing a lyrical metalanguage of history, an illusory fusing of subject with object in a *transcendental metabolism*."[118] Surrealist praxis overemphasized language, "overloaded meaning—and changed nothing." The productions of techno-surrealist art perhaps represent something more: by de-emphasizing the individual unconscious, and acknowledging the dynamism of our technological unconscious, the transcendental metabolisms of techno-surrealism might describe a trajectory for real change.

TERMINAL

FLESH

5 TERMINAL RESISTANCE/
CYBORG ACCEPTANCE

The nineteenth and twentieth centuries have given us as much terror as we can take. We have paid a high enough price for the nostalgia of the whole and the one, for the reconciliation of the concept and the sensible, of the transparent and the communicable experience. Under the general demand for slackening and for appeasement, we can hear the mutterings of the desire for a return of terror, for the realization of the fantasy to seize reality. The answer is: Let us wage a war on totality; let us be witnesses to the unpresentable; let us activate the differences and save the honor of the name.

—Jean-François Lyotard ¶ Anthropologists of possible selves, we are technicians of realizable futures.—Donna Haraway

TERMINAL RESISTANCE   Is there some deviant logic un-

folding more powerful than that provided by reason?—J. G. Ballard ¶

Vaughan died yesterday in his last car crash. . . .—J. G. Ballard

The Armored Body (and the Armored Arnold)

What I have described in the preceding chapters is a set of fictions—in literature, philosophy, cinema, television, comics, and theme parks—that present a movement away from the traditional experience of the body and toward some sort of ecstatic activity of cybernetic fusion. The discourses of science fiction and philosophy have constructed a metaphorical subject redefined to permit its situation as a biological being within an electronic world. But this rarely occurs without a simultaneous retention of an older notion of the subject based on mastery rather than symbiosis, a subject that ultimately *retains* power through the "displacement" of cybernetic reconstruction. Within the fictions of terminal identity, the subject is brought to the limits of self-definition, but the metaphorical solutions to the problems posed by a postmodern existence often recenter subject power as an untested, unchanging, and eternal phenomenon.

TRON features no far-flung machine-civilizations, but it does offer the near-future equivalent: the computer that tries to take over the world. This is another idea familiar to *Star Trek* enthusiasts (who can forget the wryly human Captain Kirk immobilizing super-rational super-computers with the fancy footwork of logical paradox?). TRON is the champion who plays games against the Master Control Program on behalf of the Users: the disembodiment of cyberspace meets the hyperbolically embodied figure of the athlete. The film therefore denies the denial of the body by investing cyberspace with an overly literal bodily presence. Mark Pomerantz has proposed that science fiction sports films constitute a significant subgenre of science fiction film, a subgenre entirely constituted around bodily anxiety in the face of overwhelming technology. Sports constitutes an "arena" in which biology and "natural ability" remain paramount. In such films as *Mad Max: Beyond Thunderdome* (1985) the bread and circuses barbarism of the future-archaic society masks a deeper utopianism: the "perverse hope that someday conditions will indeed warrant a similar return to the body" as technology collapses into ruins.[1]

Rollerball (1975) is a fascinating piece of schlock set in a world governed by a single mega-corporation. All needs are filled, and the only price is unquestioning obedience. The devaluation of labor implies the obsolescence of the body, and the pristine, "mod" decadence of the mise-en-scène (over)emphasizes the alienation of the subject. A hyperviolent sport is again presented, but Rollerball represents the barbaric underside of this indolent society of the spectacle. One player, Jonathan E, dominates the game until the corporation tries to retire him. The secret of Rollerball is that it is designed to convey the *futility* of individual effort, while Jonathan's heroic prowess has produced precisely the opposite result. The rules of the game are changed to destroy Jonathan, but he will not surrender; he will not "quit the game." Ultimately, "he punishes his body in the final game he was forbidden to play and, dripping with blood, wins the contest, thus reaffirming the importance of the body to an audience anxious about the status of their own."[2] The importance of the body implies the importance of the individual: *you have a body,* the scifi sports film insists. *You exist.*

The star of the SF sports film *The Running Man* (1987) is a former athlete—ex-body builder Arnold Schwarzenegger, whose hyper-commodified body has come to represent the figure of the cyborg in the popular imagination, as Claudia Springer notes. The representation of the cyborg has been more consistent in cinema than in other media, Springer argues, "in part because many mainstream commercial films remain entrenched in a tradition that upholds conventional gender roles and maintains a stable masculine subject position."[3] The cyborg is a killing machine, whether nasty (*Terminator*) or nice (*Robocop, Termi-*

nator 2). Schwarzenegger fuses the natural ability of the athlete with a symbiotic relation to technology. The first *Terminator* cast Arnold as a transtemporal assassin created by yet another computer out to destroy all human life, while in the second he becomes humanity's cyborg protector.

Claudia Springer, Hal Foster, and Mark Dery all turned to Klaus Theweleit's massive research into the psychology of the *Freikorps* to understand the underpinnings of the cinematic cyborg. The ego was, in Freud's view, more than a mental function, it was "first and foremost a bodily ego"; it was "a mental projection of the surface of the body."[4] A disruption of, or threat to, ego development might result in the defensive formation of a mental "armor," in which the subject attains invulnerability by aligning itself with the rationalistic predictability of the machine. Foster cites Bettelheim's case study of Joey, the autistic child who believed he was a machine living in a "world of mire,"[5] noting that the machines with which he surrounded himself "were attempts to abject this world, to reestablish his boundaries."[6] Armor substitutes for the "desiring-machine" of a functional self: "The armor of these men can be seen as constituting their ego."[7]

Under fascism the body almost explicitly becomes part of a machine, delibidinalized through the imposition of boundaries drawn from the outside by the massive deployment of disciplinary and military technologies. The ego is further delibidinalized through pain, severed from the weakness and frailty of the flesh. Meanwhile, subjects augment their armor through acts and attitudes of aggressivity against a range of "outsiders." The men of the *Freikorps* externalize their fear of dissolution by killing what is not "them." An obfuscating ideology unifies body and psyche—the subject as weapon, the subject as machine. The subject becomes an armored figure, hiding both the erotic and the mortal truth of its being. This is what Theweleit refers to as "*the conservative utopia of the mechanized body*" (2:162).

Dery and Springer both emphasize an aspect of Theweleit's study that Foster bypasses: the characteristic masculine aversion to the soft, the liquid, and the gooey—elements associated with the monstrous feminine. The fear of women among the *Friekorps*-men, Theweleit points out, is more than mere castration anxiety: soldier males exhibited the desire to annihilate the female and reduce her to a "bloody mass." The woman is associated with feared libidinal energies that are not beholden to reason, instrumental or otherwise. Ultimately, women exemplify that *flow* that threatens to wash away all that is rational (all that is *the subject*) in a final, cataclysmic flood, and thus "anti-woman" is a code for anti-*life* (1:218). Theweleit even establishes a class relationship wherein the working class becomes a metamorphosing, flowing mass of aggressive, sexualized women.

In the wake of such profound technological and political traumas as followed World War I, Foster argues that surrealism and dada created their own armored bodies. Ernst's fascination with automata, for example, or Bellmer's obsessively deconstructed *poupées,* grappled with deep ambivalences regarding subject and social structure within a newly intensified, and seemingly objectified, technological paradigm. Foster observes "the tension between binding and shattering tendencies, the play between sadistic and masochistic impulses." Surrealism is defined by the struggle "between the erotic and the destructive, the one never pure of the other" (94). He digresses on his "sense that the figure of the armored body pervades the imaginary of American commercial culture" (a photo of Schwarzenegger illustrates his point). Foster ties his argument to recent SF cinema: "Though sometimes parodic, even critical, the armored figures of commercial culture symbolically treat fantasmatic threats to the normative social ego: for instance, visions of cities given over to drugged minorities (e.g., Robocop)" (69n).

In the current era of techno-surrealism similar ambivalences pertain, and as the represented body moves ever more emphatically toward a symbiosis with electronic technology, it becomes ever more emphatically armored. Robocop is only one example of the *defensive* drive toward a techno-humanoid fusion (the science fiction sports film represents another). Springer and Dery both concentrate on *Terminator 2* and the conflict between Arnold's old-fashioned T-100 cyborg model and the new, "liquid metal" T-1000. To understand the intra-Terminator battles, both writers stress the feared flow of the feminine. Dery, writing in *Mondo 2000,* is disturbed by the digital technology of *morphing* used by Dennis Muren to create the T-1000: morphing becomes a paradigm for the surfeit of body-reshaping technologies available today, from aerobics to cosmetic surgery to Michael Jackson's videos and lifestyle ("In his privileged ability to transmogrify himself, Jackson lives in the future").[8] Dery sees morphing as the site of new "micropolitical power struggles between an information-rich technocratic elite and the information poor masses" (his argument is also borne out in the 1992 morphing-comedy, *Death Becomes Her,* in which the technology is explicitly tied to the body of the Beverly Hills female).[9] The T-1000 combines the mutability of the Thing with the techno-organicism of the Alien. Electronic technology becomes a new site of anxiety: it can't even be relied upon to keep its shape. By contrast, Schwarzenegger, as the

The reassuringly armored body of Arnold Schwarzenegger in *Terminator 2*. (Carolco Pictures)

"nice" Terminator, is predictably mechanical and trustworthy—he always looks like Arnold.[10]

The men of the *Freikorps* "fortif[ied] themselves with hard leather body armor to assert their solidity against the threat of fluid women."[11] Hence, Robocop and Terminator: bodies armored against a new age (political and technological). The cyborg adorns itself in leather and introjects the machine, becoming part punk, part cop, part biker, part bike, part tank, part *Freikorps*-superhero. Springer writes that these cyborg figures "perpetuate, and even exaggerate, the anachronistic industrial-age metaphor of externally forceful masculine machinery, expressing nostalgia for a time of masculine superiority" and argues that the bodily-sense of electronic technology is *internal* "with its concealed and fluid systems. . . . It is this feminization of electronic technology and the passivity of the human interaction with computers that the hypermasculine cyborg in films resists."[12] By doing battle with the fluid, and even effeminate, digitized form of the T-1000 ("The 'animal' in the mass . . . can metamorphose into a single creature, many-limbed: millipede, rat, snake, dragon" [II: 4]), the mechanical Terminator expunges the nightmare of masculine and industrial obsolescence (note that each term metaphorizes the other). The climactic battle is fought in a steel foundry.

Springer's argument is convincing and is furthered by Dery in his consideration of *T2* and *Aliens* (1986), both directed by James Cameron. "The Menschmachine's pathological fear of the glutinous feminine goo that will gum its gears is manifest" in both films but "given ironic spin by the fact that the masculinist protagonist of each is in fact a woman."[13] *Aliens* has been viewed by some as a "feminist" discourse of empowerment by critics eager to seize upon the progressive aspects of female action-heroes, but this is an argument that Dery rejects (as would, presumably, Springer). The fluidity of *Alien* has already been explored, and Dery cites Mark Crispin Miller on *Aliens* (note the Theweleit-inflected language): "*Aliens* divides the female in two," Miller argues, the "tough-guy heroine" and the slimy, reproductive alien nemesis. "Ripley manages to snuff the Alien only by turning herself hyper-masculine/robotic: she encases herself in a mammoth robot-exoskeleton, which—powerful and dry—allows her to crush the shrieking mother-figure as if it were a giant, juicy bug."[14] Dery sees a similar process working in *T2,* in which "soft squishy evil pours itself into the mercurial shape of the T-1000, a polymorphous perversity made of 'mimetic polyalloy.' . . . Linda Hamilton, morphed into a *Freikorps* cyborg, triumphs over the feminine as-

The unsettling, and androgynous, liquid metal T-1000 (Robert Patrick). Note the uselessness of the phallic weapon against the fluid interiority of this year's model. (Carolco Pictures)

pect embodied in the T-1000 with the aid of the male principle manifest in the Schwarzeneggerian model."[15]

Springer also considers *Hard Boiled,* a satirical (?) comic book by Frank Miller and Geof Darrow in which a salaryman turns out to be a killing robot. This is probably one of the most self-consciously violent comics ever produced, and the dialogue is nonsensically minimal to leave ample room for Darrow's hyper-detailed depiction of explosions, shootings, crashes, operations, gougings, and random lacerations. Springer writes that *Hard Boiled* or similar works demonstrate "that the patriarchal system, with its brutal violence covered by sugary platitudes, is indeed on the way out, even if, as a last gasp, it has rallied its forces of muscular cyborg soldiers." One might note that Frank Miller has become the poet laureate of last-gasp cyborgism: here and in *Batman: The Dark Knight Returns* and in *Robocop 2,* his characters are always "returning" to their killing ways despite their perceived obsolescence. It is also worth pointing out that comic books have long represented a haven for the "armored body" in American culture: note the orphaned and significantly named Superman with his invulnerability to bullets (and exploding planets) and Iron Man ("he's a cool exec/with a heart of steel," the TV theme song declared).[16] Cinematic cyborg Robocop owes much to Judge Dredd comics, and Tim Burton's *Batman* (1989) changed the costume from a leotard to an encasing body-armor. The armored body has a powerful legacy in America and is often aligned with issues of technology.

The stylization, exaggeration, and repetition of *Hard Boiled* place it in the tradition of French and Japanese comics. A low-budget short Japanese film, *Tetsuo: The Iron Man* (1991), also derives its structure and imagery from the endless, wordless violence of Japanese *manga*. Another armored salaryman figure battles a young "metals fetishist" who is trying to stave off rust by merging with the salaryman. Penises become electric drills, women sprout metallic tentacles, and people are swallowed in miles of metallic cabling until at the end when, "a huge metal monster with two faces stands ready to take the streets of Tokyo, convinced that the whole world can be mutated into metal." The film is mordantly obsessive and moves beyond its *manga*-roots through its dark monomania. Tony Rayns compares the film to *Crash,* with some reason, although Shinya Tsukamoto is both less transgressive and less reflexive than Ballard.[17] Nevertheless, *Tetsuo* is an impressive (and happily unpleasant) work of techno-surrealism. In its aggressive fear of female sexuality, its sense of alienation, and its willfully hyperbolic violence, the film is a discourse both *of* and *about* the armored body in techno-culture. The parodic and disturbing ultraviolence of *Hard Boiled* and *Tetsuo* recognize that in cyborg fictions there exists Joey's desire to "abject this world." The fusion with machines represents something other than a postmodern celebration of dissolving borders and boundaries, because they are often as much attempts to reseat the human (male) in a position of virile power and control.

The Mechanists of *Schismatrix* are explicit regarding the increase of power with the surrender of the unarmored body: "With the loss of mobility comes the extension of the senses." The Immobs of Bernard Wolfe's *Limbo,* busily amputating their limbs to approach a machinelike perfection (a simulacrum, perhaps, of Joey's autism), satirize this armoring in the face of Armageddon while Wolfe and Tsukamoto acknowledge the terrifying impulses hidden at the fantasy's core. By exercising the choice of becoming One with their machines, the Mechs, Immobs, Iron Men, and cyberspace cowboys are empowered. By fusing with the machine, the subject is armored against it. Hence the aversion in cyberpunk to the buttonheads, wireheads, and Charge Addicts, whose tech-

Robocop (Peter Weller): the armored body in the inner city. (Orion Pictures)

nological dependency marks their loss of power and ego. In works by Effinger and Williams, the heroes are men, individuals, trying to hold themselves rigid before an onslaught of dissolving spaces and personality modifiers. In a world of addicts they remain pure, yet still at the controls of the machine, still wielding their armor.

The analyses by Dery and Springer make clear that there are different kinds of machines operating here, and the externalized mechanical physicality of the robotic T-100, once the embodiment of an antihuman killing machine, has become positively *benign* in contrast to the noncorporeal, interiorized digitalism of the electronically generated T-1000.

The techno-organic fusion of these cinematic cyborgs thus represents only an exaggerated defensive formation, another panic subject frantically hiding its obsolescence behind a suit of armor. If this is exaggerated in the mainstream cinematic blockbusters of *Aliens* and *T2,* it is also present in the more ambivalent literary works of SF. I have argued that the cyberspace cowboys of *Neuromancer* mark a regression to an animistic conception of the universe, wherein thoughts are endowed with a new omnipotence, and *Neuromancer* is not without its armored figures. Case's watchdog, companion, and ally is Molly: "She wore tight black gloveleather jeans and a bulky black jacket cut from some matte fabric that seemed to absorb light. . . . She held out her hands, palms up, the white fingers slightly spread, and with a barely audible click, ten double-edged, four-centimeter scalpel blades slid from their housings beneath the burgundy nails. She smiled. The blades slowly withdrew" (24–25). The leather-jacketed and mirror-shaded figures of Case and Molly are exemplary armored bodies, and even in cyberspace, Case (closed object, hard case) is as much machine as human.

However, *Neuromancer* is surely to be regarded as a celebration of flow ("fluid neon origami trick," indeed). Theweleit notes that when getting a fix, the addict experiences a "rush," a "streaming of the stuff through the arteries and the body" (1:269), and Case, in his state of withdrawal, recalls the "bodiless exultation of cyberspace" from which he is now sadly excluded. The dreaded triumph of electronic technology in *T2* becomes the exultant kinesis of the passage into cyberspace. Theweleit regards capitalist space as a terrain of blocked "flow." Citing Deleuze and Guattari, who state that capitalism "institutes or restores" territorialities upon the field of flowing desires, Theweleit argues that under the instrumental rationalism of capitalism, "streams of desire were encoded as streams of money, and circulation replaced free trajectories" (1:271). Until cyberspace, that is: *Neuromancer* reencodes capitalist space as an erotic space, a space defined by the flow of desire and the circumvention of (the poaching upon) instrumental, capitalist space. Eroticism is linked to movement ("The body whose parts no longer set any streams in motion, and in, on, across, and out of which nothing flows anymore, is a body that has died" [1:267])—and we know all about cyberspace as a space of kinesis.

Yet kinesis is more than a jubilant flow—kinesis is also aggression ("Speed is a key category for the soldier body. It needs to heat up, rev up, and race psychically, before charging physically toward the site on which it expects to experience itself in the streaming of pleasure" [2:181]), and kinesis is also the province of the machine. Thus, Thewe-

TERMINAL

RESISTANCE/

CYBORG

ACCEPTANCE

Man Ray, "The Return to Reason." 1923. 18.7 x 13.9 cm. Julien Levy Collection, Special Photography Acquisitions Fund, 1979. 96, The Art Institute of Chicago.

leit's terms provide a means of tracking real ambivalences, of reading reactionary and progressive attitudes toward the fusion of human and technology. "Come with me," the Terminator says, "if you want to live."

Feminist Resistance and a Romance Novel for Cyborgs

The reification of the subject as natural, eternal, and concrete is challenged through the parameters of a feminism that has resisted the euphorias of both science fiction and the cyberpunk posturing of Baudrillard. To trace the limits of a male-produced terminal identity, here are three images to consider. The first two are by Man Ray. In one from 1929, a woman, Lee Miller, stands next to a window, her body facing the camera, her face in profile. The top of a corset is visible; otherwise, she is naked. The shadow of the mesh curtain falls across her breasts and torso, imposing a grid. The pattern responds to the topography of her body, here circling her nipple, there tracing down her arms. In the second image, from 1923, a woman's naked torso is again the site of a projection, as the shadows of the exterior world, curtain and window frame, appear to outline and circumscribe her being. The title is "The Return to Reason."

The last image is a production still from the Michael Crichton science fiction film, *Looker* (1981). In this anonymous photograph, a woman, Susan Dey, stands in an undefined and apparently barren space. She too is naked; her body also faces the camera. A projected network of crosses (crosshairs?) covers her body, literally from head to foot. It is difficult to see this woman as human, and indeed the narrative involves computer-generated mannequins. She appears vulnerable; naked in the figurative, as well as the literal, sense. This scene in the film depicts the woman being measured and digitally recorded; as in Edison Carter's replication as Max Headroom, she is being "translated into data."

The stills are notably similar; the link between terminal identity fiction and surrealism is displayed. Rosalind Krauss has written of "The Return to Reason" that "the nude torso of a woman is shown as if submitting to possession by space."[18] She cites Roger Callois's essay on mimicry (1935), paying particular attention to his analysis of "the organism's relation to space." (Mimicry, as in the adaptive coloration of the chameleon, is precisely the inscription of space upon the body.) Callois wrote: "It is with represented space that the drama becomes clear: for the living being, the organism, is no longer the origin of the coordinates, but is one point among others; it is dispossessed of its privilege and, in the strongest sense of the term, *no longer knows where to put itself.*"[19] For Krauss, the represented space of Man Ray's photographs are a powerful display on this "dispossession of privilege" as the body becomes a scene of projection, a site of cultural inscription. The metaphors are multiple: the body becomes a screen or a target or a map. My central thesis is precisely that contemporary SF is speaking from a condition of "dispossessed privilege" and a subject-condition characterized by a failure to know "where to put itself." The inscription of exterior space upon the body of the model constructed in Man Ray's photographs is replaced by an inscription of cybernetic control.

Krauss continues by linking Callois and surrealism to Freud's essay on "The Uncanny," in which he argued that adults frequently undergo a regression to "more psychologically primitive states" related to the omnipotence of thoughts. She paraphrases: "All those bonds that children and tribal man create between themselves and everything around them in order to gain mastery over an all-too-threatening and inchoate environment are first given visual form by the image of the self projected onto the external world in the form of one's shadow or one's reflection. Then, through mechanisms of projection, these doubles—invented to master and sustain the individual—become the possessors of supernatural power and turn against him."[20] Substitute the omnipotence of the electronic brain for the biological one, and the applicabil-

TERMINAL

RESISTANCE/

CYBORG

ACCEPTANCE

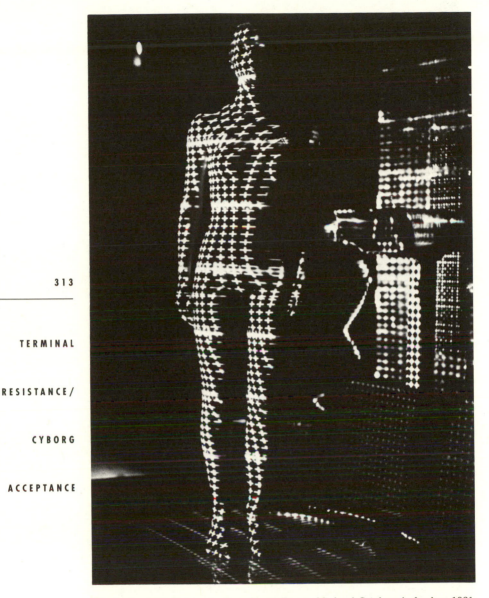

The body as digital projection: Susan Dey in Michael Crichton's *Looker,* 1981.
(Courtesy Photofest)

ity to cyberpunk and science fiction is striking: electronic "images of
the self" are "projected onto the external world." With every appearance of autonomy, these cybernetic "shadows" become the possessors
of a nonnatural, nonphysical "power" within the datascape and even
(sometimes) turn against their creators—Brian O'Blivion was Videodrome's inventor and its first victim.

That a *woman's* body should be so inscribed in these three images is hardly accidental. For the woman in Western culture, the sense of a dispossession of privilege is an unavoidable condition, extending from inequitable wage scales to the victimization before an onslaught of endemic domestic violence and sexual assault. For the female subject, "the body" is no abstract notion (as the battle for reproductive rights amply demonstrates) and is more evidently bound into a system of power relations. In SF that explicitly considers the gendered subject, the threat to the woman's body is conspicuous; the promise of physical transcendence is more dizzying but always less fulfilled. A question emerges while charting the various manifestations of terminal identity, and while this study has begged it for too long, it remains to be asked: *Why aren't there any women in cyberspace?*

There *are* women in science fiction; the genre is uniquely susceptible to feminist appropriation.[21] Science fiction is strongly heterogenous; at its most radical it approaches the heterotopic, as Foucault described it: "*Heterotopias* are disturbing, probably because they secretly undermine language, because they make it impossible to name this *and* that. . . . Heterotopias dissolve our myths." He also notes that heterotopias destroy the syntax "which causes words and things . . . to 'hold together.' "[22] These qualities are also characteristic of the language of science fiction, as deLauretis notes. Sarah Lefanu observes in her excellent critical analysis that SF "makes possible, and encourages (despite its colonization by male writers), the inscription of women as subjects free from the constraints of mundane fiction; and it also offers the possibility of interrogating that very inscription, questioning the basis of gendered subjectivity."[23] As Mary Ann Doane has stated, "[W]hen technology intersects with the body in the realm of representation, the question of sexual difference is inevitably involved."[24]

For some feminist SF writers the body—and so the subject—is understood as a cultural construction (as in the texts of the Krokers), and so the *dissolution* of the body becomes a potentially positive maneuver in a struggle for self-definition. These science fictions locate the human at the intersection of technology, politics, and history, whereas most SF posits an essential humanity that transcends such categories. The textual deconstructions of the textual "body" performed by such writers as Joanna Russ and Pamela Zoline turn the text into a tactic—a *technology*—that similarly challenges the masculinist formations of SF and culture. They "use the metaphors of science fiction to subvert it from within, without making compromises with another literary tradition—

that of the 'bourgeois' novel—that, too, glosses over the construction of sexual difference."[25]

The "real" body disappears into its postmodern master-narrative of dissolution in too many terminal identity philosophies and fictions. *Neuromancer*'s Case longs for "the bodiless exultation of cyberspace:" dissolution is *empowering*. The body is paradoxically extended by its own disappearance—the subject's control is increased by its implosion within the cyberspaces of electronic technology. *Neuromancer* is especially adept at maintaining the subject while producing its dissolution and subsequent cybernetic reconstruction. The entire "consensual hallucination" of cyberspace is specifically designed to allow an interface with electronic data which seems as "natural" as mundane bodily experience (digital interaction *becomes* lived body experience). Other writers, trying to follow Gibson's lead, have proven less deft—and less subtle—in negotiating the survival of an empowered and centralized subject within a reality which has become terminal. There is a reactionary face to cyberpunk, as technology becomes incorporated with a subject position that is strengthened but otherwise unchanged—a highly romantic view.

Only in Gibson's writing is the exuberance of the interface accompanied by the subsequent dependency that leads to withdrawal. Case is no longer fully defined as a subject *except* in cyberspace (was he a complete subject *before* he "jacked in?" Are any of us?). In cyberspace, Case becomes pure kinesis, and the automobile again is the metaphor, as it is for figures as diverse as Mark Pauline, Michael Crichton, and J. G. Ballard. The driver is already a cyborg, wedded to the technology which defines him. Todd Gitlin's remarks on car advertising apply to the hero's plight in *Neuromancer*: "And yet there is pathos on top of irony in all these . . . claims that the Real Man gets to be Real only when he slides into the right driver's seat. For as Dodge's deserted city inadvertently (or brilliantly?) suggests, the car's pilot is all but helpless without his equipment. The blank expression he has displayed up to this point could be read as a self-protective response to the anguish of his uprootedness."[26] As discussed by Springer and Dery, the armored body of the cyborg (the Real Man) represents a fantasied state of masculine invulnerability that carries disturbing echoes of the misogyny of German fascism. Fears of the "interior spaces" of female sexuality conflate with anxieties around "invisible technologies." What holds for cyborg symbiosis is also valid for the visualization and occupation of cyberspace by rogue, male "cowboys." While I would not want to reduce science fiction and cyberpunk to these castration anxieties, I would neither deny their presence nor their power.

Science fiction by women simply does not indulge such fantasies of technological "oneness." The interface with the cyberspatial realities takes a toll on the female subject rarely acknowledged by the cowboy heroes of cyberpunk. In cyberpunk the desire to merge with the machine is romanticized as a necessary but voluntary action, the next evolutionary step. In feminist science fiction, this desire to merge with the machine is viewed as aberrant, and is often presented as an act of surrender rather than empowerment. James Tiptree, Jr.'s, "The Girl Who Was Plugged In" (1973) is a fascinating novella, sometimes cited as an important proto-cyberpunk work. In its relation to technology, however, Tiptree's tale is far from the bodiless exultation of cyberspatial transcendence. Instead, the body is figured as a pronounced limit point.

James Tiptree, Jr., was the pseudonym of Alice Sheldon, an employee of the intelligence branch of the United States government and the child of prominent anthropologists. In her middle-age, she returned to school to receive a degree in psychology and shortly thereafter began to produce her dense, pseudonymous science fiction. That "Tiptree" was female was known to none in the field, although these remarkable tales of aliens and sexuality earned "him" a following among feminist writers and scholars in the early and middle 1970s. After she was "outed," she continued to write significant (if less remarkable) fiction until her death in 1982.[27]

Tiptree's prose is paradigmatic of Delany's propositions regarding the language of science fiction, and her writing is often telegraphically compact. "The Girl Who Was Plugged In" opens in the following manner:

> Listen zombie. Believe me. What I could tell you—you with your silly hands leaking sweat on your growth-stocks portfolio. One-ten lousy hacks of AT&T on twenty-point margin and you think you're Evel Knievel. AT&T?—You doubleknit dummy, how I'd love to show you something. Look, dead daddy, I'd say. See for instance that rotten girl? In the crowd over there, that one gaping at her gods. One rotten girl in the city of the future. (That's what I said.) Watch. She's jammed among bodies, craning and peering with her soul yearning out of her eyeballs. Love! Oo-ooh, love them! Her gods are coming out of a store called Body East.[28]

In this story involving a deformed woman who is chosen to cybernetically operate a beautiful "remote body," Tiptree's first sentences create a complex address. Who in the world (and in what world) is speaking here? Perhaps it isn't possible to assume that the narrator is female, but it is likely that the target of this seemingly oral address is male—a "doubleknit dummy" from the world of high-finance. The narrator quickly punctures the listener's patriarchal authority through disparaging comparisons to commercial daredevil Evel Knievel and twists the knife with a castrating title ("dead daddy").

Only then does this bilious discourse announce its status as science fiction. By referring to the city of the future as something surprising, something *not* to be taken for granted by the reader ("That's what I said"), Tiptree ruptures the unity between reader and diegesis while she positions the "ideal reader" (or ideal listener) close to the actual reader (both are located in "our" present). Nearly all science fiction texts seem to disguise the gap between the world of the reader and the world of the fiction by inserting unfamiliar details (drinks, foods) in rhetorically nonchalant ways.[29] This nonchalance is a blind for that play of unfamiliar signifiers which defines the genre. Tiptree *announces* the estranging function of science fiction by dragging her pathetic and infantilized reader forcibly into the future.

The language of the narrator is thus retrospectively understood as a futuristic, and youthful, slang (composed of dead daddies, rotten girls, and zombies). In the remainder of the passage, while the notion of love, youthful or otherwise, is mocked, the body emerges as a dominant figure. The body is introduced in a state of putrescence: the undead bodies of "zombies" and the decaying forms of "dead daddies" and "rotten girls" all present the body as unclean. The rotten girl is "jammed among bodies," her yearning pouring out of her "eyeballs." The zombie listener's hands are sweaty. And these teen idol gods are emerging from what must be an exclusive shop called Body East.

The publication date of 1973 places this text squarely within the era of glitter rock, in which chameleonlike androgynes such as David Bowie and Bryan Ferry overturned gender conventions in an ambivalent celebration of the body's own malleability. "Bowie's metamessage was escape—from class, from sex, from personality, from obvious commitment—into a fantasy past . . . or a science-fiction future," Dick Hebdige wrote in his analysis of youth-culture styles. "Bowie was responsible for opening up questions of sexual identity which had previously been repressed, ignored or merely hinted at in rock and youth culture." He also notes that "Every Bowie concert performed in drab provincial cinemas and Victorian town halls attracted a host of startling Bowie lookalikes." Angela Carter (herself a writer of revisionist fantasy, both dark and light, as well as science fiction) wrote of glitter rock's "ambivalent triumph of the oppressed."[30]

In Tiptree's version it is difficult to see the triumph of which Hebdige and Carter write. The malleability of identity is seen as a further sign of oppression and not an ambivalent release from that status. The body is now thoroughly commodified and thoroughly spectacular. Pity, then, poor P. Burke, "a tall monument to pituitary dystrophy. . . . The crowd is pushing her along now, treating you to glimpses of her jumbled torso, her mismatched legs" (3). Burke is adopted by a cartel that use her brain to animate a beautiful body, named Delphi, "who" appears in a futuristic serial. Through Delphi, Burke is able to participate in the jet-set world she has desired from afar. In a way, Delphi functions as a "virtual body" for Burke, one which negotiates the virtual reality of spectacular culture.

The language of the telematic body is consistently linked to the position of the reader in contemporary culture: "But Delphi is in no sense a robot. Call her a waldo if you must. The fact is she's just a girl, a real live girl with her brain in an unusual place. A simple real-time on-line system with plenty of bit-rate—even as you and you." In fact, Delphi is a literal "embodiment" of the vicarious pleasures available in the society of the spectacle. As Debord wrote, in language with uncanny applicability (once the gender has been switched): "The externality of the spectacle in relation to the active [woman] appears in the fact that *[her] own gestures are no longer [hers] but those of another who represents them to [her].* This is why the spectator feels at home nowhere, because the spectacle is everywhere" (Thesis 30, emphasis mine). Burke's gestures are no longer hers, and her life in an underground isolation ward is irrelevant. Only the actions of Delphi—who represents Burke's own desires and reflects them back to her—only those distant actions are "real." Delphi literalizes the alienated spectator—the split subject—as well as the surrogate reality of the spectacle. The function of the spectacle, after all, is "to make one *see* the world by means of various specialized mediations (it can no longer be grasped directly)" (Thesis 18). Tiptree's extrapolation replaces *seeing* with a more phenomenally advanced condition of total *being*.

Debord's text becomes still more relevant when Tiptree introduces the theme of advertising in "the future." Ads have been legally banned, and Delphi represents an attempt to subvert that prohibition by becoming a "living" example of what is now called "lifestyle advertising": when Delphi/Burke publically uses a product, millions of P. Burkes will follow suit. Thus the purest form of spectacle, the advertisement, moves beyond its boundaries to become more generalized; more diffused through a culture that is becoming more completely spectacular. Tiptree's text narrates exactly this diffusion through an oracle named Delphi.

Thus, in "The Girl Who Was Plugged In," a human body is "jacked in" to a computer system which permits the user an extended mobility, a heightened phenomenal awareness, and an entry into a previously closed realm of experience. The comparisons to *Neuromancer* are thus farfetched neither on the level of plot nor rhetoric (Gibson's "razor-girls" vs. Tiptree's "rotten girls," for example). The differences, though, are telling.

There is a careful ambiguity in Tiptree's provocative title as to whether "the girl" has plugged *herself* in or whether she has been plugged in by others. This points to the limited agency which Burke has, compared to Case. If Case is subject to the plots and counterplots of Wintermute, the artificial intelligence, or the mysterious Armitage, then the *film noir* aesthetic of *Neuromancer* also guarantees the character his own rugged individuality and ultimate revenge. Case is not comparable to the passive and malleable flesh that is P. Burke—a pathetic and even stupid character. In addition, Burke's state is not "bodiless exultation." The reader is always aware of Burke's deformed flesh hovering just out of view: "And again Delphi proves apt. Of course it's really P. Burke down under Carbondale who's doing it, but who remembers that carcass? Certainly not P. Burke, she hasn't spoken through her own mouth for months. Delphi doesn't even recall dreaming of her when she wakes up" (30). This very disavowal renews our awareness of Burke, preventing the reader from surrendering to the cathartic fantasy of her spectacular incarnation as Delphi. (Once again, as in Spinrad's *The Void Captain's Tale,* the reader is directed to reflect on the very mechanisms of fantasy which operate transparently in most genre fiction.) Here the feminist appropriation of the tropological systems of the romance and SF deconstructs the function of the fantasy for the reader.[31]

In the climactic scene, Delphi's true love, Paul, attempts to rescue her from her controllers, hardly suspecting the existence of Burke in the secret laboratories: " 'Paul darling!' croaks the voice of love and the arms of love reach for him. And he responds. Wouldn't you, if a gaunt she-golem flab-naked and spouting wires and blood came at you clawing with metal studded paws—'Get away!' He knocks wires. It doesn't matter which wires, P. Burke has so to speak her nervous system hanging out." Tiptree's discourse here participates in the tropes of the romance, the oral tale, science fiction and horror, as well as the metaphorically "extended nervous system" described by Marshall Mc-Luhan. What emerges is not a misogynist text, but a complex language which links its own spectacular rhetorical tactics to the strategic colonization of the woman's image, the woman's subjectivity, and, finally, the woman's very being.[32]

Other feminist texts have been concerned with the control of women by and through the spread of technologies, such as spectacular or reproductive technologies. Zoline's "The Heat Death of the Universe" and Tiptree's "The Girl Who Was Plugged In" are overtly condemning of the technologies of consumerism, and Octavia Butler's Xenogenesis series has been uniquely, brilliantly, structured around issues of reproduction and miscegnation. It is extraordinary to consider how many works of science fiction are actually "about" issues of reproduction: in this study alone—*2001, Blood Music, 20 Minutes into the Future, Robocop, Terminator* (1 and 2), *Neuromancer, Schismatrix, The Incal, Alien, Aliens, Alien³*—they are too numerous to mention.[33] As Sobchack has argued, sexuality and reproduction are displaced onto technologies of exploration and sagas of evolution. If science fiction is frequently (over)determined in its desire to retain the organic as a fundament of the human, it equally avoids the realities of reproduction and the presence of the woman. Thus technological progress in science fiction often represents only a further inscription of (a sometimes literal) phallic power. In this sense, Tiptree's title refers to the state of being *plugged in* to male definitions of the feminine image and being; *plugged in* to the power structures of male technology. When the cybernetic cyborg is female, transcendence does not await her in the form of bodiless—or embodied—exultations nor in the satisfying multiplicity of subjectivities experienced by Edison Carter/Max Headroom nor in the guidance of the artificial intelligences that await *Neuromancer*'s Case in the interstices of the telematic web. In her interface with the electronic landscape, the woman is reconstituted as a figure of subjugation, and her body exists only as a sign of her own repression and incompleteness.[34]

James Tiptree, Jr., produces ambivalent, densely structured texts that participate in the technologized and estranging language structures of science fiction, undermining the authority of these structures while retaining the imbrication with "science" and "technology" as experiential and ideological categories. Terminal identity is only attained through a *destruction* of the self, which is very different from the liberatory potentials of a *dissolution* or *transcendence*.

CYBORG ACCEPTANCE   A cyborg body is not innocent;

it was not born in a garden; it does not seek unitary identity and so generate

antagonistic dualities without end (or until the world ends); it takes irony for

granted.—Donna Haraway

The End of Eden

Donna Haraway has extensively rethought the emergence of the cyborg in the mid-twentieth century, and the very term has become nearly synonymous with her formulations: "Linguistically and materially a hybrid of cybernetic device and organism, a cyborg is a science fiction chimera from the 1950s and after; but a cyborg is also a powerful social and scientific reality in the same historical period" (*Primate Visions* [*PV*], 138). The cyborg as a category (outside of science fiction, and *not* by name) materialized in the pervasive wartime (and postwar) intersection between cybernetics and information system studies on the one hand and the life sciences of biology, sociology, and primatology on the other (*PV* 102–4). In 1947 Norbert Weiner published his *Cybernetics: Or Control and Communication in the Animal and the Machine*. The human sciences produce a "functional analogy" between the human and the computer—an *analogy,* not an identity (but within the functionalist paradigm that dominated the human sciences at that time, privileging the functionality of parts within an overall and unifying system, the distinction has little meaning).

Haraway further points out that cybernetics was not a disinterested analysis of communication systems: "Since communication was here measured in terms of altered probabilities of behavior of the receiving organism, cybernetics provided simultaneously a theory of communication and a promising technology of control through statistical procedures" (*PV* 106). What occurs, in Haraway's terms, is "the reconstitution of natural-technical objects in biology as command-control-communication systems ordered by a teleology of reproduction" (*PV* 105). More specifically, animals or humans become "biotic components in technological communication systems" (*PV* 108). The human is analogized as a machine, susceptible to rationalist assimilation, measurement, and control (*Crash* resists precisely this functionalism).

Here are the beginnings of the human/machine overlap within cultural discourse (the notion of the human as an information-processing system is obviously reductive, but Haraway is at pains to be fair to the scientists involved, most of whom recognized the analogy as a functional, but limited, model). These are the origins of the overlap as an epistemological and analytic category. With the emergent proliferation of electronic simulations technologies that began in the early postwar era, the category becomes more than merely academic, or even political, as an ontological shift in the definition of the human takes shape. The overlap of technology and biology ceases to be a categorical question and becomes instead a fundamental, existent, cyborg fact. Science fiction repeatedly illustrates and/or explores the definition of the human within this cybernetic-functionalist matrix in both directions: either SF stages the implications of these technologies of control (Vonnegut's *Player Piano*), emphasizing the functionalist shift in the understanding of "the human" as an epistemological category, or SF confronts the ontological redefinition which renders "the human" problematic on purely biological grounds (*Blade Runner*). In both cases the human is presented as one part of a broader technological matrix; a science fiction in a much broader sense:

TERMINAL

> Like any important technology, a cyborg is simultaneously a myth and a tool, a representation and an instrument, a frozen moment and a motor of social and imaginative reality. A cyborg exists when two kinds of boundaries are simultaneously problematic: 1) that between animals (or other organisms) and humans, and 2) that between self-controlled, self-governing machines (automatons) and organisms, especially humans (models of autonomy). The cyborg is the figure born of the interface of automaton and autonomy. (*PV* 139)

RESISTANCE/

CYBORG

ACCEPTANCE

In her well-known "manifesto," Haraway has argued for a positive feminist rereading of the cyborg mythos in a world that has blurred distinctions between organism and machine in a "border war" with high stakes: "Late-twentieth-century machines have made thoroughly ambiguous the difference between natural and artificial, mind and body, self-developing and externally-designed, and many other distinctions that used to apply to organisms and machines. Our machines are disturbingly lively, and we ourselves frighteningly inert" (Cyborg Manifesto [CM] 152). Thus, "by the late twentieth century, our time, a mythic time, we are all chimeras, theorized and fabricated hybrids of machine and organism; in short, we are cyborgs. The cyborg is our ontology; it gives us our politics" (CM 150).

The polemical advantage of the cyborg, for Haraway, is that it resists being encoded as natural. "The cyborg skips the step of original unity, of identification with nature in the Western sense" (CM 151). "We cannot go back ideologically or materially" she writes (CM 162), recalling a speech in *Schismatrix:* "There's no going back. That's a game for those who still have flesh." For both writers the cyborg inhabits a posthuman solar system, in the ideological sense of the "human" as a particular mythos of "natural" individualism. It is as Foucault indicated: "man is only a recent invention, a figure not yet two centuries old, a new wrinkle in our knowledge; he will disappear again as soon as that knowledge has discovered a new form."[35]

One finds in Haraway's writing a rejection of the instrumental forces of the technocracy in favor of a pleasurable and playful excess. The interplay of continuities and discontinuities is striking in her discussion: "So my cyborg myth is about transgressed boundaries, potent fusions and dangerous possibilities which progressive people might explore as one part of needed political work" (CM 154). The dualisms which structure too much socialist and feminist thought need to be supplanted: "A cyborg body is not innocent; it was not born in a garden; it does not seek unitary identity and so generate antagonistic dualities without end (or until the world ends); it takes irony for granted." Haraway's new cyborg mythology assails the dispassionate rationality of power structures and overturns the artificial discontinuities of a gender-based ideology. "Haraway's originality," Istvan Csicsery-Ronay, Jr. has argued, "in terms equally valid for critical theory and SF, is her notion of imagining utopia by moving through the 'heart' of dystopia. Recovering the cyborg from [its] role as ideological legitimator (for conservative humanists and naive technophiles both), Haraway attempts to clear a new path for utopian rationality through the sprawl of instrumental rationalization."[36] "Cyborg politics" opens the prospect of technological symbiosis as a progressive alternative, rather than a simple masculine fantasy of "natural" mastery and domination. In fact, that symbiosis has already been attained: "The boundary between science fiction and social reality is an optical illusion," she declares (CM 149). While this recalls Baudrillard's proclamation that we no longer need to read science fiction because we are *in* it, Haraway's utopian impulse is far from Baudrillard's cyborg nightmare.

Feminist science fiction recognizes the interface of human with technology as already pervasive, but also as already producing an ambivalent and profound dilemma. Clearly it is the patriarchal ideology that is simplistic here—even within Gibson's finely wrought labyrinth there still remains some notion of an essential humanity untainted by the electronic conditions of being. In the writing of more politically sophisticated writers, on the other hand, the body is always-already in crisis. If cyberpunk is defined by the illusory relation between the disembodied freedoms of electronic reality and the physical, bounded limitations of the "meat," then feminist science fiction has proved more capable of recognizing the significance of the body as a site of ongoing struggle.

The revisionist writings and readings in feminist SF enable the critic to locate some of the more reactionary aspects of science fiction and cyberpunk, but it would be a mistake to then ignore the complexity and ambiguity of many of those texts. *Schismatrix,* for example, posits a complex network of structures within which the human takes up a provisional position and from a perspective which surely derives from feminist discourse. The new formations of the human which are encountered in the "posthuman solar system" of *Schismatrix* or the "new flesh" of *Videodrome* represent a fundamental ambivalence toward a technologically defined reality and a rejection of any "essential" definition of humanity. There is an absence of moral outrage in cyberpunk, Charles Platt points out, "as if dehumanization is so inevitable, we might as well learn to like it."[37] *Like* may be too strong a term here, but Platt is correct regarding this shift. The cyborg of Tom Maddox's "Snake Eyes" (1986) is told, "You want to go back, but there's no place to go, no Eden. This is it, all there is."[38] So much science fiction is Edenic—either the unspoiled, pretechnological past or the Utopian promise of a pristine future serves as the Paradise to be either lost or regained. By rejecting Edenism, cyberpunk moves toward a more ambivalent position. The nostalgia for the fixed values of the perfect world must be replaced. Cyberpunk moves us closer to the cyborg culture celebrated (in feminist-Utopian, but *not* Edenic, terms) by Haraway: The cyborg "was not born in a garden. . . . The cyborg would not recognize the Garden of Eden" (CM 151).

Donna Haraway's "ironic political myth" of the cyborg acknowledges technology as holding a possibility for liberation within a new epoch, a new "posthuman" and "postgendered" era. She overtly acknowledges that her myth owes much to science fictions by Russ, Delany, John Varley, Tiptree, Octavia Butler, Monique Wittig, and Vonda McIntyre. "These are our storytellers exploring what it means to be embodied in high-tech worlds," she writes (CM 173). Feminist science fiction (and

TERMINAL

RESISTANCE/

CYBORG

ACCEPTANCE

theories of science fiction) does not simply account for the absence of women from cyberspace, nor does it merely recapitulate the dominance of patriarchal systems of power. Such scriptors of terminal identity fictions as Haraway and Russ deconstruct the ambivalent definition of the subject within a postmodern, electronic culture, and with astonishing clarity, but all the works considered here have contributed to the deployment of a provocative set of new posthuman contours that necessarily contain the germ of new political and philosophical orientations to accompany their new spatial and bodily configurations. As Haraway notes, these are fiction writers who have transcended their genre to become "theorists for cyborgs."

The Body without Organs

In contradistinction to the *armored body,* we find the Body without Organs, a concept elaborated by Gilles Deleuze and Félix Guattari, who have inherited Bataille's anthropological/psychoanalytic discourse of excess and transgression and rewritten it within the terms of a technological—even electronic—culture. The Body without Organs (the BwO), a fantasy they encounter in Artaud and other discourses of madness, is an abstraction of subject annihilation—*being degree zero:* "Where psychoanalysis says, 'Stop, find your self again,' we should say instead, 'Let's go further still, we haven't found our BwO yet, we haven't sufficiently dismantled our self.' "[39] The BwO is opposed to the "depth" of the subject: "We come to the gradual realization that the BwO is not at all the opposite of the organs. The organs are not its enemies. The enemy is the organism. The BwO is opposed not to the organs but to that organization called the organism . . . the organic organization of the organs. The *judgement of God,* the system of the judgement of God, the theological system, is precisely the operation of He who makes an organism" (58). The Body without Organs stands against the *telos* of theology and the order of instrumental reason. It is also *anti-armor.*

The Body without Organs is a heterogeneous system defined by the *malleability* of the organs and not just their absence. They cite Burroughs: "The physical changes were slow at first, then jumped forward in black klunks, falling through his slack tissue, washing away the human lines. . . . In his place of total darkness mouth and eyes are one organ that leaps forward to snap with transparent teeth, . . . but no organ is constant as regards either function or position; . . . sex organs sprout anywhere; . . . rectums open, defecate and close; . . . the entire organism changes color and consistency in split-second adjustments."[40] In the fantasy of the BwO, the body resists the finality of the organism, of the subject. But this ideal status isn't so easily attained: "You never reach the Body without Organs, you can't reach it, you are forever attaining it, it is a limit." (150)

This is especially fascinating in relation to *new flesh, antibodies, cyberspace cowboys,* and electronic existences, the fantasied perfection of the *machine*. The body becomes a desiring machine: "The question posed by desire is not 'What does it mean?' but rather 'How does it work?'" (109). The BwO "works" against the totality of the organism, Deleuze and Guattari observe: "This drawing together, this reweaving is what Joyce called *re-embodying,*" but the re-embodying of the Body without Organs does not totalize (43). *Crash* is a compendium of atrocities that never subsumes them within a totalizing system of meaning. Vaughan seeks to *crash through,* to attain that state of being without organs. The sounds of Stelarc's bodily functions are amplified to become electronic music as he reforms his organs to suit a changing world. Max Renn, in *Videodrome,* has a hand that sometimes becomes a gun and a slit that sometimes appears in his stomach ("sex organs sprout anywhere"). Renn might be approaching the Body without Organs when he fires at his temple, but that's the point at which the film has to end. This *re-embodying* is inconceivable—even the imagination can only approach it.

The BwO is not alone: by dismantling the self, the body fuses with the world: "If the BwO is already a limit, what must we say of the totality of all BwO's? It is a problem not of the One and the Multiple but of a fusional multiplicity that effectively goes beyond any opposition between the one and the multiple" (154). The disembodied fusion with the fields and arrays of electronic space, the dissolution of the body into the self-aware noocytes of intelligent bloodcells, the graphic loss of bodily organs by a half-fly/half-man, and the cybernetic existence behind the screen are all manifestations of this transcendence. Deleuze and Guattari here present a disembodied subject and a trajectory through a space defined and anchored by the machine: "the points of disjunction on the body without organs form circles that converge on the desiring-machines; then the subject—produced as a residuum alongside the machine, as an appendix, or as a spare part adjacent to the machine—passes through all the degrees of the circle, and passes from one circle to another. This subject itself is not at the center, which is occupied by the machine, but on the periphery, with no fixed identity, forever decentered, *defined* by the states through which it passes" (20). Deleuze and Guattari are cyberpunks, too, constructing fictions of terminal identity in the nearly familiar language of a techno-surrealism—note that the body is described biologically (*an appendix*) and mechanically (*a spare*

TERMINAL

RESISTANCE/

CYBORG

ACCEPTANCE

Andy Warhol, android, from Neil Gaiman and Mark Buckingham's *Miracleman* #19. (Eclipse Enterprises, Inc., story copyright 1990 Neil Gaiman, art copyright 1990 Mark Buckingham)

part). The subject is always on the periphery: on the verge of the BwO, but always in a state of continual passage.

The Body without Organs is the state in which we aspire to dissolve the body and regain the world. So the contemporary drama of the subject, *terminal flesh,* is played out upon the *surface* of the body—"depth" is an illusion that belongs to a passing moment of a particular subjectivity. The surface of the body becomes the arena for dissolving the governing instrumental reason of the organism. The flat, affectless oeuvre of Andy Warhol stands as a paradigmatic aesthetic experience in the posthuman solar system (and yet one also thinks of the shocking photography by Avedon of Warhol displaying his wounds; the wounds that proved that he *was* of the flesh after all). And so the last word should be given to, not Andy Warhol exactly, but "Andy Warhol"—an android copy of the original (one of many, of course) as presented in a Neil Gaiman script for the comic book *Miracleman.*[41] "Andy" (the ultimate armored body) has attained the Body without Organs: "Do you like this existence, Andy?" he is asked:

> "Oh, sure. It's wonderful. I *like* being a machine.
> It's what I always *wanted* to be. You see, I used to carry a camera with me everywhere I went.
> Now my eyes are cameras, recording all they see. I don't *need* tape recorders any more—I *am* a tape recorder. This is *heaven.*
> And the *comics.* That's what I read, when I was a child. Superman and Popeye and Nancy and Uncle Scrooge.
> And *this* is a comic book *world.*"

CONCLUSION

Feminist critiques and productions of science fiction confront the anxieties and contradictions that remain latent in so many of the genre's fantasies of technological being, but cyberpunk remains the most sustained manifestation of *terminal identity* in contemporary culture. At the same time that it produces an anxious subject armored against the terrors of a reality turned terminal, its techno-surrealist fusions eroticize the technological. In cyberpunk the cyborg is at once a delibidinalized body and a sexualized machine. If Gibson is indisputably the finest of the cyberpunk writers, it is because he is the most poetic and the most physical—the most erotic. Despite its ideological limits, *Neuromancer* remains a consequential bricolage that moves us further from

Edenic fantasies of essentialism. As in Ballard's *Crash,* random juxtapositions release the erotic tensions that the armored body seeks to resist. In the climactic cyberspatial transcendence at the end of *Neuromancer,* Case's mouth fills with "the aching taste of blue" (257)—perhaps the taste of the machine, the taste of technology.

Terminal identity speaks with voices of repressed desire and repressed anxiety about terminal culture. In postmodern science fiction, a pervasive parallel population comprised of genetically engineered wetware wonders, electrically addicted buttonheads, fragmented posthuman enclaves, and terminal cyborgs has arisen to embody our new, and inescapable, state of being. Terminal identity negotiates a complex trajectory between the forces of instrumental reason and the abandon of a sacrificial excess. The texts promise and even produce a transcendence which is also always a surrender.

329

TERMINAL

RESISTANCE/

CYBORG

ACCEPTANCE

NOTES

Introduction

1 Jean Baudrillard, "The Ecstasy of Communication," in *The Anti-Aesthetic,* ed. Hal Foster (Port Townsend, Wash.: Bay Press, 1983), 128.

2 Walter A. McDougall, *The Heavens and the Earth: A Political History of the Space Age* (New York: Basic Books, 1985), 7.

3 McDougall, 9.

4 McDougall, 382. He also observes that "where Khrushchev and the Soviets expected the new age to fulfill their dream of a future utopia, Webb and the American technocrats expected it to restore a past apotheosis" (388).

5 Donna Haraway, *Primate Visions: Gender, Race, and Nature in the World of Modern Science* (New York: Routledge, 1989), 102–4.

6 Satellites, for example, were not only a communications technology, they were also tools of reconnaissance, and anxiety about satellite surveillance pervades such works as Philip K. Dick's early SF novel *Eye in the Sky.* Lynn Spigel has written about the concurrent fear of television as a panoptic technology of surveillance in "Installing the Television Set: Popular Discourses on Television and Domestic Space, 1948–1955." *Camera Obscura* 16 (1988).

7 McDougall, 12. My emphasis.

8 See 118–22, and 191. This is not a period of *postindustrialism,* as some, including Daniel Bell, would have it, but a period of *full industrialization.* In each case, Mandel argues, the new "leap" soaks up the excess capital accumulated during the previous era's phase of declining surplus-profits, greatly reduces the cost per unit, and boosts profits significantly (albeit temporarily). Jameson is careful to note, incidentally, that Mandel's model

is based on capital's need to absorb accumulated resources which then drives the adoption of new power technologies. This, then, is a model rooted in an *economic*, rather than a *technological*, determinism. I would add that technology frequently serves as a visible icon of these invisible, economically derived power relations.

9   Leo Marx, *The Machine in the Garden: Technology and the Pastoral Ideal in America* (New York: Oxford University Press, 1968); Richard Guy Wilson, Dianne H. Pilgrim, and Dickran Tashjian, *The Machine Age in America: 1918–1941* (New York: Brooklyn Museum in association with Harry N. Abrams, 1986), 24.

10 Wilson et al., 339.

11 Paul Strand, "The New God," *Classic Essays on Photography,* ed. Alan Trachtenberg (New Haven, Conn.: Leete's Island Books, 1980), 151.

12 Don Ihde, *Technology and the Lifeworld: From Garden to Earth,* the Indiana Series in the Philosophy of Technology, ed. Don Ihde (Bloomington and Indianapolis: Indiana University Press, 1990), 75.

13 Larry McCaffery, "Introduction: The Desert of the Real," *Storming the Reality Studio: A Casebook of Cyberpunk and Postmodern Fiction,* ed. Larry McCaffery (Durham, N.C.: Duke University Press, 1992), 8.

14 J. G. Ballard, "The Dead Astronaut," *Memories of the Space Age* (Sauk City, Wis.: Arkham House, 1988), 67.

15 Melvin M. Webber, "The Urban Place and the Nonplace Urban Realm," in *Explorations into Urban Structure,* eds. Melvin M. Webber, John W. Dyckman, Donald L. Foley, Albert Z. Guttenberg, William L. C. Wheaton, and Catherine Bauer Wurster (Philadelphia: University of Pennsylvania Press, 1964).

16 Fredric Jameson, "Postmodernism, or the Cultural Logic of Late Capitalism," *New Left Review* 146 (1984): 58.

17 Bruce Sterling, "Preface," in *Mirrorshades: The Cyberpunk Anthology,* ed. Bruce Sterling (New York: Arbor House, 1986), ix; Marshall McLuhan, "Notes on Burroughs," in *William S. Burroughs at the Front: Critical Reception, 1959–1989,* ed. Jennie Skerl and Robin Lydenberg (Carbondale, Ill.: Southern Illinois University Press, 1991), 73; J. G. Ballard, "Introduction to *Crash,"* *Re/Search* 8/9 (1984), 97; Larry McCaffery, "Introduction," in *Across the Wounded Galaxies: Interviews with Contemporary American Science Fiction Writers,* ed. Larry McCaffery (Urbana and Chicago: University of Illinois Press, 1990), 1; Kenny Scharf, artwork published in *Interview* 19, no. 1 (January 1988), 114.

18 Ivan Chtcheglov, "Formulary for a New Urbanism," in *Situationist International Anthology,* ed. and trans. Ken Knabb (Berkeley, Calif.: Bureau of Public Secrets, 1981), 2.

19 Fredric Jameson, *Postmodernism, or, the Cultural Logic of Late Capitalism,* Post-Contemporary Interventions, eds. Stanley Fish and Fredric Jameson (Durham, N.C.: Duke University Press, 1991), 419n.

20 J. G. Ballard, "Introduction to *Crash,"* *Re/Search* 8/9 (1984), 96.

21 See J. G. Ballard, *Empire of the Sun* (New York: Simon and Schuster, 1984), and *The Kindness of Women* (New York: Farrar, Straus, Giroux, 1991).

22 William S. Burroughs, "My Purpose Is to Write for the Space Age," in *William S. Burroughs at the Front: Critical Reception, 1959–1989,* ed. Jennie Skerl

and Robin Lydenberg (Carbondale, Ill.: Southern Illinois University Press, 1991).

23 Note that the *discontinuities* being referred to here are very different from those that are so favored by poststructuralist theories of history and discourse. The replacement of the human into the continuum of nature is to be understood as the radical maneuver here.

24 Bruce Mazlish, "The Fourth Discontinuity," in *Technology and Culture*, ed. Kranzberg, Melvin, and Davenport (New York: New American Library, 1972), 217–18. Freud's remarks are from the eighteenth lecture of the *General Introduction to Psychoanalysis*. Bruner's analysis is from his "Freud and the Image of Man," *Partisan Review* 23, no. 3 (Summer 1956).

25 McDougall, 449.

26 McCaffery, *Across the Wounded Galaxies*, 7 & 5.

27 McCaffery, *Across the Wounded Galaxies*, 232.

28 William S. Burroughs, *Nova Express* (New York: Grove Press, 1964), 19.

29 Frank Miller, Howard Chaykin, and Dan O'Bannon have written screenplays and comics; Moebius has done comics, book illustration, and costume design; Samuel Delany writes fiction and criticism; Rudy Rucker writes fiction as well as artificial life computer programs; William Burroughs has involved himself in almost every medium of the postmodern era.

30 Jameson cites Perry Anderson's interesting argument that one shared feature of the various modernisms was their hostility to the market. He continues: "Modern art, in this respect, drew its power and its possibilities from being a backwater and an archaic holdover within a modernizing economy: it glorified, celebrated, and dramatized older forms of individual production which the new mode of production was elsewhere on the point of displacing and blotting out" (*Postmodernism*, 305–7).

31 I am tempted to add such fictional terminal identity figures to the list as Professor Brian O'Blivion (*Videodrome*) and Max Headroom.

32 Joanna Russ, "Interview," *Khatru*, ed. Jeffrey D. Smith (Baltimore: Phantasmicon Press, 1975), 3, 4, and 47.

33 McCaffery, *Across the Wounded Galaxies*, 6.

34 Jameson, *Postmodernism*, ix.

35 Jameson, *Postmodernism*, 284.

36 Jameson, *Postmodernism*, 285. Jameson is here discussing Philip Dick's *Time Out of Joint*, a novel set in a "parallel" present, but his comments are appropriate to other science fictions as well, as his own "Progress vs. Utopia; or, Can We Imagine the Future?" (*Science Fiction Studies* 9, no. 2 [1982]) makes clear.

37 Jameson, "Progress vs. Utopia," 152.

38 Jameson refers to the discourse of postmodernism, which has produced an aesthetization of reality that is nevertheless far from the fascism that Walter Benjamin once feared. Jameson writes "we know it's only fun: a prodigious exhilaration with the new order of things, a commodity rush, our 'representations' of things tending to arouse an enthusiasm and a mood swing not necessarily inspired by the things themselves" (*Postmodernism*, x).

39 McCaffery, *Across the Wounded Galaxies*, 3–4.

40 Teresa deLauretis, "Signs of W[a/o]nder," *The Technological Imagination:*

NOTES

Theories and Fictions, ed. Teresa deLauretis, Andreas Huyssen, and Kathleen Woodward (Madison, Wis.: Coda Press, 1980), 160.

41 Samuel R. Delany, "About 5,750 Words," *The Jewel-Hinged Jaw: Notes on the Language of Science Fiction* (Elizabethtown, N.Y.: Dragon Press, 1977), 36–40.

42 Samuel R. Delany, *Starboard Wine: More Notes on the Language of Science Fiction* (Elizabethtown, N.J.: Dragon Press, 1984), 88. Delany is aware of the common meaning of the word as well. The later writings of Delany are collected in this volume and in *The American Shore: Meditations on a Tale of Science Fiction by Thomas M. Disch—"Angouleme"* (Elizabethtown, N.Y.: Dragon Press, 1978).

43 Delany, *Starboard Wine,* 50–52.

44 Most writers on SF cinema privilege thematic or narrative relations over the visual experience of special effects. See, for example, John Baxter, *Science Fiction in the Cinema,* International Film Guide Series, ed. Peter Cowie (New York: New American Library, 1970). Here the very title constitutes SF as a preexistent form grafted onto the medium of film. However, I am hardly the first to emphasize the centrality of effects to the genre or, indeed, the medium itself. Annette Michelson's analysis of *2001,* in "Bodies in Space: Film as 'Carnal Knowledge'," *Artforum* 7, no. 6 (1969) was truly groundbreaking in its application of nonnarrative theoretical precepts to the maligned genre of science fiction. My own study also owes much to the phenomenological emphasis of Vivian Sobchack in her *Screening Space: The American Science Fiction Film,* 2d ed. (New York: Ungar, 1987) and in other works. Both Michelson and Sobchack emphasize the defamiliarizing aspects of spatiality in the SF film in terms commensurate with those of Delany, deLauretis, Jameson, and McCaffery.

45 Tom Gunning, "The Cinema of Attractions: Early Film, Its Spectator and the Avant-Garde," *Early Cinema: Space, Frame, Narrative,* ed. Thomas Elsaesser (London: British Film Institute, 1990), 57; Miriam Hansen, *Babel & Babylon: Spectatorship in American Silent Film* (Cambridge, Mass.: Harvard University Press, 1991), 34.

46 Hansen, 83 and 137.

47 Gunning, "Cinema of Attractions," 57.

48 McCaffery, "Introduction: The Desert of the Real," 6.

49 Although it is true that much video mimics cinematic styles and structures—the rapid montage of MTV is hardly innovative in and of itself.

50 Stanley Cavell, "The Fact of Television," *Video Culture: A Critical Investigation,* ed. John Hanhardt (Rochester, N.Y.: Visual Studies Workshop Press, 1986), 209–10.

51 Thomas Pynchon, *Gravity's Rainbow* (New York: Bantam Books, 1973), 727.

52 Jean Baudrillard, *The Ecstasy of Communication,* Foreign Agents Series, ed. Jim Fleming and Sylvere Lotringer (New York: Semiotext(e), 1988), 50–51.

53 The narrative of Clair's *A Nous La Liberté* (1931) might seem antitechnological, but when viewed as an allegory of sound cinema, the joys of technological control become evident. Vertov and Clair both humanize technology brilliantly—the former through his extraordinary portrait shots, the latter through his seemingly improvised appropriations of technology.

54 Arthur Kroker and Marilouise Kroker, "Theses on the Disappearing Body in

the Hyper-Modern Condition," in *Body Invaders: Panic Sex in America,* eds. Arthur Kroker and Marilouise Kroker (New York: St. Martin's Press, 1987), 21.

55 Jameson, *Postmodernism,* 365.

56 Baudrillard, *Simulations,* 124.

57 Timothy Leary, "The Cyber-Punk: The Individual as Reality Pilot," in *Storming the Reality Studio,* ed. L. McCaffery (Durham: Duke Press, 1992), 252.

58 Maurice Merleau-Ponty, *Phenomenology of Perception,* trans. Colin Smith (London: Routledge & Keagan Paul, 1962), 132.

59 In virtual reality, a computer user wears an apparatus that allows the computer to track and respond to movement. The computer can then generate, in real time, an array of interactive visual and auditory environments.

60 Walter Jon Williams, *Hardwired* (New York: Tor Books, 1986), 130–31.

61 Istvan Csicsery-Ronay, Jr., "The SF of Theory: Baudrillard and Haraway," *Science Fiction Studies* 18, no. 3 (1991): 387–404.

62 Mazlish, "Fourth Discontinuity," 229.

63 Ballard, "Introduction to *Crash,*" 98.

64 Jean Baudrillard, "Symbolic Exchange and Death," in *Jean Baudrillard: Selected Writings,* ed. Mark Poster (Stanford, Calif.: Stanford University Press, 1988), 147.

65 Jameson, *Postmodernism,* 67.

NOTES

1 Terminal Image

1 A similar sense of Japan as the perfect "floating signifier" is to be found in Roland Barthes, *Empire of Signs,* trans. Richard Howard (New York: Hill and Wang, 1982).

2 The electronic soundtrack has been a staple of the science fiction genre since at least *The Day the Earth Stood Still* (1951) and *Forbidden Planet* (1956).

3 Alvin Toffler, *The Third Wave* (New York: Bantam Books, 1981), 165.

4 For the earlier examples, see *Fahrenheit 451* by Ray Bradbury, *The Space Merchants* by Frederik Pohl and C. M. Kornbluth, and "The Seventh Victim" by Robert Sheckley, all from 1953. For the later texts, see Sterling's *Schismatrix,* Ballard's *The Atrocity Exhibition,* Gibson's Cyberspace trilogy, and Chaykin's *American Flagg!* and *Time².* These latter works will be discussed in the following chapters.

5 But Marker is never "colonized" as is Bowie's media-addicted character, Thomas Newton.

6 See, for instance, Samuel R. Delany, "About 5,750 Words," in *The Jewel-Hinged Jaw: Notes on the Language of Science Fiction* (Elizabethtown, N.Y.: Dragon Press, 1977) and Teresa deLauretis, "Signs of W[a/o]nder," in *The Technological Imagination: Theories and Fictions,* eds. Teresa deLauretis, Andreas Huyssen, and Kathleen Woodward (Madison, Wis.: Coda Press, 1980).

7 For an example of this overtly political analysis, see Ben H. Bagdikian, *The Media Monopoly* (Boston: Beacon Press, 1990).

8 An episode of the public television series *Television,* for example, aired on

February 23, 1988, in New York City, speaks of "the power of the *images* it sends into our homes." Presumably, Edwin Newman's sober narration, written for him by Michael Winship and read from an invisible, state of the art teleprompter, exists above such spectacular power.

9   For the most hysterical examples, see Jerry Mander, *Four Arguments for the Elimination of Television* (New York: William Morrow, 1978), and Marie Winn, *The Plug-in Drug: TV, Children, and the Family* (New York: Viking, 1977). Of course, I would not *entirely* separate myself from such a view.

10 Truffaut's film unfortunately fails to engage with its own status as spectacle, as image-commodity—as though film were somehow inherently exempt from the field of spectacle, as books and written language seem to be.

11 A more complex relationship between word and image is to be found in the work of Truffaut's contemporary, Jean-Luc Godard. See his "science fiction" film, *Alphaville, Un Femme Mariée* (1964), and *Le Gai Savoir* (1968).

12 See Patrick Brantlinger, *Bread and Circuses: Theories of Mass Culture as Social Decay* (Ithaca, N.Y.: Cornell University Press, 1983) for a complete discussion of the discourse on the "barbarization" of culture.

13 Andy Grundberg, "Ask It No Questions: The Camera Can Lie," *New York Times,* August 12, 1990.

14 See Alan Trachtenberg, ed., *Classic Essays on Photography* (New Haven, Conn.: Leete's Island Books, 1980), a fascinating collection of essays on the medium, for more information.

15 This opening "hook" is actually followed by a more sufficient historical overview. The article notes that the new electronic technology "allows *anyone* to alter a photographic image at will" (emphasis mine)—an unintentional irony suggesting that this ability should perhaps remain the province of a select few.

16 This has been nowhere more evident than in the "morphing" technologies used to produce the liquid metal T-1000 in *Terminator 2* and the dazzling kaleidoscope of mutable ethnicity presented in Michael Jackson's "Black or White" video (1991). Television commercials for diet colas have also constructed digital duets between Louis Armstrong and Elton John, and Ray Charles and his "twin brother"—the real thing?

17 Paul de Man, *Allegories of Reading: Figural Language in Rousseau, Nietzsche, Rilke, and Proust* (New Haven: Yale University Press, 1979), 77.

18 David Porush, *The Soft Machine: Cybernetic Fiction* (New York: Methuen, 1985).

19 Ballard, "Introduction to *Crash,*" 97.

20 Toffler, *Third Wave,* 165.

21 Arthur Kroker and David Cook, *The Postmodern Scene: Excremental Culture and Hyper-Aesthetics,* Culture Texts, ed. Arthur Kroker and Marilouise Kroker (New York: St. Martin's Press, 1986), 279.

22 "Design Decade," *Architectural Forum* 73 (October 1940). Cited in Richard Guy Wilson, Dianne H. Pilgrim, and Dickran Tashjian, *The Machine Age in America: 1918–1941* (New York: Brooklyn Museum in association with Harry N. Abrams, 1986), 57.

23 Thomas Hine, *Populuxe* (New York: Alfred A. Knopf, 1986), 107–22.

24 Karrie Jacobs, "Identity Crisis," *Metropolis* 7, no. 2 (1987).

25 Jacobs, 75.

26 Jacobs, 51.

27 Kroker and Cook, 275—the internal citation is to Baudrillard.

28 Jean Baudrillard, *In the Shadow of the Silent Majorities,* trans. Paul Foss, Paul Patton, and John Johnston, Foreign Agents Series, ed. Jim Fleming and Sylvere Lotringer (New York: Semiotext[e], 1983), 21.

29 Baudrillard, *Silent Majorities,* 97.

30 Baudrillard, *Silent Majorities,* 101.

31 This variation on Oscar Wilde is to be found in Kroker and Cook, 268.

32 Jameson, *Postmodernism,* 69 and 76.

33 Alvin Toffler, *Future Shock* (New York: Bantam Books, 1971), 161.

34 John Sladek, *The Müller-Fokker Effect* (New York: Carroll & Graf, 1990), 28.

35 Kroker and Cook, 274.

36 Guy Debord, *Society of the Spectacle* (Detroit: Black & Red, 1983).

37 Greil Marcus, *Lipstick Traces: A Secret History of the Twentieth Century* (Cambridge, Mass.: Harvard University Press, 1989), 99.

38 Kroker and Cook, 279.

39 Marcus, 101. In *Lipstick Traces,* Marcus illustrates Debord's arguments with striking effectiveness, using Michael Jackson's *Thriller* album and subsequent Jacksons tour as his examples ("the first pop explosion not to be judged by the subjective quality of the response it provoked, but to be measured by the number of objective commercial exchanges it elicited" [96–112]).

40 This is where Debord's "spectacle" differs from Daniel Boorstin's "image." In his 1961 study, *The Image: A Guide to Pseudo-Events in America,* Boorstin discusses news, celebrity, travel, and American self-image—all of which depend upon the citizen's interface with public existence (Daniel J. Boorstin, *The Image: A Guide to Pseudo-Events in America* [New York: Atheneum, 1985]). Boorstin's analysis is rooted entirely in the realm of public life and does not continue to track the incursion of the simulacrum into more privatized and personal realms.

41 Like Marker in *Sans Soleil,* she is infantilized by her television-dominated environment. The three wall-sized screens recall the holographic nursery in the same author's tale of "The Veldt" (1950) while a form of interactive programming combines the form of the soap opera with the childhood game of House (and an early example of a virtual reality system, incidentally). Television is conceived as a form of Debordian social control in *Fahrenheit 451:* a control characterized by distraction, pacification, and ultimate neutralization. The control status is rendered explicit by the government edicts which ban all books—television viewing is the entertainment which carries the official sanction of the state.

42 William S. Burroughs, *Naked Lunch* (New York: Grove Press, 1959), xxxviii and xxxix.

43 As the protagonist of Wim Wenders's *Alice in the Cities* (1974) once noted.

44 Burroughs, *Naked Lunch,* 36.

45 Herbert Marcuse, *One-Dimensional Man* (Boston: Beacon Press, 1964), 65.

46 See the texts by Mander and Winn; also see Nicolas Johnson, *How to Talk Back to Your Television Set* (New York: Bantam Books, 1970), and Fred W.

Friendly, *Due to Circumstances Beyond Our Control* (New York: Vintage Books, 1968). A more theorized polemic can be found in Max Horkheimer and Theodor Adorno, *The Dialectic of Enlightenment,* trans. John Cummings (New York: Continuum Publishing, 1972). Dziga Vertov's writings on the cinema are also relevant in their emphasis on spectacle as opiate and are collected in Annette Michelson, ed., *Kino-Eye: The Writings of Dziga Vertov* (Berkeley: University of California Press, 1984).

47 Brantlinger's *Bread and Circuses* is an excellent examination of the metaphor of cultural "barbarism." See especially chapter 8, "Television: Spectacularity vs. McLuhanism."

48 Jean Baudrillard, "Requiem for the Media," *For a Critique of the Political Economy of the Sign,* trans. Charles Levin (St. Louis: Telos Press, 1981), 172.

49 William Burroughs, "The Cut-Up Method of Brion Gysin," *Re/Search* 4/5 (1982): 36.

50 Burroughs, "Cut-Up Method," 35.

51 William S. Burroughs, "The Electronic Revolution," in *Ah Pook is Here and Other Texts* (New York: Riverrun Press, 1979), 125.

52 Burroughs, *Ah Pook,* 126–27.

53 J. G. Ballard, "Mythmaker of the 20th Century," *Re/Search* 8/9 (1984), 106.

54 Don Delillo, *White Noise* (New York: Viking Penguin, 1986).

55 Kroker and Cook, 13.

56 See J. G. Ballard, "Time, Memory, and Inner Space," *Re/Search* 8/9 (1984), for example.

57 Lawrence Alloway, "The Development of British Pop," in *Pop Art,* ed. Lucy Lippard (New York: Oxford University Press, 1966), 40.

58 David Robbins, ed., *The Independent Group: Postwar Britain and the Aesthetics of Plenty* (Cambridge, Mass.: MIT Press, 1990), 61.

59 James Colvin, "A Literature of Acceptance," in *New Worlds: An Anthology,* ed. Michael Moorcock (London: Flamingo Books, 1983), 348. Article originally published in 1968.

60 J. G. Ballard, "Fictions of Every Kind," *Re/Search* 8/9 (1984), 99 (emphasis mine).

61 The Space Age was frequently perceived from the perspective of those on the ground. See, for example, "Gravity," by Harvey Jacobs, or "The Dead Astronaut," by Ballard.

62 Moorcock's "Jerry Cornelius" stories and novels took place in a similar landscape, as *New Worlds* writer Brian Aldiss—not a Ballard fan—has noted: "In a sense it was the same contemporary world coldly glimpsed in Ballard's work, but a world in which warm pastiche breathed, a world with far greater animation and personality. . . . The novels themselves, cluttered with images and objects—vibrators, Sikorsky helicopters, Mars bars among them—are deliberately less meaningful. Of course this was a kind of fictional in-joke amongst the writers of *New Worlds:* consequently, a comic book quality often pervades much of the writing." *Trillion Year Spree: The History of Science Fiction* (New York: Atheneum, 1986), 303.

63 William S. Burroughs, *The Soft Machine* (New York: Grove Press, 1966), 152.

64 David Pringle, "Media Landscape," in *The Encyclopedia of Science Fiction,* ed. Peter Nicholls (New York: Doubleday, 1979), 391.

65 J. G. Ballard, "Quotations by Ballard," *Re/Search* 8/9 (1984), 158.

66 J. G. Ballard, "The Intensive Care Unit," in *Myths of the Near Future* (London: Triad Books, 1984), 198.

67 Ballard, "Introduction to *Crash,*" 98.

68 J. G. Ballard, "The Assassination Weapon," in *The Atrocity Exhibition* (San Francisco, Calif.: Re/Search Publications, 1990), 34.

69 Ballard, "Fictions," 100.

70 Ballard, "Fictions," 99.

71 These have been collected under the title *The Atrocity Exhibition.* The original title was *Love and Napalm: Export USA,* a title which evokes Godard, whose mid-60s fascination with consumer culture and narrative experimentation is well known.

72 James Goddard and David Pringle, eds., *J. G. Ballard: The First Twenty Years* (Middlesex: Bran's Head Books, 1976), 4.

73 J. G. Ballard, "Coming of the Unconscious," *Re/Search* 8/9 (1984), 103. See chapters 4 and 5 for more on science fiction and surrealism.

74 Pamela Zoline, "The Heat Death of the Universe," in *The Heat Death of the Universe and Other Stories* (Kingston, N.Y.: McPherson, 1988).

75 The story also anticipates the use of entropy as a structuring metaphor in Pynchon's *Gravity's Rainbow* (Pynchon had already used entropy as an extensive metaphor in "Entropy" as well as in *The Crying of Lot 49*). Zoline's story also intersects in fascinating ways with Chantal Akerman's massive film of domestic isolation and breakdown, *Jeanne Dielmann, 23 Quai du Commerce, 1080 Bruxelles* (1975). The Akerman film, for example, emphasizes extremely long takes and sequence shots, giving each shot a discrete existence which is reminiscent of Zoline's numbered paragraphs. The emphasis on household chores in Jeanne Dielmann is anticipated in "The Heat Death of the Universe."

76 Ballard, "Quotations," 160.

77 Goddard and Pringle, 33.

78 The film is thus only an apparent reversal of *Sans Soleil.* In the later, somewhat more autocritical film, science fiction is invoked more explicitly as a metaphor than it is in Roeg's commercial release of 1976.

79 The images include movies, war footage, mating animals—another similarity to Marker's film—and, in what is surely a reflexive joke on Bowie's pop-star status—an Elvis Presley movie.

80 See Guiliana Bruno, "Ramble City: Postmodernism and Blade Runner," *OCTOBER* 41 (1987), for more on this Barthesian view of the photograph.

81 Fredric Jameson, "Postmodernism, or the Cultural Logic of Late Capitalism," *New Left Review* 146 (1984), 79.

82 I do not want to suggest that Jameson is unsympathetic to Dick. In fact, Jameson has produced effective analyses of Dick's work: see "After Armageddon: Character Systems in *Dr. Bloodmoney,*" *Science Fiction Studies,* 2 no. 1 (1975), and *Postmodernism,* 279–87.

83 Page references are to Philip K. Dick, *The Simulacra* (London: Methuen, 1977).

84 Richard Sennett, *The Fall of Public Man* (New York: Vintage Books, 1978), 282. Sennett views this phenomenon as an impersonal consequence of the

"rationality" of capitalist development, while Dick's pervasive paranoia attributes the decline of public existence to a heinous government/technocratic conspiracy.

85 Philip K. Dick, *The Three Stigmata of Palmer Eldritch* (New York: Bantam Books, 1977).

86 Philip K. Dick, *Now Wait for Last Year* (London: Granada Publishing, 1979), 23. Jameson refers to this work in *Postmodernism,* 118.

87 Philip K. Dick, *Martian Time-Slip* (New York: Ballantine Books, 1964).

88 Charles Jencks, *The Language of Post-Modern Architecture* (New York: Rizzoli Books, 1981), 9–10.

89 Ernest Mandel, *Late Capitalism,* trans. Joris de Bres (London: Verso Editions, 1978), 216.

90 Kim Stanley Robinson, *The Novels of Philip K. Dick,* Studies in Speculative Fiction, ed. Robert Scholes (Ann Arbor: UMI Research Press, 1984), 90.

91 Robinson, *Novels of Philip K. Dick,* 90.

92 Howard Chaykin (Evanston, Ill.: First Comics, 1983). The original three issue story of the series was reprinted in a single volume entitled *Hard Times* in 1985.

93 Brantlinger, 251.

94 William S. Burroughs, *Nova Express* (New York: Grove Press, 1964), 18.

95 "The provocative adventures of a fearless vice cop walking the streets of an unnamed, untamed and sexually-transmitted-disease-ridden sector of a great urban metroplex."

96 Chaykin's *Time²* features a newspaper *called* "The Postmodern Times."

97 Robert Smithson, "Language to be Looked at and/or Things to be Read," in *The Writings of Robert Smithson,* ed. Nancy Holt (New York: New York University Press, 1979), 104.

98 For an extensive analysis of the underlying importance of such a use of language, see Rosalind Coward and John Ellis, *Language and Materialism: Developments in Semiology and the Theory of the Subject* (London: Routledge & Kegan Paul, 1977). See also Jacques Derrida, *Of Grammatology,* trans. Gayatri Chakravorty Spivak (Baltimore: Johns Hopkins University Press, 1976).

99 Eric Mottram, *William Burroughs: The Algebra of Need* (London: Marion Boyars, 1977), 65.

100 Charles Jencks, *Late Modern Architecture* (New York: Rizzoli Books, 1980), 32.

101 Jameson, "Postmodernism," 81.

102 Jameson, "Postmodernism," 83.

103 Robert Venturi, Denise Scott Brown, and Steven Izenour, *Learning from Las Vegas* (Cambridge, Mass.: MIT Press, 1977), 35.

104 Jim Hoberman, "What's Stranger Than Paradise? or How We Stopped Worrying and Learned to Love the 'Burbs," *Village Voice Film Special,* June 30, 1987, 8.

105 "A cartoon character flew across the waitress's stomach . . . to be replaced instantly by a car crashing head-on into another, both bursting into flames. 'Cars are crashing in your stomach,' Purchase told her." John Shirley, *Eclipse* (New York: Bluejay Books, 1985), 76.

106 Nam June Paik, "Electronic Video Recorder," in *Nam June Paik: Video and Videology 1959–1973* (Syracuse: Everson Museum of Art, 1974), 11.

107 Jean Baudrillard, "Design and Environment, or How Political Economy Escalates into Cyberblitz," *For a Critique of the Political Economy of the Sign,* ed. and trans. Charles Levin (St. Louis: Telos Press, 1981).

108 Alan Moore and Dave Gibbons, *The Watchmen* (New York: DC Comics, 1987), chapter XI, 1. The same is true of the collision of panels in comics, making the statement autoreferential.

109 David Ross, "Nam June Paik's Videotapes," in *Nam June Paik,* ed. John Hanhardt (New York: Whitney Museum of American Art, 1982), 109.

110 The attribution of authorship to this work is difficult, but the contributions of producer Peter Wagg, writer Steve Roberts, and directors Rocky Morton and Annabelle Jankel were all crucial.

111 Max "himself" will receive some attention in chapter 4, "Terminal Flesh."

112 The sets, for example, with their end-of-empire shoddiness, derive equally from Ridley Scott's *Blade Runner* and Terry Gilliam's *Brazil* (1985), while its rapid editing suggests the montage effects in George Miller's postapocalyptic Mad Max films.

113 Frederik Pohl and C. M. Kornbluth, *The Space Merchants* (New York: Ballantine Books, 1953), 10.

114 See, for one very good example, Mark Crispin Miller, "Virtù, Inc.," in *Boxed In: The Culture of TV* (Evanston, Ill.: Northwestern University Press, 1988).

115 On the topic of the supplement, see Derrida's *Of Grammatology,* especially pages 144–46.

116 Sean Cubitt, *Timeshift: On Video Culture* (London; New York: Routledge, 1991), 156. Even the neo-Dadaist comic strip "Zippy the Pinhead" has commented on the change in viewing habits. In a 1987 strip the rational narrator discusses the matter with the absurdist Zippy:

> *Griffy:* Channel-hopping is a nasty habit, Zip. . . . Once you start it's like a monkey on your back. . . .
> *Zippy:* Stop on Sixteen!! I don't want to miss th' "RAID" commercial!!
> *Griffy:* These clickers have destroyed what little continuity was left in modern life. . . . No matter how "interested" you become in a show, you can't resist th' POWER you have to switch to ANOTHER! . . . After a while, everything equals everything else and your mind goes numb and your soul is sucked into th' tube and you're just a pair of eyes and a thumb . . . clicking . . . clicking . . . clicking. . . .
> *Zippy:* FASTER!! I almost formed an opinion of Madonna's new video!!
> (Bill Griffith, "Excess Access")

117 Toffler, *Third Wave,* 163. Artificial reality designer Myron Krueger writes that through zipping, "The ultimate passive medium is being made interactive by its audience." *Artificial Reality,* 2d ed. (Reading, Mass.: Addison-Wesley Publishing, 1991), 76.

118 Again, see Jameson on the "cartographic failure" of the subject within contemporary culture in "Postmodernism," 83.

119 Jean Baudrillard, *The Mirror of Production,* trans. Mark Poster (St. Louis: Telos Press, 1975), 169–70.

120   Codirectors Morton and Jankel made their reputation with a fine series of music videos.

121   Jean Baudrillard, *Simulations*, trans. Paul Foss, Paul Patton, and Philip Beitchman, Foreign Agents Series, ed. Jim Fleming and Sylvere Lotringer (New York: Semiotext[e], 1983), 23–26.

122   Citing, among other things, a disrespectful attitude toward the sponsors: a gambit already familiar to viewers of *Late Night with David Letterman*, not to mention *Alfred Hitchcock Presents*. Harry F. Waters, Janet Huck, and Vern E. Smith, "Mad About M-M-Max," *Newsweek*, April 20, 1987, 59.

123   By the end of the 1980s, evil corporations were the requisite villain in almost every science fiction film, from *Robocop* to *Who Framed Roger Rabbit?* (1988). See Thomas B. Byers, "Commodity Futures," in *Alien Zone: Cultural Theory and Contemporary Science Fiction Cinema*, ed. Annette Kuhn (London: Verso, 1990) for more on this recurrent cinematic motif.

124   Marshall McLuhan, *Understanding Media* (New York: New American Library, 1964).

125   Michel Foucault, *The Archaeology of Knowledge*, trans. A. M. Sheridan Smith (New York: Pantheon Books, 1972), 8.

126   Ballard, "Introduction to *Crash*," 96.

127   A. J. Liebling, *The Press* (New York: Ballantine Books, 1975), 32.

128   T. J. Clark, *The Painting of Modern Life: Paris in the Art of Manet and His Followers* (Princeton, N.J.: Princeton University Press, 1984), 9–10.

129   On this subject, see of course George Lukacs, "Reification and the Consciousness of the Proletariat," in *History and Class Consciousness: Studies in Marxist Dialectics*, trans. Rodney Livingstone (Cambridge, Mass.: MIT Press, 1971).

130   See Baudrillard, "Requiem for the Media."

131   Baudrillard, *The Mirror of Production*.

132   Jean Baudrillard, *Forget Foucault*, trans. Nicole Dufresne, Foreign Agents Series, ed. Jim Fleming and Sylvere Lotringer (New York: Semiotext[e], 1987). Arthur Kroker argues that this deconstruction of Marx (a deconstruction strategically absent from Derrida's work) is not tantamount to an anti-Marxist polemic. Baudrillard's writing does not contradict or obviate the economic analyses of capitalism, by Mandel, for example; nor does it negate much of the Hegelian Marxist tradition of the Frankfurt School or its inheritors, such as Jameson or Sennett (Kroker and Cook, 170–88). In its nihilistic rejection of the "transcendental signified" of labor power, the Baudrillard position does demolish the utopian trajectory of revolutionary Marxism but, for the purposes of this analysis, the work of these theorists is largely commensurable.

133   Baudrillard, *Forget Foucault*, 11.

134   Jean Baudrillard, "The Ecstasy of Communication," in *The Anti-Aesthetic*, ed. Hal Foster (Port Townsend, Wash.: Bay Press, 1983), 128.

135   Baudrillard, *Simulations*, 54–55.

136   Lynn Spigel, "Installing the Television Set: Popular Discourses on Television and Domestic Space, 1948–1955," *Camera Obscura* 16 (1988), 34.

137   Spigel, 34–35.

138   Baudrillard, "Ecstasy," 128.

139 The trilogy includes *Nova Express* (1964), *The Soft Machine* (1966), and *The Ticket That Exploded* (1967).

140 Cited in Mottram, 40.

141 Mottram, 56.

142 Marshall McLuhan, "Notes on Burroughs," in *William S. Burroughs at the Front: Critical Reception, 1959–1989,* eds. Jennie Skerl and Robin Lydenberg (Carbondale, Ill.: Southern Illinois University Press, 1991), 69.

143 Cited in Mottram, 40.

144 The desire to construct a myth intersects with at least two other important conceptions of mythic structures. For Claude Lévi-Strauss, myth is a cultural attempt at the reconciliation of irreconcilables. The contradictions which arise between natural and cultural phenomena are thereby explained and fixed into a system of meaning—typically with culture being subsumed within the forces of the natural (Claude Lévi-Strauss, "The Structural Anthropology of Myth," in *Structural Anthropology,* trans. Claire Jacobson, Brooke Schoepf [New York: Basic Books, 1963]). Burroughs's use of mythic structure also functions on an explicitly metaphorical level, as a mode of comprehending and regarding the irrational and invisible in culture. Culture is liberated in Burroughs's mythology: a "mythology for the space age." Nature is not immediately evident within his corpus of tales involving power, technology, addiction, and control.

Nietzsche privileged myth as an *overt* aestheticizing and ordering of the world. The "prison house of language" prevents the direct experience of reality, structuring as it does cognitive activity and conceptualization. Language seems grounded in the world, in nature, while myth does not. Myth is clearly a cultural product; in fact, it is almost a defining characteristic of culture. For Nietzsche, science served as an adequate basis for myth, while the mythic form aestheticized the cold logic of science, providing distance and order, free play and structure. Nietzsche also advocated the creation of new myths *ex nihilo,* the better to consciously apprehend the cultural specificity of the mythic structure (Alan Megill, *Prophets of Extremity: Nietzsche, Heidegger, Foucault, Derrida* [Berkeley: University of California Press, 1985]). It is evident that the importance and function of myth coincide for both Nietzsche and Burroughs, and here lies the source of Burroughs's appropriation of the forms and tropes of science fiction.

145 This is also discussed by Jennie Skerl in *William S. Burroughs* (Boston: Twayne Publishers, 1985), 77.

146 Ballard, "Mythmaker," 106.

147 Roland Barthes, "The Death of the Author," in *Image-Music-Text* (New York: Hill and Wang, 1977), 147.

148 William S. Burroughs, *The Ticket That Exploded* (New York: Grove Press, 1967), 51.

149 Christopher Sharrett, "Myth and Ritual in the Post-Industrial Landscape: The Horror Films of David Cronenberg," *Persistence of Vision* 1, nos. 3/4 (1986), 113.

150 Baudrillard, *Silent Majorities,* 109.

151 Porush, 101.

152 Baudrillard, *Silent Majorities,* 25.

153 Baudrillard, *Silent Majorities,* 25.

154 Burroughs, *Ticket,* 50.

155 Fredric Jameson, "Science Fiction as a Spatial Genre: Generic Discontinuities and the Problem of Figuration in Vonda McIntyre's *The Exile Waiting,*" *Science Fiction Studies* 14, no. 1 (1987), 54.

156 Annette Michelson, "Bodies in Space."

157 "The Shape of Rage" is a phrase that recalls Burroughs's "the algebra of need." The title has also been used, very appropriately, as the title of a collection of essays on Cronenberg's films.

158 William Beard, "The Visceral Mind: The Films of David Cronenberg," in *The Shape of Rage: The Films of David Cronenberg,* ed. Piers Handling (New York: New York Zoetrope, 1983), 4.

159 See Arthur Kroker, Marilouise Kroker, and David Cook, eds., *Panic Encyclopedia* (New York: St. Martin's Press, 1989), a funny and disturbing compendium. Further discussion of the body in science fiction can be found in chapters 4 and 5 of the present work.

160 Carrie Rickey, "Make Mine Cronenberg," *The Village Voice,* February 1, 1983, 64 (my emphasis).

161 Beard, 8.

162 Baudrillard, "Ecstasy," 128.

163 See Guy Debord, "Perspectives for Conscious Alterations in Everyday Life," in *Situationist International Anthology,* ed. Ken Knabb (Berkeley, Calif.: Bureau of Public Secrets, 1981), for a transcript of one of these performances.

164 Burroughs, *Ticket,* 213.

165 The acronym suggests the computer term, *Random Access Memory.*

166 For an important analysis of the figuration of the body in *Videodrome,* from an explicitly feminist theoretical position, see Tania Modleski, "The Terror of Pleasure: The Contemporary Horror Film and Postmodern Theory," in *Studies in Entertainment: Critical Approaches to Mass Culture,* ed. Tania Moledski (Bloomington: Indiana University Press, 1986).

167 After detailing the similarities between the work of Burroughs and Cronenberg, I must admit that *Naked Lunch* reveals their profound differences; most notably in the area of sexuality.

168 Baudrillard, *Simulations,* 54.

169 Baudrillard, "Ecstasy," 132.

170 Burroughs, *Soft Machine,* 155.

171 Philip K. Dick, *UBIK* (New York: DAW Books, 1983).

172 This is discussed in Peter Fitting, "*UBIK:* The Deconstruction of Bourgeois SF," in *Philip K. Dick,* ed. Joseph D. Olander and Martin Harry Greenberg (New York: Taplinger Publishing, 1983), especially 155–56.

173 Philip K. Dick, *UBIK: The Screenplay* (Minneapolis, Minn.: Corroboree Press, 1985).

174 William S. Burroughs, *The Last Words of Dutch Schultz* (New York: Seaver Books, 1975).

175 Dick, *UBIK: The Screenplay,* 120. This description is strikingly reminiscent of Cronenberg's *Naked Lunch* adaptation.

176　Karl Marx, *Capital,* trans. Ben Fowkes (New York: Vintage Books, 1977), vol. 1, 177.

177　Burroughs, *Soft Machine,* 43.

178　Baudrillard, *Simulations,* 12 and 2.

179　Baudrillard, *Simulations,* 11–12.

180　Baudrillard, *Simulations,* 12; Jameson, "Postmodernism," 66–68.

181　Kroker and Cook, *Postmodern Scene,* 27.

2 Terminal Space

1　Steward Brand, *The Media Lab: Inventing the Future at MIT* (New York: Viking Penguin, 1987), 98.

2　Interested readers should see Steven Levy, *Artificial Life: The Quest for a New Creation* (New York: Pantheon Books, 1992).

3　Heinz R. Pagels, *The Dreams of Reason: The Computer and the Rise of Sciences of Complexity* (New York: Simon and Schuster, 1989), 104.

4　Pagels, 106.

5　Brochure for Compuserve Information Service.

6　Brand, 241.

7　Bruce Sterling, *Islands in the Net* (New York: Arbor House, 1988), 177.

8　A. K. Dewdney, *The Armchair Universe: An Exploration of Computer Worlds* (New York: W. H. Freeman, 1988).

9　John Shirley, *Eclipse Corona* (New York: Popular Library, 1990), 33.

10　John Shirley, *Eclipse* (New York: Bluejay Books, 1985); William Gibson, *Neuromancer* (New York: Ace Science Fiction Books, 1984).

11　Vivian Sobchack, "The Scene of the Screen: Towards a Phenomenology of Cinematic and Electronic Presence," *Post-Script* 10 (1990), 56.

12　Pagels, 143.

13　Jameson, "Postmodernism," 58. One definition of cyberspace in this era of electronic banking is that *cyberspace is where your money is.*

14　See, in addition to Rifkin's history, the rise of a culture of "simultaneity" as described in Stephen Kern, *The Culture of Time and Space: 1880–1918* (Cambridge, Mass.: Harvard University Press, 1983).

15　Hayden White, "The Historical Text as Literary Artifact," in *Tropics of Discourse* (Baltimore: Johns Hopkins University Press, 1978).

16　Much of this hurried discussion derives from the arguments developed in Fredric Jameson, *The Political Unconscious: Narrative as a Socially Symbolic Act* (Ithaca, N.Y.: Cornell University Press, 1981), especially the first and second chapters.

17　Jean-François Lyotard, *The Postmodern Condition: A Report on Knowledge,* trans. Geoff Bennington, Brian Massumi (Minneapolis: University of Minnesota Press, 1984), xxiv.

18　Baudrillard, *Forget Foucault,* 11.

19　Baudrillard, *Simulations,* 10.

20　Sobchack, "The Scene of the Screen," 57.

21　Sobchack, "The Scene of the Screen," 56.

22　Maurice Merleau-Ponty, "Eye and Mind," in *The Primacy of Perception,* trans. Carleton Dallery, ed. James M. Edie (Northwestern University Press, 1964), 186.

23 Mihai Nadin, "Emergent Aesthetics—Aesthetic Issues in Computer Arts," in *Computer Art in Context: SIGGRAPH 1989 Art Show Catalog,* ed. Mark Resch (Oxford: Pergamon Press, 1989), 43.

24 Sobchack, "The Scene of the Screen," 57–58.

25 John Berger has argued that the material richness of the medium of oil paints is emblematic of the era of merchant capitalism (John Berger, *Ways of Seeing* [Middlesex: Penguin Books, 1972], 86–87). Perhaps the pixel-lated bytes of the terminal screen are paradigmatic of the implosive forces pulsing through the age of late capitalism, the Dataist Era.

26 Jameson, "Postmodernism," 91–92.

27 The ecstasy accompanying these texts often recall earlier works of film theory, which frequently narrated the potentials of cinema as a perceptual tool through its manipulation of temporality (through time-lapse photography, reverse motion, and montage) and spatiality (through exotic camera placements and, again, montage). See, for celebrated examples, Annette Michelson, ed., *Kino-Eye: The Writings of Dziga Vertov* (Berkeley: University of California Press, 1984); Jean Epstein, "Magnification and Other Writings," *OCTOBER* 3 (1976); and Walter Benjamin, "The Work of Art in the Age of Mechanical Reproduction," in *Illuminations,* trans. Harry Zohn, ed. Hannah Arendt (New York: Schocken Books, 1969).

28 H.-O. Peitgen and H. Richter, eds., *The Beauty of Fractals* (Berlin and New York: Springer-Verlag, 1986), 3.

29 Margot Lovejoy, *Postmodern Currents: Art and Artists in the Age of Electronic Media* (Ann Arbor: UMI Research Press, 1989), 247–48.

30 Cara McCarty, *Information Art: Diagramming Microchips* (New York: Museum of Modern Art, 1990), 6.

31 Timothy Binkley, "Camera Fantasia," *Millenium Film Journal* 20/21 (1989), 20.

32 Lovejoy, 291. J. David Bolter notes that the phenomenon of computer space is based in mathematical logic and empirical, physical, reality (Bolter, *Turing's Man: Western Culture in the Computer Age* [Chapel Hill, N.C.: University of North Carolina Press, 1984], 97).

33 Dewdney, *Armchair Universe,* 65.

34 Philip Elmer-DeWitt, "Invasion of the Data Snatchers!," *Time,* September 26, 1988. The *New York Times* used similarly simple graphics, but this time further schematized to a series of simple icons (similar to those used by the Apple Macintosh) in John Markoff, "A 'Virus' Gives Business a Chill," *New York Times,* March 17, 1988.

35 Andrew Ross, "Hacking Away at the Counterculture," in *Technoculture,* eds. Constance Penley and Andrew Ross (Minneapolis: University of Minnesota Press, 1991), 108. These biological metaphors are problematic, as Ross acknowledges, and have met with approbation from AIDS awareness groups that believe the metaphor trivializes the very real viral invasion of their communities. Arthur Kroker argues, however, that the term does not represent a biologizing of technology so much as the reverse: "biology is cyberneticized with such speed and intensity that it takes on a second,

processed life as the genetic language of the computerscape" (*Panic Encyclopedia,* 236). One must further recognize and accept the pervasiveness of the viral trope within postmodernism (already encountered in the previous chapter) and understand the ontological confusion (and ideological anxiety) which it carries.

36   James Gleick, *Chaos* (New York: Viking Books, 1987), 98.

37   Richard Mark Friedhoff and William Benzon, *Visualization: The Second Computer Revolution* (New York: Harry Abrams, 1989), 113.

38   It has also been used as a logo and recurrent image in *Big Numbers,* an ambitious comic by Alan Moore and Bill Sienkiewicz (Northampton, England: Mad Love, 1990). Moore explicitly uses the Mandelbrot set as a metaphor for his narrative evocation of social chaos (*The Mandelbrot Set* was the work's original title). For Moore's explanation, see Liz Evans, "Massive Mathematics," *Deadline,* April 1990.

39   Michelson, "Bodies in Space"; also Annette Michelson, "About Snow," *OCTOBER* (1973).

40   See Vivian Sobchack, "A Theory of Everything: Meditations on Total Chaos," *Artforum International* (October 1990), 148–55.

41   Ronald Lusk, "The First Encounter," *Amygdala,* April 1987, 2–3.

42   Baudrillard, *Silent Majority,* 9.

43   Istvan Csicsery-Ronay, Jr., "Cyberpunk and Neuromanticism," in McCaffery, ed., *Storming the Reality Studio,* 188.

44   One sees a similar struggle between antitechnological narrative and hypertechnological aesthetic in *Star Wars.* Here the obfuscation is more successful; the film less interesting.

45   Ballard, "Introduction to *Crash,*" 4–5.

46   Sobchack, "The Scene of the Screen," 50.

47   Edmund Husserl, "Phenomenology," in *Deconstruction in Context: Literature and Philosophy,* ed. Mark C. Taylor (Chicago: University of Chicago Press, 1986), 125.

48   Maurice Merleau-Ponty, *Phenomenology of Perception,* trans. Colin Smith (London: Routledge & Kegan Paul, 1962), 70.

49   In fact, Merleau-Ponty is explicit on this point in his discussions of case studies in the history of abnormal psychology. See, for example, *The Phenomenology of Perception,* 228–29.

50   Gibson, *Neuromancer,* 261.

51   Robert Smithson, "Entropy and the New Monuments," in *The Writings of Robert Smithson,* ed. Nancy Holt (New York: New York University Press, 1979), 10.

52   Jameson, "Postmodernism," 53.

53   Smithson, "Entropy," 12.

54   Smithson, "Entropy," 11.

55   Michael Sorkin, "Introduction," in *Variations on a Theme Park: The New American City and the End of Public Space* (New York: Noonday Press, 1992), xiv.

56   William Sharpe and Leonard Wallock, "From 'Great Town' to 'Nonplace Urban Realm': Reading the Modern City," in *Visions of the Modern City:*

Essays in History, Art, and Literature, ed. William Sharpe and Leonard Wallock (New York: Hayman Center for the Humanities, 1983), 7.

57 Melvin M. Webber, "The Urban Place and the Nonplace Urban Realm," in *Explorations into Urban Structure,* ed. Melvin M. Webber et al. (Philadelphia: University of Pennsylvania Press, 1964), 89.

58 Jameson, "Science Fiction as a Spatial Genre," 54.

59 Webber, "The Urban Place and the Nonplace Urban Realm."

60 Brian Stableford, "Cities," in *The Science Fiction Encyclopedia,* ed. Peter Nicholls (Garden City, N.Y.: Doubleday, 1979), 120.

61 Stableford, 120.

62 See, in addition to the volume by Sharpe and Wallock, the writings of Robert Venturi or Charles Jencks, or *The Image of the City* by Kevin Lynch. For the city in SF cinema, see Vivian Sobchack, "Cities on the Edge of Time: The Urban Science Fiction Film," *East-West Film Journal* 3, no. 1 (1988), 4–19.

63 Jameson, "Postmodernism," 81.

64 Paul Virilio, "The Overexposed City," *ZONE* 1/2 (1984), 21.

65 The IMAX screening rooms around the country, but especially at the Smithsonian Institute's Air and Space Museum in Washington D.C., have such sharply raked floors that it is possible to sit halfway up the screen, as it were. In films about flight or space travel, the experience of weightless suspension is extraordinary.

66 Raoul Vaneigem, "Basic Banalities," in *Situationist International Anthology,* ed. Ken Knabb (Berkeley, Calif.: Bureau of Public Secrets, 1981), 128.

67 J. G. Ballard, "The Concentration City," in *The Best Short Stories of J. G. Ballard* (New York: Holt, Rinehart, and Winston, 1978), 1–20.

68 The former was originally scripted by John Wagner and was most effectively drawn by Brian Bolland and Mike McMahon. *Ranxerox* is by Tanino Liberatore (art) and Stefano Tamburini.

69 Moebius, "The Long Tomorrow," in *The Long Tomorrow and Other Science Fiction Stories,* ed. Jean-Marc Lofficier and Randy Lofficier (New York: Marvel Entertainment Group, 1987); Moebius, *The Incal,* ed. Jean-Marc Lofficier and Randy Lofficier (New York: Marvel Entertainment Group, 1988), 3 vols. Moebius has extensive connections to science fiction cinema: both works cited were produced in collaboration with filmmakers: the former with Dan O'Bannon, scripter of *Dark Star* (1974) and *Alien* (1979), and the latter with Alexander Jodorowsky. In addition, Moebius contributed costume designs to both *Alien, Tron,* and *The Abyss* (1990).

70 The series ends, six books later, with a repetition of the same image, constructing a temporal as well as a spatial looping.

71 Jameson, "Science Fiction as a Spatial Genre," 54.

72 Fredric Jameson, "Progress vs. Utopia; or, Can We Imagine the Future?" *Science Fiction Studies* 9, no. 2 (1982), 152.

73 "We thus need to explore the proposition that the distinctiveness of SF as a genre has less to do with time (history, past, future) than with space" (Jameson, "Science Fiction as a Spatial Genre," 58).

74 See, for example, Bruno, "Ramble City," and Sobchack, *Screening Space.*

75 James Verniere, "Blade Runner," *Twilight Zone Magazine* 2, no. 3 (1982).

76 Eric Alliez and Michael Feher, "Notes on the Sophisticated City," *ZONE* 1/2 (1984), 49. To my mind, the authors are less successful in adapting to *Blade Runner* Virilio's thesis regarding the usurpation of surveillance by simulation.

77 The work has been collected in Angus McKie, *So Beautiful and So Dangerous* (New York: Heavy Metal Communications, 1979). McKie also produced paintings for *Crystal Gazing,* a film by Peter Wollen and Laura Mulvey. McKie's striking book covers have been widely reprinted and are on display, along with work by Chris Foss and other contemporaries, in two fictional illustrated "histories" of the future: Stewart Cowley, *Spacecraft: 2000–2100 A.D.* (Seacaucus, N.J.: Chartwell Books, 1978), and Stewart Cowley and Charles Herridge, *Great Space Battles* (Seacaucus, N.J.: Chartwell Books, 1979). Further illustrations by Foss, who contributed spaceship designs to *Alien,* can be found in his own future "history": Chris Foss, *Diary of a Spaceperson* (Surrey, England: Paper Tiger, 1990).

78 Gert Elienberger, "Freedom, Science and Aesthetics," in *The Beauty of Fractals,* ed. Heinz-Otto Peitgen and Peter H. Richter (Heidelberg: Springer-Verlag, 1986), 179.

79 Gleick, 117.

80 Merleau-Ponty, "Eye and Mind," 186.

81 Gleick, 117.

82 Epstein, "Magnification."

83 *Blade Runner* was rereleased in 1992 in a "director's cut" that eliminated the irritating voiceover and thereby improved the film immensely. See Scott Bukatman, "Fractal Geographies," *Artforum International* 31:4 (December 1992): 6–7.

84 There is, in cyberpunk, no shortage of references to the artworks and primary figures of surrealism: in *Angel Station* by Walter Jon Williams, the main character is named Ubu Roy; Cornell boxes are prominent in Gibson's *Count Zero;* Burroughs is quoted in John Shirley's *Eclipse Corona;* in *Neuromancer,* Case stumbles upon Duchamp's "Bride Stripped Bare" glass; a chapter in Richard Kadrey's *Metrophage* is titled "The Exquisite Corpse"; a punk band plays an ode to "Guernica" in the same novel; and Ballard's fiction is, of course, rife with references to Ernst, Breton, and Dali. According to cyberpunk, it seems that a major surrealist revival can be expected in the early part of the twenty-first century. The significance of this return to surrealism will be examined in chapter 4.

85 *TRON* is discussed in chapter 3.

86 Michael Moorcock, ed., *New Worlds: An Anthology* (London: Flamingo Books, 1983), 16.

87 This account of allegory is elaborated in Walter Benjamin, *The Origin of German Tragic Drama,* trans. John Osborne (London: New Left Books, 1977).

88 Fred Pfeil, "These Disintegrations I'm Looking Forward To," in *Another Tale to Tell: Politics and Narrative in Postmodern Culture* (London: Verso, 1990), 85.

89 Pfeil, 86.

90 Pfeil, 84.

91 Christopher Johnston, "Remember Timothy Leary?," *Village Voice Fast Forward,* November 25, 1986, 11.

92 Rudy Rucker, "Report from Silicon Valley," *Science Fiction Eye* 1, no. 4 (1988), 23.

93 Jay Stevens, *Storming Heaven: LSD and the American Dream* (New York: Harper & Row, 1987), 29.

94 Norman Spinrad, "The Neuromantics," *Issac Asimov's Science Fiction Magazine,* May 1986, 184.

95 Bruce Sterling, "Preface," in *Mirrorshades: The Cyberpunk Anthology,* ed. Bruce Sterling (New York: Arbor House, 1986), viii–ix.

96 Larry McCaffery, "Cutting Up: Cyberpunk, Punk Music, and Urban Decontextualizations," *Storming the Reality Studio: A Casebook of Cyberpunk and Postmodern Fiction,* ed. Larry McCaffery (Durham, N.C.: Duke University Press, 1992), 288.

97 Sterling, "Preface," xi.

98 William Gibson, "The Gernsback Continuum," *Burning Chrome* (New York: Arbor House, 1986).

99 Science fiction often coexists with other genres: there are science fiction Westerns (*Outland, Andromeda Gun*), science fiction war stories (*The Empire Strikes Back, Starship Troopers*), science fiction fantasies (*Star Wars, Hiero's Journey*), and even science fiction pornography (*Flesh Gordon, Cafe Flesh,* John Norman's Gor novels). Obviously there is an extensive overlap between the genres of science fiction and horror (examined in chapter 4).

100 Roland Barthes, *S/Z,* trans. Richard Miller (New York: Hill and Wang, 1974) 75–76, 84–88.

101 Dennis Porter, *The Pursuit of Crime: Art and Ideology in Detective Fiction* (New Haven: Yale University Press, 1981), 24–52.

102 Brian Stableford and Peter Nicholls, "Crime and Punishment," in *The Science Fiction Encyclopedia,* ed. Peter Nicholls (Garden City, N.Y.: Doubleday, 1979), 144.

103 The *Encyclopedia* is also correct in pointing out that Issac Asimov was one of the few writers to *consistently* combine the forms of science fiction and the "classic" detective story, although one would certainly also cite Poe and Chesterton as important progenitors (of both genres).

104 Fredric Jameson, "On Chandler," in *The Poetics of Murder: Detective Fiction and Literary Theory,* ed. Glenn W. Most and William W. Stowe (New York: Harcourt Brace Jovanovich, 1983), 131.

105 Jameson, "Postmodernism," 89.

106 The surrealism of cyberpunk is explored in chapter 4.

107 Clute, "Introduction," viii.

108 See Csicsery-Ronay's "Cyberpunk and Neuromanticism," 184, for a hilarious template for a cyberpunk narrative.

109 Mike Davis, *City of Quartz* (New York: Vintage Books, 1991), 229. A similarly negative view of contemporary urbanism is found in Michael Sorkin's *Variations on a Theme Park.*

110 Ross contrasts the burnt-out future metropoles of cyberpunk (and its music video inheritors) with "the hip-hop aesthetic" of *real* urban residents who bring "color, style and movement . . . transforming bleak back-

drops by graffiti that speaks to the act of creative landscaping." Andrew Ross, "Cyberpunk in Boystown," in *Strange Weather: Culture, Science, and Technology in an Age of Limits* (London: Verso, 1991), 144. It has been a *long* time since hip-hop has been this thoroughly romanticized. It is as though Ross has never heard of gangster rap, which operates by a rather different set of aesthetic principles.

111 David Tomas, "Old Rituals for New Space: 'Rites of Passage' and William Gibson's Cultural Model of Cyberspace," *Cyberspace: First Steps,* ed. Michael Benedikt (Cambridge, Mass.: MIT Press, 1991), 33.

112 Allucquere Rosanne Stone, "Will the Real Body Please Stand Up? Boundary Stories About Virtual Cultures," *Cyberspace: First Steps,* ed. Michael Benedikt (Cambridge, Mass.: MIT Press, 1991), 95.

113 In conversation, January 30, 1991.

114 This last term is borrowed from the rock group, demonstrating Gibson's eclecticism.

115 Jameson, "Postmodernism," 84.

116 Michael Herr, *Dispatches* (New York: Avon Books, 1978), 8.

117 Jameson, "Postmodernism," 81.

118 Thomas Disch, "Lost in Cyberspace," *New York Times Book Review,* November 6, 1988.

NOTES 119 One also notes the echoes of Pynchon's opening sentence in *Gravity's Rainbow:* "A screaming comes across the sky." In both, nature is redefined by the presence of technology.

120 There is a similar scene in *20 Minutes into the Future* (see chapter 4).

121 Sobchack, *Screening Space,* 234.

122 Brand, 139. See also Howard Rheingold, *Virtual Reality* (New York: Summit Books, 1991) for a thorough overview of cyberspace's prehistory.

123 Bolter, 98.

124 Bolter, 93.

125 Merleau-Ponty, "Eye and Mind," 178.

126 William Gibson, *Mona Lisa Overdrive* (New York: Bantam Books, 1988), 13.

127 William Gibson, "Introduction," in *Neuromancer: The Graphic Novel,* ed. David M. Harris (New York: Epic Comics, 1989).

128 Scott Rockwell and Darryl Banks, *Cyberpunk* (Wheeling, W.V.: Innovative Corporation, 1989); Mike Saenz, *IRON MAN: CRASH* (New York: Marvel Entertainment Group, 1988); Pepe Moreno, *Batman: Digital Justice* (New York: DC Comics, 1990); Tom DeHaven and Bruce Jensen, *Neuromancer: The Graphic Novel* (New York: Epic Comics, 1989). In the *Neuromancer* adaptation, the cyberspace is a cool blue, peppered with the solid geometrical "clusters and constellations of data;" it is, ironically, also more solidly rendered, more photographic in its detail, than the overview of the BAMA urbanscape which looks like a production drawing from *Blade Runner* (Japan's *Akira* [Katsuhiro Otomo]—comic book and 1988 animated film—also depicts this vertically impacted, post-*Blade Runner* urbanism, but with a more hyperbolized hyperrealism).

129 Henri Lefebvre, *The Production of Space,* trans. Donald Nicholson-Smith (Oxford: Blackwell, 1991), 9. This paragraph has relied on 7–9.

130 Michael Benedikt, "Introduction," *Cyberspace: First Steps,* ed. Michael Benedikt (Cambridge, Mass.: MIT Press, 1991), 1.

131 Benedikt, 6. Allucquere Rosanne Stone and David Tomas also take anthropological approaches. See Stone, "Will the Real Body Please Stand Up? Boundary Stories About Virtual Cultures," *Cyberspace: First Steps,* ed. Michael Benedikt (Cambridge, Mass.: MIT Press, 1991), 81–118; and Tomas, "Old Rituals for New Space."

132 Merleau-Ponty, "Eye and Mind," 187.

133 Merleau-Ponty, "Eye and Mind," 187.

134 Samuel R. Delany, "Is Cyberpunk a Good Thing or a Bad Thing?" *Mississippi Review* 47/48 (1988): 31.

135 Alfred Bester, *The Stars My Destination,* 1953.

136 A term which describes not only the teleportation technique, but also Bester's hyperactive narrative structure and "jaunty" writing style.

137 Roger Zelazny, "He Who Shapes," in *The Best of the Nebulas,* ed. Ben Bova (New York: TOR Books, 1989).

138 Takayuki Tatsumi, "Some *Real* Mothers: An Interview with Samuel R. Delany," *Science Fiction Eye* 1, no. 3 (1988), 6.

139 Michelson, "Bodies in Space."

140 The film was produced by Albert Zugsmith, whose notorious predilection for arcana extended to Orson Welles's *Touch of Evil* (1958) and Douglas Sirk's *The Tarnished Angels* (1958).

141 In-class observation. This section owes a large debt to Michelson's course in science fiction cinema at New York University, which I attended in the summer of 1984.

142 Sobchack, *Screening Space,* 133–34.

143 Brian McHale, *Postmodernist Fiction* (New York: Methuen, 1987).

144 Robert Coover, "The Phantom of the Movie Palace," in *A Night at the Movies* (New York: Simon & Schuster, 1987), 22.

145 Note *Alphaville's* labyrinthine urban space, which is analogized to the world, the galaxy, the universe—also note the cybernetic core of this hyperbolic space.

146 In Porush's text, it is as though Burroughs, Vonnegut, and Pynchon produced texts in a high-art vacuum. Fortunately, Porush's recent writings indicate that this "ghettoization" of high-literary and genre texts has outlived its usefulness.

147 Samuel R. Delany and Howard Chaykin, *Empire* (New York: Berkeley/Windhover Books, 1978).

148 Darko Suvin, *Metamorphoses of Science Fiction: On the Poetics and History of a Literary Genre* (New Haven: Yale University Press, 1979).

149 McHale wants to separate Farmer from postmodernism, but I would hesitate. In Farmer's fiction, including the Riverworld series, historical and fictional characters interact. He also wrote a book as Kilgore Trout, previously the fictional alter ego of Kurt Vonnegut (as well as an homage to SF writer Theodore Sturgeon), and his Tarzan story as written by *William S.* as opposed to *Edgar Rice* Burroughs, "The Jungle Rot Kid On the Nod," should not be ignored. Farmer seems a knowing participant in the shifting textual ontologies of postmodernism.

150 He notes, for example, that Ballard's fiction retains the modernist paradigm in its evident dependence upon the perspective of a single, world-weary observer; a solitary chronicler of the end of the world (or the end of Empire, as Jameson observes ["Progress vs. Utopia," 152]). It is only with *The Atrocity Exhibition* that "Ballard finally frees his ontological projections from their epistemological constraints," replacing his allusions to the Conrad's modernism with an attention to the postmodernism of Roussel (69). Allegiances to both modernist and postmodernist paradigms similarly informs his reading of two Delany novels, *Dhalgren* and *Triton*.

151 Csicsery-Ronay, "Cyberpunks and Neuromanticism," 190 and 188.

152 Delany, "Some *Real* Mothers," 8.

153 Csicsery-Ronay, "Cyberpunk and Neuromanticism," 193; Jameson, *Postmodernism*, 1 and 419.

154 "Pynchon may even be partly responsible for what is arguably the most characteristic of all cyberpunk motifs, that of human-computer symbiosis, and the associated motif of the 'Electroworld' (Pynchon's term), the computer-generated world of Gibson's 'Matrix' trilogy and other cyberpunk texts." Brian McHale, "POSTcyberMODERNpunkISM," in *Storming the Reality Studio: A Casebook of Cyberpunk and Postmodern Science Fiction*, ed. Larry McCaffery (Durham, N.C.: Duke University Press, 1992), 316.

155 Brian McHale, "Elements of a Poetics of Cyberpunk," *Critique* 33, no. 3 (1992), 149.

156 McHale, "Elements of a Poetics of Cyberpunk," 158.

157 William Gibson, "Academy Leader," in *Cyberspace: First Steps*, ed. Michael Benedikt (Cambridge, Mass.: MIT Press, 1991), 27.

158 Veronica Hollinger, "Cybernetic Deconstructions: Cyberpunk and Postmodernism," in *Storming the Reality Studio: A Casebook of Cyberpunk and Postmodern Science Fiction*, ed. Larry McCaffery (Durham, N.C.: Duke University Press, 1992), 204.

159 While the Sharpe and Wallock essay predates Jameson's more complete elaboration of postmodernism in the *New Left Review*, it postdates his contribution to *The Anti-Aesthetic*.

160 Brian Aldiss and David Wingrove, *Trillion Year Spree: The History of Science Fiction* (New York: Atheneum, 1986), 303.

161 Delany, "Some *Real* Mothers," 7.

162 Ivan Chtcheglov, "Formulary for a New Urbanism," in *Situationist International Anthology*, trans. and ed. Ken Knabb (Berkeley, Calif.: Bureau of Public Secrets, 1981), 4.

163 Jonathan Raban, *Soft City* (1974). Cited in Jon Savage, *England's Dreaming: Anarchy, Sex Pistols, Punk Rock, and Beyond* (New York: St. Martin's Press, 1992), 3.

164 John Clute, "The Repossession of Jerry Cornelius," in *The Cornelius Chronicles* (New York: Avon, 1977), ix. Moorcock's *Mother London* completes his underlying trajectory by centering the city as protagonist and mythic object.

165 Gilbert Hernandez, Mario Hernandez, Jaime Hernandez, and Dean Motter, *The Return of Mr. X* (E. Fullerton, Calif.: Graphitti Designs, 1986). While the comic never quite maintained its quality once the Hernandez brothers

moved on to other projects, an adaptation of a *Mr. X* comic appeared on a
CD-ROM disk with animation, sound effects, and music, and there are plans
to produce original stories on disk. Needless to say, *Mr. X* is well-suited to
this multimedia approach (Carl Liberman, Darryl Gold, and Diana Schein,
"The Mr. X CD-ROM," Media Collision, 1991).

166 Wilson et al., *The Machine Age,* 24.

167 William Gibson, *Count Zero* (London: Victor Gollancz, 1986).

168 Gibson, *Mona Lisa Overdrive,* 238.

169 Jameson, "Postmodernism," 84.

170 A more detailed and dialectical analysis of the relation between quantum
mechanics and literary structure is presented in the work of N. Katherine
Hayles. See *The Cosmic Web: Scientific Field Models and Literary Strategies in
the Twentieth Century* (Ithaca, N.Y.: Cornell University Press, 1984) and
Chaos Bound: Orderly Disorder in Contemporary Literature and Science (Ithaca, N.Y.: Cornell University Press, 1990).

171 Donald Hofstadter, *Gödel, Escher, Bach: An Eternal Golden Braid* (New York:
Basic Books, 1979); Stephen W. Hawking, *A Brief History of Time: From the
Big Bang to Black Holes* (New York: Bantam Books, 1988); Fred Alan Wolf,
Taking the Quantum Leap: The New Physics for Non-Scientists (New York:
Harper & Row, 1989); Charles C. Mann and Edward Zuckerman, "For Start-
ers: We'd Kill Hitler, Buy Xerox at $8^{1/2}$ and Save the Dinosaurs," *SPY,* August
1989. One of the most engaging of this wave of books is Timothy Ferris,
Coming of Age in the Milky Way (New York: Doubleday, 1988).

172 Wolf, 127.

173 Barry N. Malzberg, *Galaxies* (New York: Pyramid Books, 1975).

174 Paul deMan, "The Rhetoric of Temporality," in *Blindness and Insight: Essays
in the Rhetoric of Contemporary Criticism* (Minneapolis: University of Minnesota Press, 1983), 206–7.

175 Samuel R. Delany, *Starboard Wine: More Notes on the Language of Science
Fiction* (Elizabethtown, N.J.: Dragon Press, 1984), 87–88.

176 Delany, "Some *Real* Mothers," 8.

177 deMan, *Allegories of Reading,* 10.

178 Merleau-Ponty, *Phenomenology of Perception,* 229.

179 This languor is somewhat characteristic of Kubrick's other work, especially *Barry Lyndon* (1975), but it is also very typical of the special effects
work of Douglas Trumbull. In *2001, Close Encounters, Star Trek: The Motion
Picture* (1979), and *Blade Runner,* the camera lingers upon the spectacle in a
profoundly contemplative manner.

180 *2001* is actually axiomatic of several tropes considered in this chapter. The
monolith surely qualifies as one of Smithson's "new monuments," its form
as inert and as inertial as any computer terminal (the NEXT computer,
designed by Steve Jobs, is monolith-black). The monolith also leads into
the paraspace where change and evolution occur.

181 Michelson, "Bodies in Space," 61.

182 A similar fetishization of technology is found in Disney's *Pinocchio* (1940): a
devoted craftsman wishes his creation could be "real." That the agent of
the transformation is a hyperreal, Rotoscoped fairy is further evidence of
an auto-referential, wish-fulfillment impulse.

183 Norman Spinrad, *The Void Captain's Tale* (New York: Pocket Books, 1983), 30.

184 McHale, "Elements of a Poetics of Cyberpunk," 157.

185 Baudrillard, "Ecstasy," 128.

186 Jean Baudrillard, "The Year 2000 Has Already Happened," in *Body Invaders: Panic Sex in America,* trans. Nai-fei Ding and Kuan-Hsing Chen, ed. Arthur Kroker and Marilouise Kroker (New York: St. Martin's Press, 1987), 36–37.

187 Baudrillard, "Ecstasy," 98–99.

188 The supersession of reality by fiction is, if not a master-narrative, at least a powerfully informing postmodern myth: "We live inside an enormous novel," Ballard notes.

3 Terminal Penetration

1 James D. Foley, "Interfaces for Advanced Computing," *Scientific American,* October 1987, 129.

2 A version of the Dataglove was marketed in 1989 as part of the Nintendo game system.

3 Foley, 127.

4 Comments by Minsky, Leary, and the nameless developer, as well as information on the Eyephones, are from a news report on National Public Radio's "All Things Considered," August 8, 1989. "What world am I in?" the reporter asks his guide through virtual space.

5 Scott S. Fisher, "Virtual Interface Environments," in *The Art of Human Computer Interface Design,* ed. Brenda Laurel (Cupertino, Calif.: Apple Computer, 1990), 433–38.

6 Myron Krueger, "Videoplace and the Interface of the Future," in *The Art of Human Computer Interface Design,* ed. Brenda Laurel (Cupertino, Calif.: Apple Computer, 1990), 421.

7 Rheingold, *Virtual Reality* (New York: Summit Books, 1991). Lanier observed in an interview that VR achieves "a plateau of completion of media technology" (Timothy Druckrey, "Revenge of the Nerds: An Interview with Jaron Lanier," *Afterimage,* May 1991, 6).

8 Howard Rheingold, "What's the Big Deal About Cyberspace?" in *The Art of Human Computer Interface Design,* ed. Brenda Laurel (Cupertino, Calif.: Apple Computer, 1990), 450. On the synonymity between *virtual reality* and *cyperspace,* John Walker of Autodesk (a manufacturer of one VR system) writes, "I define a cyberspace system as one that provides users with a three-dimensional interaction experience that includes the illusion they are inside a world rather than observing an image" (John Walker, "Through the Looking Glass," in *The Art of Human-Computer Interface Design,* 444).

9 Michael Heim, "The Erotic Ontology of Cyberspace," in *Cyberspace: First Steps,* ed. Michael Benedikt (Cambridge, Mass.: MIT Press, 1991), 59.

10 Jonathan Crary, *Techniques of the Observer: On Vision and Modernity in the Nineteenth Century* (Cambridge, Mass.: MIT Press, 1990), 31.

11 Michael Benedikt, "Introduction," *Cyberspace: First Steps,* ed. Michael Benedikt (Cambridge, Mass.: MIT Press, 1991), 11.

12 Vivian Sobchack, "New Age Mutant Ninja Hackers," *Artforum International,* April 1991, 25.

13 Timothy Leary, in *The Art of Human-Computer Interface Design,* ed. Brenda Laurel (Cupertino, Calif.: Apple Computer, 1990), 233.

14 Leary, 232—"*man*" added for emphasis.

15 Rheingold, "What's the Big Deal About Cyberspace?" 449.

16 Brenda Laurel, "Art and Activism in VR," *VERBUM,* Fall/Winter 1991, 14–17. Laurel is one of the more intelligent people writing about computer interfaces, but this piece is very problematic.

17 Nicole Stenger, "Mind is a Leaking Rainbow," *Cyberspace: First Steps,* ed. Michael Benedikt (Cambridge, Mass.: MIT Press, 1990), 53. This is a common cyberdrool trope.

18 Sobchack, "New Age Mutant Ninja Hackers," 26; Don Ihde, *Technology and the Lifeworld: From Garden to Earth,* Indiana Series in the Philosophy of Technology, ed. Don Ihde (Bloomington and Indianapolis: Indiana University Press, 1990), 75.

19 On McLuhan, see chapter 1.

20 André Bazin, "The Myth of Total Cinema," in *What is Cinema?* trans. and ed. Hugh Gray (Berkeley: University of California Press, 1967), 20 and 21.

21 Friedhoff and Berzon, 194.

22 Rheingold, *Virtual Reality,* 70.

23 Karrie Jacobs, "Design for the Unreal World," *Metropolis* 10, no. 2 (1990), 69.

24 Pynchon, 815.

25 Pynchon, 648.

26 Benedikt, "Introduction," 1.

27 Neal Stephenson, *Snow Crash* (New York: Bantam Books, 1992), 25.

28 Stephenson, 38–39.

29 The film also provides some digitized footage to indicate the android gunfighter's point of view, further anticipating *The Terminator* (1984) and *Robocop* (1987).

30 Ballard, "Introduction to *Crash,*" 98; Baudrillard, *Simulations,* 25.

31 This is different from, for example, models of narrative objectivity such as those found in Isherwood or Robbe-Grillet. In cybernetic fiction the text becomes a metaphorical machine that produces itself, rather than a text that operates as a representation of some exteriority.

32 Porush, x.

33 Virtual reality researchers are thinking in very similar terms to these. Howard Rheingold's report on his first experience with a Dataglove highlights the issues that have shaped the development of the technology: "the act of moving my hand in the glove and watching [a] representation of my hand and fingers move in cyberspace were like hooks, handles—*affordances*—that linked "in here" to "out there" and dragged my sense of being in a physical space from the physical room that held my body to the space defined by the 3D computer model. The hand that floated in the virtual world was more than a hand. It was me" (*Virtual Reality,* 146).

34 Shirley, *Eclipse Corona,* 33.

35 Steven Levy, *Hackers: Heroes of the Computer Revolution* (New York: Dell Books, 1984), 304.

36 Theodor Holm Nelson, "The Right Way to Think About Software Design," in *The Art of Human-Computer Interface Design,* ed. Brenda Laurel (Cupertino, Calif.: Apple Computer, 1990), 235.

37 Rheingold, *Virtual Reality,* 23.

38 See his *Mindstorms: Children, Computers and Powerful Ideas* (New York: Basic Books, 1980).

39 Johan Huizinga, *Homo Ludens* (London: Temple Smith, 1970), 31.

40 Robyn Miller and Rand Miller, *Cosmic Osmo* (Menlo Park, Calif.: Activision, 1989). Software.

41 Frank Rose, *West of Eden: The End of Innocence at Apple Computer* (New York: Viking, 1989), 128.

42 Toffler, *The Third Wave,* 186.

43 In Toffler's case the procapitalist slant is equally evident—he is a favorite lecturer at Silicon Valley corporations. Interestingly, his work is an invaluable reference for the cyberpunks.

44 More recent advertising revealed Apple's desire to win a share of IBM's business market.

45 Rheingold, *Virtual Reality,* 134–37.

46 John Clute, "Introduction," in *Interzone: The Second Anthology,* viii.

47 Vernor Vinge, "True Names," *True Names and Other Dangers* (New York: Baen Books, 1987).

48 Norman Spinrad, "Science Fiction vs. Sci-Fi," *Issac Asimov's Science Fiction Magazine,* mid-December 1986, 184.

49 In recognition of the conceptual richness of "True Names," Vinge's picture appears on the currency in Habitat, Lucasfilm's cyberspace community (see Chip Morningstar and F. Randall Farmer, "The Lessons of Lucasfilm's Habitat," in *Cyberspace: First Steps,* ed. Michael Benedikt [Cambridge, Mass.: MIT Press, 1991], 273–301). (Shades of *UBIK!*)

50 It is worth comparing this to the hero's first fix in Nelson Algren's *Man With the Golden Arm* (1949): "It hit all right. It hit the heart like a runaway locomotive, it hit like a falling wall. Frankie's whole body lifted with that smashing surge, the very heart seemed to lift up-up-up—then rolled over and he slipped into a long warm bath with one long orgasmic sigh of relief."

51 Gibson, "Introduction" to *Neuromancer: The Graphic Novel.*

52 Merleau-Ponty, *Phenomenology of Perception,* 132.

53 Merleau-Ponty, *Phenomenology of Perception,* 142.

54 Merleau-Ponty, *Phenomenology of Perception,* 133.

55 Sigmund Freud, "Animism, Magic, and the Omnipotence of Thoughts," in *Totem and Taboo,* trans. James Strachey (New York: W. W. Norton, 1950), 85.

56 Freud, 88.

57 Claudia Springer, "The Pleasure of the Interface," *Screen* 32, no. 3 (1991), 306.

58 The "armoring" of the body as a substitute for a nonemergent or damaged ego will be discussed in chapter 5.

59 Michel de Certeau, *The Practice of Everyday Life,* trans. Steven Rendall (Berkeley, Calif.: University of California Press, 1984), xxiii. My emphasis.

60 DeHaven and Jensen, *Neuromancer: The Graphic Novel.*

61 Gibson, *Count Zero,* 91.

62 Gibson, *Count Zero,* 133.

63 Gibson, *Count Zero,* 191.

64 Jameson, "Postmodernism," 79.

65 Syd Mead, *OBLAGON: Concepts of Syd Mead.*

66 Christopher Finch, *Special Effects: Creating Movie Magic* (New York: Abbeville Press, 1984), 226.

67 David Bordwell and Kristen Thompson, *Film Art: An Introduction,* 2d ed. (New York: Alfred A. Knopf, 1986), 175.

68 Hugo Münsterberg, *The Film: A Psychological Study* (New York: Dover Publications, 1970). Originally published in 1916.

69 Annette Michelson, "Dr. Crase and Mr. Clair," *OCTOBER* 11 (1979), 39.

70 Annette Michelson, "Camera Lucida, Camera Obscura," *Artforum* (1973), 32.

71 Michelson, "Bodies in Space."

72 Christian Metz, *The Imaginary Signifier: Psychoanalysis and the Cinema,* trans. Celia Britton et al. (Bloomington, Ind.: Indiana University Press, 1977), 49–51.

73 Rosalind Krauss, "Grids," *The Originality of the Avant-Garde and other Modernist Myths* (Cambridge, Mass.: MIT Press, 1986), 10–11.

74 Rosalind Krauss, "The Double Negative: A New Syntax for Sculpture," in *Passages in Modern Sculpture* (Cambridge, Mass.: MIT Press, 1977), 266 and 270.

75 As in *The Wizard of Oz,* Flynn encounters his real-world friends in cybernetic forms.

76 Sobchack, "The Scene of the Screen," 57.

77 Sobchack, *Screening Space,* 257.

78 It should be noted that the narrative, in terms of audience engagement, is so slight that its subversion is a moot point. The script (replete with such lines as, "Forget it, Mr. High-and-Mighty Master Control! You're not making me talk!") and incompetent pacing and character direction are undoubtedly responsible for the film's rapid box-office demise, rather than the "alienating effects" of its electronic effects. For the purposes of analysis, however, such flaws provide useful grist for the mill and are much in keeping with the notion of a "failure" of the human within the context of a newly, and increasingly, cyberneticized existence.

79 P. Adams Sitney, *Visionary Film: The American Avant-Garde 1943–1978,* 2d ed. (New York: Oxford University Press, 1979), 383–84.

80 Sobchack, *Screening Space,* 256.

81 Jameson, "Postmodernism," 61–64; Sobchack, "The Scene of the Screen," 56. Sobchack's discussion of *TRON* and the transition from the depth of cinematic space to the surfaces of electronically generated imagery is very perceptive. She, too, notes the conflict between these new, radically mutable spatialities and the "nostalgic humanism of the narratives in which they appear" (*Screening Space,* 261).

82 Krauss, "The Double Negative," 279.

83 Jameson, "Postmodernism," 83.

84 In *TRON* and *The Last Starfighter,* space is used reflexively. The latter film presents an Earth boy video-game whiz kid whose prowess enables him to

save the universe from evil aliens (ethno- and anthropocentrism reaching new heights). The outer space sequences were computer generated and so terminal and physical realities are, in fact, made identical. The film becomes more than an apologia for video games, it becomes a justification for its own disembodied spatiality. Terminal space *is* real space, the film tells the viewer (but our kids can handle it).

85 H. Bruce Franklin, "America as Science Fiction: 1939," *Science Fiction Studies* 9, no. 1 (1982), 46.

86 Jameson, "Progress vs. Utopia," 149.

87 Clute, "Introduction," viii.

88 Thanks to Vivian Sobchack for these suggestions.

89 Rouse cited in Richard Schickel, *The Disney Version,* rev. ed. (New York: Simon & Schuster, 1985), 23; Michael Sorkin, "See You in Disneyland," in *Variations on a Theme Park: The New American City and the End of Public Space,* ed. Michael Sorkin (New York: Noonday Press, 1992), 227; Margaret King, "Disneyland and Walt Disney World: Traditional Values in Futuristic Form," *Journal of Popular Culture* 15, no. 1 (1981), 127.

90 Guy Debord, "Report on the Construction of Situations and on the International Situationist Tendency's Conditions of Organization and Action," in *Situationist International Anthology,* trans. and ed. Ken Knabb (Berkeley, Calif.: Bureau of Public Secrets, 1981), 23.

91 Thanks to Caitlin Kelch for the Disneyland::brain analogy.

92 Debord, "Report on the Construction of Situations," 24. My emphasis.

93 Randy Bright, *Disneyland: Inside Story* (New York: Harry N. Abrams, 1987), 88.

94 William Kowinski, *The Malling of America* (New York: William Morrow, 1985), 71.

95 Kroker et al., *Panic Encyclopedia,* 208.

96 Kowinski, 67.

97 Schickel, 313.

98 William Irwin Thompson, "Looking for History in L.A.," in *At the Edge of History* (New York: Harper & Row, 1971), 21 and 18.

99 Hine, *Populuxe,* 8.

100 This perfect coinage belongs to Michael Sorkin. See his *Variations on a Theme Park.*

101 William Gibson, "The Gernsback Continuum," in *Burning Chrome* (New York: Arbor House, 1986), 37–38.

102 Sterling, "Preface," xi.

103 Norman Spinrad, "The Neuromantics," *Issac Asimov's Science Fiction Magazine,* May 1986, 186.

104 Brooks Landon, "Bet On It: Cyber/video/punk/performance" in McCaffery, ed., *Storming the Reality Studio,* 239.

105 Hine, *Populuxe,* 151.

106 King, 127.

107 King, 120.

108 Raymond Fielding, "Hale's Tours: Ultrarealism in the Pre-1910 Motion Picture," in *Film Before Griffith,* ed. John Fell (Berkeley, Calif.: University of California Press, 1983), 116.

109 Sorkin, 210.

110 Sorkin, 232.

111 Of course, one is inevitably reminded of the computerized theme park in *Westworld,* where "*nothing can go wrong . . . go wrong . . . go wrong. . . .*"

112 "Max" is a prevalent postmodern name with overtones of maximum energy: Max Headroom, Mad Max, *Videodrome's* Max Renn.

113 Bright, 56. All of these tendencies are exaggerated at Walt Disney World, whose acreage is twice that of Manhattan. The Magic Kingdom and Epcot Center are now supplemented by Typhoon Lagoon (water theme park), Pleasure Island (discos and other "entertainment), Fort Wilderness Campground, the Disney/MGM Studio Theme Park, numerous hotels, and a convention center. It is no longer possible to "do" the entire facility in a week-long vacation, although many families frantically try. In the "panic" terminology of Arthur Kroker ("Between ecstasy and fear, between delirium and anxiety" [*Panic Encyclopedia,* 16]), Disney World has become a "panic vacation."

114 Richard V. Francaviglia, "Main Street USA: A Comparison/Contrast of Streetscapes in Disneyland and Walt Disney World." *Journal of Popular Culture* 15, no. 1 (1981), 156.

115 The movement through a tube of swirling cybernetic imagery is somewhat similar to the opening images of Dante's *Explorers* and could be considered emblematic of computerized special effects.

116 Tom Gunning, "An Unseen Energy Swallows Space: The Space in Early Film and Its Relation to American Avant-Garde Film," in *Film Before Griffith,* ed. John Fell (Berkeley, Calif.: University of California Press, 1983), 363.

117 Lynne Kirby, "Male Hysteria and Early Cinema," *Camera Obscura* 17 (1989).

118 Benjamin, "The Work of Art in the Age of Mechanical Reproduction," cited in Kirby, 121.

119 Just as in Hale's Tours, a catharsis of technological breakdown is humorously, kinetically, enacted in the most popular ride these days, Star Tours (designed by George Lucas and company), in which your robot pilot malfunctions and sends you careening through space.

120 Unlike science fiction, however, Disney World's operations emphasize a process of familiarization. As I hope to have demonstrated by now, science fiction emphasizes a linguistic *de*familiarization, although this is frequently recuperated as the narrative proceeds.

121 I am not, however, arguing that this phenomenological function is the *only* purpose of narrative, nor even that it is the *primary* purpose. That narrative, and especially cinematic narrative, possesses a phenomenological component, however, seems beyond dispute, and it is to this component of narrative that I refer.

4 Terminal Flesh

1 Bruce Sterling, *Schismatrix* (New York: Ace Science Fiction, 1985), 179.

2 Bernard Wolfe, *Limbo* (New York: Carroll & Graf, 1987), 131.

3 Rudy Rucker, *Software* (New York: Avon Books, 1982), 127.

4 Gregory Benford, "Is Something Going On?" *Mississippi Review* 16, nos. 2/3 (1988), 20.

5 Jean Baudrillard, "On Seduction," in *Jean Baudrillard: Selected Writings,* ed. Mark Poster (Stanford, Calif.: Stanford University Press, 1988).

6 Mark Poster, "Introduction," in *Jean Baudrillard: Selected Writings,* ed. Mark Poster (Stanford, Calif.: University of Stanford Press, 1988), 5.

7 Baudrillard, *The Ecstasy of Communication,* 32.

8 Baudrillard, *The Ecstasy of Communication,* 53.

9 Arthur Kroker and Marilouise Kroker, "Theses on the Disappearing Body in the Hyper-Modern Condition," in *Body Invaders: Panic Sex in America,* ed. Arthur Kroker and Marilouise Kroker (New York: St. Martin's Press, 1987), 22.

10 Jean Baudrillard, *Forget Foucault, Foreign Agents Series,* ed. Jim Fleming and Sylvere Lotringer (New York: Semiotext[e], 1987), 11.

11 Kroker and Kroker, 21.

12 The work was filmed—execrably—as *Total Recall,* but the story sustains the recursivity of embedded remembrances. The film fails to raise ontological considerations, due largely to the massive and unquestionable presence of Arnold Schwarzenegger in the lead. It simply doesn't matter *who* Arnold is, because he's always-already Arnold.

13 Bruno, 190–94.

14 Norman Spinrad, "The Transmogrification of Philip K. Dick," in *Science Fiction in the Real World* (Carbondale, Ill.: Southern Illinois University Press, 1990), 89.

15 John Varley, "The Phantom of Kansas," in *The Persistence of Vision* (New York: Dell Publishing, 1978), 8.

16 Varley, "The Phantom of Kansas," 8.

17 John Varley, "Overdrawn at the Memory Bank," in *The Persistence of Vision* (New York: Dell Publishing, 1978), 240.

18 Merleau-Ponty, *Phenomenology of Perception,* 147.

19 Jon Savage, "Introduction to the *Industrial Culture Handbook,*" *Re/Search* 6/7 (1983), 4. This paragraph is entirely indebted to Savage's work.

20 Mark Dery, "Kraftwerk Redux: House Music Goes Robo-Rock," *New York Times,* June 16, 1991, 30.

21 In *Cyberpunk,* a book about outlaw computer hackers, the authors describe the West German hacker Pengo as huddled over his computer terminal. They clearly attach some insidious significance to his music of choice: "His headphones affixed to his ears, Pengo tapped the keyboard to the strains of Kraftwerk, the West German synthesizer band that sang paeans to pocket calculators and home computers in the monotone of automatons [sic]. He would listen to one album for weeks, until he couldn't stand it any longer" (Katie Hafner and John Markoff, *Cyberpunk: Outlaws and Hackers on the Computer Frontier* [New York: Simon & Schuster, 1991], 155–56).

22 Pfeil, 88. As with punk itself, however, what was radical was quickly assimilated into the mainstream, as "pop" industrial groups like The Art of Noise demonstrated. Further, the rise of sampled sounds and scratching (transforming a record on a turntable, a technology of reproduction, into a musical instrument, a technology of production) emerged in the complex

amalgams that characterized African-American hip-hop throughout the 1980s and into the 1990s.

23 See, for example, Jeff Greenfield's perceptive (and proto-Baudrillardian) analysis of campaign coverage on *Nightline* on the evening following the election, in which the manipulation of the American flag was discussed. Although the press recognized their own manipulation in permitting the "photo opportunities" of flag factories and flag waving to dominate their coverage, the candidates were still permitted to set the agenda for their own press coverage.

24 Michael Oreskes, "America's Politics Loses Way As Its Vision Changes World," *New York Times,* March 18, 1990, 22.

25 Miller, "Virtù Inc.," 87 and 88. The *New York Times* reports that "The disconnection of the public can be seen as well, over the last three decades, in sharp declines in the sort of organizations that used to serve as intermediaries between the public and government—political parties, churches, labor unions—as well as in only in [sic] voting." The report goes on to cite the attitude of Twila Martinez, who regards politics as separate from her life: "It seems like another world to me" (Oreskes, 22).

26 Robinson, 67.

27 Thomas Disch, "In the Mold of 1964: An Afterword," in *The Penultimate Truth* (New York: Bluejay Books, 1984).

28 Miller, "Virtù Inc.," 86.

29 Mark Crispin Miller, "Hollywood: The Ad," *Atlantic,* April 1990, 64.

30 Jane Feuer, "The Concept of Live TV," in *Regarding Television—Critical Approaches: An Anthology,* ed. E. Ann Kaplan (Frederick, Md.: University Publications of America, 1983).

31 Chaykin was hired to do design work for film, but the association did not come to fruition. Still, the film owes much to comics—not only to *American Flagg!,* but to Britain's *Judge Dredd* series as well. Frank Miller, who wrote and drew some of the most influential comics of the 1970s and 1980s, including *Batman: The Dark Knight Returns,* scripted *Robocop II* (1990). See chapter 5 for more on Miller.

32 Todd Gitlin, "We Build Excitement," in *Watching Television,* ed. Todd Gitlin (New York: Pantheon Books, 1986).

33 Pat Cadigan, "Pretty Boy Crossover," in *The Year's Best Science Fiction: Fourth Annual Collection,* ed. Gardner Dozois (New York: St. Martin's Press, 1987).

34 How appropriate that Max should have made his American debut in a series of commercials (directed by Ridley Scott) pitching "the real thing," Coca-cola™.

35 For a more sustained revision of the cyborg mythos, see Donna Haraway, "A Cyborg Manifesto: Science, Technology and Socialist-Feminism in the 1980s," in *Simians, Cyborgs, and Women* (New York: Routledge, 1989)— discussed in chapter 5.

36 Mention should be made of John Sladek's interesting new-wave science fiction novel, *The Müller-Fokker Effect.* In this Pynchonesque work from 1970, writer Bob Shairp is translated into data and stored on computer

tapes. He retains a subjectivity, but one represented through both flow-charts and heavily punning stream-of-consciousness prose.

37 Even the industrial robot performance art of Mark Pauline's Survival Research Laboratories made use of what its creators called "genuine components"—meat, that is; the reanimated carcasses that adorned their machinery (see "Boys' Toys from Hell" for more on SRL).

38 Some further implications of this reactionary background are traced in "Panic Subjects." It should also be noted that the "domestication" of Max Headroom reached disturbing proportions on the American television series, which privileged the power and autonomy of Edison Carter at every opportunity. Max was frequently reduced to wry commentary on human foibles, much like the basset hound Cleo on the old sitcom *The People's Choice.*

39 Miller, "Virtù, Inc.," 81.

40 In the course of his administration, Reagan appeared to many a media commentator as similar to that other simulacrum—a Max Headroom without irony. The *Village Voice* ran side-by-side pictures of Reagan and Headroom above a caption that read, "Two electronic performers." The cartoonist Garry Trudeau made the most sustained comparison in a series of Doonesbury strips that caricatured the president as "Ron Headrest," a computer-generated president who was nothing more than his own scan-lined image; an object rather than a subject: "I c-c-combine the breezy irreverence of yesteryear with the high-tech hipness of today!" Many of these cartoons are collected in G. B. Trudeau, *Talkin' About My G-G-Generation* (New York: Henry Holt, 1987).

41 Merleau-Ponty, *Phenomenology of Perception,* 106.

42 John Shirley, "Stelarc and the New Reality," *Science Fiction Eye* 1, no. 2 (1987), 59.

43 Kroker and Kroker, 25.

44 Shirley, "Stelarc and the New Reality," 59. Shirley was directed toward Stelarc by people who found his work reminiscent of the "wire dancers" in his novel *Eclipse.* He astutely notes the "conceptual synchronicity" that cut across media boundaries in the 1980s, "in *Neuromancer,* in *Schismatrix,* in *Eclipse,* in Laurie Anderson and other performance artists, which would seem to indicate a kind of 'steam engine time,' for the recognition of the new, hyper-intimate and all-encompassing phase of man's interaction with technology."

45 Ian Watson, "Introduction to 'Vile Dry Claws of the Toucan," *SEMIO-TEXT(E) SF,* ed. Rudy Rucker et al. (New York: Semiotext[e], 1989), 170.

46 Authors Stephen King and Clive Barker have each directed films; Barker, Jeter, and Nancy Collins are extensively involved in comics production and illustration; Neil Gaiman writes comics and novels; and Cronenberg has appeared as an actor in Barker's films.

47 Thanks to Richard Allen for this proposal.

48 William Gibson was also struck by the film's design: "I thought there were germs of stories implicit in the art direction. I always wanted to know more about these guys. Why were they wearing dirty sneakers in this funky

spaceship? I think it influenced my prose SF writing because it was the first funked-up, dirty kitchen-sink space ship and it made a big impression on me." Sheldon Teitelbaum, "William Gibson's *Neuroaliens*" *CINEFANTAS-TIQUE* 22, no. 6 (1922), 12.

49 Vivian Sobchack, "The Virginity of Astronauts: Sex and the Science Fiction Film," in *Alien Zone: Cultural Theory and Contemporary Science Fiction Cinema,* ed. Annette Kuhn (London: Verso, 1990), 103 and 108. Klaus Theweleit describes an eerily similar mode operating in writings by *Freikorps*-men, as women are again banished: "It is men who procreate. . . . Men create the future." Klaus Theweleit, *Male Fantasies,* trans. S. Conway, E. Carter, and C. Turner (Minneapolis: University of Minnesota Press, 1978), vol. 2, 88.

50 Of course, in linking the irrational with the position of the feminine, I am describing a dominant *construction* of femininity which seems to operate beneath these films.

51 Barbara Creed, "Gynesis, Postmodernism, and the Science Fiction Horror Film," in *Alien Zone: Cultural Theory and Contemporary Science Fiction Cinema,* ed. Annette Kuhn (New York: Verso, 1990), 215.

52 Sobchack, "The Virginity of Astronauts," 110.

53 Creed, "Gynesis, Postmodernism, and the Science Fiction Horror Film," 216.

54 Noël Carroll, *The Philosophy of Horror, or Paradoxes of the Heart* (New York: Routledge, 1990), 31–32.

55 Judith Newton, "Feminism and Anxiety in *Alien,*" in *Alien Zone: Cultural Theory and Contemporary Science Fiction Cinema,* ed. Annette Kuhn (London: Verso, 1990), 83.

56 Andrew Haase, "Body Shops: The Death of Georges Bataille," in *Body Invaders: Panic Sex in America,* ed. Arthur Kroker and Marilouise Kroker (New York: St. Martin's Press, 1987), 140.

57 Manohla Dargis, "Is This the End?" *Village Voice Film Special,* June 2, 1992, 16.

58 Michael Crichton's mass-market bestseller *The Terminal Man,* for all its hard-science trappings, is obviously reminiscent not only of *Frankenstein* (horror or science fiction?) but also of *Psycho* (Hitchcock, 1960): the psychotic's home is distinguished by its notably anachronistic decor, the dénouement occurs in a basement, and, most evidently, the narrative is predicated upon a "split" personality (here split between brain and computer functions).

59 Greg Bear, "Blood Music," in *Tangents* (New York: Warner Books, 1989); Greg Bear, *Blood Music* (New York: Ace Books, 1985).

60 John Elkington, *The Gene Factory: Inside the Science and Business of Biotechnology* (New York: Carroll & Graf, 1985), 214. The biochip industry regards genes and computer programs as theoretically identical: both represent encoded information. "One biochip pioneer, Dr. James McAlear of the US firm Gentronix, has suggested that a biochip could be a microprocessor constructed from organic molecules, like the human brain itself." Elkington continues: "He has argued that such molecular computers 'open up the possibility of three-dimensional circuits, increased speeds, reach a million billion elements per cubic centimetre. On this scale, all the

memory elements of every computer manufactured to this day could be contained in a cube one centimetre on a side' " (214).

61 Bear, "Blood Music," 13. Most references will be from the novel, but the original novella contains some significant language that was not always retained in the expanded version.

62 The link between these "inhuman" creatures and the American perception of Communists has, of course, been thoroughly analyzed.

63 Shirley, *Eclipse Corona,* 31.

64 Rucker, *Software,* 112.

65 Rudy Rucker, *Wetware* (New York: Avon Books, 1988), 41.

66 Rucker, *Wetware,* 73.

67 Vinge, "True Names," 144.

68 Bear, "Blood Music," 40.

69 In *Hyperion,* Simmons refers to "the quasi-perceptual Gibsonian matrix" and "cyberpuke" (Dan Simmons, *Hyperion* [New York: Doubleday, 1989], 382 and 340).

70 The stories have been collected, along with other short fiction, in Bruce Sterling, *Crystal Express* (New York: Ace Books, 1990).

71 Sterling has said, in an interview: "The thing I really wanted to do with *Schismatrix* is distill the weak beer of conventional space opera into a sort of whiskey. I've heard critics compare *Schismatrix* to hardcore punk, in the sense that it's something really loud and fast, and more intense. . . . *Schismatrix* is a definitive cyberpunk book, probably the most cyberpunk book I will ever write. It's in some sense, a literary experiment." Bruce Sterling, "An Interview with Bruce Sterling by Takayuki Tatsumi," *Science Fiction Eye* 1, no. 1 (1987), 36.

72 See Delany, *Starboard Wine,* 46–54.

73 Tom Maddox, "The Wars of the Coin's Two Halves: Bruce Sterling's Mechanist/Shaper Narratives," in McCaffery, ed., *Storming,* 327.

74 Insect metaphors also pervade the writings of Burroughs, especially in *The Soft Machine,* in which insects obviously represent an evil empire of slavish devotion—a hive mentality of entirely programmed functions. Insects also clearly connote decay and putrescence, emphasizing the organic limitations of bodily flesh. At the same time, insects are frequently linked to technology in these texts. The linking of insect with machine is not Burroughs's innovation, nor is it restricted to his work. One recalls the intercutting of grasshopper and scythe in Eisenstein's *Old and New* (1928), an evocative rhyme that suggests first an equivalence and then finally man's superior control over the forces of nature. And in Cronenberg's *The Fly,* Brundle's transformation to Brundle-fly is only a preparation for the final biotechnological horror as Brundle merges with the blue metal transporter itself.

75 Georges Bataille, *Erotism: Death and Sensuality,* trans. Mary Dalwood (San Francisco: City Lights Books, 1986). The phrase appears somewhat later than the introduction, on page 101.

76 For an analysis of Bataille's relation to the theorists of the Frankfurt School of philosophy, see Annette Michelson, "Heterology and the Critique of Instrumental Reason," *OCTOBER* 36 (1986).

77   Allan Stoekl, "Introduction," in *Visions of Excess: Selected Writings of Georges Bataille,* ed. Allan Stoekl (Minneapolis: University of Minnesota Press, 1985), xii.

78   Michelson, "Heterology," 121.

79   Georges Bataille, "Sacrificial Mutilation and the Severed Ear of Vincent Van Gogh," in *Visions of Excess: Selected Writings,* ed. Allan Stoekl (Minneapolis: University of Minnesota, 1985), 70.

80   Bataille's work centers so wholly upon "primitive," almost pretechnological, cultures—far from the cyborg politics of electronic culture—that any connection to science fiction might seem tenuous, if not forced. However, the appropriation of Bataille is not my own doing: it clearly informs a range of terminal identity fictions that exist on the margins of science fiction, from the condensed novels of J. G. Ballard to the philosophy of Deleuze and Guattari. Several of the works discussed here partake of the terms of Bataille's discourse with varying explicitness.

81   Bataille, *Erotism,* 78.

82   Georges Bataille, "Sacrifices," in *Visions of Excess: Selected Writings,* ed. Allan Stoekl (Minneapolis: University of Minnesota Press, 1985), 132. My emphasis.

83   Theodore Sturgeon, *More Than Human* (New York: Ballantine Books, 1953), 3.

84   Of course, Sturgeon's strategy is partially a circumlocution of the very real constraints on a genre writer in the 1950s writing about sexuality.

85   As the genre opened up to literary experimentation and a new explicitness in the 1960s, Sturgeon's fiction became far more direct in its approach to the dialectical relation between sexuality and love.

86   Gilles Deleuze and Félix Guattari, *Anti-Oedipus: Capitalism and Schizophrenia,* trans. Robert Hurley et al. (New York: Viking Press, 1977), 5.

87   Arthur C. Clarke, *2001: A Space Odyssey* (New York: Signet Books, 1968), 220.

88   It must be noted, however, that the hugely metaphysical finale of transcendence is often no more than a gesture of the genre, and Spinrad argues that it frequently represents a dramatic failure ("the characteristic failed ending of this sort of novel is a burst of unconvincing transcendentalism, an endemic failing of otherwise successful science fiction time out of mind" [Norman Spinrad, "All's Well That Ends Well," *Issac Asimov's Science Fiction Magazine,* June 1990, 178]). While this is undoubtedly valid, I think it can be seen as precisely the structural aporia against which the science fiction narrative defines itself; the limit point the genre is always addressing, if not always to any clear purpose. In the hands of Sturgeon, Clarke, Kubrick, Bear, Bester, and many others, the gesture of transcendence acquires a rare fullness of meaning which itself transcends the limitations of this frequently ethnocentric genre.

89   Thanks to Paul Arthur and Jacob Angstreich.

90   Norman Spinrad, "The Hard Stuff," *Science Fiction in the Real World* (Carbondale, Ill.: Southern Illinois University Press, 1990), 104.

91   Spinrad, "The Hard Stuff," 104–5.

92   Michael Crichton, *The Terminal Man* (New York: Avon Books, 1972): "The

idea of an electrical addict was predicated on an astonishing discovery made by James Olds in the 1950s. Olds found that there were areas in the brain where electrical stimulation produced intense pleasure—strips of brain tissue he called 'rivers of reward.' If an electrode was placed in such an area, a rat would press a self-stimulation lever to receive a shock as often as five thousand times an hour. In its quest for pleasure, it would ignore food and water. It would stop pressing the lever only when it was prostrate with exhaustion" (97).

93 Kingsley Amis, *New Maps of Hell: A Survey of Science Fiction* (New York: Harcourt, Brace, 1960), 113.

94 George Alec Effinger, *When Gravity Fails* (New York: Bantam Books, 1988), 123. Williams's characters are similarly protective of their humanity: "Buttonheads make Cowboy nervous; he doesn't trust junkies in general and has a particular aversion to this kind—it's a near desecration, an abuse of the interface. The idea is to use the interface to reach out, to touch the remotes from the inside, to access the electron world . . . to feel yourself moving *at the speed of light!* The run across the Line is the only addiction Cowboy needs, and it's something real, not just an electronic stimulation of the lizard pleasure centers" (*Hardwired* [New York: Tor Books, 1986], 95).

95 In addition to *Hardwired,* see *Voice of the Whirlwind* (New York: Tor Books, 1987) and Michael Swanwick, *Vacuum Flowers* (New York: Ace Books, 1988).

96 Stoekl, xv.

97 David Skal, *Antibodies,* Isaac Asimov Presents, ed. Gardner Dozois (New York: Worldwide Library, 1988).

98 A memoir by Factory hanger-on Ultra Violet reveals that Warhol had a metal snap embedded in his skull to hold his wig securely in place.

99 Bruno Bettelheim, *The Empty Fortress: Infantile Autism and the Birth of the Self* (New York: Free Press, 1967), 234.

100 Bettelheim, 268.

101 Richard Kadrey, "A Young Person's Guide to Chaos." *Science Fiction Eye* 1, no. 4 (1988), 52.

102 Lou Stathis, "SRL in NYC." *Science Fiction Eye* 1, no. 4 (1988), 53. Here is a description of another show; the text is by SRL: "AN UNFORTUNATE SPECTACLE OF VIOLENT SELF-DESTRUCTION (Saturday, Sept. 6, 1981/8:30 pm. Parking lot at Folsom/2nd Sts). Most complex and dangerous show staged to date, in which a wide variety of equipment (organic robots, dart guns, laser-aimed explosive rockets, land mines, and a catapult) interacted to effect a frightening illusion of ultimate misfortune. SRL's first audience injury" (V. Vale and Andrea Juno, "Mark Pauline," *Re/Search* 6/7 [1983] 41).

103 V. Vale and Andrea Juno, "(Interview with) Mark Pauline." *Re/Search* 11 (1987), 14.

104 This moment is found in the performance of EXTREMELY CRUEL PRACTICES: A SERIES OF EVENTS DESIGNED TO INSTRUCT THOSE INTERESTED IN POLICIES THAT CORRECT OR PUNISH (1985) on "VIRTUES OF NEGATIVE FASCINATION," (Jonathan Reiss and Joe Rees, videotape, 1986).

105 Jim Pomeroy, "Black Box S-Thetix: Labor, Research, and Survival in the He[Art] of the Beast," in *Technoculture,* ed. Constance Penley and Andrew Ross (Minneapolis: University of Minnesota Press, 1991), 293.

106 Kadrey, 52.

107 J. G. Ballard, *Crash* (New York: Vintage Books, 1985).

108 Bataille, "Sacrificial Mutilation," 69.

109 "Warm Leatherette," an early electronic dance record produced by the Normal in the late 1970s, adapted Ballard's imagery: "A tear of petrol is in your eye/The handbrake penetrates your thigh/Quick/Let's make love/Before you die/On warm/Leatherette." The song was later covered by androgynous disco queen Grace Jones. Baudrillard has also written on *Crash:* in "Two Essays," *Science Fiction Studies* 18, no. 3 (1991), 313–20.

110 Bernard Wolfe, *Limbo* (New York: Carroll & Graf, 1987). Wolfe, a fascinating figure, was at one time a bodyguard of Trotsky's in Mexico. J. G. Ballard, incidentally, has called *Limbo* the finest American science fiction novel.

111 Donna Haraway, *Primate Visions: Gender, Race and Nature in the World of Modern Science* (New York: Routledge, 1989), 106.

112 The rationalist drive of the superpower supercomputers to merge into one global unit had, in fact, precipitated the global conflict, as desperate humans pitted the machines against each other.

113 Pfeil, 88.

114 It is also worth remembering the backlash that quickly characterized the genre's response to cyberpunk. Writers and fans were quick to reject what was perceived as a "trendy" and antihumanist discourse (that science fiction perhaps *ought* to be trendy, and that its trendiness might be significant, was not widely debated).

115 Debord, "Report on the Construction of Situations," 19.

116 Debord, "Report on the Construction of Situations," 18.

117 Lefebvre, 18.

118 Lefebvre, 19 (emphasis mine).

5 Terminal Resistance/Cyborg Acceptance

1 Mark Pomerantz, "Sports and the Science Fiction Film," 6. The next two paragraphs are largely adapted from this interesting work, in which *Rollerball, Beyond Thunderdome, Running Man,* and (less successfully) *TRON* are examined. The essay was written for, and in response to, my course in science fiction film at Yale University in the fall of 1991 and took my arguments into new areas. My thanks to Mark for his help.

2 Pomerantz, 9.

3 Claudia Springer, "Muscular Circuitry: The Invincible Armored Cyborg in Cinema," *Genders,* in press.

4 Foster cites these provocative remarks, which are from Sigmund Freud, *The Ego and the Id* standard ed., trans. James Strachey (New York and London: W. W. Norton, 1960), 16.

5 Bruno Bettelheim, *The Empty Fortress: Infantile Autism and the Birth of the Self* (New York: Free Press, 1967).

6 Hal Foster, "Armor Fou," *OCTOBER* 56 (1991), 80.

7 See Klaus Theweleit, *Male Fantasies,* 2 vols., trans. S. Conway et al. (Minneapolis: University of Minnesota Press, 1977–78), vol. 2, 164.

8 Mark Dery, "Cyborging the Body Politic," *MONDO 2000* (1992): 101.

9   Dery, "Cyborging the Body Politic," 103.

10 In *T2*, when Arnold says his tag line, *I'll be back,* it is no longer a threat. *Total Recall,* released one year earlier, failed as drama because Arnold is too strong an icon to play an ontologically unstable character (of course, these elements probably contributed to the film's success). *T2* is ultimately a fantastic ode to metal and an oddly interesting updating of *The Day the Earth Stood Still* (1951).

11 Springer, "Muscular Circuitry," 11.

12 Springer, "Muscular Circuitry," 12.

13 Dery, "Cyborging the Body Politic," 102.

14 Mark Crispin Miller, "The Robot in the Western Mind," *Boxed In: The Culture of TV* (Evanston, Ill.: Northwestern University Press, 1988), 307.

15 Dery, "Cyborging the Body Politic," 102–3.

16 In another comic, part of a wave that either parodied or tried to "subvert" the power fantasies of the superhero genre, the "hero" wears leather and a bondage mask and is caricatured as a Super-Nazi Freikorps member. See Pat Mills (writer) and Kevin O'Neill (artist), *Marshal Law: Super Babylon* (Milwaukie, Oreg.: Dark Horse Comics, 1992). Theweleit himself is clearly well aware of both mainstream and underground comics—he uses illustrations of Spiderman, Capt. America, and Thor to accompany his discussion of armor, as well as some brilliant material by Robert Crumb on male anxiety and a stunning antiwar-story story by Greg Irons.

17 Tony Rayns, "Tetsuo: The Iron Man," *Sight and Sound* (1991): 52. All quotes about the film are taken from Rayns's review.

18 Rosalind Krauss, "Corpus Delicti," in *L'Amour Fou: Photography and Surrealism,* ed. Rosalind Krauss and Jane Livingstone (New York: Abbeville Press, 1985), 74.

19 Emphasis his; cited in Krauss, "Corpus Delicti, 78.

20 Krauss, "Corpus Delicti," 85.

21 Science fiction is often regarded as a male-dominated subliterary domain, but this is less true than it once was. The genre has developed stylistically, and the number of women, and feminist women, producing and consuming SF has also continued to grow. There has always been a tradition of women writing the "marginalia" of science fiction (or, even more acceptably, "fantasy") that extends from Mary Shelley to adventure writers including Andre Norton, Anne McCaffrey, and the brilliance of C. L. Moore and Leigh Brackett, but it was not until the middle-to-late 1960s that women were acknowledged as central to the production of the field. For a more detailed history of feminist science fictions and a thorough analysis of the appropriation of science fiction for various feminist politics, see Sarah Lefanu's excellent *Feminism and Science Fiction* (Bloomington and Indianapolis: Indiana University Press, 1989).

22 Michel Foucault, *The Order of Things: An Archeology of the Human Sciences,* trans. Alan Sheridan (New York: Random House, 1970), xviii.

23 Lefanu, *Feminism and Science Fiction,* 9.

24 Mary Ann Doane, "Technophilia: Technology, Representation, and the Feminine," *Body/Politics: Women and the Discourses of Science,* ed. Mary Jacobus, Evelyn Fox Keller, and Sally Shuttleworth (New York: Routledge, 1990), 163.

NOTES

25 Lefanu, 9.

26 Todd Gitlin, "We Build Excitement," in *Watching Television,* ed. Todd Gitlin (New York: Pantheon Books, 1986), 147.

27 In a death that seems simultaneously tragic, heroic, and mysterious, Sheldon killed her severely ailing husband and herself at an advanced age. Although most of her best work remains out of print, or in limited distribution, I suspect that Tiptree's reputation will garner increasing attention. Arkham House has published an extensive, and indispensable, collection of her best work: James Tiptree, Jr., *Her Smoke Rose Up Forever* (Sauk City, Wis.: Arkham House, 1990).

28 James Tiptree, Jr., *The Girl Who Was Plugged In,* TOR Doubles (New York: TOR Books, 1989), 7:1. Tiptree was in her late fifties when she published this piece of punk poetry.

29 Comedian Jay Leno once noticed how Star Trek "positions" itself in the future by always listing three examples, only two of which are familiar to its viewers: "Men, you all know the works of Plato . . . Socrates . . . Creemus of Rigel 7." Leno is exactly right in his deconstruction of the conventions of the genre.

30 Dick Hebdige, *Subculture: The Meaning of Style,* New Accents, ed. Terence Hawkes (New York: Methuen, 1979), 60–62.

31 One is reminded of Bobby's mother in Gibson's *Count Zero,* passively jacked into her simstim fantasies. Here again the woman is more *object* than *subject* in cyberspace.

32 "The Girl Who Was Plugged In" finds echoes in a more recent story by William Gibson, "The Winter Market" in *Burning Chrome* [New York: Ace Books, 1987]). Here, again, a disfigured woman (who must wear a prosthetic exoskeleton) dreams of abandoning her body in order to exist as data inside a mainframe computer. Superficially similar to Tiptree's story, "The Winter Market" presents a surrender of the body to attain a more questionable level of being—a "hi-tech Saint Joan burning for union with that hardwired godhead" (139). There is, however, one significant difference—Gibson's story is narrated by the woman's lover, who writes with a tragic remorse that both romanticizes the "death" of the woman and makes *him* seem like the victim: "That she threw away that poor sad body with a cry of release, free of the bonds of polycarbon and hated flesh. Well, maybe, after all, she did. Maybe it was that way. I'm sure that's the way she expected it to be" (140). There is no irony here, no complexity of rhetoric or attitude, to offset the clichéd terms of wounded masculinity and feminine sacrifice. Gibson's cyberpunk has rarely seemed more reactionary, especially when read against the stunning deconstructions of Tiptree.

Another narrative similar to "The Girl Who Was Plugged In," again with less awareness or reflection, is Michael Crichton's film, *Looker.* Once more the power of telematic culture is enlisted to "replace" the real female with her idealized and perfected simulation (however, as Bergstrom has argued, this text fails to examine its own assumptions regarding female attractiveness and desirability: "we're not really ever supposed to doubt the attractiveness of Cindy's image. Even at its most robotic, it serves to emphasize the fact that her 'real,' sensual self is present somewhere, and is a more powerful image" [Bergstrom, 47]). While Edison Carter can coexist with Max Headroom, his pixel-lated double, the woman's constitution as an *object* rather than a *subject* in these texts precludes such extensions of power and subjectivity.

33 While *Aliens* dealt with issues of reproduction in distinctly peculiar ways, *Alien³* (1992) confronted the issue head-on, with Ripley's discovery of the alien inside her. Ripley and the alien in the film are photographed in the same sidelit profile shots and silhouettes, enforcing a deliberate and self-aware confusion. For more on reproduction and SF, see essays by Paula Treichler and Mary Ann Doane in Mary Jacobus, Evelyn Fox Keller, and Sally Shuttleworth, eds., *Body/Politics: Women and the Discourses of Science* (New York: Routledge, 1990); essays by Sobchack, Constance Penley, and Barbara Creed in Annette Kuhn, ed., *Alien Zone: Cultural Theory and Contemporary Science Fiction* (London: Verso, 1990); and essays by Sobchack and Bergstrom in Constance Penley et al., eds., *Close Encounters: Film, Feminism and Science Fiction* (Minneapolis: University of Minnesota Press, 1991).

34 It is no small measure of the progressive aspect of *20 Minutes into the Future* that it presents one of the only female characters with a facility to operate in cyberspace. While Edison is the character who actually enters the cyber-spatial realm, a position largely denied science fiction's women, Theora Jones is that rarity, a female hacker (and, admittedly, secretary). Her abilities, as she "runs" Carter around Network 23, arouse far more admiration than Carter's own maneuvers as the fly caught in an electronic web. While it might be argued that Jones is merely serving "her man," in this sequence her technological dexterity is fully heroicized and even eroticized. Rather than the total physical immersion in the dataspace which marks the "natural" technological symbiosis of man and machine in *Neuromancer* and *TRON*, Jones's negotiations are clearly the result of training and work (these qualities were not presented as forcefully in the subsequent American television series, where Max's cyberspatial presence obviated much of Theora's dramatic function). See also John Varley's "Press Enter ■," in *Blue Champagne* (New York: Berkley Books, 1986), 230–90.

35 Foucault, *The Order of Things,* xxiii.

36 Istvan Csicsery-Ronay, Jr., "The SF of Theory: Baudrillard and Haraway," *Science Fiction Studies* vol. 18, No. 3 (1991), 387–404.

37 In a review of Bruce Sterling's anthology *Mirrorshades* (*Washington Post Book World,* December 28, 1986).

38 Tom Maddox, "Snake-Eyes," in *Mirrorshades: The Cyberpunk Anthology,* ed. Bruce Sterling (New York: Arbor House, 1986), 28.

39 Gilles Deleuze and Félix Guattari, *A Thousand Plateaus: Capitalism and Schizophrenia,* trans. Brian Massumi (Minneapolis: University of Minnesota Press, 1987), 151.

40 Burroughs, *Naked Lunch,* 9.

41 Neil Gaiman and Mark Buckingham, in *Miracleman* 19 (Forestville, Calif.: Eclipse Comics, 1991). The artwork, by Mark Buckingham, is a sophisticated pastiche of Warhol's serial lithography, and there is a full cognizance of

these techniques being returned to the "low culture" form that originally inspired them. *Miracleman,* once an older (and somewhat forgettable) British comic book series, had been revived in the 1980s by writer Alan Moore. It became a vehicle for exploring the nature of the superhero power fantasy before becoming a broader exploration of the ramifications of utopia.

NOTES

FILMOGRAPHY

20 Minutes into the Future. Rocky Morton and Annabelle Janke, 1985. 60 mins. Marketed on video in America as *The Max Headroom Story.*

2001: A Space Odyssey. Stanley Kubrick, 1968. 139 mins. Originally in Cinerama. Stargate sequence by Douglas Trumbull.

Akira. Katsuhiro Otomo, 1988. 124 mins. Animated film.

Alien. Ridley Scott, 1979. 117 mins. Designs by Moebius and H. R. Giger.

Aliens. James Cameron, 1986. 137 mins.

Alien³. David Fincher, 1992. 115 mins.

Alphaville. Jean-Luc Godard, 1965. 100 mins.

Andromeda Strain, The. Robert Wise, 1971. 130 mins.

Batman. Tim Burton, 1989. 126 mins.

Blade Runner. Ridley Scott, 1982. 118 mins. Based on *Do Androids Dream of Electric Sheep,* by Philip K. Dick. Special effects supervised by Douglas Trumbull, designs by Syd Mead.

Brainstorm. Douglas Trumbull, 1983. 106 mins.

Brazil. Terry Gilliam, 1985. 131 mins.

Brood, The. David Cronenberg, 1979. 90 mins.

Clockwork Orange, A. Stanley Kubrick, 1971. 137 mins.

Close Encounters of the Third Kind. Steven Spielberg, 1977. 135 mins.

Crimes of the Future. David Cronenberg, 1970. 65 mins.

Dark Star. John Carpenter, 1974. 83 mins. Scripted by Dan O'Bannon.

Dead Ringers. David Cronenberg, 1988. 115 mins.

Double Lunar Dogs. Joan Jonas, 1984. Videotape, 25 mins.

Drake's Equation. Max Almy, 1986. Videotape, 3:45 mins.

Explorers. Joe Dante, 1985. 109 mins.

Fahrenheit 451. François Truffaut, 1967. 111 mins.

Fly, The. David Cronenberg, 1986. 100 mins.

Incredible Shrinking Man, The. Jack Arnold, 1957. 81 mins.

Invasion of the Body Snatchers, The. Don Siegel, 1956. 80 mins.

Invasion of the Body Snatchers, The. Philip Kaufman, 1978. 115 mins.

Just Imagine. David Butler, 1930. 102 mins.

Last Starfighter, The. Nick Castle, 1984. 100 mins.

Lawnmower Man, The. Brett Leonard, 1992.

Leaving the 20th Century. Max Almy, Videotape. 10:17 mins.

Looker. Michael Crichton, 1981. 94 mins.

Lost in the Pictures. Max Almy, 1985. Videotape. 4:06 mins.

Mad Max: Beyond Thunderdome. George Miller, George Ogilvie, 1985. 106 mins.

Man Who Fell to Earth, The. Nicholas Roeg, 1976. 140 mins.

Metropolis. Fritz Lang, 1926. 120 mins.

Naked Lunch. David Cronenberg, 1991. 115 mins.

Paris Qui Dort. Rene Clair, 1924. 70 mins.

Perfect Leader. Max Almy, 1983. Videotape. 4:11 mins.

Région Centrale, La. Michael Snow, 1971. 190 mins.

Road Warrior, The. George Miller, 1982. 94 mins. Also known as *Mad Max II.*

Robocop. Paul Verhoeven, 1987. 107 mins.

Robocop 2. Irvin Kershner, 1990. 128 mins.

Rollerball. Norman Jewison, 1975. 128 mins.

Sans Soleil. Chris Marker, 1982. 100 mins.

Scanners. David Cronenberg, 1981. 102 mins.

Stalker. Andrei Tarkovsky, 1979. 160 mins.

Star Trek—The Motion Picture. Robert Wise, 1979. 132 mins. Special effects by Douglas Trumbull, designs by Syd Mead.

Star Trek II: The Wrath of Khan. Nicholas Meyer, 1982. 113 mins.

Star Wars. George Lucas, 1977. 121 mins.

Stereo. David Cronenberg, 1969. 65 mins.

Strike. Sergei Eisenstein, 1924. 73 mins.

Terminator, The. James Cameron, 1984. 108 mins.

Terminator 2. James Cameron, 1991. 137 mins.

Tetsuo: The Iron Man. Shinya Tsukamoto, 1989. 67 mins.

They Came from Within. David Cronenberg, 1975. 87 mins.

Thing (From Another World), The. Christian Nyby, 1951. 87 mins.

Thing, The. John Carpenter, 1982. 108 mins.

Things to Come. William Cameron Menzies, 1936. 92 mins.

THX 1138. George Lucas, 1971. 88 mins.

Total Recall. Paul Verhoeven, 1990. 109 mins. Based on Philip K. Dick's story, "We Can Remember it for You Wholesale."

TRON. Steven Lisberger, 1982. 96 mins. Designs by Moebius and Syd Mead.

Videodrome. David Cronenberg, 1982. 90 mins.

Virtues of Negative Fascination. Jonathan Reiss and Joe Rees, 1986. Videotape. 75 mins.

War of the Worlds. Byron Haskin, 1953. 85 mins. Produced by George Pal.

WarGames. John Badham, 1983. 110 mins.

Westworld. Michael Crichton, 1973. 88 mins.

BIBLIOGRAPHY

Non-Fiction

Aldiss, Brian, and David Wingrove. *Trillion Year Spree: The History of Science Fiction.* New York: Atheneum, 1986. Originally published in 1973 as "Billion Year Spree" by Brian Aldiss.

Alliez, Eric, and Michael Feher. "Notes on the Sophisticated City." *ZONE* 1/2 (1984): 40–55.

Alloway, Lawrence. "The Development of British Pop." *Pop Art.* Ed. Lucy Lippard. New York: Oxford University Press, 1966. 27–67.

Amis, Kingsley. *New Maps of Hell: A Survey of Science Fiction.* New York: Harcourt Brace, 1960.

Antin, David. "Video: The Distinctive Features of the Medium." *Video Culture: A Critical Investigation.* Ed. John Hanhardt. Rochester, N.Y.: Visual Studies Workshop Press, 1986. 147–66.

Bagdikian, Ben H. *The Media Monopoly.* 3d ed. Boston: Beacon Press, 1990.

Ballard, J. G. "Coming of the Unconscious." *Re/Search* 8/9 (1984): 102–4. Originally published in *New Worlds* in 1966.

Ballard, J. G. "Fictions of Every Kind." *Re/Search* 8/9 (1984): 98–100. Text originally published in 1971.

Ballard, J. G. "Introduction to *Crash.*" *Re/Search* 8/9 (1984): 96–98. Novel originally published 1973; introduction first published 1974.

Ballard, J. G. "Mythmaker of the 20th Century." *Re/Search* 8/9 (1984): 105–7.

Ballard, J. G. "Quotations by Ballard." *Re/Search* 8/9 (1984): 154–64. Originally appeared in *Search and Destroy* 10 (1978).

Ballard, J. G. "Time, Memory, and Inner Space." *Re/Search* 8/9 (1984): 100–101.

Barthes, Roland. *S/Z.* Trans. Richard Miller. New York: Hill and Wang, 1974.

Barthes, Roland. "The Death of the Author." *Image-Music-Text*. New York: Hill and Wang, 1977. 142–48.

Barthes, Roland. *Empire of Signs*. Trans. Richard Howard. New York: Hill and Wang, 1982.

Bataille, Georges. "Sacrifices." *Visions of Excess: Selected Writings*. Ed. Allan Stoekl. Minneapolis: University of Minnesota, 1985. 130–36.

Bataille, Georges. "Sacrificial Mutilation and the Severed Ear of Vincent Van Gogh." *Visions of Excess: Selected Writings*. Ed. Allan Stoekl. Minneapolis: University of Minnesota, 1985. 61–72.

Bataille, Georges. "Celestial bodies." *OCTOBER* 36 (1986): 75–78. Annette Michelson. This text was originally published in 1938.

Bataille, Georges. *Erotism: Death and Sensuality*. Trans. Mary Dalwood. San Francisco: City Lights Books, 1986. Originally published in English in 1962.

Baudrillard, Jean. *The Mirror of Production*. Trans. Mark Poster. St. Louis: Telos Press, 1975.

Baudrillard, Jean. "Requiem for the Media." Trans. Charles Levin. *For a Critique of the Political Economy of the Sign*. Ed. Charles Levin. St. Louis: Telos Press, 1981. 164–84. Originally published in 1972.

Baudrillard, Jean. "Design and Environment, or How Political Economy Escalates into Cyberblitz." Trans. Charles Levin. *For a Critique of the Political Economy of the Sign*. Ed. Charles Levin. St. Louis: Telos Press, 1981. 185–203. Originally published in 1972.

Baudrillard, Jean. "The Ecstasy of Communication." *The Anti-Aesthetic*. Ed. Hal Foster. Port Townsend, Wash.: Bay Press, 1983. 126–34.

Baudrillard, Jean. *In the Shadow of the Silent Majorities*. Foreign Agents Series. Trans. Paul Foss, Paul Patton, and John Johnston. New York: Semiotext(e), 1983.

Baudrillard, Jean. *Simulations*. Foreign Agents Series. Trans. Paul Foss, Paul Patton, and Philip Beitchman. New York: Semiotext(e), 1983.

Baudrillard, Jean. *Forget Foucault*. Foreign Agents Series. Trans. Nicole Dufresne. New York: Semiotext(e), 1987. Originally published in 1977.

Baudrillard, Jean. "The Year 2000 Has Already Happened." Trans. Nai-fei Ding and Kuan-Hsing Chen. *Body Invaders: Panic Sex in America*. Ed. Arthur Kroker and Marilouise Kroker. CultureTexts. New York: St. Martin's Press, 1987. 35–44.

Baudrillard, Jean. *The Ecstasy of Communication*. Foreign Agents Series. Trans. Bernard Schutze and Caroline Schutze. New York: Semiotext(e), 1988.

Baudrillard, Jean. "Fatal Strategies." *Jean Baudrillard: Selected Writings*. Ed. Mark Poster. Stanford, Calif.: Stanford University Press, 1988. 185–206.

Baudrillard, Jean "On Seduction." *Jean Baudrillard: Selected Writings*. Ed. Mark Poster. Stanford, Calif.: Stanford University Press, 1988. 149–65.

Baudrillard, Jean. "Symbolic Exchange and Death." *Jean Baudrillard: Selected Writings*. Ed. Mark Poster. Stanford, Calif.: Stanford University Press, 1988. 119–48.

Baudrillard, Jean. *Xerox and Infinity*. London: Touchepas, 1988.

Baudrillard, Jean. "Two Essays." *Science Fiction Studies* 18, no. 3 (1991): 309–20.

Baxter, John. *Science Fiction in the Cinema*. The International Film Guide Series. New York: New American Library, 1970.

Bazin, André. "The Myth of Total Cinema." Trans. Hugh Gray. *What Is Cinema?* Ed. Hugh Gray. 2 vols. Berkeley: University of California Press, 1967.

Beard, William. "The Visceral Mind: The Films of David Cronenberg." *The Shape of Rage: The Films of David Cronenberg.* Ed. Piers Handling. New York: New York Zoetrope, 1983.

Benedikt, Michael. "Introduction." *Cyberspace: First Steps.* Ed. Michael Benedikt. Cambridge, Mass.: MIT Press, 1991. 1–25.

Benford, Gregory. "Is Something Going On?" *Mississippi Review* 16, nos. 2/3 (1988): 18–23.

Benjamin, Walter. "The Work of Art in the Age of Mechanical Reproduction." Trans. Harry Zohn. *Illuminations.* Ed. Hannah Arendt. New York: Schocken Books, 1969. 217–51.

Benjamin, Walter. *The Origin of German Tragic Drama.* Trans. John Osborne. London: New Left Books, 1977.

Berger, John. *Ways of Seeing.* Middlesex: Penguin Books, 1972.

Bergstrom, Janet. "Androids and Androgyny." *Camera Obscura* 15 (1986): 37–64.

Bettelheim, Bruno. *The Empty Fortress: Infantile Autism and the Birth of the Self.* New York: Free Press, 1967.

Binkley, Timothy. "Camera Fantasia." *Millenium Film Journal* 20/21 (1989): 6–43.

Bolter, J. David. *Turing's Man: Western Culture in the Computer Age.* Chapel Hill, N.C.: University of North Carolina Press, 1984.

Boorstin, Daniel J. *The Image: A Guide to Pseudo-Events in America.* New York: Atheneum, 1985.

Bordwell, David, and Kristen Thompson. *Film Art: An Introduction.* 2d ed. New York: Alfred A. Knopf, 1986.

Brand, Stewart. *The Media Lab: Inventing the Future at MIT.* New York: Viking Penguin, 1987.

Brantlinger, Patrick. *Bread and Circuses: Theories of Mass Culture as Social Decay.* Ithaca, N.Y.: Cornell University Press, 1983.

Bright, Randy. *Disneyland: Inside Story.* New York: Harry N. Abrams, 1987. An official history of the park.

Bruno, Giuliana. "Ramble City: Postmodernism and *Blade Runner.*" *OCTOBER* 41 (1987): 61–74.

Bukatman, Scott. "Fractal Geographies." *Artforum International.* 31; 4 (December 1992): 6–7.

Burroughs, William. "The Cut-Up Method of Brion Gysin." *Re/Search* 4/5 (1982): 35–36.

Burroughs, William S. "The Electronic Revolution." *Ah Pook is Here and Other Texts.* New York: Riverrun Press, 1979. 123–57.

Burroughs, William S. "My Purpose is to Write for the Space Age." *William S. Burroughs at the Front: Critical Reception, 1959–1989.* Ed. Jennie Skerl and Robin Lydenberg. Carbondale, Ill.: Southern Illinois University Press, 1991. 265–68. Originally published in the *New York Times Book Review,* February 19, 1984.

Byers, Thomas B. "Commodity Futures." *Alien Zone: Cultural Theory and Contemporary Science Fiction Cinema.* Ed. Annette Kuhn. London: Verso, 1990. 39–50.

Carroll, Noël. *The Philosophy of Horror, or Paradoxes of the Heart.* New York: Routledge, 1990.

Cavell, Stanley. "The Fact of Television." *Video Culture: A Critical Investigation.* Ed. John Hanhardt. Rochester, N.Y.: Visual Studies Workshop Press, 1986. 192–218.

Chtcheglov, Ivan. "Formulary for a New Urbanism." Trans. Ken Knabb. *Situationist International Anthology.* Ed. Ken Knabb. Berkeley, Calif.: Bureau of Public Secrets, 1981. 1–4. Article originally published in 1953.

Clark, T. J. *The Painting of Modern Life: Paris in the Art of Manet and His Followers.* Princeton, N.J.: Princeton University Press, 1984.

Clute, John. "The Repossession of Jerry Cornelius." *The Cornelius Chronicles.* New York: Avon, 1977. vii–xv.

Clute, John. "Introduction." *Interzone: The Second Anthology.* Ed. John Clute. New York: St. Martin's Press, 1987. vii–x.

Colvin, James. "A Literature of Acceptance." *New Worlds: An Anthology.* Ed. Michael Moorcock. London: Flamingo Books, 1983. 347–52. Originally published in 1968.

Coward, Rosalind, and John Ellis. *Language and Materialism: Developments in Semiology and the Theory of the Subject.* London: Routledge & Kegan Paul, 1977.

Crary, Jonathan. *Techniques of the Observer: On Vision and Modernity in the Nineteenth Century.* Cambridge, Mass.: MIT Press, 1990.

Creed, Barbara. "Gynesis, Postmodernism, and the Science Fiction Horror Film." *Alien Zone: Cultural Theory and Contemporary Science Fiction Cinema.* Ed. Annette Kuhn. New York: Verso, 1990. 214–18.

Csicsery-Ronay, Istvan, Jr. "Cyberpunk and Neuromanticism." *Storming the Reality Studio,* Durham: Duke Univ. Press, 1992.

Csicsery-Ronay, Istvan, Jr. "The SF of Theory: Baudrillard and Haraway." *Science Fiction Studies* 18, no. 3 (1991): 387–404.

Cubitt, Sean. *Timeshift: On Video Culture.* London and New York: Routledge, 1991.

Dargis, Manohla. "Is This the End?" *Village Voice Film Special,* June 2, 1992.

Davis, Mike. *City of Quartz.* New York: Vintage Books, 1991.

Debord, Guy. "Perspectives for Conscious Alterations in Everyday Life." *Situationist International Anthology.* Ed. Ken Knabb. Berkeley, California: Bureau of Public Secrets, 1981. 68–75.

Debord, Guy. "Report on the Construction of Situations and on the International Situationist Tendency's Conditions of Organization and Action." Trans. Ken Knabb. *Situationist International Anthology.* Ed. Ken Knabb. Berkeley, Calif.: Bureau of Public Secrets, 1981. 17–25. Originally published in 1957.

Debord, Guy. *Society of the Spectacle.* Detroit: Black & Red, 1983. Originally published in 1967; originally translated in 1970, revised in 1977.

de Certeau, Michel. *The Practice of Everyday Life.* Trans. Steven Rendall. Berkeley, Calif.: University of California Press, 1984.

Delany, Samuel R. "About 5,750 Words." *The Jewel-Hinged Jaw: Notes on the Language of Science Fiction.* Elizabethtown, N.Y.: Dragon Press, 1977. 33–49.

Delany, Samuel R. *The American Shore: Meditations on a Tale of Science Fiction by Thomas M. Disch—"Angouleme."* Elizabethtown, N.Y.: Dragon Press, 1978.

Delany, Samuel R. *Starboard Wine: More Notes on the Language of Science Fiction.* Elizabethtown, N.J.: Dragon Press, 1984.

Delany, Samuel R. "Is Cyberpunk a Good Thing or a Bad Thing?" *Mississippi Review* 47/48 (1988): 28–35.

Delany, Samuel R. "Some *Real* Mothers: An Interview with Samuel R. Delany by Takayuki Tatsumi." *Science Fiction Eye* 1, no. 3 (1988): 5–11.

deLauretis, Teresa. "Signs of W[a/o]nder." *The Technological Imagination: Theories and Fictions.* Ed. Teresa deLauretis, Andreas Huyssen, and Kathleen Woodward. Madison, Wis.: Coda Press, 1980. 159–74.

Deleuze, Gilles, and Félix Guattari. *Anti-Oedipus: Capitalism and Schizophrenia.* Trans. Robert Hurley, Mark Seem, Helen R. Lane. New York: Viking Press, 1977.

Deleuze, Gilles, and Félix Guattari. *A Thousand Plateaus: Capitalism and Schizophrenia.* Trans. Brian Massumi. Minneapolis: University of Minnesota Press, 1987.

deMan, Paul. *Allegories of Reading: Figural Language in Rousseau, Nietzsche, Rilke, and Proust.* New Haven: Yale University Press, 1979.

deMan, Paul. "The Rhetoric of Temporality." *Blindness and Insight: Essays in the Rhetoric of Contemporary Criticism.* Rev. ed. Minneapolis: University of Minnesota Press, 1983. 187–228.

Derrida, Jacques. "Structure, Sign, and Play in the Discourse of the Human Sciences." *The Structuralist Controversy: The Languages of Criticism and the Sciences of Man.* Ed. Richard Macksey and Eugenio Donato. Baltimore: Johns Hopkins University Press, 1970. 247–72.

Derrida, Jacques. *Of Grammatology.* Trans. Gayatri Chakravorty Spivak. Baltimore: Johns Hopkins University Press, 1976.

Dery, Mark. "Kraftwerk Redux: House Music Goes Robo-Rock." *New York Times,* June 16, 1991: 30.

Dery, Mark. "Cyborging the Body Politic." *MONDO 2000* 7 (1992), 101–5.

Dewdney, A. K. *The Armchair Universe: An Exploration of Computer Worlds.* New York: W. H. Freeman, 1988.

Dibbell, Julian. "Reality Used to be a Friend of Mine." *Village Voice Film Special,* June 2, 1992: 3–4.

Disch, Thomas. "In the Mold of 1964: An Afterword." *The Penultimate Truth.* New York: Bluejay Books, 1984. 192–201.

Disch, Thomas. "Lost in Cyberspace." *New York Times Book Review,* November 6, 1988.

Doane, Mary Ann. "Technophilia: Technology, Representation, and the Feminine." *Body/Politics: Women and the Discourses of Science.* Ed. Mary Jacobus, Evelyn Fox Keller, and Sally Shuttleworth. New York: Routledge, 1990. 163–76.

Druckrey, Timothy. "Revenge of the Nerds: An Interview with Jaron Lanier." *Afterimage* (May 1991): 5–9.

Eco, Umberto. *Travels in Hyperreality.* Trans. William Weaver. New York: Harcourt, Brace, Jovanovich, 1985.

Eilenberger, Gert. "Freedom, Science, and Aesthetics." *The Beauty of Fractals.* Ed. Heinz-Otto Peitgen and Peter H. Richter. Heidelberg: Springer-Verlag, 1986. 175–80.

Elkington, John. *The Gene Factory: Inside the Science and Business of Biotechnology.* New York: Carroll & Graf, 1985.

Elmer-DeWitt, Philip. "Invasion of the Data Snatchers!" *Time* (September 26, 1988): 62–67.

Epstein, Jean. "Magnification and Other Writings." *OCTOBER* 3 (1976): 9–25.

Evans, Liz. "Massive Mathematics." *Deadline* (April 1990): 26–28.

Ferris, Timothy. *Coming of Age in the Milky Way.* New York: Doubleday, 1988.

Feuer, Jane. "The Concept of Live TV." *Regarding Television—Critical Approaches: An Anthology.* Ed. E. Ann Kaplan. American Film Institute Monograph Series, no. 2. Frederick, Md.: University Publications of America, 1983. 12–22.

Fielding, Raymond. "Hale's Tours: Ultrarealism in the Pre-1910 Motion Picture." *Film Before Griffith.* Ed. John Fell. Berkeley, Calif.: University of California Press, 1983. 116–30. Article originally published in 1957.

Finch, Christopher. *Special Effects: Creating Movie Magic.* New York: Abbeville Press, 1984.

Fisher, Scott S. "Virtual Interface Environments." *The Art of Human Computer Interface Design.* Ed. Brenda Laurel. Cupertino, Calif.: Apple Computer, 1990. 423–38.

Fishman, Robert. *Urban Utopias in the Twentieth Century: Ebenezer Howard, Frank Lloyd Wright, Le Corbusier.* Cambridge, Mass.: MIT Press, 1982. Originally published in 1977.

Fitting, Peter. "*UBIK:* The Deconstruction of Bourgeois SF." *Philip K. Dick.* Ed. Joseph D. Olander and Martin Harry Greenberg. New York: Taplinger Publishing, 1983. 149–59.

Fitting, Peter. "The Lessons of Cyberpunk." *Technoculture.* Ed. Constance Penley and Andrew Ross. Minneapolis: University of Minnesota Press, 1991. 295–315.

Foley, James D. "Interfaces for Advanced Computing." *Scientific American* (October 1987): 126–35.

Foster, Hal. "Armor Fou." *OCTOBER* 56 (1991): 64–97.

Foucault, Michel. *The Order of Things: An Archeology of the Human Sciences.* Trans. Alan Sheridan. New York: Random House, 1970.

Foucault, Michel. *The Archaeology of Knowledge.* Trans. A. M. Sheridan Smith. New York: Pantheon Books, 1972.

Foucault, Michel. *Discipline and Punish: The Birth of the Prison.* Trans. Alan Sheridan. New York: Vintage Books, 1979.

Francaviglia, Richard V. "Main Street USA: A Comparison/Contrast of Streetscapes in Disneyland and Walt Disney World." *Journal of Popular Culture* 15, no. 1 (1981): 141–56.

Franklin, H. Bruce. "America as Science Fiction: 1939." *Science Fiction Studies* 9, no. 1 (1982): 38–50.

Freud, Sigmund. "Animism, Magic, and the Omnipotence of Thoughts." Trans. James Strachey. *Totem and Taboo.* New York: W. W. Norton, 1950. 75–99.

Freud, Sigmund. *The Ego and the Id.* Trans. James Strachey. Standard ed. New York and London: W. W. Norton, 1960.

Friedhoff, Richard Mark, and William Benzon. *Visualization: The Second Computer Revolution.* New York: Harry Abrams, 1989.

Friendly, Fred W. *Due to Circumstances Beyond Our Control.* New York: Vintage Books, 1968.

Gibson, William. "Interview." *Science Fiction Eye* 1, no. 1 (1987): 18–26.

Gibson, William. "Introduction." *Neuromancer: The Graphic Novel.* Ed. David M. Harris. New York: Epic Comics, 1989.

Gitlin, Todd. "We Build Excitement." *Watching Television.* Ed. Todd Gitlin. New York: Pantheon Books, 1986. 136–61.

Gleick, James. *Chaos.* New York: Viking Books, 1987.

Goddard, James, and David Pringle, eds. *J. G. Ballard: The First Twenty Years.* Middlesex: Bran's Head Books, 1976.

Grundberg, Andy. "Ask It No Questions: The Camera Can Lie." *New York Times,* August 12, 1990. sec. 2: 1ff.

Gunning, Tom. "An Unseen Energy Swallows Space: The Space in Early Film and its Relation to American Avant-Garde Film." *Film Before Griffith.* Ed. John Fell. Berkeley, Calif.: University of California Press, 1983. 355–66.

Gunning, Tom. "The Cinema of Attractions: Early Film, Its Spectator, and the Avant-Garde." *Early Cinema: Space, Frame, Narrative.* Ed. Thomas Eslaesser. London: British Film Institute, 1990. 56–62.

Haase, Andrew. "Body Shops: The Death of Georges Bataille." *Body Invaders: Panic Sex in America.* Ed. Arthur Kroker and Marilouise Kroker. New York: St. Martin's Press, 1987. 120–49.

Hafner, Katie, and John Markoff. *Cyberpunk: Outlaws and Hackers on the Computer Frontier.* New York: Simon & Schuster, 1991.

Hansen, Miriam. *Babel & Babylon: Spectatorship in American Silent Film.* Cambridge, Mass.: Harvard University Press, 1991.

Haraway, Donna. "The Biopolitics of Postmodern Bodies: Constitution of Self in Immune Systems Discourse." *Simians, Cyborgs, and Women.* New York: Routledge, 1989. 203–30.

Haraway, Donna. "A Cyborg Manifesto: Science, Technology and Socialist-Feminism in the 1980s." *Simians, Cyborgs, and Women.* New York: Routledge, 1989. 149–81.

Haraway, Donna. *Primate Visions: Gender, Race, and Nature in the World of Modern Science.* New York: Routledge, 1989.

Hardison, O. B., Jr. *Disappearing Through the Skylight: Culture and Technology in the Twentieth Century.* New York: Viking, 1989.

Hawking, Stephen W. *A Brief History of Time: From the Big Bang to Black Holes.* New York: Bantam Books, 1988.

Hayles, N. Katherine. *The Cosmic Web: Scientific Field Models and Literary Strategies in the Twentieth Century.* Ithaca, N.Y.: Cornell University Press, 1984.

Hayles, N. Katherine. *Chaos Bound: Orderly Disorder in Contemporary Literature and Science.* Ithaca, N.Y.: Cornell University Press, 1990.

Hebdige, Dick. *Subculture: The Meaning of Style. New Accents.* New York: Methuen, 1979.

Heim, Michael. "The Erotic Ontology of Cyberspace." *Cyberspace: First Steps.* Ed. Michael Benedikt. Cambridge, Mass.: MIT Press, 1991. 59–80.

Herr, Michael. *Dispatches.* New York: Avon Books, 1978.

Hine, Thomas. *Populuxe.* New York: Alfred A. Knopf, 1986.

Hoberman, J. "The Mass Psychology of Disney World." *Arcade: The Comics Revue* (Fall 1976): 28.

Hoberman, Jim. "What's Stranger Than Paradise? or How We Stopped Worrying and Learned to Love the 'Burbs." *Village Voice Film Special,* June 30, 1987.

Hofstadter, Douglas R. *Gödel, Escher, Bach: An Eternal Golden Braid.* New York: Basic Books, 1979.

Hollinger, Veronica. "Cybernetic Deconstructions: Cyberpunk and Postmodernism." *Storming the Reality Studio: A Casebook of Cyberpunk and Postmodern Science Fiction.* Ed. Larry McCaffery. Durham, N.C.: Duke University Press, 1992. 203–18.

Horkheimer, Max, and Theodor Adorno. *The Dialectic of Enlightenment.* Trans. John Cummings. New York: Continuum Publishing, 1972.

Huizinga, J. (1970). *Homo Ludens.* London: Temple Smith.

Husserl, Edmund. "Phenomenology." *Deconstruction in Context: Literature and Philosophy.* Ed. Mark C. Taylor. Chicago: University of Chicago Press, 1986. 121–40.

Ihde, Don. *Technology and the Lifeworld: From Garden to Earth.* The Indiana Series in the Philosophy of Technology. Bloomington and Indianapolis: Indiana University Press, 1990.

Jacobs, Karrie. "Identity Crisis." *Metropolis* 7, no. 2 (1987).

Jacobs, Karrie. "Design for the Unreal World." *Metropolis* 10, no. 2 (1990): 40ff.

Jacobus, Mary, Evelyn Fox Keller, and Sally Shuttleworth, eds. *Body/Politics: Women and the Discourses of Science.* New York: Routledge, 1990.

Jameson, Fredric. "After Armageddon: Character Systems in *Dr. Bloodmoney.*" *Science Fiction Studies* 2, no. 1 (1975): 31–42.

Jameson, Fredric. *The Political Unconscious: Narrative as a Socially Symbolic Act.* Ithaca, N.Y.: Cornell University Press, 1981.

Jameson, Fredric. "Progress vs. Utopia; or, Can We Imagine the Future?" *Science Fiction Studies* 9, no. 2 (1982): 147–58.

Jameson, Fredric. "On Chandler." *The Poetics of Murder: Detective Fiction and Literary Theory.* Ed. Glenn W. Most and William W. Stowe. New York: Harcourt Brace Jovanovich, 1983. 122–48.

Jameson, Fredric. *Postmodernism, or, the Cultural Logic of Late Capitalism.* Durham, N.C.: Duke University Press, 1991.

Jameson, Fredric. "Science Fiction as a Spatial Genre: Generic Discontinuities and the Problem of Figuration in Vonda McIntyre's *The Exile Waiting.*" *Science Fiction Studies* 14, no. 1 (1987): 44–59.

Jameson, Fredric. *Postmodernism, or, the Cultural Logic of Late Capitalism: Post-Contemporary Interventions.* Durham, N.C.: Duke University Press, 1991.

Jencks, Charles. *Late Modern Architecture.* New York: Rizzoli Books, 1980.

Jencks, Charles. *The Language of Post-Modern Architecture.* 3d ed. New York: Rizzoli Books, 1981.

Johnson, Nicolas. *How to Talk Back to Your Television Set.* New York: Bantam Books, 1970.

Johnston, Christopher. "Remember Timothy Leary?" *Village Voice Fast Forward,* November 25, 1986.

Kadrey, Richard. "A Young Person's Guide to Chaos." *Science Fiction Eye* 1, no. 4 (1988): 48–54.

Kern, Stephen. *The Culture of Time and Space: 1880–1918.* Cambridge, Mass.: Harvard University Press, 1983.

King, Margaret. "Disneyland and Walt Disney World: Traditional Values in Futuristic Form." *Journal of Popular Culture* 15, no. 1 (1981): 116–40.

Kirby, Lynne. "Male Hysteria and Early Cinema." *Camera Obscura* 17 (1989): 113–31.

Knabb, Ken, ed. *Situationist International Anthology*. Berkeley, Calif.: Bureau of Public Secrets, 1981.

Kowinski, William. *The Malling of America*. New York: William Morrow, 1985.

Krauss, Rosalind. "The Double Negative: A New Syntax for Sculpture." *Passages in Modern Sculpture*. Cambridge, Mass.: MIT Press, 1977. 243–88.

Krauss, Rosalind. "Corpus Delicti." *L'Amour Fou: Photography and Surrealism*. Ed. Rosalind Krauss and Jane Livingstone. New York: Abbeville Press, 1985. 57–100.

Krauss, Rosalind. "Grids." *The Originality of the Avant-Garde and Other Modernist Myths*. Cambridge, Mass.: MIT Press, 1986. 10–22.

Kroker, Arthur, and David Cook. *The Postmodern Scene: Excremental Culture and Hyper-Aesthetics*. CultureTexts. New York: St. Martin's Press, 1986.

Kroker, Arthur, and Marilouise Kroker. "Theses on the Disappearing Body in the Hyper-Modern Condition." *Body Invaders: Panic Sex in America*. Ed. Arthur Kroker and Marilouise Kroker. New York: St. Martin's Press, 1987. 20–34.

Kroker, Arthur, Marilouise Kroker, and David Cook, eds. *Panic Encyclopedia*. CultureTexts. New York: St. Martin's Press, 1989.

Krueger, Myron. "Videoplace and the Interface of the Future." *The Art of Human Computer Interface Design*. Ed. Brenda Laurel. Cupertino, Calif.: Apple Computer, 1990. 417–22.

Krueger, Myron. *Artificial Reality*. 2d ed. Reading, Mass.: Addison-Wesley Publishing, 1991.

Kuhn, Annette, ed. *Alien Zone: Cultural Theory and Contemporary Science Fiction*. London: Verso, 1990.

Landon, Brooks. "Bet On It: Cyber/video/punk/performance." *Storming the Reality Studio*. Durham: Duke Univ. Press, 1992.

Laurel, Brenda. "Art and Activism in VR." *VERBUM* (Fall/Winter 1991): 14–17.

Leary, Timothy. "The Cyber-Punk: The Individual as Reality Pilot." *Storming the Reality Studio*. Durham: Duke Univ. Press, 1992.

Leary, Timothy. "The Interpersonal, Interactive, Interdimensional Interface." *The Art of Human-Computer Interface Design*. Ed. Brenda Laurel. Cupertino, Calif.: Apple Computer, 1990. 229–33.

Leary, Timothy. *The Art of Human-Computer Interface Design*. Ed. Brenda Laurel. Cupertino, Calif.: Apple Computer, 1990.

Lefanu, Sarah. *Feminism and Science Fiction*. Bloomington and Indianapolis: Indiana University Press, 1989.

Lefebvre, Henri. *The Production of Space*. Trans. Donald Nicholson-Smith. Oxford: Blackwell, 1991. Originally published in France in 1974.

Lévi-Strauss, Claude. "The Structural Anthropology of Myth." Trans. Claire Jacobson, Brooke Schoepf. *Structural Anthropology*. New York: Basic Books, 1963. 206–31.

Levy, Steven. *Hackers: Heroes of the Computer Revolution*. New York: Dell Books, 1984.

Levy, Steven. *Artificial Life: The Quest for a New Creation*. New York: Pantheon Books, 1992.

Liebling, A. J. *The Press*. 2d ed. New York: Ballantine Books, 1975.

Lovejoy, Margot. *Postmodern Currents: Art and Artists in the Age of Electronic Media*. Ann Arbor: UMI Research Press, 1989.

Lukács, Georg. "Reification and the Consciousness of the Proletariat." Trans. Rodney Livingstone. *History and Class Consciousness: Studies in Marxist Dialectics*. Cambridge, Mass.: MIT Press, 1971.

Lyotard, Jean-François. *The Postmodern Condition: A Report on Knowledge*. Trans. Geoff Bennington and Brian Massumi. Minneapolis: University of Minnesota Press, 1984.

Maddox, Tom. "The Wars of the Coin's Two Halves: Bruce Sterling's Mechanist/Shaper Narratives." *Mississippi Review* 16, nos. 2/3 (1988): 237–44.

Mandel, Ernest. *Late Capitalism*. Trans. Joris de Bres. London: Verso Editions 1978.

Mander, Jerry. *Four Arguments for the Elimination of Television*. New York: William Morrow, 1978.

Mann, Charles C., and Edward Zuckerman. "For Starters: We'd Kill Hitler, Buy Xerox at 8½ and Save the Dinosaurs." *SPY* (August 1989): 58–68.

Marcus, Greil. *Lipstick Traces: A Secret History of the Twentieth Century*. Cambridge, Mass.: Harvard University Press, 1989.

Marcuse, Herbert. *One-Dimensional Man*. Boston: Beacon Press, 1964.

Markoff, John. "A 'Virus' Gives Business a Chill." *New York Times* (March 17, 1988): D1 & D7.

Marx, Karl. *Capital*. Vol. 1. Trans. Ben Fowkes. 3 vols. New York: Vintage Books, 1977.

Marx, Leo. *The Machine in the Garden: Technology and the Pastoral Ideal in America*. New York: Oxford University Press, 1968.

Mazlish, Bruce. "The Fourth Discontinuity." *Technology and Culture*. Ed. Kranzberg, Melvin and Davenport. New York: New American Library, 1972. 216–32.

McCaffery, Larry, ed. *Across the Wounded Galaxies: Interviews with Contemporary American Science Fiction Writers*. Urbana and Chicago: University of Illinois Press, 1990.

McCaffery, Larry. "Cutting Up: Cyberpunk, Punk Music and Urban Decontextualizations." *Storming the Reality Studio: A Casebook of Cyberpunk and Postmodern Fiction*. Ed. Larry McCaffery. Durham, N.C.: Duke University Press, 1992. 286–307.

McCaffery, Larry. "Introduction: The Desert of the Real." *Storming the Reality Studio: A Casebook of Cyberpunk and Postmodern Fiction*. Ed. Larry McCaffery. Durham, N.C.: Duke University Press, 1992. 1–16.

McCarty, Cara. *Information Art: Diagramming Microchips*. New York: Museum of Modern Art, 1990. Catalog for an exhibition funded by the Intel Corporation Foundation.

McDougall, Walter A. *The Heavens and the Earth: A Political History of the Space Age*. New York: Basic Books, 1985.

McHale, Brian. *Postmodernist Fiction*. New York: Methuen, 1987.

McHale, Brian. "Elements of a Poetics of Cyberpunk." *Critique* 33, no. 3 (1992): 149–75.

McHale, Brian. "POSTcyberMODERNpunkISM." *Storming the Reality Studio: A*

Casebook of Cyberpunk and Postmodern Science Fiction. Ed. Larry McCaffery. Durham, N.C.: Duke University Press, 1992. 308–23.

McLuhan, Marshall. *Understanding Media*. New York: New American Library, 1964.

McLuhan, Marshall. "Notes on Burroughs." *William S. Burroughs at the Front: Critical Reception, 1959–1989*. Ed. Jennie Skerl and Robin Lydenberg. Carbondale, Ill.: Southern Illinois University Press, 1991. 69–73. Originally published in *The Nation*, December 28, 1964.

Megill, Alan. *Prophets of Extremity: Nietzsche, Heidegger, Foucault, Derrida*. Berkeley: University of California Press, 1985.

Merleau-Ponty, Maurice. *Phenomenology of Perception*. Trans. Colin Smith. London: Routledge & Kegan Paul, 1962.

Merleau-Ponty, Maurice. "Eye and Mind." Trans. Carleton Dallery. *The Primacy of Perception*. Ed. James M. Edie. Northwestern University Studies in Phenomenology and Existential Philosophy. Northwestern University Press, 1964. 159–90.

Metz, Christian. *The Imaginary Signifier: Psychoanalysis and the Cinema*. Trans. Celia Britton, Annwyl Williams, Ben Brewster, and Alfred Guzzetti. Bloomington, Ind.: Indiana University Press, 1977.

Michelson, Annette. "Bodies in Space: Film as Carnal Knowledge." *Artforum* 7, no. 6 (1969): 54–63.

Michelson, Annette. "Camera Lucida, Camera Obscura." *Artforum* (1973): 30–37.

Michelson, Annette. "About Snow." *October* 8 (1978): 111–24.

Michelson, Annette. "Dr. Crase and Mr. Clair." *October* 11 (1979): 31–53.

Michelson, Annette, ed. *Kino-Eye: The Writings of Dziga Vertov*. Berkeley: University of California Press, 1984.

Michelson, Annette. "Heterology and the Critique of Instrumental Reason." *OCTOBER* 36 (1986): 111–27.

Miller, Mark Crispin. "The Robot in the Western Mind." *Boxed In: The Culture of TV*. Evanston, Ill.: Northwestern University Press, 1988. 285–307.

Miller, Mark Crispin. "Virtù, Inc." *Boxed In: The Culture of TV*. Evanston, Ill.: Northwestern University Press, 1988. 79–94.

Miller, Mark Crispin. "Hollywood: The Ad." *Atlantic* (April 1990): 41–68.

Modleski, Tania. "The Terror of Pleasure: The Contemporary Horror Film and Postmodern Theory." *Studies in Entertainment: Critical Approaches to Mass Culture*. Ed. Tania Modleski. Bloomington: Indiana University Press, 1986. 155–66.

Moorcock, Michael, ed. *New Worlds: An Anthology*. London: Flamingo Books, 1983.

Morningstar, Chip, and F. Randall Farmer. "The Lessons of Lucasfilm's Habitat." *Cyberspace: First Steps*. Ed. Michael Benedikt. Cambridge, Mass.: MIT Press, 1991. 273–301.

Mottram, Eric. *William Burroughs: The Algebra of Need*. London: Marion Boyars, 1977.

Münsterberg, Hugo. *The Film: A Psychological Study*. New York: Dover Publications, 1970.

Nadin, Mihai. "Emergent Aesthetics—Aesthetic Issues in Computer Arts." *Com-*

puter Art in Context: SIGGRAPH 1989 Art Show Catalog. Ed. Mark Resch. Oxford: Pergamon Press, 1989. 43–48. Actually a supplemental issue of *Leonardo,* the Journal of the International Society for the Arts, Sciences, and Technology.

Nelson, Theodor Holm. "The Right Way to Think About Software Design." *The Art of Human-Computer Interface Design.* Ed. Brenda Laurel. Cupertino, Calif.: Apple Computer, 1990. 235–43.

Newton, Judith. "Feminism and Anxiety in *Alien.*" *Alien Zone: Cultural Theory and Contemporary Science Fiction Cinema.* Ed. Annette Kuhn. London: Verso, 1990. 82–87.

Oreskes, Michael. "America's Politics Loses Way As Its Vision Changes World." *New York Times,* March 18, 1990: 1 ff.

Pagels, Heinz R. *The Dreams of Reason: The Computer and the Rise of the Sciences of Complexity.* New York: Simon and Schuster, 1989.

Paik, Nam June. "Electronic Video Recorder." *Nam June Paik: Video and Videology 1959–1973.* Syracuse: Everson Museum of Art, 1974. Exhibition catalogue.

Papert, S. (1980). *Mindstorms: Children, Computers and Powerful Ideas.* New York: Basic Books.

Peitgen, H.-O., and P. H. Richter, ed. *The Beauty of Fractals.* Berlin and New York: Springer-Verlag, 1986.

Penley, Constance, et al., ed. *Close Encounters: Film, Feminism, and Science Fiction.* Minneapolis: University of Minnesota Press, 1991.

Pfeil, Fred. "These Disintegrations I'm Looking Forward To." *Another Tale to Tell: Politics and Narrative in Postmodern Culture.* London: Verso, 1990. 83–94.

Platt, Charles. "*Mirrorshades.*" *Washington Post Book World,* December 28, 11.

Pomerantz, Mark. "Sports and the Science Fiction Film." Yale student essay, 1991.

Pomeroy, Jim. "Black Box S-Thetix: Labor, Research, and Survival in the He[Art] of the Beast." *Technoculture.* Ed. Constance Penley and Andrew Ross. Minneapolis: University of Minnesota Press, 1991. 271–94.

Porter, Dennis. *The Pursuit of Crime: Art and Ideology in Detective Fiction.* New Haven: Yale University Press, 1981.

Porush, David. *The Soft Machine: Cybernetic Fiction.* New York: Methuen, 1985.

Poster, Mark. "Introduction." *Jean Baudrillard: Selected Writings.* Ed. Mark Poster. Stanford, Calif.: University of Stanford Press, 1988. 1–9.

Pringle, David. "Media Landscape." *The Encyclopedia of Science Fiction.* Ed. Peter Nicholls. New York: Doubleday, 1979. 390–91.

Rayns, Tony. "*Tetsuo: The Iron Man.*" *Sight and Sound* (1991): 52.

Rheingold, Howard. "What's the Big Deal About Cyberspace?" *The Art of Human Computer Interface Design.* Ed. Brenda Laurel. Cupertino, Calif.: Apple Computer, 1990. 449–53.

Rheingold, Howard. *Virtual Reality.* New York: Summit Books, 1991.

Rickey, Carrie. "Make Mine Cronenberg." *Village Voice,* February 1, 1983: 62ff.

Rifkin, Jeremy. *Time Wars: The Primary Conflict in Human History.* New York: Henry Holt, 1987.

Robbins, David, ed. *The Independent Group: Postwar Britain and the Aesthetics of Plenty.* Cambridge, Mass.: MIT Press, 1990.

Robinson, Kim Stanley. *The Novels of Philip K. Dick: Studies in Speculative Fiction.* Ann Arbor, Mich.: UMI Research Press, 1984.

Rosinsky, Natalie M. *Feminist Futures: Contemporary Women's Speculative Fiction.* Studies in Speculative Fiction. Ann Arbor, Mich.: UMI Research Press, 1984.

Rose, Frank. *West of Eden: The End of Innocence at Apple Computer.* New York: Viking, 1989.

Ross, Andrew. "Cyberpunk in Boystown." *Strange Weather: Culture, Science, and Technology in an Age of Limits.* London: Verso, 1991. 137–67.

Ross, Andrew. "Hacking Away at the Counterculture." *Technoculture.* Ed. Constance Penley and Andrew Ross. Minneapolis: University of Minnesota Press, 1991. 107–34.

Ross, David. "Nam June Paik's Videotapes." *Nam June Paik.* Ed. John Hanhardt. New York: Whitney Museum of American Art, 1982. 101–10. Exhibition catalogue.

Rucker, Rudy. "Report from Silicon Valley." *Science Fiction Eye* 1, no. 4 (1988): 22–25.

Russ, Joanna. "Interview." *Khatru.* Ed. Jeffrey D. Smith. Baltimore: Phantasmicon Press, 1975. 3 and 4. This fan publication is cited by Sarah Lefanu in her *Feminism and Science Fiction.*

Savage, Jon. "Introduction to the *Industrial Culture Handbook.*" *Re/Search* 6/7 (1983): 4–5.

Savage, Jon. *England's Dreaming: Anarchy, Sex Pistols, Punk Rock, and Beyond.* New York: St. Martin's Press, 1992.

Schickel, Richard. *The Disney Version.* Rev. ed. New York: Simon & Schuster, 1985.

Sennett, Richard. *The Fall of Public Man.* New York: Vintage Books, 1978.

Sharpe, William, and Leonard Wallock. "From 'Great Town' to 'Nonplace Urban Realm': Reading the Modern City." *Visions of the Modern City: Essays in History, Art, and Literature.* Ed. William Sharpe and Leonard Wallock. New York: Hayman Center for the Humanities, 1983. 7–46.

Sharrett, Christopher. "Myth and Ritual in the Post-Industrial Landscape: The Horror Films of David Cronenberg." *Persistence of Vision* 1, no. 3/4 (1986): 111–30.

Shirley, John. "Stelarc and the New Reality." *Science Fiction Eye* 1, no. 2 (1987): 56–61.

Sitney, P. Adams. *Visionary Film: The American Avant-Garde 1943–1978.* 2d ed. New York: Oxford University Press, 1979.

Skerl, Jennie. *William S. Burroughs.* Boston: Twayne Publishers, 1985.

Smithson, Robert. "Entropy and the New Monuments." *The Writings of Robert Smithson.* Ed. Nancy Holt. New York: New York University Press, 1979. 9–18. Originally published in 1966.

Smithson, Robert. "Language to be Looked at and/or Things to be Read." *The Writings of Robert Smithson.* Ed. Nancy Holt. New York: New York University Press, 1979. 104. Originally published in 1967.

Sobchack, Vivian. *Screening Space: The American Science Fiction Film.* 2d ed. New York: Ungar, 1987.

Sobchack, Vivian. "Cities on the Edge of Time: The Urban Science Fiction Film." *East-West Film Journal* 3, no. 1 (December 1988): 4–19.

Sobchack, Vivian. "The Scene of the Screen: Towards a Phenomenology of Cinematic and Electronic Presence." *Post-Script* 10 (1990): 50–59.

Sobchack, Vivian. "The Virginity of Astronauts: Sex and the Science Fiction Film." *Alien Zone: Cultural Theory and Contemporary Science Fiction Cinema.* Ed. Annette Kuhn. London: Verso, 1990. 103–15.

Sobchack, Vivian. "New Age Mutant Ninja Hackers." *Artforum International* (April 1991): 24–26.

Sorkin, Michael. "See You in Disneyland." *Variations on a Theme Park: The New American City and the End of Public Space.* Ed. Michael Sorkin. New York: Noonday Press, 1992. 205–32.

Sorkin, Michael, ed. *Variations on a Theme Park: The New American City and the End of Public Space.* New York: Noonday Press, 1992.

Spigel, Lynn. "Installing the Television Set: Popular Discourses on Television and Domestic Space, 1948–1955." *Camera Obscura* 16 (1988): 11–46.

Spinrad, Norman. "The Neuromantics." *Issac Asimov's Science Fiction Magazine* (May 1986): 180–90.

Spinrad, Norman. "Science Fiction vs. Sci-Fi." *Issac Asimov's Science Fiction Magazine* (Mid-December 1986): 178–91.

Spinrad, Norman. "All's Well That Ends Well." *Issac Asimov's Science Fiction Magazine* (June 1990): 175–90.

Spinrad, Norman. "Books into Movies." *Science Fiction in the Real World.* Carbondale, Ill.: Southern Illinois University Press, 1990. 77–89.

Spinrad, Norman. "The Transmogrification of Philip K. Dick." *Science Fiction in the Real World.* Carbondale, Ill.: Southern Illinois University Press, 1990. 198–216.

Springer, Claudia. "The Pleasure of the Interface." *Screen* 32, no. 3 (1991): 303–23.

Springer, Claudia. "Muscular Circuitry: The Invincible Armored Cyborg in Cinema." *Genders,* in press.

Stableford, Brian. "Cities." *The Science Fiction Encyclopedia.* Ed. Peter Nicholls. Garden City, N.Y.: Doubleday, 1979. 118–21.

Stableford, Brian. "Cyborgs." *The Encyclopedia of Science Fiction.* Ed. Peter Nicholls. Garden City, N.Y.: Doubleday, 1979. 151.

Stableford, Brian, and Peter Nicholls. "Crime and Punishment." *The Science Fiction Encyclopedia.* Ed. Peter Nicholls. Garden City, N.Y.: Doubleday, 1979. 142–44.

Stathis, Lou. "SRL in NYC." *Science Fiction Eye* 1, no. 4 (1988): 52–53.

Stenger, Nicole. "Mind is a Leaking Rainbow." *Cyberspace: First Steps.* Ed. Michael Benedikt. Cambridge, Mass.: MIT Press, 1991. 49–58.

Sterling, Bruce. "Preface." *Mirrorshades: The Cyberpunk Anthology.* Ed. Bruce Sterling. New York: Arbor House, 1986. vii–xiv.

Sterling, Bruce. "An Interview with Bruce Sterling by Takayuki Tatsumi." *Science Fiction Eye* 1, no. 1 (1987): 27–42.

Stevens, Jay. *Storming Heaven: LSD and the American Dream.* New York: Harper & Row, 1987.

Stoekl, Allan. "Introduction." *Visions of Excess: Selected Writings of Georges Bataille.* Ed. Allan Stoekl. Minneapolis: University of Minnesota Press, 1985. ix–xxv.

Stone, Allucquere Rosanne. "Will the Real Body Please Stand Up? Boundary

Stories About Virtual Cultures." *Cyberspace: First Steps.* Ed. Michael Benedikt. Cambridge, Mass.: MIT Press, 1991. 81–118.

Strans, Paul. "The New God." *Classic Essays on Photography.* Ed. Alan Trachtenberg. New Haven, Conn.: Leete's Island Books, 1980. 144–51.

Suvin, Darko. *Metamorphoses of Science Fiction: On the Poetics and History of a
Literary Genre.* New Haven: Yale University Press, 1979.

Theweleit, Klaus. *Male Fantasies.* Trans. S. Conway, E. Carter, C. Turner. 2 vols.
Minneapolis: University of Minnesota Press, 1977–78.

Thompson, William Irwin. "Looking for History in L.A." *At the Edge of History.*
New York: Harper & Row, 1971.

Toffler, Alvin. *Future Shock.* New York: Bantam Books, 1971.

Toffler, Alvin. *The Third Wave.* New York: Bantam Books, 1981.

Tomas, David. "Old Rituals for New Space: 'Rites of Passage' and William Gibson's Cultural Model of Cyberspace." *Cyberspace: First Steps.* Ed. Michael
Benedikt. Cambridge, Mass.: MIT Press, 1991. 31–47.

Trachtenberg, Alan, ed. *Classic Essays on Photography.* New Haven, Conn.: Leete's
Island Books, 1980.

Trudeau, G. B. *Talkin' About My G-G-Generation.* New York: Henry Holt, 1987.

Vale, V., and Andrea Juno. "Mark Pauline." *Re/Search* 6/7 (1983): 20–41.

Vale, V., and Andrea Juno. "(Interview with) Mark Pauline." *Re/Search* 11 (1987):
6–17.

Vaneigem, Raoul. "Basic Banalities." *Situationist International Anthology.* Ed. Ken
Knabb. Berkeley, Calif.: Bureau of Public Secrets, 1981. 118–33.

Venturi, Robert, Denise Scott Brown, and Steven Izenour. *Learning from Las
Vegas.* Rev. ed. Cambridge, Mass.: MIT Press, 1977.

Verniere, James. "Blade Runner." *Twilight Zone Magazine* 2, no. 3 (1982): 53–56.

Virilio, Paul. "The Overexposed City." *ZONE* 1/2 (1984): 15–31.

Walker, John. "Through the Looking Glass." *The Art of Human-Computer Interface
Design.* Ed. Brenda Laurel. Cupertino, Calif.: Apple Computer, 1990. 439–47.

Walser, Randal. "Is it Live . . . or is it Autodesk?" *Mondo 2000* (Fall 1989): 16–17.

Waters, Harry F., Janet Huck, and Vern E. Smith. "Mad About M-M-Max." *Newsweek* (April 20, 1987): 58–64.

Watson, Ian. "Introduction to 'Vile Dry Claws of the Toucan.'" *SEMIOTEXT(E) SF.*
Ed. Rudy Rucker, Peter Lamborn Wilson, and Robert Anton Wilson. New
York: Seimotext(e), 1989. 170.

Webber, Melvin M. "The Urban Place and the Nonplace Urban Realm." *Explorations into Urban Structure.* Ed. Melvin M. Webber et al. Philadelphia: University of Pennsylvania Press, 1964. 79–153.

White, Hayden. "The Historical Text as Literary Artifact." *Tropics of Discourse.*
Baltimore: Johns Hopkins University Press, 1978.

Wilson, Richard Guy, Dianne H. Pilgrim, and Dickran Tashjian. *The Machine Age
in America: 1918–1941.* New York: Brooklyn Museum in Association with
Harry N. Abrams, 1986.

Winn, Marie. *The Plug-in Drug: TV, Children, and the Family.* New York: Viking,
1977.

Wolf, Fred Alan. *Taking the Quantum Leap: The New Physics for Non-Scientists.* Rev.
ed. New York: Harper & Row, 1989.

Fiction

Ballard, J. G. "The Concentration City." *The Best Short Stories of J. G. Ballard.* New York: Holt, Rinehart, and Winston, 1978. 1–20. Story originally published in 1957.

Ballard, J. G. "The Intensive Care Unit." *Myths of the Near Future.* London: Triad Books, 1984. 195–205.

Ballard, J. G. *Empire of the Sun.* New York: Simon and Schuster, 1984.

Ballard, J. G. *Crash.* New York: Vintage Books, 1985. Originally published in 1973.

Ballard, J. G. "The Dead Astronaut." *Memories of the Space Age.* Sauk City, Wis.: Arkham House, 1988. 65–78. Originally published in 1968.

Ballard, J. G. "The Assassination Weapon." *The Atrocity Exhibition.* Revised, expanded, annotated, illustrated ed. San Francisco, Calif.: Re/Search Publications, 1990. 31–37. Story originally published in 1966.

Ballard, J. G. *The Kindness of Women.* New York: Farrar, Straus, Giroux, 1991.

Bellamy, Edward. *Looking Backward.* New York: Penguin Books, 1982. Originally published in 1888.

Bester, Alfred. *The Stars My Destination.* 1953.

Burroughs, William S. *Naked Lunch.* New York: Grove Press, 1959.

Burroughs, William S. *Nova Express.* New York: Grove Press, 1964.

Burroughs, William S. *The Soft Machine.* Rev. ed. New York: Grove Press, 1966.

Burroughs, William S. *The Ticket That Exploded.* Rev. ed. New York: Grove Press, 1967.

Burroughs, William S. *The Last Words of Dutch Schultz.* New York: Seaver Books, 1975.

Clarke, Arthur C. *2001: A Space Odyssey.* New York: Signet Books, 1968.

Coover, Robert. "The Phantom of the Movie Palace." *A Night at the Movies.* New York: Simon & Schuster, 1987.

Crichton, Michael. *The Terminal Man.* New York: Avon Books, 1972.

Delillo, Don. *White Noise.* New York: Viking Penguin, 1986.

Dick, Philip K. *Martian Time-Slip.* New York: Ballantine Books, 1964.

Dick, Philip K. *The Simulacra.* London: Methuen, 1977. Originally published in 1964.

Dick, Philip K. *The Three Stigmata of Palmer Eldritch.* New York: Bantam Books, 1977. Originally published in 1964.

Dick, Philip K. *Now Wait for Last Year.* London: Granada Publishing, 1979. Originally published in 1966.

Dick, Philip K. *UBIK.* New York: DAW Books, 1983.

Dick, Philip K. *UBIK: The Screenplay.* Minneapolis: Corroboree Press, 1985.

Lusk, Ronald. "The First Encounter." *Amygdala,* April 1987: 2–3.

Malzberg, Barry N. *Galaxies.* New York: Pyramid Books, 1975.

Pohl, Frederik, and C. M. Kornbluth. *The Space Merchants.* New York: Ballantine Books, 1953.

Pynchon, Thomas. *Gravity's Rainbow.* New York: Bantam Books, 1973.

Russ, Joanna. *The Female Man.* New York: Bantam Books, 1975.

Sladek, John. *The Müller-Fokker Effect.* New York: Carroll & Graf, 1990. Originally published in 1970.

Spinrad, Norman. *The Void Captain's Tale.* New York: Pocket Books, 1983.

Sturgeon, Theodore. *More Than Human.* New York: Ballantine Books, 1953.

Tiptree, James, Jr. *The Girl Who Was Plugged In.* Vol. 7 of TOR *Doubles.* New York: TOR Books, 1989. Originally published in 1973.

Tiptree, James, Jr. *Her Smoke Rose Up Forever.* Sauk City, Wis.: Arkham House, 1990.

Varley, John. "Overdrawn at the Memory Bank." *The Persistence of Vision.* New York: Dell Publishing, 1978. 228–62.

Varley, John. "The Phantom of Kansas." *The Persistence of Vision.* New York: Dell, 1978. 1–42.

Varley, John. "Press Enter ■." *Blue Champagne.* New York: Berkley Books, 1986. 130–60.

Varley, John. "Just Another Perfect Day." *The Year's Best Science Fiction: Seventh Annual Collection.* Ed. Gardner Dozois. New York: St. Martin's Press, 1990. 460–71.

Wolfe, Bernard. *Limbo.* New York: Carroll & Graf, 1987. First published in 1952.

Zelazny, Roger. "He Who Shapes." *The Best of the Nebulas.* Ed. Ben Bova. New York: TOR Books, 1989. 72–141. Originally published in 1965.

Zoline, Pamela. "The Heat Death of the Universe." *The Heat Death of the Universe and Other Stories.* Kingston, N.Y.: McPherson, 1988. 13–28. Originally published in 1967.

Cyberpunk

Bear, Greg. *Blood Music.* New York: Ace Books, 1985.

Bear, Greg. "Blood Music." *Tangents.* New York: Warner Books, 1989. 11–41. Story originally published in 1983.

Cadigan, Pat. "Pretty Boy Crossover." *The Year's Best Science Fiction: Fourth Annual Collection.* Ed. Gardner Dozois. New York: St. Martin's Press, 1987. 106–14.

Cadigan, Pat. *Synners.* New York: Bantam Books, 1991.

Effinger, George Alec. *When Gravity Fails.* New York: Bantam Books, 1988. Originally published in 1986.

Gibson, William. *Neuromancer.* The New Ace Science Fiction Specials. New York: Ace Books, 1984.

Gibson, William. *Count Zero.* London: Victor Gollancz, 1986.

Gibson, William. "The Gernsback Continuum." *Burning Chrome.* New York: Arbor House, 1986. 23–35. Originally published in 1981.

Gibson, William. *Burning Chrome.* New York: Ace Books, 1987.

Gibson, William. "The Winter Market," *Burning Chrome.* New York: Ace Books, 1987. 117–141. Originally published in 1986.

Gibson, William. *Mona Lisa Overdrive.* New York: Bantam Books, 1988.

Gibson, William. "Academy Leader." *Cyberspace: First Steps.* Ed. Michael Benedikt. Cambridge, Mass.: MIT Press, 1991. 27–29.

Jeter, K. W. *Dr. Adder.* New York: Bluejay Books, 1984.

Jeter, K. W. *The Glass Hammer.* New York: Bluejay Books, 1985.

Kadrey, Richard. *Metrophage.* The New Ace Science Fiction Specials. New York: Ace Books, 1988.

Maddox, Tom. "Snake-Eyes." *Mirrorshades: The Cyberpunk Anthology.* Ed. Bruce Sterling. New York: Arbor House, 1986. 12–33.

Rucker, Rudy. *Software.* New York: Avon Books, 1982.

Rucker, Rudy. *Wetware.* New York: Avon Books, 1988.

Shirley, John. *Eclipse.* New York: Bluejay Books, 1985.

Shirley, John. *Eclipse Penumbra.* New York: Popular Library, 1987.

Shirley, John. *Eclipse Corona.* New York: Popular Library, 1990.

Simmons, Dan. *Hyperion.* New York: Doubleday, 1989.

Skal, David. *Antibodies.* Isaac Asimov Presents. New York: Worldwide Library, 1988.

Stephenson, Neal. *Snow Crash.* New York: Bantam Books, 1992.

Sterling, Bruce. *Schismatrix.* New York: Ace Science Fiction, 1985.

Sterling, Bruce. *Islands in the Net.* New York: Arbor House, 1988.

Sterling, Bruce. *Crystal Express.* New York: Ace Books, 1990.

Swanwick, Michael. *Vacuum Flowers.* New York: Ace Books, 1988.

Vinge, Vernor. "True Names." *True Names and Other Dangers.* New York: Baen Books, 1987.

Williams, Walter Jon. *Hardwired.* New York: TOR Books, 1986.

Williams, Walter Jon. *Voice of the Whirlwind.* New York: TOR Books, 1987.

Williams, Walter Jon. *Angel Station.* New York: TOR Books, 1989.

Womack, Jack. *Ambient.* New York: TOR Books, 1987.

Womack, Jack. *Terraplane.* New York: TOR Books, 1988.

Womack, Jack. *Heathern.* New York: TOR Books, 1990.

Comics, Illustration, and Software

Chaykin, Howard. *American Flagg!* Evanston, Ill.: First Comics, 1983.

Chaykin, Howard, *Time²: The Epiphany.* Evanston, Ill.: First Comics, 1986.

Chaykin, Howard. *Time²: The Satisfaction of Black Mariah.* Evanston, Ill.: First Comics, 1987.

Cowley, Stewart. *Spacecraft: 2000–2100 A.D.* Seacaucus, N.J.: Chartwell Books, 1978.

Cowley, Stewart, and Charles Herridge. *Great Space Battles.* Seacaucus, N.J.: Chartwell Books, 1979.

DeHaven, Tom, and Bruce Jensen. *Neuromancer: The Graphic Novel.* New York: Epic Comics, 1989.

Delany, Samuel R. and Howard Chaykin. *Empire.* Berkeley/Windhover Books, 1978.

Foss, Chris. *Diary of a Spaceperson.* Surrey, England: Paper Tiger, 1990.

Gaiman, Neil, and Mark Buckingham. "Notes from the Underground." *Miracleman* 19. Forestville, Calif.: Eclipse Comics, 1991.

Hernandez, Gilbert, et al. *The Return of Mr. X.* East Fullerton, Calif.: Graphitti Designs, 1986. This volume reprints the first four issues, which originally appeared in 1983–84.

Liberman, Carl, Darryl Gold, and Diana Schein. *The Mr. X CD-ROM.* Media Collision, 1991. Software.

McKie, Angus. *So Beautiful and So Dangerous.* New York: Heavy Metal, 1979.

Mead, Syd. *OBLAGON: Concepts of Syd Mead.*

Miller, Frank, and Geof Darrow. *Hard Boiled.* Milwaukie, Oreg.: Dark Horse Comics, 1990. Three issue series, appeared from 1990–1992.

Miller, Robyn, and Rand Miller. *Cosmic Osmo.* Menlo Park, Calif.: Activision, 1989. Software.

Mills, Pat, and Kevin O'Neill. *Marshal Law: Super Babylon.* Milwaukie, Oreg.: Dark Horse Comics, 1992.

Moebius. "The Long Tomorrow." *The Long Tomorrow and Other Science Fiction Stories.* Ed. Jean-Marc Lofficier and Randy Lofficier. 6 vols. Collected Fantasies of Jean Giraud. New York: Marvel Entertainment Group, 1987. Vol. 4.

Moebius. *The Incal.* Vol. 1 of 3 vols. New York: Marvel Entertainment Group, 1988.

Moore, Alan, and Dave Gibbons. *The Watchmen.* New York: DC Comics, 1987.

Moore, Alan, and Bill Sienkeiwicz. *Big Numbers.* Northampton, England: Mad Love, 1990.

Moreno, Pepe. *Batman: Digital Justice.* New York: DC Comics, 1990.

Rockwell, Scott, and Darryl Banks. *Cyberpunk.* Wheeling, W.V.: Innovative Corporation, 1989.

Saenz, Mike. *IRON MAN: CRASH.* New York: Marvel Entertainment Group, 1988.

Scharf, Kenny. *The Future Was Now.* 1988. Painting.

Wagner, John, et al. *The Chronicles of Judge Dredd: Blockmania.* London: Titan Books, 1981, 1984.

393

"Hence, the academic grappling with his computer, ceaselessly correcting, reworking, and complexifying, turning the exercise into a kind of interminable psychoanalysis, memorizing everything in an effort to escape the final outcome, to delay the day of reckoning of death, and that other—fatal— moment of reckoning that is writing, by forming an endless feedback loop with the machine. . . .[H]e has at last found the equivalent of what the teenager gets from his stereo and his walkman: a spectacular desublimation of thought, his concepts as images on a screen."—Jean Baudrillard

INDEX

Scott Bukatman teaches film at New York University.

Library of Congress Cataloging-in-Publication Data

Bukatman, Scott, 1957–

Terminal identity : the virtual subject in postmodern science

fiction / Scott Bukatman.

ISBN 0-8223-1332-4. — ISBN 0-8223-1340-5 (pbk.)

1. Science fiction, American—History and criticism.   2. American

fiction—20th century—History and criticism.   3. Postmodernism

(Literature)—United States.   4. Identity (Psychology) in

literature.   5. Virtual reality in literature.   I. Title.

PS374.S35B84   1993

813′.0876209—dc20   92-39981 CIP